Understanding Inequality

The Intersection of Race/Ethnicity, Class, and Gender

Edited by
Barbara A. Arrighi

ROWMAN & LITTLEFIELD PUBLISHERS, INC.
Lanham • Boulder • New York • Oxford

ROWMAN & LITTLEFIELD PUBLISHERS, INC.

Published in the United States of America
by Rowman & Littlefield Publishers, Inc.
4720 Boston Way, Lanham, Maryland 20706
http://www.rowmanlittlefield.com

12 Hid's Copse Road, Cumnor Hill, Oxford OX2 9JJ, England

Library of Congress Cataloging-in-Publication Data

Understanding inequality : the intersection of race/ethnicity, class, and gender / edited by
Barbara A. Arrighi
    p. cm.
Includes bibliographical references and index.
ISBN 0-8476-9914-5 — ISBN 0-8476-9915-3 (pbk.)
        1. Equality—United States.   2. United States—Social conditions.   3. Minorities—
United States—Social conditions.   4. Social classes—United States.
5. Sex role—United States.   I. Arrighi, Barbara A.
HN90.S6 U53 2001
305'.0973—dc21   00-033275

Printed in the United States of America

∞™ The paper used in this publication meets the minimum requirements of
American National Standard for Information Sciences—Permanence of
Paper for Printed Library Materials, ANSI/NISO Z39.48–1992.

Contents

Preface

My primary goal in editing this text was to create a reader that would encourage students to think in new ways about old issues. In order to achieve that goal, I felt it was imperative to include a mixture of scholarly, research-oriented readings and essays that would spur classroom discussion. As a writer and researcher, the highest praise I can offer my colleagues who allowed their work to be included is that I wish I had been the author of the fine writing assembled in this reader.

The selections have been excerpted to a digestible length and degree of difficulty suitable for undergraduate courses. I think readability has been achieved without jeopardizing the integrity of the writing or intent of the authors. Having said that, it is my sincere hope the selections will whet your appetitie so that you will read the original sources in their entirety. You will not be disappointed.

Acknowledgments

Many people have influenced the writing of this book. First and foremost, I pay tribute to the students in my classes from whom I continue to learn much about difference, tolerance, patience, humor, and of course teaching.

My heartfelt appreciation is extended to the contributors for granting permission to have their writing included in this work. It speaks to the high value these scholars place on the continued pedagogical discourse about race/ethnicity, class, and gender. I am grateful, too, for the helpful comments of anonymous reviewers who assisted me in thinking outside of the box, both in terms of content and context. Many ongoing discussions and debates with numerous colleagues from various disciplines have influenced my thinking about race/ethnicity, gender, and class. Fearing that I might omit someone who should be named, I think it best to leave it with an unspecified but very sincere thank you. I feel fortunate for the opportunity to have worked on this project with Dean Birkenkamp, editor for Rowman and Littlefield, and have benefited from his assistance in bringing this text to fruition.

Finally, this book is dedicated to my daughters, Elena and Eiler, who always inspire me to think outside of the box; to Megan, who makes the world new for me every day; and to my mother, Ernesta, and those of her generation who knowingly and unknowingly laid the groundwork for the measure of equality we enjoy today.

Introduction

In . . . most America, it was the well-off white boys who counted most. Their girls ran a far second. Few others counted, and some who didn't were told so in so many words. . . . [T]he big social things affect us, often, in silence, but affect and produce us they do.

Charles Lemert, *Social Things*

Lemert's quote is a succinct summary of the way things were before 1964. That year, the Civil Rights Act—a federal mandate—compelled us as a nation to rid our public institutions, especially our schools and workplaces, of everyday patterns of segregation and discrimination that were thought to contribute significantly to inequality in our society. However, because attitudes cannot be legislated—laws can legislate behaviors but not change minds—and because deeply held biases are not easily given up, thirty years later we continue to examine the remnants of segregation, prejudice, and discrimination. Indeed, as I write this introduction a young man sits on death row in a Texas prison because he chained an African American man to a pickup truck and dragged him to his death. Why did he kill him? Because the victim was born with brown skin. This generation of students, as our next leaders, will undertake the most critical tasks of understanding and remedying these issues.

Although this reader addresses the divisive issues surrounding race/ethnicity, gender, and class, it is not a book about diversity or multiculturalism; that is, it does not focus on celebrating the uniqueness of individuals or groups. Although this text does examine the many ways in which we are separated from each other, it is a book about connectedness. It is my hope that as you read the articles, you will think of how we are bound to each other. I hope, too, that you will think about the fact that women and men are more alike than different, no matter what their shape or the color of their skin. What a powerful statement! If we are more alike than not, couldn't many of our differences be constructed, manufactured, or created? Why do we feel the need to divide, segregate, dominate, subordinate? What are the benefits to society and to individuals? What are the costs? Think about the ways in which physical differences are translated into social differences in our everyday lives. And then think about how the more we see ourselves in the faces of others, the greater our ability to understand, empathize, compromise, and accept other points of view.

Understanding inequality requires looking at the pattern of distribution of resources and opportunities in a society. Simply put: Who gets what? Do certain groups consistently have greater access to society's most desirable resources? If so, at whose expense? If distribution is structured—if it is built into the system—what does it mean for individual effort? Put another way, what is one's chance of getting a piece of the pie? Is the deck stacked?

WHAT'S MISSING?

Familiar themes about inequality are touched upon here as well as what is missing from the literature. For example, one of the ways that the exclusion of women and other minorities from the sociological literature has been remedied is by excising white males from the discourse—except as the group that bears the blame. However, when one group is discarded in order to include other groups, we are in danger of employing zero-sum tactics. And when we summarily dismiss or scapegoat a group, one possible consequence is the intensification of intergroup conflict (whites against blacks or men against women). Using marginalization or exclusion as a form of domination or as a mechanism for social control grants tacit permission for the arbitrary debarment of others. Another possible effect is that by limiting the input of a select few, we run the risk of extracting only partial knowledge on any given subject. How effective are decisions made without full information? Excluding or denigrating white males because women and other minorities have been denied active participation in matters of the intellect for centuries does little to advance equality in society.

NEW SCAPEGOATS: WHITE MALES

While it might seem expeditious to attribute all things negative to white males, consider some of the consequences. First, excluding them ignores the disparate economic and/or social conditions among members of that group. Second, if equalizing opportunity and reducing intergroup conflict are desirable societal goals, then understanding the position of white males vis-à-vis other groups is useful. Perhaps in the process, intergroup commonalities will become evident. The inclusion of white males in the discussion can increase our understanding of the complexities of issues surrounding race/ethnicity, gender, and class. It then becomes possible to think of men not as a monolithic group of elite oppressors but as a heterogeneous group—in terms of race/ethnicity and class—fulfilling rather narrow gender roles.

THE ROLE OF PATRIARCHY

Bear in mind that the definition of patriarchy is that of a system of domination by a few men over *all* others, including children, women, *and* men. By definition then, women and most men are subordinated in some form. It is true that within a patriarchal system women have ranked only slightly above children (if even that) and many of the pieces herein will direct your attention to women's ongoing subordinate position. However, finding the connections that bind as well as the forces that divide women and men will provide a greater understanding than will simply focusing on the latter.

EQUALITY ELUDES US

There is no question that we have a long road to travel to achieve equality on the basis of sex and race/ethnicity. Since the passage of the Civil Rights Act, additional laws have been enacted as well as modified to lessen inequality, thereby heightening public awareness. Scholarly writing and research, which previously ignored or marginalized minority voices, have slowly begun to integrate the thinking of others into the sociological mainstream. Yet after three decades of legislation, patriarchy continues, and full equality eludes us.

More than a few selections in this volume call attention to the embeddedness of patriarchy in our institutions. Still other readings suggest that to some extent, women, like other oppressed groups, have internalized or taken in the sexist thinking of their oppressors. In this way, the oppressed then unwittingly become complicit in their subordination.

THROWING OFF COLONIAL MENTALITY

Colonization is useful in understanding the position of minority groups. It means control by a dominant force over a dependent people. Aimé Césaire summarized the crippling effect of colonization on indigenous populations as "millions of men in whom fear has been cunningly instilled, who have been taught to have an inferiority complex, to tremble, kneel, despair."[1] To think as one who has been colonized is to accept the limitations and constraints, and to unleash the colonizer within, to think *inside the box.* How does the colonized throw off the colonizer? Frantz Fanon wrote: "In decolonization, there is therefore the need of a complete calling in question of the colonial situation."[2] Question the constraints, question the box. The decolonized person thinks and acts *outside of the box*. Martin Luther King acted outside of the box. Rosa Parks acted outside of the box. Suffragettes acted outside of the box. Perhaps Lemert is on to something when he says, "Parents and teachers could be said to be the colonizers of the minds of children."[3]

HELPFUL CONCEPTUAL TOOLS

In addition to colonization, other terms will be useful in guiding you through the readings. Using accessible language, Charles Lemert introduces the notion of social structure—the patterned constraints, opportunities, and invisible but powerful forces in our lives that sort us out, work on us as we play, sleep, and work—pushing and pulling us as we go about our everyday lives. The next chapter, Stephen Worchel's short, cogent explanation about stereotyping, goes a long way to enlighten readers about the process by which we tend to pigeonhole members of various groups with our preconceived ideas about them. Worchel also makes us aware of the consequences of making judgments about others based on stereotypes.

EMBEDDED IDEOLOGY: RACISM/ETHNOCENTRISM AND SEXISM

When reading this section, consider the similarities and differences between racism and sexism. Do women think sexism is embedded within the social structure in the way that racism and ethnocentrism are? bell hooks examines how the vestiges of racism and sexism have worked to keep African American women and white women from forming an effective alliance to dismantle the "isms." Following hooks is Derrick Bell's treatise on racism, in which he argues that if racist behavior is to change, so too must racist ideology. As you read hooks's and Bell's essays, think of other ways in which racism and sexism are embedded within this society. Next, Laura Goodstein's chapter reminds us that there is always a new minority group to scapegoat and stereotype. She demonstrates the role the media play in creating and perpetuating stereotypes. Finally, Gambino's (now Huberty) pithy essay examines the stereotyping judgments that are formed about someone simply on the basis of a surname—especially one that has been made infamous by the media.

THE *OTHER* WEARS MANY FACES

This section addresses the issue of *otherness*—alienation, isolation, invisibility, and/or exclusion. Arturo Madrid, who is an American of Mexican heritage, poignantly describes what it feels like to be excluded, to be made to feel like the *other* in the United States, a country in which Madrid's ancestors predate the earliest European immigrants. Implicit in Madrid's article is the intersection of class with race/ethnicity (discussed more fully in the following section). When you are reading Madrid's words, think of a time when you have felt like the other. Perhaps the discomfort was only temporary, like being the new person among old friends. Then imagine if the feeling were imposed on you wherever you went. As you read, think about whether there is a pattern to otherness.

The chapter by Billie Wright Dziech addresses the otherness of white males, a group we rarely think of as being excluded or alienated. Dziech emphasizes the importance of finding common ground and the need to balance the needs of all students if positive change is to occur. Dziech's piece responds to white males' complaints about feeling marginalized in college classrooms. She maintains that no student should be made to feel excluded in the classroom.

In a different vein, the selection by Simone de Beauvoir maintains that woman has been defined as the other by man. Although subordinated like members of other minority groups, woman is in a unique situation because of the nature of her intimate relationship with man. Rather than flee, woman clings to her oppressor, and de Beauvoir explains why.

SOCIAL CLASS: THE DIRTY LITTLE SECRET

The first thing I must tell you about social class is that the sections designated for race/ethnicity, gender, and class represent arbitrary divisions. The three concepts are interrelated. It is difficult to discuss race/ethnicity without including social class in the analysis. The same can be said of gender and class. The separation of the three is done primarily for the purpose of simplifying the discussion. Keep in mind what was stated above about *patterns*. There is a pattern to the distribution of material resources in this society that consistently places the majority of women and other minorities in lower classes than white males. Even when discussion focuses on gender and/or race/ethnicity, social class is in the equation, whether explicitly stated or implied.

Since the social and political upheaval of the 1960s and '70s, social class, a central tenet of the inequality literature, has vied with race/ethnicity and gender for scholarly attention. In the United States, our embedded ideology promotes individualism and upward mobility, which contribute to widespread denial of social class barriers.

Although there is a section of the text dedicated to the discussion of class, I encourage you to think outside of the box; consider the aspects of social class that can be uncovered in the articles that are *not* included under the class heading. Who wrote the article? What clues do you have about the author's social class? What is the research question or essay thesis? What is the social class of those being researched? Because social class intersects with race/ethnicity and gender, it will be one of your tasks to uncover the clues about class in each article.

Remember as a child how you would find the hidden pictures in a *Highlights* magazine? Take a similar tack in those articles in which the author has not specified social class; that is, find social class as it lurks beneath the surface waiting for you to extract it. For example, a reading about cosmetic surgery implies resources and discretionary time far beyond the reach of people scrounging for the necessities of life. Although the role class plays in shaping us is something we are not conscious of in our daily lives, it is there, embedded, working in tandem with gender and/or race/ethnicity.

Another example of class/race intersection would be the pattern that exists for African American males, who, on average, earn less than White males. Are African American men less productive, less skilled than white males? When a significant proportion of a group's members have similar economic experiences, it compels us to consider many things, including educational opportunity and/or occupational opportunity, and how the two are connected with the class structure. Explanations that focus on characteristics of the individual will not suffice.

STRUCTURED INEQUALITY—THE INVISIBLE IRON CAGE OF CLASS

The three chapters in this section give readers an inkling of the role of social class in sorting out women and men in this society. First, Messner's examination of the interaction of race, class, and athletics for adolescent males reveals that high-school athletics give lower-class boys (white and black) "public masculine status" but not much else. Diane Reay's selection demonstrates that working-class women also feel marked and constrained by their class status. Reay recounts her struggle to feel a sense of belonging in academia, first as a working-class student, then as a professor with a working-class background. Reay's work shows the persistence of otherness that frequently follows working-class people, even when they achieve upward social mobility. Michelle Fine, Lois Weis, Judi Addelston, and Julia Marusza's jarring chapter brutally reminds us of some of the prevailing attitudes among poor and working-class men who feel their unfulfilled privileges are being undermined by the *other*—women and African Americans. To what extent do you think the attitudes revealed in the selection are prevalent in the United States?

STRUCTURED INEQUALITY—RACE/ETHNICITY

In Haya Stier and Marta Tienda's chapter, they conclude that, even in the face of dire economic conditions, lower-class fathers attempt to support their families. The authors' findings counter the stereotypes of African American and Hispanic fathers as absent, irresponsible, and/or disengaged. Note the interaction of race/ethnicity and class here. The following chapter presents the findings of a study by William J. Chambliss concerning the treatment of young African American males by the Washington, D.C., metropolitan police. Chambliss found that the police stopped members of this group of drivers an average of every twenty minutes during a shift. The chapter by Robyn Meredith relates a similar experience for African American males in Detroit. When reading this, keep in mind what it means when a pattern of this kind of behavior toward a segment of the population is revealed.

Next, the analysis of discriminatory treatment shifts to other minority ethnic groups. First, Leslie Marmon Silko reports behavior on the part of the Border Patrol that depicts similar police tactics to Chambliss and Meredith's accounts, only the location and the minority group are different. Silko is followed by Marc Cooper, who offers a chilling glimpse of the collusion between the meat-packing industry and the Immigration and Naturalization Service. Cooper charges that legal as well as illegal workers are exploited by the industry.

STRUCTURED INEQUALITY—ACQUIRING GENDER

A number of chapters here explain gender as socially constructed. This perspective maintains that gender, rather than fixed and innate, is fluid and acquired. "Gender . . . is not a set of traits, not a variable, nor a role, but the product of social doings of some sort."[4] Although gender is relational and nonessential, it is presented as an essential, natural, innate, interactional process.[5] In the chapter by Judith Butler, the notion of gender as performance is critiqued. Butler asks insightful questions: If gender is constructed, who does the constructing? When does it occur, and how does it occur? Does our acceptance of gender as inherent keep us from questioning? Next, Judith Lorber makes the case for questioning. Lorber argues that becoming women and men in western society has more to do with ideology and power than physical attributes. Using sports and technological competence to illustrate her argument, Lorber maintains that social practices, not biology, fit individuals into a gender category.

The excerpt from Laureen Snider's comprehensive article about building safer societies addresses the violence that permeates culturally appropriate masculine socialization. Snider discusses men's loss of traditional prerogatives due to economic restructuring and women's changing roles. Next Barbara Arrighi maintains that while girl children have narrow gender performance parameters, the expectations for boys are perhaps even more narrow and become entrenched at an earlier age. Anne Fausto-Sterling's examination of data relating to premenstrual conditions suggests that long-held biases about women continue to inform contemporary gynecological research.

CORPORATE GATEKEEPING: FITTING IN

The excerpt from Deborah Tannen's book introduces the reader to this section and explores the double bind for women: those who use forceful communication styles at work are negatively sanctioned as *masculinized* women, and women whose communication styles are perceived as *feminine* typically are labeled ineffective. Richard L. Zweigenhaft and G. William Domhoff present a sobering picture of women's slow rise to the director level of the corporate world, raising the question of why women continue to be tokens in high places. However, the authors indicate that in some ways corporate women have more in common with corporate men than with other women. As you read this, ponder: what could be at work here?

Sally Ann Davis-Netzley's study is an excellent follow-up to Domhoff and Zweigenhaft. She interviewed female and male executives, and, though she found some overlap in their responses, she detected a gendered pattern to their perceptions. The final chapter in the section, by Michael S. Kimmel, shifts the focus to the dilemma of corporate men: when they try to seek a balance between work and family, they are viewed as uncommitted to the workplace.

WOMEN'S EQUALITY: PROGRESS AND RESISTANCE

This section turns to the progress of women's pursuit of equality and offers a timely analysis of the unevenness of women's struggle as well as the lack of women's unity in that pursuit. It is not only man who constrains women; it is also woman who sometimes acts to censure and impede the progress of other women. Why is it that some women have advocated for change, while other women have defended the status quo? Three selections provide a context within which to understand the slow progress toward gender equality. An excerpt from Jane Jerome Camhi's book is apropos here. She recounts the concerted effort of antisuffragettes in the early part of the century to block women's right to vote. Camhi's work does not, however, focus on the issue of social class, which was a major factor in the antis' opposition to suffrage: The antis were fearful that women's enfranchisement would signal the downfall of the status of elite women.

In the next chapter, Susan J. Douglas fast-forwards us to the late 1960s and finds that resistance to women's equality is continued—from men in the legislature, from the media, and from women in positions to influence public opinion at the time. Barbara Arrighi brings us to the late 1990s with a survey of college freshmen's attitudes and expectations regarding mating, marriage, and the marketplace. The findings indicate that while young women and men have egalitarian expectations and attitudes concerning home, neither group seems annoyed by a gender-segregated workplace.

AGING: DEVALUED WOMEN *AND* MEN

The first chapter addresses women's predicament: acceptance of or resistance to aging. Myra Dinnerstein and Rose Weitz offer a thought-provoking critique of Jane

Fonda's resistance and Barbara Bush's acceptance. As you are reading, consider the media's role in disseminating both points of view. Think too, about the limited resources lower-income women have to ward off aging. A fitting follow-up is the qualitative study by Doris G. Bazzini, William D.McIntosh, Stephen M. Smith, Sabrina Cook, and Caleigh Harris of popular films, which provides evidence that, in film, aging women fare worse than men.

Are men immune to the sociological ravages of age? The paucity of articles in general and here specifically might suggest that is the case; however, from the viewpoint of the readings in this selection, it seems masculinity for men, like beauty for women, is reserved for the young. Edward H. Thompson maintains that early masculinizing of young males dissipates as men age. Images of older men frequently reflect dependency and an emasculated status rather than the machismo of their youth.

THE PRICE OF DEVIANCE

This section includes three analyses of the consequences for those who act outside of the box. First, Kathleen Rowe considers the fate of *unruly women*—women like Roseanne Arnold, women who do not fit the scripted feminine model. The second selection comes from Christine Craft's account of her protracted sex discrimination suit against her employer. Craft argues that she was fired because she was considered too old and too unattractive; Craft was in her thirties at the time. She could have done nothing as most people in her predicament do, but she was deviant and instead fought back. Eleanor Randolph brings the issue to 1999 and provides evidence that Craft's case was not an anomaly. Finally, Lawrence Otis Graham's provocative essay about his decision to have cosmetic surgery is both a reminder of the powerful push to conform to some arbitrary societal standard of attractiveness and the unique dimension that race/ethnicity brings to the issue.

PATRIARCHY AND ITS CONSEQUENCES

John Stuart Mill's remarkable essay condemning the subordination of women is as timely and powerful today as it was when he first presented it. What courage Mill displayed by writing such a controversial piece more than a hundred years ago! Next is an excerpt from Susan Estrich's book *Real Rape*. A discussion of rape might seem out of place here until you consider the relationship between patriarchy and rape. The incidence of rape is an important indicator of inequality between males and females. The last entry in this section is Mary F. Rogers's astute dissection of the Anita Hill-Clarence Thomas Senate hearings. In it Rogers analyzes the unusual circumstances that resulted in the teamwork between the white and black patriarchs in their effort to discredit Anita Hill.

EQUALITY AND THE MILLENNIUM:
THE CRISIS IN HIGHER EDUCATION

Walda Katz-Fishman offers a blistering and insightful treatise of the status of higher education. She reports facts and figures that present education as a purveyor of inequality. It is an appropriate ending to our discussion, as Katz-Fishman dispels the traditionally held view that education is the universal elixir for inequality.

NOTES

1. Aimé Césaire.

2. Frantz Fanon, *The Damned*, trans. by Constance Farrington (Paris: Présence Africaina, 1963), pp. 20–25.

3. Charles Lamart, *Social Things: An Introduction to the Sociological Life* (Lanham, Md.: Rowman & Littlefield, 1997), p. 97.

4. Candace West and Don H. Zimmerman, "Doing Gender," *Gender and Society* 1 (1987): 125–51.

5. Myra Marx Ferree, "Beyond Separate Spheres: Feminism and Family Research," *Journal of Marriage and the Family* 38 (1990): 473–832.

Part One

Helpful Conceptual Tools

1

Mysterious Power of Social Structures

Charles Lemert

Today, if you are born poor, you will grow up to be poor. There are exceptions, of course, but the exceptions are rare when measured against the ideals of social progress in which [modern democratic] societies believe. In the mid-1980s, shortly after Frankie and the Hangers[1] entered adult life, the wealthiest 40 percent of all Americans gained 67 percent of the country's total income, while the poorest 40 percent received only 15 percent. The United States is one of the modern societies most honorably committed to the ideals of equal opportunity and social progress. Yet the gap between the income and wealth of the richest Americans has remained in roughly this range for most of the last two centuries. By the 1990s, the gap had grown into a canyon. In 1994, the wealthiest 20 percent of the population raked in 56 percent of the total income, while the poorest 20 percent eked out but 4 percent of all that was earned that year. Or, worse yet, the richest 5 percent of the population earned 18 percent of all income, more than four times that earned by the poorest 20 percent. Some who are poor better their situation, but most do not. The problem is getting worse, not better.

Though the facts of social inequality raise many questions, three are the most important for a sociologist: (1) What goes on in the larger structures of society to produce the reality with which Frankie and millions of others must live? (2) How do people, whether poor or not, live with the effects of those structures that so obviously shape their thinking about whether or not, as Frankie put it, they are going to fuck up? And (3) how do individuals measure their own social chances in comparison with whatever opportunities their world provides? Simply put, these are questions of social *structures*, of the individual *subjects* who must live with them, and

From *Social Things: An Introduction to the Sociological Life* by Charles Lemert (Lanham, Md.: Rowman & Littlefield Publishers, 1997), pp. 124–135, 152. Reprinted with permission.

of the social *differences* these structures create. Hardly a person alive does not face these questions one way or another, even if only in the crude but astute way Frankie did. All sociologies, practical and professional, must address them.

It would be nice if the answers were as straightforward as the questions, but they are not. One (but only one) of the reasons the answers are so hard to come by is that there is a good deal of mystery surrounding the stark facts Frankie knew so well. This chapter . . . will consider . . . most difficult of all—the mysterious power of social structures.

What, after all, is a structure? We use the word often, but, as with many common terms in our daily speech, we seldom examine it.

We may speak, for example, of doghouses, apartments, caves, nests, rocks, or even subway grates as structures within, under, or upon which a creature sleeps or, even, "lives." We recognize that most living things are themselves well-enough structured. Flowers have stems, trees have roots, beetles have shells, other bugs have wings; on it goes. An animal's body, for example, is structured around or within skeletons of some kind, just as most plants can be said to be structured with respect to a system of trunks and roots. Rising a bit higher in the food chain, it is not uncommon to speak of the structure of one's marriage, the structure of one's work organization or school, or the structure of professional sports, network television, or the American family. We seem to recognize that things are structured in certain ways, as if by nature.

Even when the word "structure" is not the one used, people recognize that, for the most part, it is a word that applies to the ordering of some set of things. Once, astronomers even spoke with confidence of the structure of the universe, just as physicists used to speak definitively of the structure of subatomic particles. Even though, now, science in its wisdom has progressed to such a point that we know that neither universes nor subatomic matter are particularly stable or orderly structures, still, it is not wrong to speak of them, and other things, as though they were "structured." "Structure" is a word of many applications, from the largest to the smallest of things. Yet, again, it is very hard to say exactly what one of them is.

A structure can, on occasion, be a most temporary, even artificial, sort of thing. One day, when I was about ten or so, the bulldozers came to the woods behind my house. I loved those hills and creeks, shaded by tall trees inviting play. For many summers, this had been the garden of my dreams. I slept out overnight beside the creek, pretending I was a true man of the woods. Daniel Boone, someone like that. Other times I leapt from limb to limb as Tarzan. On a path that had been beaten down over the years, I even practiced my losing effort in the fifty-yard dash at the grade-school track meet. When the bulldozers came to carve the land for still another postwar subdivision I was angry—at first.

In the first days of clear-cutting, the workers left a huge stack of fallen trees. With the limbs unsevered, and slowly dying leaves still attached, this accidental, unintended, temporary structure was for a few weeks a place of summer play. My pals and I climbed high on the fallen wood, slithered down into hidden crevices, cut away hiding places amid the branches. In those crevices and caves that would soon be hauled away, I had many an adventure, including even the first memorable, if futile, sexual act of my dimly approaching adolescence. For so long as it endured, this pile of construction rubbish had become a temporary, but wonderful, structure in and around which I organized a moment in my young life.

I have since heard of other children doing much the same. Even children who are poor—or those, poor or not, who are deprived of parental attentions—make their rooms, or their beds, or a corner of a closet into some little structure that, for a time, shelters their emotional lives, allowing them as best they can to organize their understanding of the world about. Dollhouses, train sets, Barbies, and toy soldiers are the occasional furnishings of the worlds imagined and played with in these corners. Structures like these (which, in the end, may not be all that different from social structures of all kinds) are able to support life, and give it order, even when they endure only for a short while.

Perhaps, to begin, we can agree that structures, including social ones, have at least two defining characteristics: (1) They make *order* out of some set of things—cells, stars, bodies, sleeping places, playrooms, imaginations, sex, and the like. (2) They do this work because they *endure* for a time, even if a very short time. In other words, structures organize some set of things because they lend them at least a minor degree of permanence. The set of things may eventually decay, come apart, or fade away, as did that stack of fallen trees and the fanciful experiments of my late childhood. But while they remain, they remain because some hard-to-define structure holds them together.

Of all the things sociologists concern themselves with, structures are, as I said, the most distinctive subject of their professional attentions. The same might be said of scientists of all kinds. Astronomers concern themselves with the structure of stellar things, just as psychologists are preoccupied with the structure of mental things, and microbiologists with the structure of organic matter.

This fascination with structures is especially remarkable among the social sciences. Economists study *markets* (a name for the structures within which economic transactions take place, fixing prices and values of other kinds). Political scientists study the structure of *political systems* (a name for the systematic, if not always fair, methods by which social groups decide who gets what among scarce resources). Cultural anthropologists, and many students of literature and the arts, study the varieties of *culture* (a name for the structures whereby societies organize myths, legends, stories, and other representations of what they value, hate, or wish to repress).

Sociology, it has been said, studies all of the above; it studies, that is, the structure of *social worlds* or, it is sometimes said, of *societies*. Unfortunately, though we often think we know what structures are, this confidence does not bear up under attempts to say with compelling precision just what realities terms like "social world" or "society" are meant to name. Social structures, somehow, are even less definite than others. A social world obviously includes everything that constitutes the collective life of groups of people, up to and including societies—their economics, their politics, their shared mental lives, their cultures, and more. Even when the social world is very small, like Frankie's hallway in Clarendon Heights, reference is made to some coherent order of social life that encompasses the economic, political, and cultural life of its members. This was an idea that Talcott Parsons made famous in the 1950s and for which his opponents, thinking he was a bit too ambitious, never forgave him. But Parsons was surely right in believing that sociology is in some sense the social science that aims to provide a general account of all that takes place in all the social worlds. Sociology, thus, is supremely interested in structures.

However uncertain social worlds may be, we know that social structures are real because differences among societies are easily spotted. Any particular enduring organization of an ongoing *social world* of people like the Lakota, the Russians, or the British is, simply, a *society*. The ongoing social worlds of members of a recognizable society can, therefore, be said to be structured such that their economic, political, and cultural practices, including any number of peculiar customs and manners, are as a whole distinct. Of this, illustrations are everywhere. Though the practices and structural forces of American society assault the Lakota society, still the social world of Lakota society is different and unlike any other. When we recognize differences of this kind, we understand that the very existence of a variety of social worlds is evidence of the powerful work of structures.

Still, structures appear to people in the course of daily life as through a mysterious fog. As I've said, it is very hard to say with precision exactly what a social structure is. Yet we must, if only because the practical sociologies by which people live and move are constantly drawn toward attempts to explain how and why structures so inexorably determine what individuals can and cannot do, even who they are. Behind the swagger, Frankie was bemoaning the structured destiny of his pals to be fuck-ups with few real options in life. Others, who might have been luckily born among the wealthiest 20 percent, have many more options than the Hallway Hangers, or for that matter the Lakota people. The privileged enjoy many more options than they need. But they, too, are who they are, and they do what they do, because of the mysterious work of social structures.

Power is the means by which social structures do this not-exactly-fair work of sorting people according to the few or many life-chances they get. Power may simply, if incompletely, be defined as the social energy of structures. Power is the determining force that causes some people to get less and some more of whatever is considered desirable in a social world.

It is power that accounts for the most important difference between social and other kinds of structures. In the structure of the universe, some stars die, while others burn on for eons. Yet no one but a poet would consider the uneven fates of stellar bodies far into darkest space a matter of unfairness. Still, strictly speaking, the death of some stars and the eternal spinning of others are the effects of cosmic energy empowering the shape of the universe into a definite structure. Though one can say that the extinction of some species of animal life is a tragedy, even this sad fate is normally felt to be a far lesser injustice than the suffering of colonized people or, even, of the urban poor like Frankie. It is only in relation to social things, to life in social worlds, that the question of power becomes a matter of binding moral intrigue. And, until we know what exactly the ants and dolphins truly think and feel, it is safe to assume that it is only in human society that the lack of power with all its sad consequences is felt so bitterly, with such terrible loss of possibility.

Perhaps the reason that is so is that power comes into serious consideration only when scarcity affects the moral as well as physical well-being of living creatures. All living beings, we know very well, are subject to the effects of scarcity, but these effects are different when the loss of life, or life's chances, is found to be a consequence of one group's theft of that to which another has a preexisting claim, perhaps a prior right of possession or ownership. Some people think that animals and plants have their distinctive rights to life. But, inasmuch as cows and trees are unable, at the present moment, to argue their case, their rights can be viewed as of a different kind. Yet, when human avarice enters in, suddenly the problem is beyond reasonable doubt.

The great herds of buffalo that possessed the American plains before the white people came died as much because their home grazing lands were divided artificially by the railroad as by the voracious stupidity of hunters for sport. When their natural access to food was diminished, the buffalo began to die. This was one scarcity-effect. But also, as the buffalo herds disappeared, the people native to the plains, including the Lakota, suffered a scarcity of meat upon which their way of life depended. Scarcity injured the buffalo as it did the Plains Indians. But its effect on the human societies can more reasonably be viewed as a sociologically interesting effect of social power. The white settlers and corporate bosses who took the plains for their use made life marginal for both the buffalo and the Indian. Only the moral confusion that did, indeed, prevail in the period of pioneer settlement could treat the danger to animals and people with equal indifference. What the Lakota lost was a direct and unequivocal result of the social power of the American society forming itself by a greedy grasp of the vast continental lands. That the whites viewed the theft of land and life as a right of their god's providence only masks the harsh reality. The current social structure of American society, based on its absolute control of a resource-rich continental landmass, was built and energized by social power taking a vast, but ultimately scarce, land from a weaker people.

When power works in these ways, it is relatively easy to see its effects in the structures that arise from the struggle for scarce but desirable goods like food, land, water, and much else. The sociological imagination would not be as demanding as it is if power always worked so openly. Sometimes it does; sometimes not. It is one thing, for example, to see the powerful effects of slavery on slaves and of colonization on the colonized, but quite another to see the effects of social power in the lives of people like Frankie. Compare, for example, Frankie's complaint at the beginning of this chapter to the reflections of Black Elk, an Oglala Lakota holy man, on the massacre at Wounded Knee:

I did not know then how much was ended. When I look back now from this high hill of my old age, I can still see the butchered women and children lying heaped and scattered all along the crooked gulch as plain as when I saw them with eyes still young. And I can see that something else died there in the bloody mud, and was buried in the blizzard. A people's dream died there. It was a beautiful dream.[2]

Black Elk saw clearly that what had happened to his people by the force of American power was devastating to the structures of his Lakota world. He was a holy man, a visionary. But this alone does not account for the greater clarity of Black Elk's understanding. Frankie's complaint is much more uncertain in that he places the responsibility (and blame) on himself and his fellow Hallway Hangers. Their plight was, he felt, a result of their own fuckings up.

It is true that poor people, including the Lakota, are perfectly capable of screwing up their own lives. But it is just as true that the energizing power of modern social structures does not very often do its work openly as it did at Wounded Knee and, thus, may be a powerful, but hidden, cause of trouble for many. This is the difference. The Lakota knew beyond any reasonable doubt that the land was theirs to use and respect and that the slaughter at Wounded Knee was a result of terrifyingly direct power. But Frankie did not so clearly see the wider powers of American social structures, even though it was these structures, every bit as much as the boys themselves, that caused their social failure.

Why could not Frankie see as clearly as Black Elk? This question leads to a still finer aspect of the mysterious workings of structuring power.

In most modern societies, most (but not all) of the time, people encounter powerful structures, not directly, but indirectly by the effects those structures cause, such as the ways teachers treated the Hallway Hangers as the losers they came to believe they were. Power may even sometimes work in the events that structures cause *not* to happen, as in Frankie's slim prospects for a good life. Either way, as bad as the consequences were for the Hallway Hangers, these effects of power are a far cry from the slaughter at Wounded Knee or the overt cruelty of slavery. The discouragement of the Hallway Hangers is one of the sneaky effects of powerful structures, an effect that challenges the sociological imagination.

One generic form of the sneaky epiphanies of power appears in the structures of *prestige*, that is, in the remarkable and systematic consistency with which nearly everyone in a society seems to agree that some persons ought to be respected highly, others less so, and some not at all. The way a society structures the distribution of prestige assigns to some people—certain championship prizefighters, for example—an incomprehensibly high status from which they usually become wealthy. At the same time, the prestige structure prevents others—most kindergarten teachers, for example—from achieving either status or wealth even though the worth of their work is certifiably more valuable than the entertainment value of public beatings rendered for pay and pleasure by boxers. We never see the actual structure of a status or prestige system, but schoolteachers (and their pupils) and boxers (and their excitable fans) experience it in all kinds of ways.

We know social structures more often by their consequences than by seeing them as such. In this sense, social structures are less like trees than stars. Trees we see. We can, as a consequence, well imagine their structures, which is why they are so often the subjects of photography, painting, art, poetry, and music. Distant stellar worlds, on the other hand, we never see. The thrill we get from those distant stars is always light-years away, long gone by the time we see it. Whatever may be the structure of the universe, its "reality" to astronomers, or lovers on a summer night, is at best a well-informed conjecture about something no one will *ever* see. Yet, were the sun to turn cold, or Jupiter to veer crazily out of its orbit, or were Darth Vader truly to invade our system, we would experience the consequences no more than we already do without realizing it. Most social structures are like this.

Most of us, for example, have distant relatives living in social worlds far from our own. They constitute the structure of our family (or kin) relations, and they make a difference. Not long ago my uncle Edwin, a quite famous professional sociologist, died after a long and productive life. At the funeral in California, I met a cousin I had not seen for half a century—when he was two and I was five. As he and his sisters and I and my brother shared our stories of their father, my father's brother, I felt a surprising (to use the correct term) *kinship* with them. Though differently, we were all shaped by many of the same family forces. In such ways, it is possible to catch an occasional glimpse of the social structures we otherwise experience by their effects, without ever seeing them all at once. After the funeral stories were told, we Lemerts had learned a great deal more about the particular, not-to-be-exaggerated prestige our fathers and uncles, their mothers and fathers, and each of us had come to possess, for better or worse. We understood, that is, a little more about how and why we each came to be who we are because of our kinship in this one structure among the many that influence us. Prestige bestows on individuals a sense of their status, whether high or low, in the structure of social things. This too is power, as anyone assigned an inferior status like Frankie's knows most painfully.

Alongside its sly workings in the structure of prestige, power also works through the structure of *authority*—the rules and regulations that assign to some people a limited right to tell others what they can and cannot do. Erving Goffman—the same Goffman who said "universal human nature is not a very human thing"—was one of sociology's most astute observers of the hidden effects of social structures like authority. In an intriguing footnote in one of his books, Goffman told a story of an event in the 1960s when the authority structures were very much in turmoil.

The event took place at Columbia University in the late spring of 1968 in the office of the university's president, Grayson Kirk. Rebel students, protesting the injustices of American society as they saw them in their own university, had taken over President Kirk's office and, quite literally, trashed it. This was not an uncommon form of student protest in those days, often inspiring outrage on the part of the authorities, including Mr. Kirk. Goffman begins his footnote by quoting a long paragraph from a book about the Columbia office trashing, then provides his own observation:

"One and a half hours after the President's suite had been cleared of student demonstrators, Grayson Kirk stood in the center of his private office looking at the blankets, cigarette butts and orange peels that covered his rug. Turning to A.M. Rosenthal of the *New York Times* and several other reporters who had come into the office with him he murmured, 'My God, how could human beings do a thing like this?' It was the only time, Truman [Kirk's dean] recalled later, that he had ever seen the President break down. Kirk's windows were crisscrossed with tape and on one hung a large sign reading 'Join Us.' His lampshades were torn, his carpet was spotted, his furniture was displaced and scratched. But the most evident and disturbing aspect of the scene was not the minor damage inflicted by the students. The everything-in-its-place decor to which Kirk had grown accustomed was now in disarray—disarray that was the result of the transformation of an office into the living quarters of 150 students during the past six days."

The great sociological question, of course, is not how could it be that human beings would do a thing like this, but rather how is it that human beings do this sort of thing so rarely. How come persons in authority have been so overwhelmingly successful in conning those beneath them into keeping the hell out of their offices?[3]

This is indeed the great sociological question. Just more than fifty years before President Kirk's office was trashed, Max Weber, a more sober commentator than Goffman, had asked the same question: "Why do men obey?" Why, indeed, do people obey authorities and their rules? It may be that no question comes closer than this one to opening up the hidden workings of power. We may be drawn to people of high prestige for the magic they sometimes seem to possess. But respect for authority is more complicated by far, thus more intriguing.

The remarkable fact that people tend to keep the hell out of the offices of the authorities, and otherwise respect the rules and regulations, even those nowhere written down, is perhaps the most impressive general evidence for the power of social structures in ordinary life. While there are many kinds of social structures, those that stand behind obedience to authority—norms, customs, rules, etiquettes, and the like—are among the more telling ones. When they work in our favor, we seldom notice. When they work against us, we notice the pain of punishment or exclusion. And, in the case of President Kirk and other authorities astonished by the actions of rebels, when authoritative structures *fail* to work any longer, such an occurrence is the subject of widespread interest. Throughout the spring of 1968 when students trashed Kirk's office, there were hundreds of demonstrations on college campuses worldwide. Everyone noticed, as well they should when the authoritative structures of such a valued institution as higher education are no longer respected.

Hence another curious feature of social structures: They tend to be invisible to those who enjoy their benefits until such time as they fail to deliver. But, even then, when workers and students, journalists, sociologists, and other rebels exercise their sociological imaginations to account for their failures in life, the collapsed social structure can only be reconstructed, *after the fact*. And, like the structure of prestige, it is never a totally present entity upon which hands can be laid. . . .

Social structures are salient enough to organize the small deeds of social worlds because they endure, for better or worse. Their duration, like that of mountains bearing the fossils and relics of life long gone, can only be the carrying forth of effects of the deep past. The class structure that, if you are young, may be at this very moment sorting you for a good chance at life, even as it assigns others lesser chances, did not spring up all at once like the dinosaurs of *Jurassic Park*. Structures are working on you as you read or nap, but their working is the slow-moving, leading edge of a social mountain, long enduring, not soon to tumble. The sociological imagination must always look up to the far peaks that define the dark valleys or pleasant streams where people live.

Mysteries abound. But it is not all that eerie to suppose that structures, like voices from the grave, press upon us out of the deep past of lost, but still powerful, worlds. Their weight may be deadly for many, or inspiring for those more privileged, but they are dead in the sense that structures do not, ever, have the same vital force as the actions individuals are generally able to take. Where the mystery persists is in how it happens that dead and invisible structures send forth so much power. Such a notion confounds the more common experience that the actions of social life rise up, instead, from individuals clustered in their many and different, but local, groups.

NOTES

1. [Frankie and the Hallway Hangers were students who lived in Clarendon Heights, a public housing project for the poor. The Hangers, whose families were broken either by death or by separation, were on the verge of social and criminal trouble. –Ed.]

2. *Black Elk Speaks: Being the Life Story of a Holy Man of the Oglala Sioux As Told through John C. Neihardt (Flaming Rainbow)* (New York: W. Morrow, 1932); reprint (University of Nebraska Press, 1974), p. 270.

3. Erving Goffman, *Relations in Public* (New York: Harper Torchbooks, 1971), p. 288.

2

"They" Are All the Same, But Each Member of My Group Is Unique

Stephen Worchel

. . . Some years ago, I took my first trip to China. During my visit, I probably interacted with 20 to 30 Chinese for any length of time. Upon returning, I encountered a Chinese colleague, and during our conversation I proclaimed that I finally had a good picture of the Chinese people: "They are bright, hardworking, happy, and friendly." My colleague smiled and asked me to describe Americans. I was taken aback, but after considerable thought I politely informed him that Americans are so diverse that it is really impossible to describe them in a few words. He never stopped smiling as he reminded me that there are over a billion people in China, including 28 distinct minority groups, yet I had no trouble describing "Chinese people" after meeting only 20 to 30 of them.

There is considerable evidence that we often view out-groups as homogeneous, while we see considerable diversity within our own group. For example, Quattrone and Jones (1980) asked students at Princeton and Rutgers university to describe the student body at their own and the other university. In both cases, the students perceived considerably more variability within the student body at their own university. Linville, Fischer, and Salavoy (1989) found that residents of an elderly people's home and a student group rated the other age group as more homogenous than their own group. There are some exceptions to this tendency. For example, people in minority groups often see their group as more homogeneous than the majority group (Simon & Brown, 1987), and members of new groups see their groups as more homogeneous than out-groups (Worchel, Coutant-Sassic, & Grossman, 1992). However, the inclination to see homogeneity in an out-group is very pervasive.

It has been argued that this effect occurs because we generally have more information from a greater variety of experiences with members of our own group than with members of out-groups. I've interacted with thousands of Americans in work, social, and religious settings, but my interactions with the Chinese were limited to professional situations in which we were strangers to each other. I failed to take this difference into account when forming my mental image of the Chinese. Another possibility is that because our in-group is more important to us and we have a higher motivation to perceive it correctly, we develop a more varied picture of it (Park, Judd, & Ryan, 1991).

But whatever the basis, consider the implications of this process. First, if I believe that members of other ethnic groups are similar, I will quickly form an impression of the whole group after meeting only a few of its members: "Know one, know them all." Second, I can justify limiting my interaction with an out-group because I'll know about the group and its members after only a few contacts. This reduced contact will ensure that my representation of the group is rarely challenged. I felt little need to return to China or meet other Chinese, because I now had a "good" picture of the group. I was ready to expand my growing knowledge of the world's people by taking a week's trip to Brazil. . . .

MORE THAN A PICTURE: THE INFLUENCE OF STEREOTYPES

. . . At a benign level, stereotypes help order our world and keep us from becoming overwhelmed by information. But this benefit comes at a cost. By putting people into categories, we tend to overlook differences between people in a category. And we tend to hold on to a stereotype as if it were our last friend on earth. Indeed, we humans have employed an elaborate array of mental activities to maintain our views.

First, we employ *selective attention*. Our stereotypes guide us to pay attention to certain details of a situation and ignore the rest (Schaller & Maass, 1989). For example, if my stereotype of your group includes the trait clumsiness, I will be quick to notice when you trip over a fold in the carpet. Without that component in the stereotype, I would most likely overlook this behavior. When I guide my attention to certain behaviors (and ignore others), my chance of finding support for my stereotype increases dramatically.

But we don't stop there. Next, our stereotypes induce *selective interpretation* of events, especially ambiguous events. In an early study, white participants watched either a black or a white person interacting with a white person (Duncan, 1976). During an animated conversation, the first person gave the second an "ambiguous shove." When the observers were asked about the shove, they viewed it as playing around or emphasizing a point when it came from a white actor. However, when the actor was black, the shove was interpreted as hostile and aggressive. Other research has shown that we are most likely to interpret events in line with our stereotypes when we are busy and have little time to pay close attention to actions that are unfolding (Gilbert & Hixon, 1991). The point is that our stereotypes prime us to interpret events in ways that confirm our expectations. This tendency not only causes us to interpret actions at times but also helps our stereotypes resist pressure to change.

Stereotypes also affect our *memory* of events: we often recall details and situations that support our stereotypes. When I was a college student, a group of Brazilians lived next door. That year, I had attended Mardi Gras and came home with the impression that Brazilians were great party animals. Three years later I saw one of my former neighbors in medical school. I was quite surprised because all I remembered of him was the parties he and his roommates had during the year he lived next to me. I couldn't recall that he had ever studied or that there had been any moments of silence in his apartment. In an interesting demonstration of selective memory, Cohen (1981) showed people a video of a woman having a birthday dinner with her husband. When the viewers were told that the woman was a waitress, they recalled that she had a television set and drank beer. But when they were told that she was a librarian, they remembered that she wore glasses and listened to classical music during the dinner. All of the points recalled were correct, but the expectations of the perceivers influenced which points they remembered.

Not only do stereotypes affect how we store and interpret information; they also guide our attitudes and behaviors. Because many stereotypes involve out-groups and we are motivated to enhance the image of our own group, many, if not most, stereotypes are relatively negative. On the basis of negative information, we are apt to develop *prejudice* toward individuals from these out-groups. *Prejudice* is "a negative attitude toward, or evaluation of, a person based on his or her membership in a group other than one's own" (Worchel, Cooper, & Goethals, 1991, p. 360). In other words, we dislike an individual because he or she belongs to a different ethnic group, religion, sex, or nation. Our dislike is based not on the individual's behavior but on his or her group. From this base of prejudice, discrimination is likely to follow. *Discrimination* is action taken to harm a group, or a member of a group, on the basis of membership in the group. In its extreme form, the combination of prejudice and discrimination can lead to *delegitimization* of a target group (Bar-Tal, 1988), determining that it does not deserve fair treatment according to a code of norms calling for proper and decent behavior. This view opens the door for the exploitation of the target group and even justifies resorting to violence. . . .

REFERENCES

Bar-Tal, D. 1988. Delegitimizing Relations between Israeli Jews and Palestinians: A Social-Psychological Analysis. In *Arab-Jewish Relations in Israel: A Quest for Human Understanding*, ed. J. Hoffman. Bristol, Ind.: Wyndham Hall Press.

Cohen, C. 1981. Person Categories and Social Perception: Testing Some Boundaries of the Processing Effects of Prior Knowledge. *Journal of Personality and Social Psychology* 40: 441–52.

Duncan, D. 1976. Differential Social Perception and Attribution of Intergroup Violence: Testing the Lower Limits of Stereotyping of Blacks. *Journal of Personality and Social Psychology* 34: 590–98.

Gilbert, D., & J. Hixon. 1991. The Trouble of Thinking: Activation and Application of Stereotypic Beliefs. *Journal of Personality and Social Psychology* 50: 509–17.

Linville, P., G. Fisher, & P. Salavoy. 1989. Perceived Distributions of the Characteristics of In-groups and Out-group Members: Empirical Evidence and A Computer Simulation. *Journal of Personality and Social Psychology* 57: 165–88.

Park, B., C. Judd, & C. Ryan. 1991. Social Categorization and the Representation of Variability Information. In *European Review of Social Psychology*, vol. 2., edited by W. Stroeber & M. Hewstone. London: Wiley.

Quattrone, G., & E. Jones. 1980. The Perception of Variability Within In-groups and Out-groups: Implications for the Law of Small Numbers. *Journal of Personality and Social Psychology* 38: 141–52.

Schaller, M., & A. Maass. 1989. Illusory Correlations and Social Categorization: Toward an Integration of Motivational and Cognitive Factors in Stereotype Formation. *Journal of Personality and Social Psychology* 56: 709–21.

Simon, B., & R. Brown. 1987. Perceived Intragroup Homogeneity in Minority-Majority Contexts. *Journal of Personality and Social Psychology* 53: 703–11.

Worchel, S., J. Cooper, & G. Goethals. 1991. *Understanding Social Psychology*, 5th ed. Pacific Grove, Ga.: Brooks Cole.

Worchel, S., D. Coutant-Sassic, & M. Grossman. 1992. A Developmental Approach to Group Dynamics: A Model and Illustrative Research. In *Group Process and Productivity*, edited by S. Worchel, W. Wood, & J. Simpson. Newbury Park, Calif.: Sage.

Part Two

Embedded Ideology:
Racism/Ethnocentrism and Sexism

3

Black Women and Feminism

bell hooks

Toward the end of 1987 I spoke at Tufts University at an annual dinner for black women. My topic was "Black Women in Predominantly White Institutions." I was excited by the idea of talking with so many young black women but surprised when these women suggested that sexism was not a political issue of concern to black women, that the serious issue was racism. I've heard this response many times, yet somehow I did not expect that I would need to prove over and over that sexism ensures that many black females will be exploited and victimized. Confronted by these young black women to whom sexism was not important, I felt that feminism had failed to develop a politics that addresses black women. Particularly, I felt that black women active in black liberation struggles in the 1960s and early 1970s, who had spoken and written on sexism (remember the anthology *The Black Woman*, edited by Toni Cade Bambara?) had let our younger sisters down by not making more of a sustained political effort so that black women (and black people) would have greater understanding of the impact of sexist oppression on our lives.

When I began to share my own experiences of racism and sexism, pointing to incidents (particularly in relationships with black men), a veil was lifted. Suddenly the group acknowledged what had been previously denied—the ways sexism wounds us as black women. I had talked earlier about the way many black women students in predominantly white institutions keep silent in classes, stating emphatically that our progress in such places requires us to have a voice, to not remain silent. In the ensuing discussion, women commented on black fathers who had told their daughters "nobody wants a loud-talking black woman." The group expressed ambivalent

From *Talking Back: Thinking Feminist, Thinking Black* by bell hooks (Boston: South End Press, 1989), pp. 177–83. Reprinted with permission.

feelings about speaking, particularly on political issues in classroom settings where they were often attacked or unsupported by other black women students.

Their earlier reluctance to acknowledge sexism reminded me of previous arguments with other groups of women about both the book and the film *The Color Purple*. Our discussions focused almost solely on whether portraying brutal sexist domination of a black female by a black male had any basis in reality. I was struck by the extent to which folks will go to argue that sexism in black communities has not promoted the abuse and subjugation of black women by black men. This fierce denial has its roots in the history of black people's response to racism and white supremacy. Traditionally it has been important for black people to assert that slavery, apartheid, and continued discrimination have not undermined the humanity of black people, that not only has the race been preserved but that the survival of black families and communities are the living testimony of our victory. To acknowledge, then, that our families and communities have been undermined by sexism would not only require an acknowledgement that racism is not the only form of domination and oppression that affects us as a people; it would mean critically challenging the assumption that our survival as a people depends on creating a cultural climate in which black men can achieve manhood within paradigms constructed by white patriarchy.

Often the history of our struggle as black people is made synonymous with the efforts of black males to have patriarchal power and privilege. As one black woman college student put it, "In order to redeem the race we have to redeem black manhood." If such redemption means creating a society in which black men assume the stereotypical male role of provider and head of household, then sexism is seen not as destructive but as essential to the promotion and maintenance of the black family. Tragically, it has been our acceptance of this model that has prevented us from acknowledging that black male sexist domination has *not* enhanced or enriched black family life. The seemingly positive aspects of the patriarchy (caretaker and provider) have been the most difficult for masses of black men to realize, and the negative aspects (maintaining control through psychological or physical violence) are practiced daily. Until black people redefine in a nonsexist revolutionary way the terms of our liberation, black women and men will always be confronted with the issue of whether supporting feminist efforts to end sexism is inimical to our interests as a people.

In her insightful essay, "Considering Feminism as a Model for Social Change," Sheila Radford-Hill makes the useful critique that black women producing feminist theory, myself included, focus more on the racism of white women within feminist movement, and on the importance of racial difference, than on the ways feminist struggle could strengthen and help black communities. In part, the direction of our work was shaped by the nature of our experience. Not only were there very few black women writing feminist theory, but most of us were not living in or working with black communities. The aim of *Ain't I A Woman* was not to focus on the racism of white women. Its primary purpose was to establish that sexism greatly determines the social status and experience of black women. I did not try to examine the ways that struggling to end sexism would benefit black people, but this is my current concern.

Many black women insist that they do not join the feminist movement because they cannot bond with white women who are racist. If one argues that there really are some white women who are resisting and challenging racism, who are genuinely committed to ending white supremacy, one is accused of being naive, of not acknowledging history. Most black women, rich and poor, have contact with white women, usually in work settings. In such settings black women cooperate with white women despite racism. Yet black women are reluctant to express solidarity with white feminists. Black women's consciousness is shaped by internalized racism and by reactionary white women's concerns as they are expressed in popular culture, such as daytime soap operas or in the world of white fashion and cosmetic products, which masses of black women consume without rejecting this racist propaganda and devaluing of black women.

Emulating white women or bonding with them in these "apolitical" areas is not consistently questioned or challenged. Yet I do not know a single black woman advocate of feminist politics who is not bombarded by ongoing interrogations by other black people about linking with racist white women (as though we lack the political acumen to determine whether white women are racists, or when it is in our interest to act in solidarity with them).

At times, the insistence that feminism is really "a white female thing that has nothing to do with black women" masks black female rage towards white women, a rage rooted in the historical servant-served relationship where white women have used power to dominate, exploit, and oppress. Many black women share this animosity, and it is evoked again and again when white women attempt to assert control over us. This resistance to white female domination must be separated from a black female refusal to bond with white women engaged in feminist struggle. This refusal is often rooted as well in traditional sexist models: women learn to see one another as enemies, as threats, as competitors. Viewing white women as competitors for jobs, for companions, for valuation in a culture that only values select groups of women, often serves as a barrier to bonding, even in settings where radical white women are not acting in a dominating manner. In some settings it has become a way of one-upping white women for black women to trivialize feminism.

Black women must separate feminism as a political agenda from white women or we will never be able to focus on the issue of sexism as it affects black communities. Even though there are a few black women (I am one) who assert that we empower ourselves by using the term feminism, by addressing our concerns as black women as well as our concern with the welfare of the human community globally, we have had little impact. Small groups of black feminist theorists and activists who use the term "black feminism" (the Combahee River Collective is one example) have not had much success in organizing large groups of black women, or stimulating widespread interest in feminist movement. Their statement of purpose and plans for action focus exclusively on black women acknowledging the need for forms of separatism. Here the argument that black women do not collectively advocate feminism because of an unwillingness to bond with racist white women appears most problematic. Key concerns that serve as barriers to black women advocating feminist politics are heterosexism, the fear that one will be seen as betraying black men or promoting hatred of men and as a consequence becoming less desirable to male companions; homophobia (often I am told by black people that all feminists are lesbians); and deeply ingrained misogynist attitudes toward one another, perpetuating sexist thinking and sexist competition.

Recently I spoke with a number of black women about why they are not more involved in feminist thinking and feminist movement. Many of them talked about harsh treatment by other black women, about being socially ostracized or talked about in negative and contemptuous ways at all-female gatherings or at conferences on gender issues. A few people committed to feminist politics described times when they found support from white women and resistance from black women peers. A black woman scheduled on a panel arrived late and couldn't find a seat in the room. When she entered and had been standing for a while, I greeted her warmly from the podium and encouraged her to join me as there were seats in front. Not only did she choose to stand, during the break she said to me, "How dare you embarrass me by asking me to come up front." Her tone was quite hostile. I was disturbed that she saw this gesture as an attempt to embarrass her rather than as a gesture of recognition. This is not an isolated case. There are many occasions when we witness the failure of black women to trust one another, when we approach one another with suspicion.

Years ago I attended a small conference with about 20 black women. We were to organize a national conference on black feminism. We came from various positions, politics, and sexual preferences. A well-known black woman scholar at a prestigious institution, whose feminist thinking was not deemed appropriately advanced, was treated with contempt and hostility. It was a disturbing time. A number of the black women present had white women companions and lovers. Yet concerning the issue of whether white women should be allowed to attend the conference, they were adamant that it should be for black women only, that white women all too often try to control us. There was no space for constructive critical dialogue. How could they trust white women lovers to unlearn racism, to not be dominating, and yet in this setting act as though all white women were our enemies? The conference never happened. At least one black woman went away from this experience determined never to participate in an activity organized around black feminists or any other feminists. As a group we failed to create an atmosphere of solidarity. The only bonds established were along very traditional lines among the folks who were famous, who talked the loudest and the most, who were more politically correct. And there was no attempt to enable black women with different perspectives to come together.

It is our collective responsibility as individual black women committed to feminist movement to work at making space where black women who are just beginning to explore feminist issues can do so without fear of hostile treatment, quick judgments, dismissals, etc.

I find more black women than ever before are appearing on panels that focus on gender. Yet I have observed, and other black women thinkers have shared as well, that often these women see gender as a subject for discourse or for increased professional visibility, not for political action. Often professional black women with academic degrees are quite conservative politically. Their perspectives differ greatly from our foremothers who were politically astute, assertive, and radical in their work for social change.

Feminist praxis is greatly shaped by academic women and men. Since there are not many academic black women committed to radical politics, especially with a gender focus, there is no collective base in the academy for forging a feminist politics that addresses masses of black women. There is much more work by black women on gender and sexism emerging from scholars who do literary criticism and from creative fiction and drama writers than from women in history, sociology, and political science. While it does not negate commitment to radical politics, in literature it is much easier to separate academic work and political concerns. Concurrently, if black women academics are not committed to feminist ethics, to feminist consciousness-raising, they end up organizing conferences in which social interactions mirror sexist norms, including ways black women regard one another. For the uninitiated coming to see and learn what feminism centered on black women might be like, this can be quite disillusioning.

Often in these settings the word "feminism" is evoked in negative terms, even though sexism and gender issues are discussed. I hear black women academics laying claim to the term "womanist" while rejecting "feminist." I do not think Alice Walker intended this term to deflect from feminist commitment, yet this is often how it is evoked. Walker defines womanist as black feminist or feminist of color. When I hear black women using the term womanist, it is in opposition to the term feminist; it is viewed as constituting something separate from feminist politics shaped by white women. For me, the term womanist is not sufficiently linked to a tradition of radical political commitment to struggle and change. What would a womanist politic look like? If it is a term for black feminist, then why do those who embrace it reject the other?

Radford-Hill makes the point:

> Not all black feminists practice or believe in black feminism. Many see black feminism as a vulgar detraction from the goal of female solidarity. Others of us, myself included, see black feminism as a necessary step toward ending racism and sexism, given the nature of gender oppression and the magnitude of society's resistance to racial justice.

I believe that women should think less in terms of feminism as an identity and more in terms of "advocating feminism"; to move from emphasis on personal lifestyle

issues toward creating political paradigms and racial models of social change that
emphasize collective as well as individual change. For this reason I do not call myself a black feminist. Black women must continue to insist on our right to participate in shaping feminist issues. Current feminist scholarship can be useful to black
women in formulating critical analyses of gender issues about black people, particularly feminist work on parenting. (When I first read Dorothy Dinnerstein, it was
interesting to think about her work in terms of black mother-son relationships.)

Black women need to construct a model of feminist theorizing and scholarship
that is inclusive, that widens our options, that enhances our understanding of black
experience and gender. Significantly, the most basic task confronting black feminists
(irrespective of the terms we use to identify ourselves) is to educate one another and
black people about sexism, about the ways resisting sexism can empower black
women, a process which makes sharing feminist vision more difficult. Radford-Hill
identifies "the crisis of black womanhood" as a serious problem that must be considered politically, asserting that "the extent to which black feminists can articulate
and solve the crisis of black womanhood is the extent to which black women will
undergo feminist transformation."

Black women must identify ways feminist thought and practice can aid in our
process of self-recovery and share that knowledge with out sisters. This is the base
on which to build political solidarity. When that grounding exists, black women will
be fully engaged in feminist movement that transforms self, community, and society.

4

Divining Our Racial Themes

Derrick Bell

. . . The fact of slavery refuses to fade, along with the deeply embedded personal attitudes and public policy assumptions that supported it for so long. Indeed, the racism
that made slavery feasible is far from dead in the last decade of twentieth-century America;
and the civil rights gains, so hard won, are being steadily eroded. Despite undeniable
progress for many, no African Americans are insulated from incidents of racial discrimination. Our careers, even our lives, are threatened because of our color. Even the most
successful of us are haunted by the plight of our less fortunate brethren who struggle for
existence in what some social scientists call the "underclass." Burdened with life-long
poverty and soul-devastating despair, they live beyond the pale of the American Dream.
What we designate as "racial progress" is not a solution to that problem. It is a regenera-
tion of the problem in a particularly perverse form.

According to data compiled in 1990 for basic measures of poverty, unemployment,
and income, the slow advances African Americans made during the 1960s and 1970s
have definitely been reversed. The unemployment rate for blacks is 2.5 times the
rate for whites. Black per-capita income is not even two thirds of the income for
whites; and blacks, most of whom own little wealth or business property, are three
times more likely to have income below the poverty level than whites.[1] If trends of
the last two decades are allowed to continue, readers can safely—and sadly—assume
that the current figures are worse than those cited here.[2]

Statistics cannot, however, begin to express the havoc caused by joblessness and
poverty: broken homes, anarchy in communities, futility in the public schools. All
are the bitter harvest of race-determined unemployment in a society where work
provides sustenance, status, and the all-important sense of self-worth. What we now

call the "inner city" is, in fact, the American equivalent of the South African home-lands. Poverty is less the source than the status of men and women who, despised because of their race, seek refuge in self-rejection. Drug-related crime, teenaged par-enthood, and disrupted and disrupting family life all are manifestations of a despair that feeds on self. That despair is bred anew each day by the images on ever-playing television sets, images confirming that theirs is the disgraceful form of living, not the only way people live.

Few whites are able to identify with blacks as a group—the essential prerequisite for feeling empathy with, rather than aversion from, blacks' self-inflicted suffering. . . . Unable or unwilling to perceive that "there but for the grace of God, go I," few whites are ready to actively promote civil rights for blacks. Because of an irrational but easily roused fear that any social reform will unjustly benefit blacks, whites fail to support the programs this country desperately needs to address the ever-widening gap between the rich and the poor, both black and white.

Lulled by comforting racial stereotypes, fearful that blacks will unfairly get ahead of them, all too many whites respond to even the most dire reports of race-based disadvantage with either a sympathetic headshake or victim-blaming rationalizations. Both responses lead easily to the conclusion that contemporary complaints of racial discrimination are simply excuses put forward by people who are unable or unwill-ing to compete on an equal basis in a competitive society.

For white people who both deny racism and see a heavy dose of the Horatio Alger myth as the answer to blacks' problems, how sweet it must be when a black person stands in a public place and condemns as slothful and unambitious those blacks who are not making it. Whites eagerly embrace black conservatives' homilies to self-help, however grossly unrealistic such messages are in an economy where millions, white as well as black, are unemployed and, more important, in one where racial discrimi-nation in the workplace is as vicious (if less obvious) than it was when employers posted signs "no negras need apply."

Whatever the relief from responsibility such thinking provides those who embrace it, more than a decade of civil rights setbacks in the White House, in the courts, and in the critical realm of media-nurtured public opinion has forced retrenchment in the tattered civil rights ranks. We must reassess our cause and our approach to it, but repetition of time-worn slogans simply will not do. As a popular colloquialism puts it, it is time to "get real" about race and the persistence of racism in America.

To make such an assessment—to plan for the future by reviewing the experiences of the past—we must ask whether the formidable hurdles we now face in the elu-sive quest for racial equality are simply a challenge to our commitment, whether they are the latest variation of the old hymn "One More River to Cross." Or, as we once again gear up to meet the challenges posed by these unexpected new setbacks, are we ignoring a current message with implications for the future which history has already taught us about the past?

Such assessment is hard to make. On the one hand, contemporary color barriers are certainly less visible as a result of our successful effort to strip the law's endorsement from the hated Jim Crow signs. Today one can travel for thousands of miles across this country and never see a public facility designated as "Colored" or "White." Indeed, the very absence of visible signs of discrimination creates an atmosphere of racial neutrality and encourages whites to believe that racism is a thing of the past. On the other hand, the general use of so-called neutral standards to continue exclusionary practices reduces the effectiveness of traditional civil rights laws, while rendering discriminatory actions more oppressive than ever. Racial bias in the pre-*Brown* era was stark, open, unalloyed with hypocrisy and blank-faced lies. We black, when rejected, knew who our enemies were. They were not us! Today, because bias is masked in unofficial practiced and "neutral" standards, we must wrestle with the question whether race or some individual failing has cost us the job, denied us the promotion, or prompted our being rejected as tenants for an apartment. Either conclusion breeds frustration and alienation—and a rage we dare not show to others or admit to ourselves.

Modern discrimination is, moreover, not practiced indiscriminately. Whites, ready and willing applaud, even idolize black athletes and entertainers, refuse to hire, or balk at working with, blacks. Whites who number individual blacks among their closest friends approve, or do not oppose, practices that bar selling or renting homes or apartments in their neighborhoods to blacks they don't know. Employers, not wanting "too many of them," are willing to hire one or two black people, but will reject those who apply later. Most hotels and restaurants who offer black patrons courteous—even deferential—treatment, uniformly reject black job applicants, except perhaps for the most menial jobs. When did you last see a black waiter in a really good restaurant?

Racial schizophrenia is not limited to hotels and restaurants. As a result, neither professional status nor relatively high income protects even accomplished blacks from capricious acts of discrimination that may reflect either individual "preference" or an institution's bias. The motivations for bias vary; the disadvantage to black victims is the same.

Careful examination reveals a pattern to these seemingly arbitrary racial actions. When whites perceive that it will be profitable or at least cost-free to serve, hire, admit, or otherwise deal with blacks on a nondiscriminatory basis, they do so. When they fear—accurately or not—that there may be a loss, inconvenience, or upset to themselves or other whites, discriminatory conduct usually follows. Selections and rejections reflect preference as much as prejudice. A preference for whites makes it harder to prove the discrimination outlawed by civil rights laws. This difficulty, when combined with lackluster enforcement, explains why discrimination in employment and in the housing market continues to prevail more than two decades after enactment of the Equal Employment Opportunity Act of 1965[3] and the Fair Housing Act of 1968.[4]

Racial policy is the culmination of thousands of these individual practices. Black people, then, are caught in a double bind. We are, as I have said, disadvantaged unless whites perceive that nondiscriminatory treatment for us will be a benefit for them. In addition, even when nonracist practices might bring a benefit, whites may rely on discrimination against blacks as a unifying factor and a safety valve for frustrations during economic hard times.

Almost always, the injustices that dramatically diminish the rights of blacks are linked to the serious economic disadvantage suffered by many whites who lack money and power. Whites, rather than acknowledge the similarity of their disadvantage, particularly when compared with that of better-off whites, are easily detoured into protecting their sense of entitlement vis-à-vis blacks for all things of value. Evidently, this racial preference expectation is hypnotic. It is this compulsive fascination that seems to prevent most whites from even seeing—much less resenting—the far more sizable gap between their status and those who occupy the lofty levels at the top of our society.

Race consciousness of this character, as Professor Kimberlè Crenshaw suggested in 1988 in a pathbreaking *Harvard Law Review* article, makes it difficult for whites "to imagine the world differently. It also creates the desire for identification with privileged elites. By focusing on a distinct, subordinate 'other,' whites include themselves in the dominant circle—an arena in which most hold no real power, but only their privileged racial identity."[5]

The critically important stabilizing role that blacks play in this society constitutes a major barrier in the way of achieving racial equality. Throughout history, politicians have used blacks as scapegoats for failed economic or political policies. Before the Civil War, rich slave owners persuaded the white working class to stand with them against the danger of slave revolts—even though the existence of slavery condemned white workers to a life of economic privation.[6] After the Civil War, poor whites fought social reforms and settled for segregation rather than see formerly enslaved blacks get ahead.[7] Most labor unions preferred to allow plant owners to break strikes with black scab labor rather than allow blacks to join their ranks.[8] The "them against us" racial ploy—always a potent force in economic bad times—is working again: today whites, as disadvantaged by high-status entrance requirements as blacks, fight to end affirmative action policies that, by eliminating class-based entrance requirements and requiring widespread advertising of jobs, have likely helped far more whites than blacks. And in the 1990s, as through much of the 1980s, millions of Americans—white as well as black—face steadily worsening conditions: unemployment, inaccessible health care, inadequate housing, mediocre education, and pollution of the environment. The gap in national incomes is approaching a crisis as those in the top fifth now earn more than their counterparts in the bottom four fifths combined. The conservative guru Kevin Phillips used a different but no less disturbing comparison: the top two million income earners in this country earn more than the next one hundred million.[9]

Shocking. And yet conservative white politicians are able to gain and hold even the highest office despite their failure to address seriously any of these issues. They rely instead on time-tested formula of getting needy whites to identify on the basis of their shared skin color, and suggest with little or no subtlety that white people must stand together against the Willie Hortons, or against racial quotas, or against affirmative action. The code words differ. The message is the same. Whites are rallied on the basis of racial pride and patriotism to accept their often lowly lot in life, and encouraged to vent their frustration by opposing any serious advancement by blacks. Crucial to this situation is the unstated understanding by the mass of whites that they will accept large disparities in economic opportunity in respect to other whites as long as they have a priority over blacks and other people of color for access to the few opportunities available.

This "racial bonding" by whites[10] means that black rights and interests are always vulnerable to diminishment if not to outright destruction. The willingness of whites over time to respond to this racial rallying cry explains—far more than does the failure of liberal democratic practices (re black rights) to coincide with liberal democratic theory—blacks' continuing subordinate status. This is, of course, contrary to the philosophy of Gunnar Myrdal's massive midcentury study *The American Dilemma.* Myrdal and two generations of civil rights advocates accepted the idea of racism as merely an odious holdover from slavery, "a terrible and inexplicable anomaly struck in the middle of our liberal democratic ethos."[11] No one doubted that the standard American policy making was adequate to the task of abolishing racism. White America, it was assumed, *wanted* to abolish racism.[12]

Forty years later, in *The New American Dilemma,* Professor Jennifer Hochschild examined what she called Myrdal's "anomaly thesis," and concluded that it simply cannot explain the persistence of racial discrimination.[13] Rather, the continued viability of racism demonstrates "that racism is not simply an excrescence on a fundamentally healthy liberal democratic body, but is part of what shapes and energizes the body."[14] Under this view, "liberal democracy and racism in the United States are historically, even inherently, reinforcing; American society as we know it exists only because of its foundation in racially based slavery, and it thrives only because racial discrimination continues. The apparent anomaly is an actual symbiosis."[15]

The permanence of this "symbiosis" ensures that civil rights gains will be temporary and setbacks inevitable. Consider: In this last decade of the twentieth century, color determines the social and economic status of all African Americans, both those who have been highly successful and their poverty-bound brethren whose lives are grounded in misery and despair. We rise and fall less as a result of our efforts than in response to the needs of a white society that condemns all blacks to quasi citizenship as surely as it segregated our parents and enslaved their forebears. The fact is that, despite what we designate as progress wrought through struggle over many generations, we remain what we were in the beginning: a dark and foreign presence, always the designated "other." Tolerated in good times, despised when things go wrong, as a people we are scapegoated and sacrificed as distraction or catalyst for compromise to facilitate resolution of political differences or relieve economic adversity.

We are now, as were our forebears when they were brought to the New World, objects of barter for those who, while profiting from our existence, deny our humanity. It is in the light of this fact that we must consider the haunting questions about slavery and exploitation contained in Professor Linda Myers's *Understanding an Afrocentric World View: Introduction to an Optimal Psychology*, questions that serve as their own answers.[16]

We simply cannot prepare realistically for our future without assessing honestly our past. It seems cold, accusatory, but we must try to fathom with her "the mentality of a people that could continue for over 300 years to kidnap an estimated 50 million youth and young adults from Africa, transport them across the Atlantic with about half dying unable to withstand the inhumanity of the passage, and enslave them as animals."[17]

As Professor Myers reminds us, blacks were not the only, and certainly not America's most, persecuted people. Appropriate, she asks about the mindset of European Americans to native Americans. After all, those in possession of the land were basically friendly to the newcomers. And yet the European Americans proceeded to annihilate almost the entire race, ultimately forcing the survivors onto reservations after stealing their land. Far from acknowledging and atoning for the atrocities, American history portrays whites as the heroes, the Indian victims as savage villains. "What," she wonders, "can be understood about the world view of a people who claim to be building a democracy with freedom and justice for all, and at the same time own slaves and deny others basic human rights?"[18]

Of course, Americans did not invent slavery. The practice has existed throughout recorded history, and Professor Orlando Patterson, a respected scholar, argues impressively that American slavery was no worse than that practiced in other parts of the world.[19] But it is not comparative slavery policies that concern me. Slavery is, as an example of what white America has done, a constant reminder of what white America might do.

We must see this country's history of slavery, not as an insuperable racial barrier to blacks, but as a legacy of enlightenment from our enslaved forebears reminding us that if they survived the ultimate form of racism, we and those whites who stand with us can at least view racial oppression in its many contemporary forms without underestimating its critical importance and likely permanent status in this country.

To initiate the reconsideration, I want to set forth this proposition, which will be easier to reject than refute: *Black people will never gain full equality in this country. Even those herculean efforts we hail as successful will produce no more than temporary "peaks of progress," short-lived victories that slide into irrelevance as racial patterns adapt in ways that maintain white dominance. This is a hard-to-accept fact that all history verifies. We must acknowledge it, not as a sign of submission, but as an act of ultimate defiance.*

We identify with and hail as hero the man or woman willing to face even death without flinching.[20] Why? Because, while no one escapes death, those who conquer their dread of it are freed to live more fully. In similar fashion, African Americans must confront and conquer the otherwise deadening reality of our permanent subordinate status. Only in this way can we prevent ourselves from being dragged down by society's racial hostility. Beyond survival lies the potential to perceive more clearly both a reason and the means for further struggle. . . .

I realize that even with the challenge to rethinking these stories pose, many people will find it difficult to embrace my assumption that racism is a permanent component of American life. Mesmerized by the racial equality syndrome, they are too easily reassured by simple admonitions to "stay on course," which come far too easily from those—black and white—who are not on the deprived end of the economic chasm between blacks and whites.

The goal of racial equality is, while comforting to many whites, more illusionary than real for blacks. For too long, we have worked for substantive reform, then settled for weakly worded and poorly enforced legislation, indeterminate judicial decisions, token government positions, even holidays. I repeat. If we are to seek new goals for our struggles, we must first reassess the worth of the racial assumptions on which, without careful though, we have presumed too much and relied on too long.

Let's begin.

NOTES

1. David Swinton, "The Economic Status of African Americans: 'Permanent' Poverty and Inequality," in *The State of Black America* (National Urban League, 1991), 25.

2. Not all the data are bleak. While the median family income for black families declined in the 1970s and 1980s, the proportion of African-American families with incomes of $35,000 to $50,000 increased from 23.3 to 27.5 percent. The proportion with incomes above $50,000 increased by 38 percent, from 10.0 to 13.8 percent. The overall median income for blacks declined, though: while the top quarter made progress, the bottom half was sliding backward, and the proportion of blacks receiving very low income (less than $5,000) actually increased. Swinton, 36–37.

3. Act of 2 July 1964, P.L. 88–352, 42 U.S.C.A. 2000e–2000e–17.

4. Fair Housing Act of 1968 (1970) (as amended 1988 in 13(a) of Pub. L. 100–430, short title "Fair Housing Amendments Act of 1988").

5. Kimberle Crenshaw, "Race, Reform, and Retrenchment: Transformation and Legitimation in Antidiscrimination Law," *Harvard Law Review* 101 (1988): 1331, 1380–81.

6. Edmund Morgan, *American Slavery, American Freedom* (New York: Norton, 1975), 8.

7. Derrick Bell, "The Racial Imperative in American Law," in *The Age of Segregation: Race Relations in the South, 1890–1945* (Jackson: University Press of Mississippi, 1978).

8. Herbert Hill, *Black Labor and the American Legal System* (Washington: Bureau of National Affairs, 1977); William Gould, *Black Workers and White Unions* (Ithaca: Cornell University Press, 1977).

9. Kevin Phillips, *Politics of Rich and Poor* (New York: Random House, 1990).

10. bell hooks, *Feminist Theory from Margin to Center* (Cambridge: South End Press, 1984), 54.

11. Gunnar Myrdal, *An American Dilemma* (New York: Harper and Bros.,1944), xix.

12. According to Myrdal, the "Negro problem in America represents a moral lag in the development of the nation and a study of it must record nearly everything which is bad and wrong in America. . . . However, . . . not since Reconstruction has there been more reason to anticipate fundamental changes in American race relations, changes which will involve a development toward the American ideals." Ibid.

13. Jennifer Hochschild, *The New American Dilemma* (New Haven: Yale University Press, 1984), 203.

14. Ibid., 5.

15. Ibid.

16. Linda Myers, *Understanding an Afrocentric World View: Introduction to an Optimal Psychology* (Dubuque: Kendall/Hunt, 1988), 8.

17. Ibid.

18. Ibid.

19. He suggests, "The dishonor of slavery . . . came in the primal act of submission. It was the most immediate human expression of the inability to defend oneself or to secure one's livelihood. . . . The dishonor the slave was compelled to experience sprang instead from that raw, human sense of debasement inherent in having no being except as an expression of another's being." Patterson, *Slavery and Social Death* (Cambridge: Harvard University Press, 1982), 76.

20. Ernest Becker, *The Denial of Death* (New York: Free Press, 1973), 11–12.

5

Cowboys and Arabs

Laurie Goodstein

The Arab-American actor Sayed Badreya has had no problem finding work in Hollywood. With his dark beard and his accented English he has had his pick of parts as terrorists, hijackers, kidnappers, and Islamic militants.

"Usually I play the bad guy role, a terrorist or someone," Mr. Badreya said by telephone from Egypt, where he is on a film shoot with Al Pacino, playing the head of the military wing of Hezbollah.

"When I got to Hollywood, at first I couldn't get a lot of jobs," Mr. Badreya said. "So I grew a beard and look like a really bad Arab, and I started to get a lot of work because that's what they want."

After years of virtual invisibility, Arab-Americans are finding prominence in Hollywood movies—as terrorists and villains. They are only the latest in a long line of ethnic groups and nationalities cast in stereotypical bad-guy roles, from American Indians to Germans to Japanese to African Americans to Russians.

Each set of villains reflected the headlines and the anxieties of its era. Each passed into obsolescence as the headlines changed. Now, with Soviet pretensions shattered and aliens from outer space passé, the new cinematic enemy is the Muslim extremist. . . .

Despite this rather mixed portrayal of Arab-Americans as both victims and prepetrators, several antidefamation organizations representing American Muslims and Arabs are undertaking a leaflet-distributing campaign outside theaters showing "The Siege." They point out that there is no avoiding the fact that its villains are Arabs who quote the Koran and perform ablutions before heading off to blow up innocent civilians. The antidefamation groups' leaflets emphasize that Islam is a peaceful, monotheistic religion and invite moviegoers to attend open houses at local mosques.

The sensitivities of American Muslims and Arabs are so raw right now because "The Siege" follows a succession of more than a dozen films and made-for-television movies produced in the 1980's and 90's featuring murderous Muslim fanatics, among them "Executive Decision," "True Lies," "Voyage of Terror," and "Terrorist on Trial."

"The problem is, you take the lunatic fringe and make the lunatic fringe represent the majority," said Jack G. Shaheen, a professor emeritus of broadcast journalism at Southern Illinois university. "It would be like showing that every Catholic is an I.R.A. member, or every Jew was a member of the Kach party."

There are between four and six million Muslims living in the United States. Some are white or African American converts. Some are new immigrants. Many are first- and second-generation Americans striving for acceptance and success, much like the other ethnic groups who came before them.

The voices of the small circle of Muslims and Arab-Americans who work in Hollywood are rarely heard in the discussion about movie stereotypes. They have never formed any group to represent their concerns. But among them, while there is less outrage than that expressed by the anti-defamation groups based in Washington, there is more frustration. The Muslim actors and writers, and the sole identifiable Muslim director-producer, have an insider's perspective on the reasons their religion is so often stereotyped in Hollywood, and whether anything can be done about it.

They acknowledge that one reason Muslim terrorists have become frequent Hollywood fare is that terrorists who kill in the name of Islam are a genuine threat in international politics.

"We cannot say there are no Arab and no Muslim terrorists," said Moustapha Akkad, an Arab-American producer and director who was born in Syria and has worked in Hollywood for 45 years. "Of course there are.

"But at the same time, balance it with the image of the normal human being, the Arab-American, the family man." Mr. Akkad said. "The lack of anyone showing the other side makes it stand out that in Hollywood, Muslims are only terrorists."

Earlier in his career, Mr. Akkad produced and directed two films portraying Muslims as heroes. "The Message" (1977) told the story of the beginning of Islam, and "Lion of the Desert" (1981) starred Anthony Quinn as the real-life Bedouin leader Omar Mukhtar, who fought Mussolini's invading troops in the deserts of Libya.

But Mr. Akkad said that raising money for such films was difficult, and that to achieve financial success and creative freedom, he had had to turn to another genre. He is now better known as the executive producer of all seven movies in the "Halloween" horror series, the most recent, "Halloween H20," released in August.

And like many Muslims interviewed for this story, including the actor Mr. Badreya, Mr. Akkad is at work on a screenplay that he hopes will help contradict the stereotypes about Muslims. Mr. Akkad's project is about the Crusades.

Anyone acquainted with real Muslims and Arab-Americans living in this country knows that their lives are rich with potential plot lines: crises of faith, cross-cultural tensions, daughters and sons marrying outside the religion. These are some of the same dramatic themes often tapped in movies about Roman Catholics or Jews.

But J. D. Hall, an actor and scriptwriter who is Muslim, said: "I've never come across a script about Muslims where they weren't terrorists. Islam as a way of life, and the people that follow it—I've seen documentaries but never a dramatic adaptation involving that. My suspicion, based on experience, is that if you came up with something like that, you'd have a devil of a time getting it made because it doesn't involve hate."

Mr. Hall, an African American who has appeared in numerous black family sitcoms like "Fresh Prince of Bel Air," says that while African Americans have had a modest measure of success as writers and directors in Hollywood, Muslims and Arab-Americans are far behind.

"We don't have any political power in this country," Mr. Hall said of Muslims in America. "And we don't have the decision-making capacity in the motion picture industry, so we can't control our own image."

. . . The more pervasive reason for stereotyping is that few Americans, in Hollywood and elsewhere, have firsthand knowledge of Islam, say American Muslim leaders.

"It is not intentional," said Aslam Abdullah, the Los Angeles-based editor of Minaret Magazine, who recently helped found a Muslim resource center for filmmakers. "It is primarily ignorance. People do not know us. And we have not made any systematic effort to reach out to people."

The most obvious evidence of ignorance is that many movies and television shows, and undoubtedly many Americans, make the mistake of equating Arabs with Muslims. In fact, only about 12 percent of the world's Muslims are Arabs. Far more Muslims live in Malaysia, Indonesia and India than in the Middle East. And most Americans wrongly assume that, conversely, all Arabs are Muslims. The truth is that many Arabs, particularly Palestinians, Lebanese and Egyptians, are Christians. Of the three million or so Arab-Americans in the United States, a large majority are Christians.

The outlook for Arabs and Muslims in Hollywood is not all bleak. Even Mr. Badreya, so often cast as a terrorist, played a heroic Arab pilot in 1996's "Independence Day." And a handful of Arab-American and Muslim actors whose skin tone and accent allow them to "pass" have consistently avoided being typecast as terrorists.

F. Murray Abraham, who received an Academy Award for his portrayal of Salieri in "Amadeus" (1984), is among them. (Early in his career Mr. Abraham dropped his first name "Fahrid" to avoid being typecast "as a sour Arab out to kill everyone," he once told an interviewer.) An Orthodox Christian, Mr. Abraham is the son of a Syrian father and an Italian-American mother.

Tony Shalhoub, an American of Lebanese heritage, has played a Russian, a Jew, several Italians (he was the hapless cab driver on NBC's "Wings" and the temperamental Italian chef in "Big Night") and many nondescript Caucasian Americans. When he first began acting, he was offered roles as a terrorist, he said in an interview. But "once you start turning them down," he added, "they stop calling with those roles."

6

What's in a Name:
Confessions of a Mafia Princess

Erica-Lynn Huberty (formerly Gambino)

My friends and I are watching a B-movie of the vampire genre. In one scene, the modern-day vampires are suddenly involved in a crime more serious, even, than neck biting. Concerned about being discovered, one vampire exclaims, "How should I know who knows? It could be anybody . . . the Feds, the police, the Gambinos!" My friends all laugh heartily. It is the first real laugh this movie has gotten us, myself included, as all eyes are on me.

My earliest recollection of being questioned about my identity was the first time I arrived late for junior high school. Running into the principal's office to get a pass, I gave my name.

"*Gambino?*" the secretary enunciated slowly, a slight gleam in her eye.

"Um—yes," I stammered uncomfortably. I wasn't that late, was I?

The secretary leaned forward, lowering her voice. "C'mon, you can tell me."

"Tell you what?" I asked, leaning in, too.

"You're one of . . . them. *The* Gambinos."

I thought a moment. "Well, my mom is the music teacher at the elementary school and . . ."

"Uh-huh. *Shoo-uh* [Long Island for 'sure']." The gleam in her eye intensified. Her blue-gray bouffant was prickly with excitement, fear, repulsion, and honor, that she was actually in the presence of one of . . . them.

Who were they, those other Gambinos? Their image was already conjuring up wild criminal scenarios in my twelve-year-old mind; they robbed banks like Patty Hearst, roamed huge dark mansions in search of victims like Dracula, made fake money in their basement like Fred Flintstone. When I came home that day and told my parents

Reprinted from *Newsday Viewpoints*, by permission of the author.

what had happened, their immediate response was, "Ignore it," something I myself have never been able to do.

I've learned a lot about those other Gambinos since my days at John Philip Sousa Junior High. For instance, that they are a notorious crime family from the Five Towns, and that people believe if you cross them, you might end up buried somewhere in New Jersey.

Fifteen years and many Mario Puzo novels later, I am now on the phone reserving an AMTRAK ticket to New York. "G-a-m-b-i-n-o," I spell, waiting for the wisecrack. The operator snickers. Instead of asking me for my Visa number, he asks. "Know where Jimmy Hoffa is?"

"You'll have to ask the Kennedys about that," I say curtly.

As it is, I have had a bad week as a Gambino. I had sent out articles and essays to various local New England publications, and was subsequently scolded by my new Rhode Island friends: "You sent it under your *real* name? Are you crazy?"

Almost everybody I know is under the opinion that "The Mafia" owns and/or runs Providence, so you might wonder why a woman who has been mistaken for the heiress to a legacy of murder and drug-peddling chose to move to a city where Raymond Patriarca made a name for himself as a leader of organized crime. The answer is ridiculously simple: it seemed like a nice place to live.

Before I moved to Providence, I lived in the picturesque mind-your-own-beeswax state of Vermont, where I obtained my master's degree at Bennington. I spent three blissful years with interesting, unusual people who never judged books by their covers, so to say. Last week one of my Bennington friends admitted that "of course we just assumed you were Erica Gambino . . . of the Gambino family. We thought it was great." Great. Bret Easton Ellis couldn't have dreamed up a better character. Artsy Mafia Princess goes to small, elite, liberal arts college, discreetly driving a bottom-of-the-line Honda Civic, and living in a small, nondescript apartment. She's so *a couvert!*

As an NYU undergraduate, I had scrounged Avenue B for a cheap hole in the wall to live and study in. Landlord after landlord would ask me, as he assured me I could squeeze my twin futon into the studio and still avoid the cockroaches who lived in the sink of the junior kitchen, "So, Gambino—as in . . . ?"

As in what? As in someone who could afford to live on Sutton Place but actually dreamed of spending her nights with a view of a crack house? Oh, yes, that must be me.

Every time I think I am at the point where I can finally laugh off people's reactions and insinuations—I mean, it could be worse, my name could be Manson—something happens to remind me that my name, and people's ethnic stereotyping, are part of a larger concern of mine that goes beyond inconvenience and harassment. This spring I was in London visiting my half-sister, whose blissfully Irish last name—Beatty—connotes gorgeous Hollywood actors to most. Thousands of miles away from anything remotely American, let alone Italian-American, I stood at a currency exchange booth in Portobello markets where a friendly Pakistani man patiently counted my travelers checks. He looked up at me with eyes wide, a grin of sheer fascination and—fear?—across his face. "Gambino!" he exclaimed, "*the Mafia . . .*"

I could not help but think of all the American imagery this man must have picked up during his excursions to movie theaters in Piccadilly Circus or even, perhaps, Rawalpindi, and that Don Corleone must have made quite an impression. It seems to me that people everywhere have bought the stereotype of the thuggish, murdering Italian, Italian-Americans included. As I watch Joe Pesci accept an Oscar for playing a psychopathic hoodlum, I cringe as he accepts role after role of illiterate fall-guys, mobsters, and an embarrassingly idiotic lawyer named Gambini. Most recently, Mario Puzo made an appearance on Good Morning America, shamelessly (and inarticulately) promoting his new novel about—surprise!—"the last Don." As Martin Scorcese continues to promote a glamorous image of organized crime, movie reviewers across the country now feel they have license to refer to DeNiro's character in *Casino* as a member of the Mafia, neglecting to mention that the character is Jewish.

In regard to people's reaction to my own name: perhaps someday, instead of smirking awkwardly, making snide counter-remarks, or cowering helplessly, I'll be able to be more like my mother, a Jew from the Upper West Side of Manhattan who revels in the proclamation of our last name. Being madly in love with my father has always made her madly in love with his name, without regard to its connotations. A sweet sentiment, for me it is nevertheless disconcerting to hear her proudly bellow (in that projecting New York Schubert Alley way), "Gam-BEE-Noooo" when asked who our dinner reservation is for.

The son of a poor, hard-working immigrant, my father has chosen to plow through the barriers of ignorance with academic zeal. He is the founder of the first Italian American studies program in the United States, and the author of several best-selling books on Italian-American ethnicity. In short, he has become an expert at being himself—a Gambino.

Since my junior high school induction into the Crime Lords Hall of Fame, I have become an expert myself, at those little tricks which help me avoid having to say my last name at all. I long to be compared with Ann Bancroft (née Ann Italiano) rather than Marissa Tomei in *My Cousin Vinny*. I have a secret career as an historical romance writer named Veronica Stephens, a maiden-name ode to that blue-blooded genius Virginia Woolf, who so gallantly fought the stereotype of womanhood. And, like my wonderfully unself-conscious mother, I prefer to make dinner reservations under my beloved's name. He, on the other hand, thinks it's thoroughly amusing and interesting to use *my* last name (his own, Huberty, causes people to become suddenly hard of hearing and very embarrassed).

The word *gambino*, incidentally, means shrimp-fisherman in Italian. Not every name is what it seems, after all. I actually went to Bennington with people named Mohammed Ali, Matt Dillon, Mark Spitz, and, of all Long Islanders, Amy Fisher. Perhaps it's the Bennington Curse—destined to be associated, by one's birth-given name, with celebrities (some more bizarre than others). There are other ways to look at it, of course. Being a person with a Societally and Ethnically Challenging Last Name can't be all bad. Or can it? Maybe the real reason why author Henry James fled the States for dear ol' Great Britain is because he was tired of being confused with that deviant bandit Jesse. If only I could have warned him that not even England would be safe.

Part Three

The *Other* Wears Many Faces

7

Diversity and Its Discontents

Arturo Madrid

My name is Arturo Madrid. I am a citizen of the United States, as are my parents and as were my grandparents and my great-grandparents. My ancestors' presence in what is now the United States antedates Plymouth Rock, even without taking into account any American Indian heritage I might have.

I do not, however, fit those mental sets that define America and Americans. My physical appearance, my speech patterns, my name, my profession (a professor of Spanish) create a text that confuses the reader. My normal experience is to be asked, "And where are *you* from?" My response depends on my mood. Passive-aggressive, I answer, "From here." Aggressive-passive, I ask, "Do you mean where I am originally from?" But ultimately my answer to those follow-up questions that will ask about origins will be that we have always been from here.

Overcoming my resentment I try to educate, knowing that nine times out of ten my words fall on inattentive ears. I have spent most of my adult life explaining who I am not. I am exotic, but—as Richard Rodriguez of *Hunger of Memory* fame so painfully found out—not exotic enough . . . not Peruvian, or Pakistani, or whatever. I am, however, very clearly the *other*, if only your everyday, garden-variety, domestic *other*. I will share with you another phenomenon that I have been a part of, that of being a missing person, and how I came late to that awareness. But I've always known that I was the *other*, even before I knew the vocabulary or understood the significance of otherness.

I grew up in an isolated and historically marginal part of the United States, a small mountain village in the state of New Mexico, the eldest child of parents native to that region, whose ancestors had always lived there. In those vast and empty spaces

The original version of this essay was delivered as the Tomás Rivera lecture at the 1988 meeting of the American Association for Higher Education.
Reprinted from *Academe* (November–December 1990) by kind permission of the author.

people who look like me, speak as I do, and have names like mine predominate. But the *americanos* lived among us: the descendants of those nineteenth-century immigrants who dispossessed us of our lands; missionaries who came to convert us and stayed to live among us; artists who became enchanted with our land and humanscape and went native; refugees from unhealthy climes, crowded spaces, unpleasant circumstances; and, of course, the inhabitants of Los Alamos, whose sociocultural distance from us was accentuated by the fact that they occupied a space removed from and proscribed to us. More importantly, however, they—*los americanos*—were omnipresent (and almost exclusively so) in newspapers, newsmagazines, books, on radio, in movies, and, ultimately, on television.

Despite the operating myth of the day, school did not erase my otherness. It did try to deny it, and in doing so only accentuated it. To this day what takes place in schools is more socialization than education, but when I was in elementary school—and given where I was—socialization was everything. School was where one became an American, because there was a pervasive and systematic denial by the society that surrounded us that we were Americans. That denial was both explicit and implicit.

Quite beyond saluting the flag and pledging allegiance to it (a very intense and meaningful action, given that the United States was involved in a war and our brothers, cousins, uncles, and fathers were on the frontlines), becoming American was learning English, and its corollary: not speaking Spanish. Until very recently ours was a proscribed language, either *de jure*—by rule, by policy, by law—or *de facto*—by practice, implicitly if not explicitly, through social and political and economic pressure. I do not argue that learning English was not appropriate. On the contrary. Like it or not, and we had no basis to make any judgments on that matter, we were Americans by virtue of having been born Americans and English was the common language of Americans. And there was a myth, a pervasive myth, to the effect that if only we learned to speak English well—and particularly without an accent—we would be welcomed into the American fellowship.

Sam Hayakawa and the official English movement folks notwithstanding, the true text was not our speech, but rather our names and our appearance, for we would always have an accent, however perfect our pronunciation, however excellent our enunciation, however divine our diction. That accent would be heard in our pigmentation, our physiognomy, our names. We were, in short, the *other*.

Being the *other* involves contradictory phenomena. On the one hand being the *other* frequently means being invisible. Ralph Ellison wrote eloquently about that experience in his magisterial novel, *Invisible Man*. On the other hand, being the *other* sometimes involves sticking out like a sore thumb. What is she/he doing here?

For some of us being the *other* is only annoying; for others it is debilitating; for still others it is damning. Many try to flee otherness by taking on protective colorations that provide invisibility, whether of dress or speech or manner or name. Only a fortunate few succeed. For the majority of us otherness is permanently sealed by physical appearance. For the rest, otherness is betrayed by ways of being, speaking, or doing.

The first half of my life I spent downplaying the significance and consequences of otherness. The second half has seen me wrestling to understand its complex and deeply ingrained realities; striving to fathom why otherness denies us a voice or visibility or validity in American society and its institutions; struggling to make otherness familiar, reasonable, even normal to my fellow Americans.

I spoke earlier of another phenomenon that I am a part of: that of being a missing person. Growing up in northern New Mexico I had only a slight sense of us being missing persons. *Hispanos,* as we called (and call) ourselves in New Mexico, were very much a part of the fabric of the society, and there were *hispano* professionals everywhere about me: doctors, lawyers, schoolteachers, and administrators. My people owned businesses, ran organizations, and were both appointed and elected public officials.

My awareness of our absence from the larger institutional life of the society became sharper when I went off to college, but even then it was attenuated by the circumstances of history and geography. The demography of Albuquerque still strongly reflected its historical and cultural origins, despite the influx of Midwesterners and Easterners. Moreover, many of my classmates at the University of New Mexico were *hispanos*, and even some of my professors. I thought that would obtain at UCLA, where I began graduate studies in 1960. Los Angeles had a very large Mexican population and that population was visible even in and around Westwood and on the campus. Many of the groundskeepers and food-service personnel at UCLA were Mexican. But Mexican-American students were few and mostly invisible, and I do not recall seeing or knowing a single Mexican-American (or, for that matter, African-American, Asian, or American Indian) professional on the staff or faculty of that institution during the five years I was there. Needless to say, people like me were not present in any capacity at Dartmouth College, the site of my first teaching appointment, and of course were not even part of the institutional or individual mindset. I knew then that we—a we that had come to encompass American Indians, Asian-Americans, African-Americans, Puerto Ricans, and women—were truly missing persons in American institutional life.

Over the past three decades the *de jure* and *de facto* types of segregation that have historically characterized American institutions have been under assault. As a consequence, minorities and women have become part of American institutional life. Although there are still many areas where we are not to be found, the missing persons phenomenon is not as pervasive as it once was. However, the presence of the *other*, particularly minorities, in institutions and in institutional life resembles what we call in Spanish a *flor de tierra* (a surface phenomenon): we are spare plants whose roots do not go deep, vulnerable to inclemencies of an economic, or political, or social, nature.

Our entrance into and our status in institutional life are not unlike a scenario set forth by my grandmother's pastor when she informed him that she and her family were leaving their mountain village to relocate to the Rio Grande Valley. When he asked her to promise that she would remain true to the faith and continue to involve herself in it, she asked why he thought she would do otherwise. "Doña Trinidad," he told her, "in the Valley there is no Spanish church. There is only an American church." "But," she protested, "I read and speak English and would be able to worship there." The pastor responded, "It is possible that they will not admit you, and even if they do, they might not accept you. And that is why I want you to promise me that you are going to go to church. Because if they don't let you in through the front door, I want you to go in through the back door. And if you can't get in through the back door, go in the side door. And if you are unable to enter through the side door I want you to go in through the window. What is important is that you enter and stay."

Some of us entered institutional life through the front door; others through the back door; and still others through the side doors. Many, if not most of us, came in through windows, and continue to come in through windows. Of those who entered through the front door, some never made it past the lobby; others were ushered into corners and niches. Those who entered through back and side doors inevitably have remained in back and side rooms. And those who entered through windows found enclosures built around them. For, despite the lip service given to the goal of the integration of minorities into institutional life, what has frequently occurred instead is ghettoization, marginalization, isolation.

Not only have the entry points been limited, but in addition the dynamics have been singularly conflictive. Gaining entry and its corollary, gaining space, have frequently come as a consequence of demands made on institutions and institutional officers. Rather than entering institutions more or less passively, minorities have of necessity entered them actively, even aggressively. Rather than waiting to receive, they have demanded. Institutional relations have thus been adversarial, infused with specific and generalized tensions.

The nature of the entrance and the nature of the space occupied have greatly influenced the view and attitude of the majority population within those institutions. All of us are put into the same box; that is, no matter what the individual reality, the assessment of the individual is inevitably conditioned by a perception that is held of the class. Whatever our history, whatever our record, whatever our validations, whatever our accomplishments, by and large we are perceived unidimensionally and dealt with accordingly. I remember an experience I had in this regard, atypical only in its explicitness. A few years ago I allowed myself to be persuaded to seek the presidency of a well-known state university. I was invited for an interview and presented myself before the selection committee, which included members of the board of trustees. The opening question of that brief but memorable interview was directed at me by a member of that august body. "Dr. Madrid," he asked, "why does a one-dimensional person like you think he can be the president of a multidimensional institution like ours?"

Over the past four decades America's demography has undergone significant changes. Since 1965 the principal demographic growth we have experienced in the

United States has been of peoples whose national origins are non-European. This population growth has occurred both through birth and through immigration. A few years ago discussion of the national birthrate had a scare dimension: the high—"inordinately high"—birthrate of the Hispanic population. The popular discourse was informed by words such as "breeding." Several years later, as a consequence of careful tracking by government agencies, we now know that what has happened is that the birthrate of the majority population has decreased. When viewed historically and comparatively, the minority populations (for the most part) have also had a decline in birthrate, but not one as great as that of the majority.

There are additional demographic changes that should give us something to think about. African-Americans are now to be found in significant numbers in every major urban center in the nation. Hispanic-Americans now number over 15 million people, and although they are a regionally concentrated (and highly urbanized) population, there is a Hispanic community in almost every major urban center of the United States. American Indians, heretofore a small and rural population, are increasingly more numerous and urban. The Asian-American population, which has historically consisted of small and concentrated communities of Chinese-, Filipino-, and Japanese-Americans, has doubled over the past decade, its complexion changed by the addition of Cambodians, Koreans, Hmongs, Vietnamese, et al.

Prior to the Immigration Act of 1965, 69 percent of immigration was from Europe. By far the largest number of immigrants to the United States since 1965 have been from the Americas and from Asia: 34 percent are from Asia; another 34 percent are from Central and South America; 16 percent are from Europe; 10 percent are from the Caribbean; the remaining 6 percent are from other continents and Canada. As was the case with previous immigration waves, the current one consists principally of young people: 60 percent are between the ages of 16 and 44. Thus, for the next few decades, we will continue to see a growth in the percentage of non-European-origin Americans as compared to European-Americans.

To sum up, we now live in one of the most demographically diverse nations in the world, and one that is increasingly more so.

During the same period social and economic change seems to have accelerated. Who would have imagined at mid-century that the prototypical middle-class family (working husband, wife as homemaker, two children) would for all intents and purposes disappear? Who could have anticipated the rise in teenage pregnancies, children in poverty, drug use? Who among us understood the implications of an aging population?

We live in an age of continuous and intense change, a world in which what held true yesterday does not today, and certainly will not tomorrow. What change does, moreover, is bring about even more change. The only constant we have at this point in our national development is change. And change is threatening. The older we get the more likely we are to be anxious about change, and the greater our desire to maintain the status quo.

Evident in our public life is a fear of change, whether economic or moral. Some who fear change are responsive to the call of economic protectionism, others to the message of moral protectionism. Parenthetically, I have referred to the movement to require more of students without in turn giving them more as academic protectionism. And the pronouncements of E. D. Hirsch and Allan Bloom are, I believe, informed by intellectual protectionism. Much more serious, however, is the dark side of the populism which underlies this evergoing protectionism—the resentment of the *other*. An excellent and fascinating example of that aspect of populism is the cry for linguisitic protectionism—for making English the official language of the United States. And who among us is unaware of the tensions that underlie immigration reform, of the underside of demographic protectionism?

A matter of increasing concern is whether this new protectionism, and the mistrust of the *other* which accompanies it, is not making more significant inroads than we have supposed in higher education. Specifically, I wish to discuss the question of whether a goal (quality) and a reality (demographic diversity) have been erroneously placed in conflict, and, if so, what problems this perception of conflict might present.

As part of my scholarship I turn to dictionaries for both origins and meanings of words. Quality, according to the *Oxford English Dictionary*, has multiple meanings. One set defines quality as being an essential character, a distinctive and inherent feature. A second describes it as a degree of excellence, of conformity to standards, as superiority in kind. A third makes reference to social status, particularly to persons of high social status. A fourth talks about quality as being a special or distinguishing attribute, as being a desirable trait. Quality is highly desirable in both principle and practice. We all aspire to it in our own person, in our experiences, in our acquisitions and products, and of course we all want to be associated with people and operations of quality.

But let us move away from the various dictionary meanings of the word and to our own sense of what it represents and of how we feel about it. First of all we consider quality to be finite; that is, it is limited with respect to quantity; it has very few manifestations; it is not widely distributed. I have it and you have it, but they don't. We associate quality with homogeneity, with uniformity, with standardization, with order, regularity, neatness. All too often we equate it with smoothness, glibness, slickness, elegance. Certainly it is always expensive. We tend to identify it with those who lead, with the rich and famous. And, when you come right down to it, it's inherent. Either you've got it or you ain't.

Diversity, from the Latin *divertere*, meaning to turn aside, to go different ways, to differ, is the condition of being different or having differences, is an instance of being different. Its companion word, diverse, means differing, unlike, distinct; having or capable or having various forms; composed of unlike or distinct elements. Diversity is lack of standardization, of regularity, of orderliness, homogeneity, conformity, uniformity. Diversity introduces complications, is difficult to organize, is troublesome to manage, is problematical. Diversity is irregular, disorderly, uneven, rough. The way we use the word diversity gives us away. Something is too diverse, is extremely diverse. We want a little diversity.

When we talk about diversity, we are talking about the *other*, whatever that other might be: someone of a different gender, race, class, national origin; somebody at a greater or lesser distance from the norm; someone outside the set; someone who possesses a different set of characteristics, features, or attributes; someone who does not fall within the taxonomies we use daily and with which we are comfortable; someone who does not fit into the mental configurations that give our lives order and meaning.

In short, diversity is desirable only in principle, not in practice. Long live diversity . . . as long as it conforms to my standards, my mind set, my view of life, my sense of order. We desire, we like, we admire diversity, not unlike the way the French (and others) appreciate women; that is, *Vive la différence!*—as long as it stays in its place.

What I find paradoxical about and lacking in this debate is that diversity is the natural order of things. Evolution produces diversity. Margaret Visser, writing about food in her latest book, *Much Depends on Dinner*, makes an eloquent statement in this regard:

> Machines like, demand, and produce uniformity. But nature loathes it: her strength lies in multiplicity and in differences. Sameness in biology means fewer possibilities and therefore weakness.

The United States, by its very nature, by its very development, is the essence of diversity. It is diverse in its geography, population, institutions, technology; its social, cultural, and intellectual modes. It is a society that at its best does not consider quality to be monolithic in form or finite in quantity, or to be inherent in class. Quality in our society proceeds in large measure out of the stimulus of diverse modes of thinking and acting; out of the creativity made possible by the different ways in which we approach things; out of diversion from paths or modes hallowed by tradition.

One of the principal strengths of our society is its ability to address, on a continuing and substantive basis, the real economic, political, and social problems that have faced and continue to face us. What makes the United States so attractive to immigrants is the protections and opportunities it offers; what keeps our society together is tolerance for cultural, religious, social, political, and even linguistic difference; what makes us a unique, dynamic, and extraordinary nation is the power and creativity of our diversity.

The true history of the United States is one of struggle against intolerance, against oppression, against xenophobia, against those forces that have prohibited persons from participating in the larger life of the society on the basis of their race, their gender, their religion, their national origin, their linguistic and cultural background. These phenomena are not consigned to the past. They remain with us and frequently take on virulent dimensions.

If you believe, as I do, that the well-being of a society is directly related to the degree and extent to which all of its citizens participate in its institutions, then you will have to agree that we have a challenge before us. In view of the extraordinary changes that are taking place in our society we need to take up the struggle again, irritating, grating, troublesome, unfashionable, unpleasant as it is. As educated and educator members of this society we have a special responsibility for ensuring that all American institutions, not just our elementary and secondary schools, our juvenile halls, or our jails, reflect the diversity of our society. Not to do so is to risk greater alienation on the part of a growing segment of our society; is to risk increased social tension in an already conflictive world; and, ultimately, is to risk the survival of a range of institutions that, for all their defects and deficiencies, provide us the opportunity and the freedom to improve our individual and collective lot.

Let me urge you to reflect on these two words—quality and diversity—and on the mental sets and behaviors that flow out of them. And let me urge you further to struggle against the notion that quality is finite in quantity, limited in its manifestations, or is restricted by considerations of class, gender, race, or national origin; or that quality manifests itself only in leaders and not in followers, in managers and not in workers, in breeders and not in drones; or that it has to be associated with verbal agility or elegance of personal style; or that it cannot be seeded, nurtured, or developed.

Because diversity—the *other*—is among us, will define and determine our lives in ways that we still do not fully appreciate, whether that other is women (no longer bound by tradition, house, and family); or Asians, African-Americans, Indians, and Hispanics (no longer invisible, regional, or marginal); or our newest immigrants (no longer distant, exotic, alien). Given the changing profile of America, will we come to terms with diversity in our personal and professional lives? Will we begin to recognize the diverse forms that quality can take? If so, we will thus initiate the process of making quality limitless in its manifestations, infinite in quantity, unrestricted with respect to its origins, and more importantly, virulently contagious.

I hope we will. And that we will further join together to expand—not to close—the circle.

8

Coping With the Alienation of White Male Students

Billie Wright Dziech

Beyond noting a sharp shift toward the Republican Party among white male voters in November, most post-election analyses devoted comparatively little consideration to the reasons for their political preference. Higher education, however, cannot afford to ignore the resentment expressed by some of those voters, who complained in exit polls that minority groups and other "special interests" were dominating the concerns of policy makers. Whether we like it or not, we must consider the possibility that higher education is one of the sectors of society at which their message was directed.

Frustration and anger have been cited as partial causes of the rightward trend that led 63 per cent of white male voters to cast ballots for Republicans and only 37 per cent for Democrats. Even more significant for colleges is one finding of a recent MTV poll: "The shift toward Republican affiliation is most evident among white men aged 23 to 29."

Obviously more than one factor affects voting behavior. But if young white men do, in fact, prefer the political party that questions affirmative action and multiculturalism, higher education must do some self-assessment. Support for both concepts has become almost universal at colleges and universities, albeit, in the case of affirmative action, only after initial pressure from the federal government.

I do not intend to debate the merits and limitations of multiculturalism and affirmative action here. Instead, I want to suggest that if we are to achieve the equality, civility, and mutual respect that we seek on campus, we must consider the possibility that our policies not only have failed to achieve their goals but also may have succeeded in alienating many young white men.

From "Coping with the Alienation of White Male Students" by Billie Wright Dziech in *Chronicle of Higher Education* (January 13, 1995). Reprinted with permission.

Those of us familiar with white male students know that a slow but inexorable process has been at work among them while the attention of campus leaders largely has been focused on other groups. As I have traveled across the country during the past several years speaking about sexual harassment—generally regarded as a "female" issue—I have at the same time learned a lot about male students. For example:

- A student—the first in his family to attend college—working his way through a small private college told me: "You know what affirmative action means to me? It means that even with a 3.9, I have less chance of getting into med school than someone with a 3.4 who's lucky enough to be a 'victim'—whatever that means."
- Hundreds of miles away at a huge urban university, another white male student explained his hostility to his institution this way: "I guess you could say I'm mad. All they ever do around here is lecture me about how I have to care about people who would blow my brains out if they could get away with it. Nobody gives a damn about me."
- Yet another such student confided: "I'm sick of being blamed for everyone else's problems. I just want to be left alone so I can finish school and get on with my life."

It is easy to ascribe such remarks to the arrogant indifference of the empowered and to maintain that they are resisting change and refusing to acknowledge the predicament of women and members of minority groups. It is more difficult, more painful to consider that in responding to students from historically oppressed groups, we may have overlooked and alienated others to whom we have equal responsibility. The revised curricula and the educational programs and support services that we have designed to bring civility and justice to our campuses apparently have made many mainstream students feel ostracized and castigated for conditions over which they have no control.

They have heard exhortations and sermons about the white-male, racist, Eurocentric hold on American history, but they have not always responded as we hoped they would. Outside of class, when they talk to parents, peers, and faculty members whom they trust, many of them say that they believe they are being forced to pay for history they had no part in and that they feel weary, angry, and alienated.

"We are always coming up with the emphatic facts of history in our private experience and verifying them here," Emerson once wrote. "All history becomes subjective; in other words there is no history, only biography. Every mind must know the whole lesson for itself—must go over the whole ground. What it does not see, what it does not live, it will not know."

What academe has forgotten is that the "whole ground" and the "emphatic facts of history" for an 18-year-old living in the last decade of the 20th century differ radically from those that shaped many of his professors. The emphatic facts of the professors' lives may be freedom rides in Mississippi or bra burnings in Boston, but these are not the history today's student has known. While one cannot deny that generations of women and members of minority groups suffered deprivation and degradation at the hands of a power structure dominated by white men, today's white male student generally has had little personal experience to help him appreciate the struggles of the groups that now appear to be favored.

He sees no academic departments equivalent to women's or African-American studies that address *his* history. He receives no special admission considerations and no special support services. Justifiably or not, the most authentic, the most vivid lesson that he may draw from his experience is that he is expected to pay for the transgressions of his ancestors and that the truly disadvantaged are people like himself, not those whose stories of victimization dominate the headlines.

There are no simple ways to alter such a perception. Even as I write, I feel trepidation at the prospect of having my words misinterpreted or exaggerated, despite my long-standing commitment to women's concerns. But it is this commitment to inclusion that should motivate us to address the complex challenge confronting us. At this point, it is impossible to say definitely how—or even whether—equitable remedies can be found for the frustration and resentment some white men feel, but we can take some steps in that direction.

Colleges must begin by acknowledging that the resentment felt by some white male students represents a legitimate concern. Then we must initiate genuinely open discussion about its causes and about ways to defuse it. This will be an arduous process, because of the new wounds and enmities that have developed along with the positive changes of the last two decades. We must undertake passionate, informed debate about how to balance our obligations to all of our constituencies—females, males, minorities, heterosexuals, and homosexuals. Such discussions must be conducted with reason and civility, the two attributes we most often cite as characteristic of our profession. Our intent should be not to prove that the claims of one interest group are superior to another's but rather to discover ways of honoring differences among students without appearing to favor some at the expense of others. The task will require considerably more honesty than we have exhibited in the past.

The admission process provides a cogent example. A source of widespread skepticism, it deserves immediate attention. Unpopular as the suggestion might be to those justifiably concerned about the problems of historically disenfranchised groups, colleges must begin to tell the truth about the use of different admission standards for different people. An institution either does or does not subscribe to affirmative-action principles. If it does, it should be capable of explaining its position articulately and intelligently, with reference to the federal statutes and laws that support its right to make exceptions for some applicants and not for others. Denial and evasion of the truth result not in protection of women and members of minority groups but in exaggerated assumptions about the special treatment they receive. Lack of candor about admission standards only exacerbates the resentment that many white male students feel about the harm that they, in their view, suffer from affirmative action. At worst, candor will stimulate debate and bring the hostility toward affirmative action out into the open. At best, it will help diminish the image of deceptiveness that plagues our institutions.

We would also benefit from more honest, clear descriptions of course content. Many classes are taught by professors with decidedly exclusionary agendas. Their defense is that the courses fulfill the specialized needs of minority and female students. That may be acceptable as long as students are given precise preliminary information about the content and environment they will experience in such politicized classes. But some white male students report a "chilly," even hostile, reception in courses in which they had no reason to expect problems. That women and members of minority groups have suffered similar or greater alienation does not excuse this injury. There can be no redressing of past injustices, no progress for the future, if any student feels estranged or subjected to ridicule in the classroom.

Historical domination by white men does not mean that their experiences are well understood. Some people would argue that today white men are the least studied of all groups in the population. Positive symbolic gain could be derived form developing courses on the white male's experience, but, more important, scholars could learn much from the process.

Despite limited resources, colleges also have a responsibility to determine whether white men, like women and members of minority groups, require some special support services. White male students are acutely aware that their institutions have demonstrated little interest in them as a group, and this is clearly a source of frustration affecting their behavior and attitudes after they leave academe.

Symposia, lectures, and discussions addressing white-male experience would show colleges' commitment to increased understanding of all campus constituencies. We need to talk about how white men were viewed in the past and are viewed today and about how both men and women have been burdened by stereotypes. Furthermore, if existing institutional grievance procedures do not adequately respond to white men who complain about sexual harassment or racial discrimination, we must devise procedures that do.

In addition, we should review the class activities, extracurricular groups, educational programs, and institutional policies intended to teach tolerance, which typically are designed and controlled by faculty or staff members. Despite our good intentions, we sometimes act simplistically and autocratically in our efforts to encourage sensitivity. Perhaps we should talk less and listen more, guide rather than direct. Our students are, after all, only one step removed from the "real world" during their sojourn on campus. Tomorrow we will not be there to instruct or harangue them about their behavior toward one another. A wide spectrum of students, not just typical student-government types, should be enlisted to explore the issues of respect and civility. Students must be genuinely engaged if they are to be moved to examine their attitudes and perhaps modify their perspectives. That engagement is less likely to occur when someone who is not a student invents and controls the process. . . .

White men, as well as women and minority groups, may suffer if our efforts at empowering the disenfranchised stop short of the most crucial goal—motivating people to share power and live in harmony. We will not achieve our goals if we focus exclusively on individual groups. In the classroom and in extracurricular programs, we must alert students to the existence of common interests beyond the particular concerns that they may have as men or women or as members of racial or ethnic groups.

Whether affirmative action is discriminatory, whether multiculturalism dilutes the college curriculum, whether remedying social injustice is an appropriate role for higher education—these are important but debatable points. Less ambiguous and far more significant is the need for Americans to accept a collective history, distinguished by both its failures and its successes, and to get on with the task of building a more equitable and moral society.

White men will be a part of that endeavor. Rightly or wrongly, many white male students feel ignored and maligned as they, like all students, struggle for respect, opportunity, and support on our campuses. Dismissing and denigrating their perceptions of how they are being treated have led only to increased misunderstanding and intolerance, as they carry their frustrations and anger from the campuses to their workplaces and communities. Old wounds will not be healed by inflicting new ones. Our task now is to use wisely the time we have with all of our students, so that when they leave us they will understand not only their country's weaknesses and the sources of its divisions but also its strengths and the bonds that unite people and give them hope for the future.

9

The Second Sex

Simone de Beauvoir

For a long time I have hesitated to write a book on woman. The subject is irritating, especially to women; and it is not new. Enough ink has been spilled in the quarreling over feminism, now practically over, and perhaps we should say no more about it. It is still talked about, however, for the voluminous nonsense uttered during the last century seems to have done little to illuminate the problem. After all, is there a problem? And if so, what is it? Are there women, really? Most assuredly the theory of the eternal feminine still has its adherents who will whisper in your ear: "Even in Russia women still are *women*"; and other erudite persons—sometimes the very same—say with a sigh: "Woman is losing her way, woman is lost." One wonders if women still exist, if they will always exist, whether or not it is desirable that they should, what place they occupy in this world, what their place should be. "What has become of women?" was asked recently in an ephemeral magazine.[1] . . .

If her functioning as a female is not enough to define woman, if we decline also to explain her through "the eternal feminine," and if nevertheless we admit, provisionally, that women do exist, then we must face the question: what is a woman?

To state the question is, to me, to suggest, at once, a preliminary answer. The fact that I ask it is in itself significant. A man would never get the notion of writing a book on the peculiar situation of the human male.[2] But if I wish to define myself, I must first of all say: "I am a woman"; on this truth must be based all further discussion. A man never begins by presenting himself as an individual of a certain sex; it goes without saying that he is a man. The terms *masculine* and *feminine* are used symmetrically only as a matter of form, as on legal papers. In actuality the relation of the two sexes is not quite like that of two electrical poles, for man represents both the positive and the neutral, as is indicated by the common use of *man* to designate human beings in general; whereas woman represents only the negative, defined by limiting criteria, without reciprocity. In the midst of an abstract discussion it is vexing to hear a man say: "You think thus and so because you are a woman"; but I know that my only defense is to reply: "I think thus and so because it is true," thereby removing my subjective self from the argument. It would be out of the question to reply: "And you think the contrary because you are a man," for it is understood that the fact of being a man is no peculiarity. A man is in the right in being a man; it is the woman who is in the wrong. It amounts to this: just as for the ancients there was an absolute vertical with reference to which the oblique was defined, so there is an absolute human type, the masculine. Woman has ovaries, a uterus; these peculiarities imprison her in her subjectivity, circumscribe her within the limits of her own nature. It is often said that she thinks with her glands. Man superbly ignores the fact that his anatomy also includes glands, such as the testicles, and that they secrete hormones. He thinks of his body as a direct and normal connection with the world, which he believes he apprehends objectively, whereas he regards the body of a woman as a hindrance, a prison, weighed down by everything peculiar to it. "The female is a female by virtue of a certain *lack* of qualities," said Aristotle; "we should regard the female nature as afflicted with a natural defectiveness." And St. Thomas for his part pronounced woman to be an "imperfect man," an "incidental" being. This is symbolized in Genesis where Eve is depicted as made from what Boussuet called "a supernumerary bone" of Adam.

Thus humanity is male and man defines woman not in herself but as relative to him; she is not regarded as an autonomous being. Michelet writes: "Woman, the relative being. . . ." And Benda is most positive in his *Rapport d'Uriel:* "The body of man makes sense in itself quite apart from that of woman, whereas the latter seems wanting in significance by itself. . . . Man can think of himself without woman. She cannot think of herself without man." And she is simply what man decrees; thus she is called "the sex," by which is meant that she appears essentially to the male as a sexual being. For him she is sex—absolute sex, no less. She is defined and differentiated with reference to man and not he with reference to her; she is the incidental, the inessential as opposed to the essential. He is the Subject, he is the Absolute—she is the Other.[3]

The category of the *Other* is as primordial as consciousness itself. In the most primitive societies, in the most ancient mythologies, one finds the expression of a duality—that of the Self and the Other. This duality was not originally attached to the division of the sexes; it was not dependent upon any empirical facts. It is revealed in such works as that of Granet on Chinese thought and those of Dumézil on the East Indies and Rome. The feminine element was at first no more involved in such pairs as Varuna-Mitra, Uranus-Zeus, Sun-Moon, and Day-Night than it was in the contrasts between Good and Evil, lucky and unlucky auspices, right and left, God and Lucifer. Otherness is a fundamental category of human thought.

Thus it is that no group ever sets itself up as the One without at once setting up the Other over against itself. If three travelers chance to occupy the same compartment, that is enough to make vaguely hostile "others" out of all the rest of the passengers on the train. In small-town eyes all persons not belonging to the village are "strangers" and suspect; to the native of a country all who inhabit other countries are "foreigners"; Jews are "different" for the anti-Semite, Negroes are "inferior" for American racists, aborigines are "natives" for colonists, proletarians are the "lower class" for the privileged. . . .

But the other consciousness, the other ego, sets up a reciprocal claim. The native traveling abroad is shocked to find himself in turn regarded as a "stranger" by the natives of neighboring countries. As a matter of fact, wars, festivals, trading, treaties, and contests among tribes, nations, and classes tend to deprive the concept *Other* of its absolute sense and to make manifest its relativity; willy-nilly, individuals and groups are forced to realize the reciprocity of their relations. How is it, then, that this reciprocity has not been recognized between the sexes, that one of the contrasting terms is set up as the sole essential, denying any relativity in regard to its correlative and defining the latter as pure otherness? Why is it that women do not dispute male sovereignty? No subject will readily volunteer to become the object, the inessential; it is not the Other who, in defining himself as the Other, establishes the One. The Other is posed as such by the One in defining himself as the One. But if the Other is not to regain the status of being the One, he must be submissive enough to accept this alien point of view. Whence comes this submission in the case of woman?

There are, to be sure, other cases in which a certain category has been able to dominate another completely for a time. Very often this privilege depends upon inequality of numbers—the majority imposes its rule upon the minority or persecutes it. But women are not a minority, like the American Negroes or the Jews; there are as many women as men on earth. Again, the two groups concerned have often been originally independent; they may have been formerly unaware of each other's existence, or perhaps they recognized each other's autonomy. But a historical event has resulted in the subjugation of the weaker by the stronger. The scattering of the Jews, the introduction of slavery into America, the conquests of imperialism are examples in point. In these cases the oppressed retained at least the memory of former days; they possessed in common a past, a tradition, sometimes a religion or a culture.

The parallel drawn by Bebel between women and the proletariat is valid in that neither ever formed a minority or a separate collective unit of mankind. And instead of a single historical event it is in both cases a historical development that explains their status as a class and accounts for the membership of *particular individuals* in that class. But proletarians have not always existed, whereas there have always been women. They are women in virtue of their anatomy and physiology. Throughout history they have always been subordinated to men,[4] and hence their dependency is not the result of a historical event or a social change—it was not something that *occurred.* The reason why otherness in this case seems to be an absolute is in part that it lacks the contingent or incidental nature of historical facts. A condition brought about at a certain time can be abolished at some other time, as the Negroes of Haiti and others have proved, but it might seem that a natural condition is beyond the possibility of change. In truth, however, the nature of things is no more immutably given, once for all, than is historical reality. If woman seems to be the inessential which never becomes the essential, it is because she herself fails to bring about this change. Proletarians say "We"; Negroes also. Regarding themselves as subjects, they transform the bourgeois, the whites, into "others." But women do not say "We," except at some congress of feminists or similar formal demonstration; men say women, and women use the same word in referring to themselves. They do not authentically assume a subjective attitude. The proletarians have accomplished the revolution in Russia, the Negroes in Haiti, the Indo-Chinese are battling for it in Indo-China; but the women's effort has never been anything more than a symbolic agitation. They have gained only what men have been willing to grant; they have taken nothing, they have only received.[5]

The reason for this is that women lack concrete means for organizing themselves into a unit which can stand face to face with the correlative unit. They have no past, no history, no religion of their own; and they have no such solidarity of work and interest as that of the proletariat. They are not even promiscuously herded together in the way that creates community feeling among the American Negroes, the ghetto Jews, the workers of Saint-Denis, or the factory hands of Renault. They live dispersed among the males, attached through residence, housework, economic condition, and social standing to certain men—fathers or husbands—more firmly than they are to other women. If they belong to the bourgeoisie, they feel solidarity with men of that class, not with proletarian women; if they are white, their allegiance is to white men, not to Negro women. The proletariat can propose to massacre the ruling class, and a sufficiently fanatical Jew or Negro might dream of getting sole possession of the atomic bomb and making humanity wholly Jewish or black; but woman cannot even dream of exterminating the males. The bond that unites her to her oppressors is not comparable to any other. The division of the sexes is a biological fact, not an event in human history. Male and female stand opposed within a primordial *Mitsein*, and woman has not broken it. The couple is a fundamental unity with its two halves riveted together, and the cleavage of society along the line of sex is impossible. . . .

Master and slave, also, are united by a reciprocal need, in this case economic, which does not liberate the slave. In the relation of master to slave the master does not make a point of the need that he has for the other; he has in his grasp the power of satisfying this need through his own action; whereas the slave, in his dependent condition, his hope and fear, is quite conscious of the need he has for his master. Even if the need is at bottom equally urgent for both, it always works in favor of the oppressor and against the oppressed. That is why the liberation of the working class, for example, has been slow.

Now, woman has always been man's dependent, if not his slave; the two sexes have never shared the world in equality. And even today woman is heavily handicapped, though her situation is beginning to change. Almost nowhere is her legal status the same as man's,[6] and frequently it is much to her disadvantage. Even when her rights are legally recognized in the abstract, long-standing custom prevents their full expression in the mores. In the economic sphere men and women can almost be said to make up two castes; other things being equal, the former hold the better jobs, get higher wages, and have more opportunity for success than their new competitors. In industry and politics men have a great many more positions and they monopolize the most important posts. In addition to all this, they enjoy a traditional prestige that the education of children tends in every way to support, for the present enshrines the past—and in the past all history has been made by men. At the present time, when women are beginning to take part in the affairs of the world, it is still a world that belongs to men—they have no doubt of it at all and women have scarcely any. To decline to be the Other, to refuse to be a party to the deal—this would be for women to renounce all the advantages conferred upon them by their alliance with the superior caste. Man-the-sovereign will provide woman-the-liege with material protection and will undertake the moral justification of her existence; thus she can evade at once both economic risk and the metaphysical risk of a liberty in which ends and aims must be contrived without assistance. Indeed, along with the ethical urge of each individual to affirm his subjective existence, there is also the temptation to forgo liberty and become a thing. This is an inauspicious road, for he who takes it—passive, lost, ruined—becomes henceforth the creature of another's will, frustrated in his transcendence and deprived of every value. But it is an easy road; on it one avoids the strain involved in undertaking an authentic existence. When man makes of woman the Other, he may, then, expect her to manifest deep-seated tendencies toward complicity. Thus, woman may fail to lay claim to the status of subject because she lacks definite resources, because she feels the necessary bond that ties her to man regardless of reciprocity, and because she is, often very well pleased with her role as the Other.

. . . But the very fact that woman *is the Other* tends to cast suspicion upon all the justifications that men have ever been able to provide for it. These have all too evidently been dictated by men's interest. A little known feminist of the seventeenth century, Poulain de la Barre, put it this way: "All that has been written about women by men should be suspect, for the men are at once judge and party to the lawsuit." Everywhere, at all times, the males have displayed their satisfaction in feeling that they are the lords of creation. "Blessed be God . . . that He did not make me a woman," say the Jews in their morning prayers, while their wives pray on a note of resignation: "Blessed be the Lord, who created me according to His will." The first among the blessings for which Plato thanked the gods was that he had been created free, not enslaved; the second, a man, not a woman. But the males could not enjoy this privilege fully unless they believed it to be founded on the absolute and the eternal; they sought to make the fact of their supremacy into a right. "Being men, those who have made and compiled the laws have favored their own sex, and jurists have elevated these laws into principles," to quote Poulain de la Barre once more.

Legislators, priests, philosophers, writers, and scientists have striven to show that the subordinate position of woman is willed in heaven and advantageous on earth. The religions invented by men reflect this wish for domination. In the legends of Eve and Pandora men have taken up arms against women. They have made use of philosophy and theology, as the quotations from Aristotle and St. Thomas have shown. Since ancient times satirists and moralists have delighted in showing up the weaknesses of women. We are familiar with the savage indictments hurled against women throughout French literature. Montherlant, for example, follows the tradition of Jean de Meung, though with less gusto. This hostility may at times be well founded, often it is gratuitous; but in truth it more or less successfully conceals a desire for self-justification. As Montaigne says, "It is easier to accuse one sex than to excuse the other." Sometimes what is going on is clear enough. For instance, the Roman law limiting the rights of woman cited "the imbecility, the instability of the sex" just when the weakening of family ties seemed to threaten the interests of male heirs. And in the effort to keep the married woman under guardianship, appeal was made in the sixteenth century to the authority of St. Augustine, who declared that "woman is a creature neither decisive nor constant," at a time when the single woman was thought capable of managing her property. Montaigne understood clearly how arbitrary and unjust was woman's appointed lot: "Women are not in the wrong when they decline to accept the rules laid down for them, since the men make these rules without consulting them. No wonder intrigue and strife abound." But he did not go so far as to champion their cause.

It was only later, in the eighteenth century, that genuinely democratic men began to view the matter objectively. Diderot, among others, strove to show that woman is, like man, a human being. Later John Stuart Mill came fervently to her defense. But these philosophers displayed unusual impartiality. In the nineteenth century the feminist quarrel became again a quarrel of partisans. One of the consequences of the industrial revolution was the entrance of women into productive labor, and it was just here that the claims of the feminists emerged from the realm of theory and acquired an economic basis, while their opponents became the more aggressive. Although landed property lost power to some extent, the bourgeoisie clung to the old morality that found the guarantee of private property in the solidity of the family. Woman was ordered back into the home the more harshly as her emancipation became a real menace. Even within the working class the men endeavored to restrain woman's liberation, because they began to see the women as dangerous competitors—the more so because they were accustomed to work for lower wages.[7]

In proving woman's inferiority, the antifeminists then began to draw not only upon religion, philosophy, and theology, as before, but also upon science—biology, experimental psychology, etc. At most they were willing to grant "equality in difference" to the *other sex*. That profitable formula is most significant; it is precisely like the "equal but separate" formula of the Jim Crow laws aimed at the North American

Negroes. As is well known, this so-called equalitarian segregation has resulted only in the most extreme discrimination. The similarity just noted is no way due to chance, for whether it is a race, a caste, a class, or a sex that is reduced to a position of inferiority, the methods of justification are the same. "The eternal feminine" corresponds to "the black soul" and to "the Jewish character." True, the Jewish problem is on the whole very different from the other two—to the anti-Semite the Jew is not so much an inferior as he is an enemy for whom there is to be granted no place on earth, for whom annihilation is the fate desired. But there are deep similarities between the situation of woman and that of the Negro. Both are being emancipated today from a like paternalism, and the former master class wishes to "keep them in their place"—that is, the place chosen for them. In both cases the former masters lavish more or less sincere eulogies, either on the virtues of "the good Negro" with his dormant, childish, merry soul—the submissive Negro—or on the merits of the woman who is "truly feminine"—that is, frivolous, infantile, irresponsible— the submissive woman. In both cases the dominant class bases its argument on a state of affairs that it has itself created. As George Bernard Shaw puts it, in substance, "The American white relegates the black to the rank of shoeshine boy; and he concludes from this that the black is good for nothing but shining shoes." This vicious circle is met with in all analogous circumstances; when an individual (or a group of individuals) is kept in a situation of inferiority, the fact is that he is inferior. But the significance of the verb *to be* must be rightly understood here; it is in bad faith to give it a static value when it really has the dynamic Hegelian sense of "to have become." Yes, women on the whole *are* today inferior to men; that is, their situation affords them fewer possibilities. The question is: should that state of affairs continue?

Many men hope that it will continue; not all have given up the battle. The conservative bourgeoisie still see in the emancipation of women a menace to their morality and their interests. Some men dread feminine competition. Recently a male student wrote in the *Hebdo-Latin*: "Every woman student who goes into medicine or law robs us of a job." He never questioned his rights in this world. And economic interests are not the only ones concerned. . . .

So it is that many men will affirm as if in good faith that women *are* the equals of man and that they have nothing to clamor for, while *at the same time* they will say that women can never be the equals of man and that their demands are in vain. It is, in point of fact, a difficult matter for man to realize the extreme importance of social discriminations which seem outwardly insignificant but which produce in woman moral and intellectual effects so profound that they appear to spring from her original nature. The most sympathetic of men never fully comprehend woman's concrete situation. And there is no reason to put much trust in the men when they rush to the defense of privileges whose full extent they can hardly measure. We shall not, then, permit ourselves to be intimidated by the number and violence of the attacks launched against women, nor to be entrapped by the self-seeking eulogies bestowed on the "true woman," nor to profit by the enthusiasm for woman's destiny manifested by men who would not for the world have any part of it.

We should consider the arguments of the feminists with no less suspicion, however, for very often their controversial aim deprives them of all real value. If the "woman question" seems trivial, it is because masculine arrogance has made of it a "quarrel"; and when quarreling one no longer reasons well. People have tirelessly sought to prove that woman is superior, inferior, or equal to man. Some say that, having been created after Adam, she is evidently a secondary being; others say on the contrary that Adam was only a rough draft and that God succeeded in producing the human being in perfection when He created Eve. Woman's brain is smaller; yes, but it is relatively larger. Christ was made a man; yes, but perhaps for his greater humility. Each argument at once suggests its opposite, and both are often fallacious. If we are to gain understanding, we must get out of these ruts; we must discard the vague notions of superiority, inferiority, equality which have hitherto corrupted every discussion of the subject and start afresh.

NOTES

1. *Franchise*, dead today.

2. The Kinsey Report [Alfred C. Kinsey and others: *Sexual Behavior in the Human Male* (W. B. Saunders Co., 1948)] is no exception, for it is limited to describing the sexual characteristics of American men, which is quite a different matter.

3. E. Lévinas expresses this idea most explicitly in his essay *Temps et l'Autre*. "Is there not a case in which otherness, alterity [*altérité*], unquestionably marks the nature of a being, as its essence, an instance of otherness not consisting purely and simply in the opposition of two species of the same genus? I think that the feminine represents the contrary in its absolute sense, this contrariness being in no wise affected by any relation between it and its correlative and thus remaining absolutely other. Sex is not a certain specific difference . . . no more is the sexual difference a mere contradiction. . . . Nor does this difference lie in the duality of two complementary terms, for two complementary terms imply a pre-existing whole. . . . Otherness reaches its full flowering in the feminine, a term of the same rank as consciousness but of opposite meaning."

I suppose that Lévinas does not forget that woman, too, is aware of her own consciousness, or ego. But it is striking that he deliberately takes a man's point of view, disregarding the reciprocity of subject and object. When he writes that woman is mystery, he implies that she is mystery for man. Thus his description, which is intended to be objective, is in fact an assertion of masculine privilege.

4. With rare exceptions, perhaps, like certain materiarchal rulers, queens, and the like.—Tr.

5. See *The Second Sex*, Part II, ch. viii.

6. At the moment an "equal rights" amendment to the Constitution of the United States is before Congress.—Tr.

7. See *The Second Sex*, Part II, pp. 115–17.

Part Four

Structured Inequality—The Invisible
Iron Cage of Class

10

Masculinities and Athletic Careers

Michael Messner

The growth of women's studies and feminist gender studies has in recent years led to the emergence of a new men's studies (Brod 1987; Kimmel 1987). But just as feminist perspectives on women have been justifiably criticized for falsely universalizing the lives and issues of white, middle-class, U.S. women (Hooks 1984; Zinn, Cannon, Higgenbotham, and Dill 1986), so, too, men's studies has tended to focus on the lives of relatively privileged men. As Brod (1983–1984) points out in an insightful critique of the middle-class basis and bias of the men's movement, if men's studies is to be relevant to minority and working-class men, less emphasis must be placed on personal lifestyle transformations, and more emphasis must be placed on developing a structural critique of social institutions. Although some institutional analysis has begun in men's studies, very little critical scrutiny has been focused on that very masculine institution, organized sports (Messner 1985; Sabo 1985; Sabo and Runfola 1980). Not only is the institution of sports an ideal place to study men and masculinity, careful analysis would make it impossible to ignore the realities of race and class differences. . . .

None of these perspectives consider the ways that gender shapes men's definitions of meaning and choices. Within the sociology of sport, gender as a process that interacts with race and class is usually ignored or taken for granted—except when it is *women* athletes who are being studied. Sociologists who are attempting to come to grips with the experiences of black men in general, and in organized sports in particular, have almost exclusively focused their analytic attention on the variable "black," while uncritically taking "men" as a given. Hare and Hare (1984), for example, view masculinity as a biologically determined tendency to act as a provider

From "Masculinities and Athletic Careers" in *Gender & Society* 3 (1989): 71–74, 76–83, 85–88. Copyright © 1989 by Charles Messner. Reprinted by permission of Sage Publications, Inc.

and protector that is thwarted for black men by socioeconomic and racist obstacles. Staples (1982) does view masculinity largely as a socially produced script, but he accepts this script as a given, preferring to focus on black men's blocked access to male role fulfillment. These perspectives on masculinity fail to show how the male role itself, as it interacts with a constricted structure of opportunity, can contribute to locking black men into destructive relationships and life-styles (Franklin 1984; Majors 1986).

This article will examine the relationships among male identity, race, and social class by listening to the voices of former athletes. I will first briefly describe my research. Then I will discuss the similarities and differences in the choices and experiences of men from different racial and social class backgrounds. Together, these choices and experiences help to construct what Connell (1987) calls "the gender order." Organized sports, it will be suggested, is a practice through which men's separation from and power over women is embodied and naturalized at the same time that hegemonic (white, heterosexual, professional-class) masculinity is clearly differentiated from marginalized and subordinated masculinities.

DESCRIPTION OF RESEARCH

Between 1983 and 1985, I conducted 30 open-ended, in-depth interviews with male former athletes. My purpose was to add a critical understanding of male gender identity to Levinson's (1978) conception of the "individual lifecourse"—specifically, to discover how masculinity develops and changes as a man interacts with the socially constructed world of organized sports. Most of the men I interviewed had played the U.S. "major sports"—football, basketball, baseball, track. At the time of the interview, each had been retired from playing organized sports for at least 5 years. Their ages ranged from 21 to 48, with the median, 33. Fourteen were black, 14 were white, and 2 were Hispanic. Fifteen of the 16 black and Hispanic men had come from poor or working-class families, while the majority (9 of 14) of the white men had come from middle-class or professional families. Twelve had played organized sports through high school, 11 through college, and 7 had been professional athletes. All had at some time in their lives based their identities largely on their roles as athletes and could therefore be said to have had athletic careers.

MALE IDENTITY AND ORGANIZED SPORTS

. . . As Rubin (1985) and Levinson (1978) have pointed out, an understanding of the lives of men must take into account the processual nature of male identity as it unfolds through interaction between the internal (psychological ambivalences) and the external (social, historical, and institutional) contexts.

To examine the impact of the social contexts, I divided my sample into two comparison groups. In the first group were 10 men from higher-status backgrounds, primarily white, middle-class, and professional families. In the second group were 20 men from lower-status backgrounds, primarily minority, poor, and working-class families. While my data offered evidence for the similarity of experiences and motivations of men from poor backgrounds, independent of race, I also found anecdotal evidence of a racial dynamic that operates independently of social class. However, my sample was not large enough to separate race and class, and so I have combined them to make two status groups.

In discussing these two groups, I will focus mainly on the high school years. During this crucial period, the athletic role may become a master status for a young man, and he is beginning to make assessments and choices about his future. It is here that many young men make a major commitment to—or begin to back away from—athletic careers.

Men from Higher-Status Backgrounds

The boyhood dream of one day becoming a professional athlete—a dream shared by nearly all the men interviewed in this study—is rarely realized. The sports world is extremely hierarchical. The pyramid of sports careers narrows very rapidly as one climbs from high school, to college, to professional levels of competition (Edwards 1984; Harris and Eitzen 1978; Hill and Lowe 1978). In fact, the chances of attaining professional status in sports are approximately 4/100,000 for a white man, 2/100,000 for a black man, and 3/1,000,000 for a Hispanic man in the United States (Leonard and Reyman 1988). For many young athletes, their dream ends early when coaches inform them that they are not big enough, strong enough, fast enough, or skilled enough to compete at the higher levels. But six of the higher-status men I interviewed did not wait for coaches to weed them out. They made conscious decisions in high school or in college to shift their attentions elsewhere—usually toward educational and career goals. Their decision not to pursue an athletic career appeared to them in retrospect to be a rational decision based on the growing knowledge of how very slim their chances were to be successful in the sports world. . . .

How and why do so many successful male athletes from higher-status backgrounds come to view sports careers as "pissing in the wind," or as "small potatoes"? How and why do they make this early assessment and choice to shift from sports and toward educational and professional goals? The white, middle-class institutional context, with its emphasis on education and income, makes it clear to them that choices exist and that the pursuit of an athletic career is not a particularly good choice to make. Where the young male once found sports to be a convenient institution within which to construct masculine status, the postadolescent and young adult man from a higher-status background simply *transfers* these same strivings to other institutional contexts: education and careers.

For the higher-status men who had chosen to shift from athletic careers, sports remained important on two levels. First, having been a successful high school or college athlete enhances one's adult status among other men in the community—but only as a badge of masculinity that is *added* to his professional status. In fact, several men in professions chose to be interviewed in their offices, where they publicly displayed the trophies and plaques that attested to their earlier athletic accomplishments. Their high school and college athletic careers may have appeared to them as "small potatoes," but many successful men speak of their earlier status as athletes as having "opened doors" for them in their present professions and in community affairs. Similarly, Farr's (1988) research on "Good Old Boys Sociability Groups" shows how sports, as part of the glue of masculine culture, continues to facilitate "dominance bonding" among privileged men long after active sports careers end. The college-educated, career-successful men in Farr's study rarely express overtly sexist, racist, or classist attitudes; in fact, in their relationships with women, they "often engage in expressive intimacies" and "make fun of exaggerated 'machismo'" (p. 276). But though they outwardly conform more to what Pleck (1982) calls "the modern male role," their informal relationships within their sociability groups, in effect, affirm their own gender and class status by constructing and clarifying the boundaries between themselves and women and lower-status men. This dominance bonding is based largely upon ritual forms of sociability (camaraderie, competition), "the superiority of which was first affirmed in the exclusionary play activities of young boys in groups" (Farr 1988, p. 265).

In addition to contributing to dominance bonding among higher-status adult men, sports remains salient in terms of the ideology of gender relations. Most men continued to watch, talk about, and identify with sports long after their own disengagement from athletic careers. Sports as a mediated spectacle provides an important context in which traditional conceptions of masculine superiority—conceptions recently contested by women—are shored up. As a 32-year-old white professional-class man said of one of the most feared professional football players today:

> A woman can do the same job as I can do—maybe even be my boss. But I'll be *damned* if she can go out on the football field and take a hit from Ronnie Lott.

Violent sports as spectacle provide linkages among men in the project of the domination of women, while at the same time helping to construct and clarify differences among various masculinities. The statement above is a clear identification with Ronnie Lott *as a man,* and the basis of the identification is the violent male body. As Connell (1987, p. 85) argues, sports is an important organizing institution for the embodiment of masculinity. Here, men's power over women becomes naturalized and linked to the social distribution of violence. Sports, as a practice, suppresses natural (sex) similarities, constructs differences, and then, largely through the media, weaves a structure of symbol and interpretation around these differences that naturalizes them (Hargreaves 1986, p. 112). It is also significant that the man who made the above statement about Ronnie Lott was quite aware that he (and perhaps 99 percent of the rest of the U.S. male population) was probably as incapable as most women of taking a "hit" from someone like Lott and living to tell of it. For middle-class men, the "tough guys" of the culture industry—the Rambos, the Ronnie Lotts who are fearsome "hitters," who "play hurt"—are the heroes who "prove" that "we men" are superior to women. At the same time, they play the role of the "primitive other," against whom higher-status men define themselves as "modern" and "civilized." . . .

Men from Lower-Status Backgrounds

For the lower-status young men in this study, success in sports was not an added proof of masculinity; it was often their only hope of achieving public masculine status. A 34-year-old black bus driver who had been a star athlete in three sports in high school had neither the grades nor the money to attend college, so he accepted an offer from the U.S. Marine Corps to play on their baseball team. He ended up in Vietnam, where a grenade blew four fingers off his pitching hand. In retrospect, he believed that his youthful focus on sports stardom and his concomitant lack of effort in academics made sense:

> You can go anywhere with athletics—you don't have to have brains. I mean, I didn't feel like I was gonna go out there and be a computer expert, or something that was gonna make a lot of money. The only thing I could do and live comfortably would be to play sports—just to get a contract—doesn't matter if you play second or third team in the pros, you're gonna make big bucks. That's all I wanted, a confirmed livelihood at the end of my ventures, and the only way I could do it would be through sports. So I tried. It failed, but that's what I tried.

Similar, and even more tragic, is the story of a 34-year-old black man who is now serving a life term in prison. After a career-ending knee injury at the age of 20 abruptly ended what had appeared to be a certain road to professional football fame and fortune, he decided that he "could still be rich and famous" by robbing a bank. During his high school and college years, he said, he was nearly illiterate. . . .

By the high school years, class and ethnic inequalities had become glaringly obvious, especially for those who attended socioeconomically heterogeneous schools. Cars, nice clothes, and others signs of status were often unavailable to these young men, and this contributed to a situation in which sports took on an expanded importance for them in terms of constructing masculine identities and status. A white, 36-year-old man from a poor, single-parent family who later played professional baseball had been acutely aware of his low-class status in his high school:

> I had one pair of jeans, and I wore them every day. I was always afraid of what people thought of me—that this guy doesn't have anything, that he's wearing the same Levi's

all the time, he's having to work in the cafeteria for his lunch. What's going on? I think that's what made me so shy. . . . But boy, when I got into sports, I let it all hang out—[laughs]—and maybe that's why I became so good, because I was frustrated, and when I got into that element, they gave me my uniform in football, basketball, and baseball, and I didn't have to worry about how I looked, because then it was *me* who was coming out, and not my clothes or whatever. And I think that was the drive.

Similarly, a 41-year-old black man who had a 10-year professional football career described his insecurities as one of the few poor blacks in a mostly white, middle-class school and his belief that sports was the one arena in which he could be judged solely on his merit:

I came from a very poor family, and I was very sensitive about that in those days. When people would say things like "Look at him—he has dirty pants on," I'd think about it for a week. [But] I'd put my pants on and I'd go out on the football field with the intention that I'm gonna do a job. And if that calls on me to hurt you, I'm gonna do it. It's as simple as that. I demand respect just like everybody else.

"Respect" was what I heard over and over when talking with the men from lower-status backgrounds, especially black men. I interpret this type of respect to be a crystallization of the masculine quest for recognition through public achievement, unfolding within a system of structured constraints due to class and race inequities. The institutional context of education (sometimes with the collusion of teachers and coaches) and the constricted structure of opportunity in the economy made the pursuit of athletic careers appear to be the most rational choice to these young men. . . .

For most young men from lower-status backgrounds, the poor quality of their schools, the attitudes of teachers and coaches, as well as the antieducation environment within their own male peer groups, made it extremely unlikely that they would be able to succeed as students. Sports, therefore, became *the* arena in which they attempted to "show their stuff." For these lower-status men, as Zinn (1982) and Majors (1986) argued in their respective studies of chicano men and black men, when institutional resources that signify masculine status and control are absent, physical presence, personal style, and expressiveness take on increased importance. What Majors (1986, p. 6) calls "cool pose" is black men's expressive, often aggressive, assertion of masculinity. This self-assertion often takes place within a social context in which the young man is quite aware of existing social inequities. . . .

Majors (1986) argues that although "cool pose" represents a creative survival technique within a hostile environment, the most likely long-term effect of this masculine posturing is educational and occupational dead ends. As a result, we can conclude, lower-status men's personal and peer-group responses to a constricted structure of opportunity—responses that are rooted, in part, in the developmental insecurities and ambivalence of masculinity—serve to lock many of these young men into limiting activities such as sports.

SUMMARY AND CONCLUSIONS

This research has suggested that within a social context that is stratified by social class and by race, the choice to pursue—or not to pursue—an athletic career is explicable as an individual's rational assessment of the available means to achieve a respected masculine identity. For nearly all of the men from lower-status backgrounds, the status and respect that they received through sports was temporary—it did not translate into upward mobility. Nonetheless, a strategy of discouraging young black boys and men from involvement in sports is probably doomed to fail, since it ignores the continued existence of structural constraints. . . .

. . . Utilizing the concept of the gender order, we can begin to conceptualize how hierarchies of race, class, age, and sexual preference among men help to construct and legitimize men's overall power and privilege over women. And how, for some black, working-class, or gay men, the false promise of sharing in the fruits of hegemonic masculinity often ties them into their marginalized and subordinate statuses within hierarchies of intermale dominance. For instance, black men's development of what Majors (1986) calls "cool pose" within sports can be interpreted as an example of creative resistance to one form of social domination (racism); yet it also demonstrates the limits of an agency that adopts other forms of social domination (masculinity) as its vehicle. As Majors (forthcoming) points out:

> Cool Pose demonstrates black males' potential to transcend oppressive conditions n order to express themselves *as men*. [Yet] it ultimately does not put black males in a position to live and work in more egalitarian ways with women, nor does it directly challenge male hierarchies.

Indeed, as Connell's (forthcoming) analysis of an Australian "Iron Man" shows, the commercially successful, publicly acclaimed athlete may embody all that is valued in present cultural conceptions of hegemonic virility. Yet higher-status men, while they admire the public image of the successful athlete, may also look down on him as a narrow, even atavistic, example of masculinity. For these higher-status men, their earlier sports successes are often status enhancing and serve to link them with other men in ways that continue to exclude women. Their decisions not to pursue athletic careers are equally important signs of their status vis-à-vis other men. Future examinations of the contemporary meaning and importance of sports to men might take as a fruitful point of departure that athletic participation, and sports as public spectacle serve to provide linkages among men in the project of the domination of women, while at the same time helping to construct and clarify differences and hierarchies among various masculinities.

REFERENCES

Brod, H. 1983–84. "Work Clothes and Leisure Suits: The Class Basis and Bias of the Men's Movement." *M: Gentle Men for Gender Justice* 11:10–12, 38–40.

Brod, H. (ed.). 1987. *The Making of Masculinities: The New Men's Studies*. Winchester, MA: Allen & Unwin.

Connell, R. W. 1987. *Gender and Power*. Stanford, CA: Stanford University Press.

———. Forthcoming. "An Iron Man: The Body and Some Contradictions of Hegemonic Masculinity." In *Sport, Men, and the Gender Order: Critical Feminist Perspectives*, edited by M. A. Messner and D. S. Sabo. Champaign, IL: Human Kinetics.

Edwards, H. 1984. "The Collegiate Athletic Arms Race: Origins and Implications of the 'Rule 48' Controversy." *Journal of Sport and Social Issues* 8:4–22.

Farr, K. A. 1988. "Dominance Bonding Through the Good Old Boys Sociability Group." *Sex Roles* 18:259–77.

Franklin, C. W. II. 1984. *The Changing Definition of Masculinity*. New York: Plenum.

Hare, N. and J. Hare. 1984. *The Endangered Black Family: Coping With the Unisexualization and Coming Extinction of the Black Race*. San Francisco, CA: Black Think Tank.

Hargreaves, J. A. 1986. "Where's the Virtue? Where's the Grace? A Discussion of the Social Production of Gender Through Sport." *Theory, Culture and Society* 3:109–21.

Harris, D. S. and D. S. Eitzen. 1978. "The Consequences of Failure in Sport." *Urban Life* 7:177–88.

Hill, P. and B. Lowe. 1978. "The Inevitable Metathesis of the Retiring Athlete." *International Review of Sport Sociology* 9:5–29.

Hooks, B. 1984. *Feminist Theory: From Margin to Center*. Boston: South End Press.

Kimmel, M. S. (ed.). 1987. *Changing Men: New Directions in Research on Men and Masculinity*. Newbury Park, CA: Sage.

Leonard, W. M. II and J. M. Reyman, 1988. "The Odds of Attaining Professional Athlete Status: Refining the Computations." *Sociology of Sport Journal* 5:162–69.

Levinson, D. J. 1978. *The Seasons of a Man's Life*. New York: Ballantine.

Majors, R. 1986. "Cool Pose: The Proud Signature of Black Survival." *Changing Men: Issues in Gender, Sex, and Politics* 17:5–6.

———. Forthcoming. "Cool Pose: Black Masculinity in Sports." In *Sport, Men, and the Gender Order: Critical Feminist Perspectives*, edited by M. A. Messner and D. S. Sabo, Champaign, IL: Human Kinetics.

Messner, M. 1985. "The Changing Meaning of Male Identity in the Lifecourse of the Athlete." *Arena Review* 9:31–60.

Pleck, J. H. 1982. *The Myth of Masculinity*, Cambridge: MIT Press.

Rubin, L. B. 1985. *Just Friends: The Role of Friendship in Our Lives*. New York: Harper & Row.

Sabo, D. 1985. "Sport, Patriarchy, and Male Identity: New Questions About Men and Sport." *Arena Review* 9:1–30.

Sabo, D. and R. Runfola (eds.). 1980. *Jock: Sports and Male Identity*. Englewood Cliffs, NJ: Prentice Hall.

Staples, R. 1982. *Black Masculinity*. San Francisco, CA: Black Scholar Press.

Zinn, M. Baca. 1982. "Chicano Men and Masculinity." *Journal of Ethnic Studies* 10:29–44.

Zinn, M. Baca, L. Weber Cannon, E. Higgenbotham, and B. Thornton Dill. 1986. "The Costs of Exclusionary Practices in Women's Studies." *Signs: Journal of Women in Culture and Society* 11:290–303.

11

The Double-Bind of the 'Working-Class' Feminist Academic: The Success of Failure or the Failure of Success?

Diane Reay

. . . Academia has rarely developed complex understandings of working-class people. Even celebrated studies like that of Willis (1977) can be read as an indictment of the working class; they are so stupid that they invest time and energy into ensuring their own oppression. However, the biggest oversight for feminist academics from working-class backgrounds is the primacy the vast majority of academic studies have given to male experience. From quantitative surveys of socio-economic categorization (Goldthorpe, 1980, 1983; Lockwood 1986) to ethnographies like that of Willis, women are invisible. In my own writing about the working classes I want to recognize what is problematic about working-class communities. Although many individuals within them challenge and combat discrimination and prejudice, they are sexist; racism and homophobia are endemic and women have to negotiate narrow, constricting versions of femininity. That is not the same as asserting that middle-class groupings in society are more enlightened. Rather sexism, racism and homophobia are hidden and denied among the middle classes, but equally prevalent (Reay, 1995a).

Currently, even mentioning social class in academia feels 'out-of-place', naively old-fashioned. The invidious influence of the 1990s academic preoccupation with postmodern identities has resulted in the relegation of social class to an intellectual backwater. Class may be mentioned on the dust-jacket in books on education but once inside the text the experiences of working-class pupils are often marginalized or subsumed within understandings of middle-class experience as normative (see, for example, Evans, 1991). . . .

The early 1990s was a period when much of the media focus seemed to be on the middle classes. Either we were all middle-class now or else the middle classes were variously viewed as under siege, in crisis or losing their privileges (for example, see Gray, 1994; Phillips, 1995). The processes impacting on working-class life have been reduced either to declarations about the disappearance of 'the working class' or to continuing pathologizations which neither of the working-class academic perspectives attempt to address. Modifying, reworking, updating theoretical understandings of the 'working classes' to match changing realities is rarely on the academic agenda. . . .

The female academic from a working-class background is the end product of very different processes to those of social reproduction. She is caught up in change and social transformation. However, the positive connotations invested in terms such as transformation and change mask an inherent negativity often overlooked in discussions of meritocracy. . . .

The contradictory positioning of the once working-class female academic juxtapose radical potentialities with confirmation of revisionist policies. There is an inherent paradox. While we bring with us insider knowledge of class inequalities, at the same time the academic from a working-class background represents a justification of right-wing rhetoric. We are the tokenistic edge of elitist policies: 'the inner-city kid with the right parents, the right teachers and the right brain'. We stand for a triumph of individualism over community; proof that equal opportunities work. . . .

Why did we work so hard in the first place? It seems incontrovertible to me that the educationally successful working-class girl has to work very hard indeed; at learning a totally new language, at undoing the silences of her childhood (Bourdieu, 1984; Borkowski, 1992); at transforming key aspects around female embodiment. Janet Zandy writes about the physicality of class difference:

> Working-class people practise a language of the body that eludes theoretical textual studies. Working-class people do not have the quiet hands or the neutral faces of the privileged classes—especially when they are within their own communities. (Zandy, 1995, p. 5)

Survival in middle-class contexts for working-class women often requires developing a decorum and reserve that fits in with middle-class standards of acceptable female sexuality (Walkerdine, 1995). It also demands a voice to replace the one that has so often been silenced in educational contexts.

How do we understand the desires and fears that accompanied such a difficult transition out of one class and into another? Kelly and Nihlen (1982) point out the gap in theories of social and cultural reproduction; the inability to explain 'the ones who got away'. Educational theorists fail to even engage with the overt psychological processes entailed in upward social mobility, let alone look beneath at the more hidden layers of compromise and compromising. However, the white working-class girl who becomes middle-class is implicated in what often feels like a treacherous process; one of shedding at least part, if not all, of her earlier class identity (Lynch and O'Neill, 1994). We have utilized one system of meritocratic individualism, the school system, in order to attain a place within another, that of higher education. How then to reconcile the working-class culture we started out with? . . .

I suggest the female academic from a working-class background is unlikely ever to feel at home in academia. For many, socialization, at least within the family, was into collective and community-based understandings of the social world, not the competitive individuals we now face in which social networks are about instrumentalism, not connection. However, this is not to valorize working-class pasts.

. . . We worked so hard at school not primarily to be acceptable to the middle classes, who were always the enemy, but to redeem our parents, to prove our family was 'just as good'. And yet when I see any documentary about miners I am overwhelmed, suffused with powerful feelings of belonging, along with a sense of outrage about their treatment. The irony is now there is no real community of coalminers, however internally divided, to belong to. There is a further irony for me as a feminist academic in that I can see my father's hand guiding my conceptions of community. It is all about his version and very little about my mother's. In spite of my aim of painting an ambivalent, tentative picture highlighting complexities of interpretation and motivation, he is the hero of my fantasy of community; this man who never really belonged to the community he valorized.

. . . Other siblings talk of my mother's ambition for her children. What I saw was her shame. She was ashamed: of the inevitable squalor from squeezing a family of ten into two bedrooms and a boxroom; of never having enough money; of being seen as profligate. Both parents felt inferior because that is what lies at the heart of working-class shame; a deeply felt sense of working-class inferiority which comes from seeing ourselves through middle-class eyes. . . .

While my parents' rage propelled me through the educational system, dealing with it subsequently in middle-class contexts has proved problematic. I regularly get angry about middle-class privilege and then guilty because I am now implicated in it. However, I have come to see that sense of unfairness as one of the most valuable things I possess.

If you have grown up working-class you know that the solution to class inequalities does not lie in making the working classes middle-class but in working at dismantling and sharing out the economic, social and cultural capital which go with middle-class status. I would suggest that the permeation of new middle-class values within the working classes has been disastrous. Collectivist understandings of self and social group have been increasingly displaced by individualistic notions premised on the self as consumer. The prevailing culture of individualism and competitiveness has given free rein to an end-of-millennium capitalism which seems increasingly out of control and unaccountable. The social groups who have had to pay the highest price for these developments are the traditional and the new working classes—the poor, manual workers, the unemployed, the low-paid in the service sectors and lone-mother families. Competition and individualism are all about hierarchy and pecking order in which the individual rather than her circumstances are judged. The working classes are no longer entitled to a sense of unfairness because everything from their financial situation and the state of their health to their children's schooling has been repackaged under late capitalism as the responsibility of the individual alone.

The answer is not to further empower ourselves within academic hierarchies but to listen to, and learn from, the still-working-class woman so that there is an erosion of status hierarchies based on educational qualifications and/or wealth. Only through work which centres class injustice, as well as the injustices of 'race' and gender, can we keep at bay 'the alienation of advantage' (Hennessy, 1993). However, therein lies the double-bind. We know that taken-for-granted middle-class superiority is a sham but we learn this just as we are growing into a sense of our own importance. The struggle is to continue questioning academic culture and values while acknowledging the extent to which we are caught up in them.

As Ladwig and Gore assert, any discussion of social privilege and power needs to pay attention to 'questions of *academic* privilege, and power, competition, and contestation' (Ladwig and Gore, 1994, p. 236; authors' emphasis). I am now in a position of inevitable complicity. Any success in promoting issues which centre social justice has become inextricably entangled with self-promotion and struggles for power within academic fields. Daphne Patai remarks that what she entitles 'tiresome self-reflexivity' would be inconceivable 'in a setting in which material want was an incontrovertible fact of life' (Patai, 1994, p. 66). We academics, despite our incessant moaning about overwork and intolerable conditions, are in a luxurious situation compared to the growing ranks of the poor (Hutton, 1995). Inevitably, my rage has been diluted with guilt. I try to see myself through my mother's eyes because then I can see just how privileged I have become.

> The fact is that those of us whose medium is words do occupy privileged positions, and we hardly give up those positions when we engage in endless self-scrutiny and anxious self-identification. (Patai, 1994, p. 67)

... There are other things at issue for academics who were once working-class; questions around loyalty and disloyalty, belonging and not belonging. We have to live with the paradox that a defining part of our identity is turning into a chimera; our 'working-classness' is a fantasy that often we alone are still engaging in. My own experience of growing up working-class has left vivid memories of the heritage and history of my social origins imprinted on my consciousness. However, that consciousness, rooted in working-class affiliation, appears increasingly to be a misfit; a sense of self both out of place and out of time. . . .

Kathleen Casey writes that for the black child to become educated is "to contradict the whole system of racist signification' (Casey, 1993, p. 123). In the same way to become educated as a working-class person is to refute the whole system of class signification. However, as Scates asserts, it is a far more contradictory and compromising process. Casey writes that 'to succeed at studying "white" knowledge is to undo the system itself, to refute its (re)production of black inferiority materially and symbolically'. I would suggest a further version in which studying middle-class knowledge presents the individual from a working-class background with a dilemma. Far from undoing the system it can represent a collusion with it and act to reproduce rather than refute the (re)production of working-class inferiority. If we are the tokenistic proof of meritocracy then our academic success serves to underscore the unworthiness of those who fail. All too often when the pervading sense of inferiority which comes with growing up working-class meets a degree of academic success and recognition, we are seduced into seeing ourselves as special and more worthy, rather than more fortunate than those we left behind. Of course the middle classes, and here we are talking of the vast majority of academics, have a vested interest in overlooking the classed nature of society. To view the world through a class lens would be to focus on their position of relative privilege.

Prevailing academic discourses construct hierarchies of oppression which have nothing to do with the world outside but are all about vying for attention within academic circles. Middle-class, white feminists who focus on their oppression to the exclusion of their privilege, the eminent white, male academics who are still 'just working-class lads', just as much as middle-class males academics from public school backgrounds who are reinventing their schooling as a source of oppression, are buying into the narcissistic competitiveness of academia. A male academic suggested that I wrote about my working-class background because I wanted to compete in the academic game of being the most oppressed. However, it is not that straightforward. There is also a sense of impossibility; the psychic refusal of becoming middle-class. It is no longer an issue of not making a good enough job of passing because the process of completing three degrees has ensured that I do. Rather, it is the sense of treachery and accedence to institutionalized and socially endemic inequalities the middle-class label holds that I continue to struggle with, while needing to recognize that I am now seen as middle-class.

How can the academic feminist from a working-class background revitalize what is left of her working-class consciousness and utilize it positively? Certainly, in academia and other middle-class contexts there is a need for people who are prepared to strip away the denial and pretence, to unmask the dissimulation which we can see clearly because it was never part of our growing up. There is a culture of contempt, class contempt that is pervasive but rarely articulated. . . .

The experiences of the working classes get left out because they have no constituency in academia. This is not to be cynical but to acknowledge that academia is primarily a self-seeking culture premised on competition where class is often conscripted as a means to academic career promotion. As bell hooks points out,

> When those of us in the academy who are working-class or from working-class backgrounds share our perspectives, we subvert the tendency to focus only on the thoughts, attitudes and experiences of those who are materially privileged. (hooks, 1994, p. 185)

... This is part of my effort to rework understandings of social class. I want to put the complexities of class inequalities on the academic agenda and have begun to try to theorize about the complicated interweavings of gender, class and 'race' in the experiences of working-class women (Reay, 1996a, 1996b). However, feminist academics from working-class backgrounds never escape those processes of compromise and compromising I described earlier. I realize that my own centering of class is part of a continuing project of reconciling what I have become with what I was, while simultaneously trying to carve out a self that I can feel at ease with.

REFERENCES

Borkowski, B. (1992) 'Ausbruch and Aufbruch durch Bildung aus Milieu-und Geschlechtsrollen-Begrenzungen' ['Breaking out and up through education from milieu and gender constraints'], in Schuluter, A. (Ed.) *Arbeitertochter und ihr sozialer Aufstieg. Zum Verhaltnis von Klasse, Geschlecht und sozialer Mobilität [Upwardly socially mobile working-class girls. On the relationship between class, gender and social mobility]*, Weinheim, Deutscher Studien Verlag.

Bourdieu, Pierre (1984) *Distinction*, London, Routledge and Kegan Paul Ltd.

Casey, Kathleen (1993) *I Answer with My Life: Life Histories of Women Teachers Working for Social Change*, New York, Routledge.

Evans, Mary (1991) *A Good School: Life at a Girls' Grammar School in the 1950s*, London, The Women's Press.

Goldthorpe, J. H. (1980) *Social Mobility and Class Structure in Modern Britain*, Oxford, Clarendon.

Goldthorpe, J. H. (1983) 'Women and Class Analysis', *Sociology*, 17, 4, pp. 465–88.

Gray, John (1994) 'Into the Abyss?', *The Sunday Times*, 30 October.

Hennessy, Rosemary (1993) *Materialist Feminism and the Politics of Discourse*, New York, Routledge, Chapman & Hall.

hooks, bell (1994) *Teaching to Transgress: Education as the Practice of Freedom*, London, Routledge.

Hutton, Will (1995) *The State We're In*, London, Cape.

Kelly, G. P. and Nihlen, A. S. (1982) 'Schooling and the Reproduction of Patriarchy: Unequal Workloads, Unequal Rewards', in Apple, Michael (Ed.) *Cultural and Economic Reproduction in Education*, London, Routledge and Kegan Paul.

Ladwig, James G. and Gore, Jennifer M. (1994) 'Extending Power and Specifying Method Within the Discourse of Activist Research', in Gitlin, Andrew (Ed.) *Power and Method: Political Activism and Educational Research*, London, Routledge.

Lockwood, D. (1986) 'Class, Status and Gender', in Crompton, R. and Mann, M. (Eds.) *Gender and Stratification*, Cambridge, Polity.

Lynch, Kathleen and O'Neill, Cathleen (1994) 'The Colonisation of Social Class in Education', *British Journal of Sociology of Education*, 15, 3, pp. 307–24.

Patai, Daphne (1994) 'When Method Becomes Power', in Gitlin, Andrew (Ed.) *Power and Method: Political Activism and Educational Research*, London, Routledge.

Phillips, Melanie (1995) 'Threatened, Lost, Self-Hating, Angry, Taxed, Envied and Insecure: Whatever Happened to the Middle-Classes?', *The Observer*, 2 July.

Reay, Diane (1995a) '"They employ cleaners to do that": Habitus in the Primary Classroom', *British Journal of Sociology of Education*, 10, 5, pp. 353–71.

Reay, Diane (1996a) 'Insider Perspectives or Stealing the Words out of Women's Mouths: Interpretation in the Research Process', *Feminist Review,* 53: *Speaking Out: Researching and Representing Women.*

Reay, Diane (1996b) 'Dealing with Difficult Differences: Reflexivity and Social Class in Feminist Research', in Walkerdine, Valerie (Ed.) *Feminism and Psychology: Special Issue on Social Class.*

Scates, Maxine (1995) 'Leaving it All Behind?', in Zandy, Janet (Ed.) *Liberating Memory: Our Work and Our Working-Class Consciousness*, New Brunswick, Rutgers University Press.

Walkerdine, Valerie (1995) 'Subject to Change Without Notice: Psychology, Postmodernity and the Popular', in Pile, Steve and Thrift, Nigel (Eds.) *Mapping the Subject: Geographies of Cultural Transformation*, London, Routledge.

Willis, Paul (1997) *Learning to Labour: How Working Class Kids Get Working Class Jobs*, Farnborough, Saxon House.

Zandy, Janet (Ed.) (1995) *Liberating Memory: Our Work and Our Working-Class Consciousness,* New Brunswick: Rutgers University Press.

12

(In)Secure Times: Constructing White Working-Class Masculinities in the Late 20th Century

Michelle Fine, Lois Weis, Judi Addelston, and Julia Marusza

. . . The poor and working-class white boys and men in this article belong to a continuum of white working-class men who, up until recently in U.S. history, have been relatively privileged. These men, however, do not articulate a sense of themselves inside that history. In current economic and social relations that felt sense of privilege is tenuous at best. Since the 1970s, the U.S. steel industry has been in rapid decline as have other areas of manufacturing and production, followed by the downward spiral of businesses that sprung up around larger industry (Bluestone and Harrison 1982). In the span of a few decades, foreign investment, corporate flight, downsizing, and automation have suddenly left members of the working class without a steady family wage, which, compounded with the dissipation of labor unions, has left many white working-class men feeling emasculated and angry (Weis, 1990; Weis, Proweller, and Centrie, 1996). It seems that overnight, the ability to work hard and provide disappeared. White working-class men, of course, are not more racist or sexist than middle-class and upper-class white men. In this analysis, however, we offer data that demonstrate how white working-class male anger takes on virulent forms as it is displaced in a climate of reaction against global economic change.

As they search for someone who has stolen their presumed privilege, we begin to understand ways in which white poor and working-class men in the 1980s and 1990s manage to maintain a sense of self in the midst of rising feminism, affirmative action, and gay/lesbian rights. We are given further insight into ways in which they sustain a belief in a system that has, at least for working- and middle-class white men, begun to crumble, "e-racing" their once relatively secure advantage over white women and women and men of color (Newman 1993). As scholars of the dominant

From "(In)Secure Times" in *Gender & Society* 11 (1997): 52–68. Copyright © 1997 by Michelle Fine, Lois Weis, Judi Addelston, Julia Marusza. Reprinted by permission of Sage Publications, Inc.

culture begin to recognize that "white is a color" (Roman 1993; Wong 1994), our work makes visible the borders, strategies, and fragilities of white working-class male culture, in insecure times, at a moment in history when many feel that this identity is under siege. . . .

ON WHITENESS

In the United States, the hierarchies of race, gender, and class are embodied in the contemporary "struggle" of working-class white men. As their stories reveal, these boys and men are trying to sustain a *place* within this hierarchy and secure the very *hierarchies* that assure their place. Among the varied demographic categories that spill out of this race/gender hierarchy, white men are the only ones who have a vested interest in maintaining both their position and their hierarchy—even, ironically, working-class boys and men who enjoy little of the privilege accrued to their gender/race status.

Scholars of colonial thought have highlighted the ways in which notions about non-Western "Others" are produced simultaneously with the production of discourse about the Western white "self," and these works become relevant to our analyses of race/gender domination. . . .

One continuing effect of colonial discourse is the production of an unnamed, unmarked white/Western self against which all others can be named and judged. It is the unmarked self that must be deconstructed, named, and marked (Frankenberg 1993). This article takes up this challenge. As we will argue here, white working-class male identity is parasitically coproduced as these men name and mark others, largely African Americans and white women. Their identity would not exist in its present form (and perhaps not at all) if these simultaneous productions were not taking place. At a moment of economic crisis in which white working-class men are being squeezed, the disparaging constructions of others proliferate.

HIGH SCHOOL STUDENTS:
RACISM AND THE CONSTRUCTION OF THE "OTHER"

. . . This is an exploration of white working-class high school students in a de-industrializing urban area called "Freeway." Data were collected in the classrooms, study halls, during extracurricular activities, and through in-depth interviews with over 60 juniors, most of their teachers, the vice-principal, social workers, guidance counselors, and others over the course of an academic year. . . .

While there are several facets to the production of the boys' identity, we focus on the ways in which young white boys coproduce African American male identities and their own identities. For the most part, these young white boys narrate a sense of self grounded in the sphere of sexuality, in which they script themselves as the protectors of white women whom they feel are in danger of what they regard as a deviant African American male sexuality. Not only are these young working-class boys unable to see themselves as belonging to a tradition of privilege in their being white and male, their felt loss of that historic status in a restructuring economy leaves them searching in their school, their neighborhood, and surrounding communities for those responsible. . . .

Freeway is a divided city and a small number of Arabs and Hispanics live among African Americans largely on one side of the "tracks," and whites on the other, although there are whites living in one section of Freeway just adjacent to the steel mill, which is in the area populated by people of color. Virtually no people of color live in the white area, unlike many large cities in the United States, where there are pockets of considerable mix. . . .

Among these white adolescent men, people of color are used consistently as a foil against which acceptable moral, and particularly sexual, standards are established. The goodness of white is always contrasted with the badness of Black—Blacks are involved with drugs, Blacks are unacceptable sexually, Black men attempt to "invade" white sexual space by talking with white women, Black women are simply filthy. The binary translates in ways that complement white boys. As described by Jim, there is a virtual denial of anything at all good being identified with Blackness and of anything bad identified with whiteness:[1]

> The minorities are really bad into drugs. You're talking everything. Anything you want, you get from them. A prime example, the ____ ward of Freeway; about 20 years ago, the ____ ward was predominantly white, my grandfather used to live there. Then Italians, Polish, the Irish people, everything was fine. The houses were maintained; there was a good standard of living. . . . The Blacks brought drugs. I'm not saying white people didn't have drugs; they had drugs, but to a certain extent. But drugs were like a social thing. But now you go down to the ____ ward; it's amazing; it's a ghetto.

Much expressed racism centers on white men's entitled access to white women, thus serving the dual purpose of fixing Blacks and white women on a ladder of social relations. . . .

These young white men construct white women as if they were in need of their protection. The young men fight for these young women. Their complaints are communicated through a language of property rights, Black boys intruding onto *white property*. It is the fact that *Black* men are invading *white* women, the property of *white* men, that is at issue here. . . .

The Black female disparaged; the Black male avenged. The elevation of white womanhood, in fact, has been irreducibly linked to the debasement of both Black women and men (Davis 1990). By this Davis asserts that in the historic positioning of Black females as unfeminine and Black males as predators, the notion of what is feminine has become an idealized version of white womanhood. It is most interesting that not one white female in this study ever discussed young Black men as a "problem." This is not to say that white women were not racist, but this discursive rendering of Black men was quite noticeably the terrain of white men.

The word *nigger* flows freely from the lips of white men and they treat Black women far worse than they say Black men treat white women. During a conversation at the lunch table, for example, Mike says that Yolanda [a Black female] should go to "Niggeria" [Nigeria]. In another conversation about Martin Luther King Day, Dave says, "I have a wet dream—about little white boys and little Black girls." On another occasion, when two African American women walk into the cafeteria, Peter comments that "Black people . . . they're yecch. They smell funny and they [got] hair under their arms." The white boys at this table follow up this sentiment by making noises to denote disgust. . . .

YOUNG ADULTS: WHITE POOR AND WORKING-CLASS MEN IN AN ECONOMIC STRANGLEHOLD

As with Freeway boys, we hear from these somewhat older men a set of identities that are carved explicitly out of territory bordered by African Americans and white women. Similar to the Freeway study, these groups are targeted by the young white adult men as they search their communities, work sites, and even the local social service office for those who are responsible for stealing their presumed privilege. While most of these men narrate hostile comparison with "Others," some offer sympathetic, but still bordered, views. Like cartographers working with different tools on the same geopolitical space, all these men—from western New York and northern New Jersey—sculpt their identities as if they were discernibly framed by, and contrasted through, race, gender, and sexuality.

As with the teens, the critique by young adult white men declares the boundaries of acceptable behavior at themselves. The white male critique is, by and large, a critique of the actions/behaviors taken by African Americans, particularly men. This circles around three interrelationship points: "not working," welfare abuse or "cheats," and affirmative action.

Because many, if not most, of the white men interviewed have themselves been out of work and/or received welfare benefits and food stamps, their critique serves to denigrate African Americans. It also draws the limits of what constitutes "deserving" circumstances for not working, receiving welfare, and relying on government-sponsored programs at themselves.

By young adulthood, the target site for this white male critique shifts from sexuality to work but remains grounded *against* men of color. . . .

The white male critique of affirmative action is that it is not "fair." It privileges Blacks, Hispanics, and at times white women, above white men. According to these men, white men are today being set up as the "new minority," which contradicts their notions of equal opportunity. Nowhere in these narrative is there any recognition that white men as a group have historically been privileged, irrespective of individual merit. The assertions about affirmative action offer white men a way of "Othering" African Americans, in particular. . . .

Many of the white men who have been out of work, or are now in a precarious economic state, speak with a strong disdain for African American men and, if less so, for white women as well. Others, however, narrate positions relative to white women and people of color within a discourse of concern and connection. This more liberal discourse is typically spoken by working-class men who occupy positions of relative economic security. But even here the borders of their identity nevertheless fall along the same fault lines of race and gender (Roediger, 1994).

The white working-class firefighters interviewed in our study narrate somewhat similar views. Joe, for instance, works in a fire department in Jersey City. He, like so many of our informants, insists that he is "not a racist," but he vehemently feels that "Civil Rights has [*sic*] gone far enough." As we discovered, the fire and police departments in Jersey City have historically garnered a disproportionate share of the city's public sector investment and growth over the last decade, and they employ a disproportionate share of white men. We began to hear these departments as the last public sector spaces in which white working-class men could at once exercise identities as white, working, and men. . . .

Mark is another white firefighter. Echoing much of what Joe has said, Mark portrays the firehouse as a relatively protected and defended space for whiteness. By extension, the firehouse represents the civic goodness of [white] public institutions. In both Joe's and Mark's interviews, there is a self-consciousness about "not sounding racist," yet both consistently link any mention of people of color and the mention of social problems—be it child neglect, violence, or vandalism. Whiteness preserves the collective good, whereas people of color periodically threaten the collective good. . . .

CONCLUSION

The U.S. economy is rapidly changing, moving from an industrial to a postindustrial society. Jobs that once served to secure the lives and identities of many working-class people are swiftly becoming a thing of the past. The corrosion of white working-class male felt privilege—as experienced by the boys and men in this analysis— has also been paralleled by the dissipation of labor unions, which are being washed away as quickly as industry. Even though capital has traditionally used fundamental cleavages such as racism and sexism as tools to fracture a working-class consciousness from forming, labor unions have typically played a strong role in U.S. history in creating a space for some workers to organize against capital for change (Roediger 1994). Historical ties to white working-class union activity are fading fast, particularly among young white working-class men, whose fathers, uncles, and older brothers no longer have a union tradition to pass on to the next generation. With the erosion of union culture and no formal space left to develop and refine meaningful critique, some white working-class men, instead, scramble to reassert their assumed place of privilege on a race/gender hierarchy in an economy that has ironically devalued all workers. Our data indicate that white working-class boys and men, unorganized and angry, consistently displace their rage toward historically and locally available groups.

We have offered two scenes in which white men in various stages of adulthood, poor and working-class, are constructing identities on the backs of people of color and white women. Clearly this is not only the case for white working-class men, nor is it generalizable to *all* white working-class men, but these men are among the best narrators of virulent oppositional hostility. It is important that the boys and young adult men in both studies in different geographic locations exhibit similar sentiments. These white men are a race/class/gender group that has been dramatically squeezed relative to their prior positions. Meanwhile, the fantasies and stereotypes of "Others" continue to be promoted, and these delicate, oppositional identities constantly require "steroids" of denigration to be maintained. As the Freeway data suggest, white working-class men also virulently construct notions of identity around another historically available "Other"—gays. Many studies, such as that by Messner and Sabo (1994), evidence how homophobia is used as a profound foil around which to forge aggressive forms of heterosexuality. Heteromasculinity, for the working class in the United States, may indeed be endangered.

As these white boys and men comment on their sense of mistreatment, we reflect, ironically, on their stone-faced fragility. The 1980s and 1990s have marked a time when the women they associate with got independent, their jobs got scarce, their unions got weak, and their privileged access to public institutions was compromised by the success of equal rights and affirmative action. Traditional bases of white male material power—head of the family, productive worker, and exclusive access to "good" public sector and/or unionized jobs—eroded rapidly. Sold out by elites, they are in panic and despair. Their reassertions of status reveal a profound fragility masked by the protection of "their women," their fight for "fairness" in the workplace, and their demand for "diversity" among (but not within) educational institutions. As they narrate a precarious white heteromasculinity, perhaps they speak for a narrow slice of men sitting at the white working-class nexus. More likely, they speak for a gendered and raced group whose privilege has been rattled and whose wrath is boiling over. Their focus, almost fetishisticaly, is on themselves as victims and "Others" as perpetrators. Research conducted by Janoff-Bulman (1979) documents that an exclusive focus on individual "perpetrators" of injustice [real or imagined] is the *least* likely strategy for transforming inequitable social conditions and the *most* likely strategy for creating poor mental health outcomes. Comforted by Howard Stern and Rush Limbaugh, these men are on a treacherous course for self, "Others," and the possibilities for broad-based social change.

The responsibility of educators, researchers, and citizens committed to democratic practice is not simply to watch passively or interrupt responsively when these boys/men get "out of hand." We must embark on serious social change efforts aimed at both understanding and transforming what we uncover here. Spaces must be located in which men/boys are working together to affirm white masculinity that does not rest on the construction of the viral "other." Such spaces must be imagined and uncovered, given the attention that they deserve. Schools, churches, and work sites all offer enormous potential for such transformative cultural activity. We need to make it our task to locate spaces in which white men and boys are reimagining what it means to be white and male in the 1990s. Activists and researchers can profitably work with such groups to chronicle new images of white masculinity that are not based on the aggressive "othering" that we find to be so prevalent.

NOTES

1. We must point out that although we focus on only the white boys' construction of Blacks, we do not mean to imply that they authored the race script in its entirety nor that they wrote the meaning of Black for the African American students. We are, for present purposes, simply focusing on the ways in which young white men discursively construct the "Other."

2. We include men of different ages and statuses to represent an array of voices that are white, male, and working-class.

REFERENCES

Bluestone, B., and B. Harrison. 1982. *The deindustrialization of America*. New York: Basic Books.

Davis, A. 1990. *Women, culture, and politics*. New York: Vintage.

Frankenberg, R. 1993. *The social construction of whiteness: White women, race matters*. Minneapolis: University of Minnesota Press.

Janoff-Bulman, R. 1979. Characterological versus behavioral self blame: Inquiries into depression and rape. *Journal of Social Psychology* 37:1798–1809.

Messner, M., and D. Sabo. 1994. *Sex, violence, and power in sports: Rethinking masculinity*. Freedom, CA: Crossing.

Newman, K. 1993. *Declining fortunes: The withering of the American dreams*. New York: Basic Books.

Roediger, D. 1994. *The wages of whiteness: Race and the making of the American working class*. New York: Verso.

Roman, L. 1993. White is a color!: White defensiveness, postmodernism, and anti-racist pedagogy. In *Race, identity and representation in education*. New York: Routledge.

Weis, L. 1990. *Working class without work: High school students in a de-industrializing economy*. New York: Routledge.

Weis, L., A. Proweller, and C. Centrie. 1996. Re-examining a moment in history: Loss of privilege inside white, working class masculinity in the 1990s. In *Off white*, edited by M. Fine, L. Powell, L. Weis, and M. Wong. New York: Routledge.

Wong, L. M. 1994. Di(s)-secting and di(s)-closing whiteness: Two tales from psychology. *Feminism and Psychology* 4:133–53.

Part Five

Structured Inequality—Race/Ethnicity

13

Are Men Marginal to the Family? Insights from Chicago's Inner City

Haya Stier and Marta Tienda

. . . Academic and policy discussion about the linkages between family structure and poverty have generated a picture of poor, unmarried minority women abandoned by irresponsible men who shirk their parental responsibilities (e.g., Murray, 1984). In fact, many noncustodial parents either never married or never lived with their children (Furstenberg, 1991; Hannerz, 1969; Sullivan, 1989). Whereas some men actually deny their fatherhood, others who acknowledge paternity renege on obligations to provide support, despite their best intentions. A third group of noncustodial fathers marry the mother of their children, but like many men who marry before children come, lose contact with the children after subsequent separation. Thus, because of rising divorce rates and high rates of nonmarital fertility, growing numbers of children receive inadequate emotional and financial support from their biological fathers.

Do declining levels of support from noncustodial fathers mean that men, especially minority men, are becoming marginal to the family? This provocative thesis is implicit in many recent accounts about the growth of an urban underclass, but it has not been explicitly posed.[1] We explore this thesis by examining the circumstances underlying father absence for a sample of parents residing in Chicago's inner city. . . .

THEORETICAL CONSIDERATIONS

Men's familial roles have undergone substantial changes since preindustrial times. Although all family members contributed to subsistence activities during preindustrial times, men were the dominant source of authority *within* the household. As family

From *Men, Work and Family*, edited by Jane C. Hood (1993), pp. 24–43. Copyright © 1993 by Haya Stier and Marta Tienda. Reprinted by permission of Sage Publications, Inc.

heads, men were considered to be primary providers because they were credited with their wives' and children's work. With the relocation of economic activity outside the household that accompanied modernization, men's family roles acquired an almost exclusive concern with economic support functions (Damos, 1986). Although fathers continued involvement with their children, particularly at an emotional level, mothers became the principals in socialization except in unusual circumstances. For example, Furstenberg (1988) noted that until the middle of the 19th century, fathers usually assumed custody over the children in case of a marital disruption. When rates of female labor force activity were low, this arrangement protected children's economic well-being. The belief that children are better off with their mother, especially during their early years of life, gradually led to changes in this practice so that by the end of the 19th century, mothers usually became custodial parents in the event of marital disruption.

The "good provider" role of fathers dominated family ideology until the 1960s, when according to Ehrenreich (1985) and others, men began to retreat from their instrumental familial roles (Bernard, 1981; Furstenberg, 1988; Rotundo, 1985). This retreat manifested itself in two ways: Men either *increased* their familial responsibilities by taking more active roles in child rearing and household duties, or greatly diminished their involvement in domestic and parenting roles.[2] Thus, changes in the division of labor within families resulted in two extreme styles of modern parenthood. Whereas some fathers have become heavily involved in child rearing and have extended their familial roles beyond that of breadwinners (Marsiglio, 1991; Pleck, 1987), other fathers deny responsibility for their children, refusing to support them altogether (Furstenberg, 1988).[3]

Many researchers have argued that men in general and minority men in particular are retreating from the family. The primary evidence for this claim derives from levels of financial and emotional support provided by noncustodial fathers. Alternative interpretations build on differences in the form and content of child support provided by men of varying economic means and ethnic group membership. These two views of child support patterns undergird our analysis of whether or not men are becoming marginal to the family.

The growing number of fathers who fail to provide child support for noncustodial children and who have minimal contact with them is socially problematic because it results in both economic and emotional deprivation (Furstenberg, Nord, Peterson, & Zill, 1983; Garfinkel & McLanahan, 1986; Weitzman, 1985). But it is unclear whether noncustodial fathers' failure to provide child support reflects their irresponsibility in dealing with familial obligations, denial of access to their children, or economic constraints. To be sure, men who lack steady incomes find it difficult to provide regular support to their noncustodial children (Furstenberg, 1991; Furstenberg et al., 1983). Before judging men's disregard of child support as evidence of their marginality to the family, it is essential to establish why they fail to provide child support. For example, learning that lack of access to jobs is the reason for neglect shifts the locus of policy debate from concerns about how to force "the scoundrels" to pay their due to concerns about the circumstances underlying their precarious labor market position (Wilson, 1987; Wilson & Neckerman, 1986). Such considerations are particularly germane to the recent debates about the growth of an urban underclass. . . .

. . . With the increasing rates of out-of-wedlock childbirth and divorce, absent fathers are becoming numerous. These men are most likely to lose interest in their nonresident children because many have limited contacts with them and do not provide adequate support. In our judgment these men are marginal to the family because they have lost their traditional roles as providers and are not involved emotionally with the rearing of their children. One consequence of this behavior is a growing number of children, but especially minority children, being reared in poverty (Eggebeen & Lichter, 1991). To date, most empirical work on living arrangements and support patterns of noncustodial fathers has been restricted to blacks or comparisons between blacks and whites. As a result, ethnic differences in parenting styles, living arrangements, and support activities are neither well documented nor understood. In particular, realitively little is known about Hispanic men's roles as fathers and providers.

There are several compelling reasons for examining the parenting behavior of Hispanic men. First, as a group, Hispanic men are more successful in the labor market than black men, although there are marked differences between Mexican and Puerto Rican men (Tienda, 1989). If labor market standing is the key factor predicting whether fathers will provide for their noncustodial children, we would expect higher levels of support from Mexican compared to Puerto Rican men. Second, the marriage behavior of Hispanic men differs markedly from that of black men (Testa, Astone, Krogh, & Neckerman, 1989). Not only are Mexican men more likely to be married at given ages, but their rates of separation are lower than those of black men (Stier & Tienda, 1992). Puerto Rican men are somewhere between these extremes, with high proportions marrying coupled with high rates of disruption, but the patterns of child support exhibited by Puerto Rican men are virtually unknown. Finally, allegations that minority men are marginal to the family require evidence showing that at comparable income levels, men of color are *less* committed to providing child support than their white counterparts.

Short of this information, prevailing stereotypes about noncustodial fathers as "irresponsible scoundrels" must be interpreted as consequences of their weak market position. Our analyses, therefore, compare black, white, Mexican, and Puerto Rican fathers residing in inner-city neighborhoods where father absence is pervasive. In addition to documenting the living arrangements of inner-city fathers and their children, we examine the circumstances that undergird their support patterns.

DATA AND METHODS

Our analyses are based on the Urban Poverty and Family Life Survey of Chicago (UPFLS) conducted by National Opinion Research Center (NORC) in 1986 and

1987. These data were collected under the auspices of a multiyear study of Urban Poverty and Family Structure in the City of Chicago.[4] The UPFLS is based on a multistage, stratified probability sample of parents aged 18–44 who resided in census tracts representing diverse socioeconomic environments. . . .

We also used the National Survey of Families and Households (NSFH) to generate baseline tabulations against which to compare family behavior and living arrangements of the inner-city sample.[5] From this survey, which is nationally representative of persons residing in families and households, we selected all men who met the age and parent status criteria used to draw the Chicago survey. To maximize comparability between the Chicago and the national sample, we restricted the NSFH sample to fathers who resided in core cities. These sample restrictions resulted in a national sample of 947 fathers.[6]

ETHNIC DIFFERENTIALS IN FAMILY BEHAVIOR AND LIVING ARRANGEMENTS

. . . Marriage behavior clearly differs along ethnic and racial lines. Both nationally and in Chicago, Mexican and white fathers were more likely to be married than their Puerto Rican and black counterparts. Further, black and Puerto Rican fathers were most likely to have never married, but Chicago's black fathers were more than twice as likely as their national counterparts to have never married.[7] Mexican fathers living in Chicago were over 10 percentage points more likely to be married than white fathers, but at the national level, the 7 point advantage was for whites. Although less than half of all black fathers residing in Chicago were married in 1987, the proportion of married black fathers nationally hovered around 60%.

Despite the considerable ethnic and geographic variation in the propensity of men to marry and stay married, there was surprisingly little diversity in the age at first marriage, which ranged between 23 and 24 years for both samples. However, there was much greater variation in the timing of fatherhood, with black men reporting younger ages at the birth of their first child (22 and 24 years, respectively for the Chicago and national samples). White men became fathers later than minority men, with virtually no difference between Chicago and urban men nationally.

The rate of nonmarital fatherhood in poor inner-city neighborhoods also is striking, particularly by comparison to all urban men. Black men are most likely to enter fatherhood prior to marriage; fathering children out of wedlock is particularly common among Chicago's inner-city black men, where nearly three out of four men acknowledged an out-of-wedlock child. Mexican and white men residing in Chicago's inner city were more likely than their national counterparts to father children prior to marriage, but ethnic differences were trivial. That is, among white and Mexican men, approximately 8% and 25%, respectively, of those in the national and the Chicago samples reported fathering children before they married. By contrast, nearly half of all Puerto Rican men reported fathering at least one child out of wedlock.

Although several of these men eventually married the mother of their child (Testa et al., 1989; see also Sullivan, 1989), there persist marked ethnic differences in the likelihood of their doing so.

. . . That Mexican men report the highest rates of co-residence with their own children reflects the larger share of fathers who were married at the time of the survey. Puerto Rican fathers are less likely to marry than Mexicans or whites, but nearly 80% of Chicago fathers reported cohabiting with their own children. The incidence of co-resident between black children and their fathers was appreciably lower—less than 50% in Chicago and just over 60% nationally. In fact, as many as one third of all black men (both in Chicago and the United States) live in households with no dependent children present. The comparable figures for all other groups are lower, especially for Mexicans.

Fathers live without children either because their offspring have already left home or because the men left their children. In most cases of divorce, and certainly most instances of out-of-wedlock births, mothers assume custody of children. Thus, half of all black and one third of all Puerto Rican fathers have dependent children who reside elsewhere. This proportion compares with 27% of white fathers in Chicago, and less than 20% of white fathers nationally. Less than one in five Mexican-origin fathers reported having dependent children who did not live with them.[8]

. . . As expected, 5% and 6% of currently married fathers residing in Chicago and U.S. cities, respectively, did not live with children compared to 43% and 55% of never-married fathers. At the other extreme, approximately 90% of currently married fathers reside with their own and other (adopted) children. Yet, between 27% and 30% of Chicago's never-married fathers reported co-residing with their own and other children, and an additional 30% of Chicago's never-wed fathers lived with children belonging to someone else—a mate, an older sibling, a friend. Among black men nationally, the latter pattern is typically rare, representing less than 5% of never-married men. However, the tendency of never-married men to reside in complex families consisting of their own and other children is more common: just over 40% of single fathers reported such living arrangements nationally.

These descriptive results raise two questions critical to our concern about men's marginality to the family: first, what circumstances explain the ethnic differences in men's propensity to marry in the first place? And second, what kind and how much support do absent fathers provide to their offspring? . . . Because of limited information on forms of child support in the National Survey of Families and Households, we restrict these analyses to the Chicago sample.

FATHERHOOD, MARRIAGE, AND PARENTAL OBLIGATIONS

The previous tabulations show that married fathers are considerably more likely than unmarried fathers to co-reside with their children. Although we lack information about the extent to which co-resident fathers fulfill their paternal obligations, it is reasonable to assume that fathers who live with their own children provide regular emotional and material support. Further, there is ample empirical evidence showing that children residing with both parents enjoy higher economic standing than those who reside with one parent—usually the biological mother (Eggebeen & Lichter, 1991; Garfinkel & McLanahan, 1986). But in light of the high rates of out-of-wedlock fathering, a first major question is: what determines transition into marriage?

Our empirical model draws from current sociological and economic theorizing about marriage behavior. One important finding from this vast literature is that the likelihood of marriage varies directly with improvements in economic standing. Thus, the low marriage rates observed among black men, parents and nonparents alike, are attributed to their weak labor market standing, as reflected by high rates of joblessness and low earnings among those who manage to secure employment. From a social point of view, men reared in broken families may find marriage less compelling when they reach adulthood because experiences with marital discord may dampen interest in permanent commitments to unattractive mates. In other words, parental life-styles may reinforce the acceptability of nonnormative living arrangements.

Our multivariate analysis considers both social and economic factors as determinants of the transition into marriage. To assess the likelihood of marriage, we estimate a proportional hazard model in which the risk of marriage (since age 14) is a function of two categories of variables: (a) background characteristics and (b) economic circumstances. Background characteristics include mother's educational level (whether mother is high school graduate), whether respondents' parents ever received welfare, and whether respondents' parents ever married. These variables capture early socialization experiences as well as the economic status of the family of origin. We expect sons of more educated mothers and those reared in married couple households to exhibit higher marriage propensities. However, experiences of poverty during childhood might depress the probability of marriage, particularly if they were chronic and severe.

The second group of variables captures respondents' economic status, represented by educational level and work status of fathers. We expected higher education (a proxy for earnings prospects) to increase the likelihood of marriage. Similarly, employed men should marry at higher rates than their jobless counterparts. Because employment status changes over time, it is measured as a time-varying covariate. In other words, it reflects respondents' work status for each year after age 14. Education is measured as high school graduation status prior to the marriage (or the survey date in case of never-married individuals) because data limitations precluded an alternative operational specification.[9] A second time-varying covariate included in the marriage model is parental status. Couples who have considered marriage, but have no definite marriage date often decide to marry because of a pregnancy. Testa and his associates (1989) found that many fathers in poor Chicago neighborhoods married the mother of their child *after* the birth. Therefore, a positive effect of birth on marriage can be anticipated. . . . No background variable exerted a significant influence on the propensity of inner-city men to marry. Surprisingly, the expected linkage between changes in work status and the propensity to marry was significant only for white men. This might cast doubt on recent arguments about the importance of employment for determining the marriageability of inner-city men. However, as a proxy for labor market status, high school graduation also increased the (log) odds that black and Puerto Rican men would marry. Specifically, the logit coefficients indicate that black high school graduates were 2.7 times and Puerto Ricans were nearly 11 times more likely to wed than their counterparts who had not completed secondary school. The birth of a child significantly *increased* the odds of marriage for all groups of roughly a factor of two for blacks and Puerto Ricans. Among whites and Mexicans the risk of marriage increased even more when a child was born— 8.7 and 3.6 times, respectively.

On balance, our results support Wilson's (1987; Wilson & Neckerman, 1986) premises about the enabling role of economic position—education or work—in raising the propensity of inner-city men to marry. That the act of fathering a child itself propels men into marriage indicates that they are inclined to accept their parental obligations when they have the means to support their children. These results also corroborate with Stack's (1974) finding that couples often do not formalize their marriage until the advent of a birth. Finally, our results show that there exist alternative pathways into adult roles in the inner city. In other words, marriage often follows rather than precedes parenting in improverished environments. The sequencing of these two life course events differs markedly by race and Hispanic origins.

. . . Although sample sizes have been reduced sharply for whites and Mexicans, over 40% of Puerto Rican fathers and nearly 60% of black fathers reported having one or more children who did not reside with them. This means that the fathers actually recognize these children as their own.[10] Of the population of fathers who reported having nonresident children, most reported providing economic support to their offspring. There is limited ethnic variation in the practice of providing financial support, except that Mexican men, who were less likely to have nonresident children to begin with, were somewhat more likely to provide financial support— probably because they often live far away from their offspring. Puerto Ricans were the least likely to support their children financially. Although there may be limited ethnic variation in the tendency of noncustodial fathers to support their children, the nature and level of support may vary greatly both in its regularity and the amounts provided.

Most fathers also report providing in-kind support (e.g., toys, clothes) to the children. That noncustodial Mexican fathers report a lower incidence of in-kind support reflects practical difficulties: For those who left dependent children in Mexico, monetary transfers are more practical than in-kind support, which often involves services and miscellaneous goods. This interpretation is consistent with other ethnic differences in child support (e.g., the actual contact with the children discussed below).

Not only do noncustodial fathers provide economic contributions to their children, but so do their relatives. This practice is especially evident among black fathers: Nearly one in four report that their noncustodial children receive financial support from other relatives, and over half reported that other relatives provide some in-kind support. Kin-based financial support to children is less common among whites, Mexicans, and Puerto Ricans, but the frequency of in-kind support from other white and Puerto Rican relatives is comparable to that of blacks.

Economic support of any kind is more frequent than direct interaction with children. However, tabulations on visitation behavior reveal that black fathers visit their children more than any other category of men. One third of black fathers reported daily contact with the nonresident children, whereas one third see the child only once or twice a month, and the remainder have no contact at all. This pattern is consistent with Stack's (1974) account of father-child interaction in a poor black community. In comparison, only 18% of the whites, 15% of the Puerto Ricans, and 9% of Mexicans reported daily visits with the children. Half of all Puerto Ricans, three fourths of Mexicans, and nearly half of the whites say they never see their children. On balance, and with the exception of blacks, noncustodial fathers have very limited if any contact with their children.

As a path to separation of fathers from their children, divorce often involves mobility of one parent, thus inhibiting frequent and regular contact with children left behind. For blacks, whose children are conceived out of wedlock at higher rates than the other groups, marriage and co-residence seem to play less decisive roles in shaping child-parent interaction. According to Stack (1974), Sullivan (1989), and Hannerz (1969), men (or their close relatives) are expected to take care of the children, regardless of the living arrangements or the marital relationships to the mother. Frequently these obligations are met. . . .

. . . Fathers who are currently employed are almost three times more likely to support their nonresident children compared to fathers who are not working. Also, high school graduates are 20% more likely to support their children compared to dropouts. That the ethnic differences are not statistically significant conveys an important message about the cultural underpinnings of distinct forms of support for noncustodial children. Stated differently, *ethnicity and race appear to be proxies for economic rather than family marginality.* This is not to dismiss the role of culture in shaping patterns of co-residence and the differential involvement of kin in providing for noncustodial children, but rather to stress that ethnic differences give way to indicators of fathers' economic status as determinants of material support to noncustodial children.

SUMMARY AND DISCUSSION

Are inner-city fathers marginal to their families? Our analyses documented the support roles of noncustodial inner-city fathers. That these men have diverse life-styles is evident in their marital behavior and fulfillment of child responsibilities.

Earnings prospects (indexed by educational status) and labor market status appear to be the key determinants of child support activity for all fathers, regardless of ethnicity. Although the black fathers are more likely than white or Hispanic men to be noncustodial parents, they compensate for this loss of family responsibility through frequent contact with their offspring and by invoking the financial contributions of their kin. Similar practices, although less prevalent, are reported by white, Mexican, and Puerto Rican fathers. Thus, it appears that through their economic, but especially their social relationships with other relatives, unmarried inner-city fathers provide an alternative family context for their noncustodial children.

Our analyses of inner-city fathers' child support patterns refute the idea that these men are becoming marginal to the family. Despite the severe financial constraints faced by minority men residing in Chicago's inner city, we were most struck by the relatively high proportions of men who reported providing financial and in-kind support to their noncustodial children. Unfortunately, we were unable to assess the regularity of the support provided or to consider whether it covered a reasonable share of their children's living expenses. Given the high rates of joblessness in the inner city (Tienda & Stier, 1991), it is unlikely that child support provided by inner-city fathers was adequate to cover all costs of child rearing. However, it is inappropriate to conclude that these men have retreated from the family, or that they are "irresponsible scoundrels" who neglect their children. Our results show that noncustodial fathers make great efforts to maintain ties with their children. That black fathers report the highest levels of contact with their noncustodial children corroborates Stack's (1974) interpretation about men's interactions with kin. When they lack financial resources, they contribute their own time and solicit support from other kin. We cannot determine whether or not visits compensate for income contributions, but visitation is certainly important for emotional development.

More generally, our study raises questions about the origins of men's marginality in the inner city. There is widespread agreement that minority men, particularly those residing in declining inner cities, have been marginalized from the labor market (Wilson, 1987). Despite their precarious economic position, it is remarkable that inner-city fathers manage to maintain ties with their noncustodial children. However, men's economic marginality, which is clearly reflected in declining rates of labor force participation and higher rates of unemployment, does reverberate in their family roles. Poor labor market standing influences the likelihood of marrying and fathering children, and the sequencing of these major life course events (Testa et al., 1989; Wilson & Neckerman, 1986). The provider roles assumed by inner-city men may not conform to the norms of middle-class whites, but this difference should not be translated as "flight from the family."

NOTES

1. We are grateful to Joan Aldous for sharpening our thinking on this issue.
2. The latter circumstance accentuated gender inequities within the family to the ex-

tent that men's retreat from the domestic arena was accompanied by an increase in women's labor force activity (Curtis, 1986; Stier, 1991).

3. Of course, there are intermediate variants between these extremes. Our focus on the extremes serves a heuristic function in sharpening our analytic goals.

4. William J. Wilson is the Principal Investigator. The original design called for a sample of census tracts where at least 20% of families had incomes below the 1980 federal poverty line. The final sample included a broader range of socioeconomic contexts.

5. Larry Bumpass was the Principal Investigator. Also fielded in 1987, this national survey contains sufficient race and ethnic variation for tabular analyses of Mexican, black, and white populations, but the sample of Puerto Ricans is limited for tabular analyses.

6. Both the UPFLS and NSFH surveys were based on cross-sectional designs, but both surveys contain several retrospective sequences on life experiences, including work behavior, marriage and fertility histories, educational histories, and welfare experiences. In addition, both surveys contain information about respondents' family backgrounds and current employment status. Because the principal investigators of both surveys exchanged instruments, many questions are directly comparable. Tabular results for both surveys are weighted to approximate the universes from which they are drawn, but the sample sizes are unweighed to indicate the actual base on which statistics are computed.

7. Among Puerto Rican fathers, the share never married did not differ between the Chicago and national samples, but the national rate is subject to a high degree of sampling variability owing to the small sample size ($N = 20$).

8. Illinois is an AFCE-U state, which means that unemployed fathers are eligible for benefits. Thus, the fact that fathers are not discouraged from living with children requires other explanations for the observed differences in living arrangements.

9. Ideally one would like a time-varying education measure that indicated whether respondent was enrolled in school each year beginning with age 14, but the UPFLS did not collect precise dates on educational outcomes. However, it is possible to ascertain the date of graduation and determine whether it occurred before or after marriage.

10. We have no indication about how many of these men had children they failed to report as their own, but they would be the most marginal fathers of all.

REFERENCES

Bernard, J. (1981). The good provider role: Its rise and fall. *American Psychologist*, 36(1), 1–12.

Curtis, R. (1986, April): Family and inequality theory. *American Sociological Review*, 51, 168–183.

Damos, J. (1986). *Past, present, and personal: The family and life course in American history*. New York: Oxford University Press.

Eggebeen, D., & Lichter, D. T. (1991). Race, family structure, and changing poverty among American children. *American Sociological Review*, 56(6), 801–817.

Ehrenreich, B. (1985). *The hearts of men: American dreams and the flight from family commitment*. New York: Anchor.

Furstenberg, F. F. (1988). Good dads—bad dads: Two faces of fatherhood. In A. J. Cherlin (Ed.), *The changing American family and public policy* (pp. 193–218). Washington, DC: Urban Institute.

Furstenberg, F. F. (1991). *Daddies and fathers: Men who do for their children and men who don't.* Unpublished manuscript, University of Pennsylvania.

Furstenberg, F. F., Nord, C. W., Peterson, J. L., & Zill, N. (1983). The life course of children of divorce: Marital disruption and parental contact. *American Sociological Review, 48,* 656–668.

Garfinkel, I., & McLanahan, S. S. (1986). *Single mothers and their children: A new American dilemma.* Washington, DC: Urban Institute.

Hannerz, U. (1969). *Soulside: Inquiring into ghetto culture and community.* New York: Columbia University Press.

Hetherington, D. E., Camara, K. A., & Featherman, D. L. (1983). Achievement and intellectual functioning of children in one-parent households. In J. Spence (Ed.), *Achievement and achievement motives* (pp. 205–284). San Francisco: W. H. Freeman.

Marsiglio, W. (1991). Parental engagement activities with minor children. *Journal of Marriage and the Family, 53,* 973–986.

Murray, C. (1984). *Losing ground: American social policy, 1950–1980.* New York: Basic Books.

Pleck, J. H. (1987). American fathering in historical perspective. In M. S. Kimmel (Ed.), *Changing men: New directions in research on men and masculinity* (pp. 83–97). Newbury Park, CA: Sage.

Rotundo, E. A. (1985). American fatherhood: A historical perspective. *American Behavioral Scientist, 29*(1), 7–25.

Stack, C. B. (1974). *All our kin: Strategies for survival in the black community.* New York: Harper & Row.

Stier, H. (1991). Immigrant women go to work: The labor supply of immigrant wives for six Asian groups. *Social Science Quarterly, 72*(1), 67–82.

Stier, H., & Tienda, M. (1992). *Love and lifestyles: Ethnic variation in marriage behavior among inner city parents.* Unpublished manuscript, University of Chicago.

Sullivan, M. L., (1989, January). Absent fathers in the inner city. *Annals of the American Academy of Political and Social Sciences, 501,* 48–58.

Testa, M., Astone, N. M., Krogh, M., & Neckerman, K. M. (1989, January). Employment and marriage among inner city fathers. *Annals of the American Academy of Political and Social Sciences, 501,* 79–91.

Tienda, M. (1989, January). Puerto Ricans and the underclass debate. *Annals of the American Academy of Political and Social Sciences, 501,* 105–119.

Tienda, M., & Stier, H. (1991). Joblessness and shiftlessness: Labor force activity in Chicago's inner city. In C. Jencks & P. Peterson (Eds.), *The urban underclass* (pp. 135–154). Washington, DC: Brookings Institution.

Weitzman, L. J. (1985). *The divorce revolution: The unexpected social and economic consequences for women and children in America.* New York: Free Press.

Wilson, W. J. (1987). *The truly disadvantaged: The inner city, the underclass, and public policy.* Chicago: University of Chicago Press.

Wilson, W. J., & Neckerman, K. M. (1986). Poverty and family structure: The widening gap between evidence and public issues. In S. H. Danziger & D. H. Weinberg (Eds.), *Fighting poverty: What works and what doesn't* (pp. 232–259). Cambridge, MA: Harvard University Press.

14

Policing the Ghetto Underclass:
The Politics of Law and
Law Enforcement

William J. Chambliss

For the past several years my students and I have been riding with the Rapid
Deployment Unit (RDU) of the Washington, D.C. Metropolitan Police. In response
to the urban riots of the 1960s, Washington, D.C., like many other cities, established specialized riot control units within the police department.[1] These units were
specially trained to respond quickly and with force to the threat of riots or urban
disturbances. Even in the United States, riots do not happen that often. For the police, the "war on drugs" provided a functional equivalent to riots: the crisis of inner-city drugs and violence.

In all we spent more than 100 hours riding with members of the RDU and other
police officers. These observations and discussions with police officers stimulated
the reflections that follow on the state of law enforcement in U.S. cities and the
impact it is having on the public's perception of crime and the lives of those most
affected.

THE RAPID DEPLOYMENT UNIT

Members of the RDU are described by other police officers as the "Dirty Harrys"
and "very serious bad-ass individuals." The RDU is deployed in teams of three patrol cars with two officers in each car. While each car may patrol in different areas,
they are never so far from one another that they cannot be summoned on short notice
to converge in one place. They patrol what Wilson (1987, 1993) calls the urban

Reprinted from *Social Problems* 41, no. 2 (May 1994): 177–94, by permission. Copyright © 1994 by
the *Society for the Study of Social Problems.*

ghetto: that is, the area of the city where 40 percent of the black population lives below the poverty level.

Vehicular Stops

The RDU patrols the ghetto continuously looking for cars with young black men in them. They are especially attentive to newer-model cars, Isuzu four-wheel-drive vehicles, BMWs and Honda Accords, based on the belief that these are the favorite cars of drug dealers. During our observations, however, the RDU officers came to the conclusion that drug dealers were leaving their fancy cars at home to avoid vehicular stops. It thus became commonplace for RDU officers to stop any car with young black men in it.

There is a nod to legality in vehicular stops in that the officers look for a violation in order to justify the stop:

Field Notes: As we pass a new-looking BMW with two black men in it the driver of the patrol car says to his partner: "Joe, check out that car for violations." The partner says quickly: "Broken tail light, hit the horn." The siren is put on and the car pulls over.

Any minor infraction is an excuse: going through a yellow light, not stopping completely at a stop sign, or having something hanging from the rear-view mirror (a violation of which almost every car in the southeast section of the city is guilty). In addition I was told confidentially by some of the officers, though neither I nor any of my students ever observed it, that if the officers feel strongly that they should stop a car, they will stop it and break a taillight as they approach the car:

"This is the jungle . . . we rewrite the constitution every day down here. . . . If we pull everyone over they will eventually learn that we aren't playing games any more. We are real serious about getting the crap off the streets."

Once a car is stopped the officers radio for backup. The two other cars in the area immediately come to the scene and triangulate the suspect's car: one car comes in close behind and the two others cars form a V in front of the suspect's car.

Vehicular stops occur on an average of every twenty minutes throughout the shift. From our observations, illegal drugs, guns, weapons, or someone who is wanted by authorities are found in only 10 percent of the cars stopped. The officers themselves believe that they find serious violations in "about a third" of the vehicular stops. . . .

. . . The RDU does not patrol the predominantly white sections of Washington, D.C. Observations of policing in this area of the city reveal an entirely different approach by the police. There are no "rips" and no vehicular stops unless there is a clear violation. Officers are not looking for cars with black drivers. If a car is stopped other cars are not called as backups, and the officer handles the infraction on his or her own. . . .

Search Warrants

[Another] major activity is carrying out search warrants. Based on information received from informants, undercover agents, or observations a warrant is issued by the court to search an apartment or home for various reasons:

Warrants: Case No. 1

"Five RDU officers enter an apartment about 10:45 P.M. Before entering the officers draw their guns, break down the door and rush in. The suspect is spotted, guns are pointed at him and he is told to 'lie down, NOW.' The suspect is handcuffed and taken outside. An elderly woman begins screaming and crying. She tells the officers to put their guns away. An officer goes to her, his gun still drawn, and tells her to 'shut up or I'll pop you in the jaw.' He physically forces her to lie down on the floor face down. The officers leave the apartment, put the suspect in the car and take him to the precinct for booking."

Observations indicate police carry out warrants differently in the predominantly white section of Washington, D.C.:

Warrants: Case No. 2

A warrant is issued by the court for the arrest of a suspected drug dealer wanted for assault and attempted murder. The third district police are in an excited state over the pending arrest. An anonymous tip has provided them with information as to the suspect's whereabouts and a discussion at the station lays out a plan for making the arrest. Twelve officers are dispatched to the house where the suspect is supposedly living. Seven officers surround the house and five others approach the front door. Most, but not all, of the officers have their guns drawn. In the dark it is not possible to see all the officers, but of those observable three have guns drawn and two do not. It is a few minutes past 1 A.M. when the officers approach the front door. The doorbell is rung and the team leader shouts, "Police, open up." Everyone appears to be on edge. There is no response to the knock or the command. The officers break open the door. Flashlights are shining in every corner, behind furniture and into people's eyes. A terrified elderly woman stands at the top of the stairs and asks what is going on. One of the officers approaches her with calmness and no gun drawn, speaks to her in a low voice, and gently removes her from the house to be watched by the team outside. The suspect is found in the basement behind a water cooler. He is identified and handcuffed. As he is being led from the house one officer says to him, "You sure have a pretty face, buddy boy. See you at the country club."

THE CONSEQUENCES

The prison population in the United States increased by 167 percent between 1980 and 1992, with the greatest percentage increase in drug law violations. . . . The United States today incarcerates a higher percentage of its population than any country in the world: a dubious distinction formerly held by the USSR and South Africa. . . . And it is minorities, especially young African Americans and Latinos, who are disproportionately arrested, convicted and sentenced to prison. In 1991, African-American males between the ages of 15 and 34 made up 14 percent of the population and more than 40 percent of the people in prison. White males made up 82 percent of this age group but less than 60 percent of the prison population (Statistical Abstracts 1993). Blacks accounted for more than 40 percent of the inmates in state and federal prisons. . . . .

In Washington, D.C. and Baltimore, 40 to 50 percent of all black males between the ages of 18 and 35 are either in prison, jail, on probation or parole, or there is a warrant for their arrest (Maurer 1990; Miller 1992). Arrests and convictions for drugs play an increasingly important part as a source of criminal convictions. Nearly 30 percent of all state and over 55 percent of all federal prisoners in 1992 were convicted on drug violations (Maguire, Pastore, and Flannagan 1993). Two-thirds of all drug arrests in 1992 were for possession, and only one-third were for the sale or manufacture of drugs. African Americans account for more than 40 percent of all drug arrests (Maguire, Pastore, and Flannagan 1993) despite the fact that self-report surveys show that, except for crack cocaine, whites are three to five times as likely to use drugs as blacks (Bureau of Justice Statistics 1992a . . .). Thus more whites than blacks use illegal drugs and more than 80 percent of the population is white. But 66 percent of the inmates in state prisons convicted of drug offenses are black, and only 33 percent are white (Maguire, Pastore, and Flannagan 1993).

Effects on Family and Education

The intensive surveillance of black neighborhoods, and the pattern of surveillance of white neighborhoods has the general consequence of institutionalizing racism by defining the problem of crime generally, and drug use in particular, as a problem of young black men. It further ghettoizes the African-American community and destroys any possibility for normal family and community relations. Young African-American and Latino men are defined as a criminal group, arrested for minor offenses over and over again, and given criminal records which justify long prison sentences. The culture of the black community and the black family is then blamed for high rates of illegitimate children and crime. Crime control policies are a major contributor to the disruption of the family, the prevalence of single parent families, and children raised without a father in the ghetto, and the "inability of people to get the jobs still available" (Anderson 1993; Wilson 1987, 1993).

But the consequences go beyond the destruction of family and community in the ghetto. Scarce resources are transferred from desperately needed social programs to criminal justice. For the first time in history, state and municipal governments are spending more money in criminal justice than education. Nationwide, expenditures on criminal justice increased by 150 percent between 1972 and 1988, while expenditures on education increased by 46 percent. Between 1969 and 1989 per capita spending on criminal justice in U.S. cities (municipal expenditures) rose from $34 to $120 and county expenditures as a percentage of total budget rose from 10 to 15 percent between 1973 and 1989. State expenditures showed even greater increases, rising tenfold from per capita expenditures on police and corrections of $8 in 1969 to $80 in 1989. State government expenditure for building prisons increased 593 percent in actual dollars. Spending on corrections—prison building, maintenance, and parole—has more than doubled in the last ten years (Chambliss 1991; Maguire and Flannagan 1990; Maguire, Pastore, and Flannagan 1992). . . .

WHY?

Many reasons have been proposed for the rapid increase in expenditures on criminal justice (or, in the words of Nils Christie, the growth of "the crime industry") in the United States (Christie 1993). One explanation is the alleged increase in crime. There is a general perception that crime, especially violent crime, has increased. The notion of a crime increase is a perception, apparently created by the law enforcement establishment, the media, and politicians. But this is not supported by the facts. The best available data, the findings of victim surveys conducted every year since 1973, show that the crime rate has not changed significantly in the last 20 years.

Victim surveys show also that it is very unlikely that anyone will be the victim of a crime in any given year. More than 90 percent of respondents report that neither they nor any member of their household was the victim of a criminal offense. Indeed, over a lifetime it is unlikely that most people will be the victim of a serious offense. The risk of being a victim of a violent crime in any given year is less than 3 percent (Bureau of Justice Statistics 1992b).

. . . The 1992 Uniform Crime Report (UCR) reported a dramatic increase in the murder rate between 1988 and 1992. The FBI used the report to demonstrate a crime rate increase. What the report failed to mention was that between 1980 and 1987 the murder rate actually declined and the 1992 rate was below that of 1980. That the murder rate has shown no appreciable increase since the 1980s is particularly noteworthy given the fact that the weapons in use today are more efficient than ever before. Pistols have been replaced with rapid firing automatic weapons that leave a victim little chance of escaping with a wound.

The Seriousness of Crime

. . . As for people in prison, Austin and Irwin's survey found that more than 50 percent of the prisoners in state and federal prisons are in for offenses that opinion surveys show the general public thinks are "not very serious crimes" (Austin and Irwin 1989). A recent study by the Bureau of Justice Statistics found that more than 20 percent of the inmates in federal prisons were in for drug offenses with no history of violent crime or other felonies (Bureau of Justice Statistics 1994). This indicates that the growth of the crime industry is not due to the seriousness of the crimes.

Crime and Public Opinion

Another explanation for the growth of the crime industry is that lawmakers are merely responding to public opinion. In explaining the creation of President Lyndon Johnson's crime commission and the spate of anti-crime legislation in the 1960s, James Q. Wilson argues that public opinion forced political action. . . .

. . . [However,] the Gallup Polls never showed that crime was perceived by the respondents as the most important problem facing the nation. Every year since 1935 the Gallup Poll has asked a sample of Americans "What do you think is the most important problem facing the country?" Between 1935 and 1993 crime rarely appears as one of the most important problems mentioned, and in the nearly 60 years the poll has been taken, crime is never chosen over other issues as "the most important problem facing the country." In 1989 and 1991 "drugs" or "drug abuse" is frequently mentioned but only once (April 1990) is it the most often chosen. Even when "drugs" is mentioned, crime in the April 1990 poll is seen as "the most important problem" by only 2 percent of the population (Gallup Poll 1989, 1990, 1991).

The politicization of crime by conservative politicians occurred at a time when the country was deeply divided over the Vietnam War and civil rights. In this historical context crime became a smokescreen behind which other issues could be relegated as less important. Crime served as well as legitimation for legislation designed primarily to suppress political dissent and overturn Supreme Court decisions (Chambliss and Sbarbaro 1993).

In addition to these political forces, and partly because of them, the crime control industry emerged as a powerful lobby. Law enforcement agencies control the information available about crime and, as noted above, manipulate the data to serve their purposes. In their effort to create moral panics, and thereby increase their budgets and power, law enforcement agencies are happily joined by the media always hungry for stories that will increase their audience. Indeed, the media has become so dependent on crime news in recent years that in 1993 crime was the most frequently reported subject on television news (Media Monitor 1994). Between 1990 and 1993 the number of crime stories appearing on ABC, CBS and NBC evening newscasts increased from 737 to 1,698.

The crime industry has become so powerful, it is virtually immune from the budgetary cuts experienced by other public services during the recent recession. On those rare occasions when a mayor or governor suggests cutting justice expenditures or even holding steady the number of police officers, propaganda, politicking and arm twisting by police officer associations (often called "benevolent" associations rather than trade unions) and lobbyists with vested interests in supplying equipment and prison facilities quickly reverse the decision. In Prince George's County, a suburb of Washington, D.C., for example, when there was talk of layoffs and pay cuts for police the police officer's association hired a public relations firm and ran television commercials citing increasing crime rates and accusing the county executive of handcuffing police officers with proposed budget cuts. The union spent more than

$10,000 in one week on television and newspaper advertisements, and the politicians acquiesced, canceling the proposed budget cuts.

With their newfound success as lobbyists and self-perpetuating bureaucracies, however, law enforcement agencies face some formidable organizational problems, the most important being how to justify their claim to more and more of the tax payer's dollars. Manipulating data, creating moral panics, and feeding the media crime stories can only go so far. Eventually arrests must be made, successful prosecutions carried out and people sent to prison. For these symbols of effective law enforcement the large population of poor black males is the perfect bureaucratic solution. For here is a population without political clout, with few resources to successfully defend against criminal charges, and a public image as a group in which crime is endemic. Enforcing the law in the black ghetto enables the police, as one officer expressed it, to "rewrite the constitution every day."

A police officer's career and even his annual income is determined by the number of "good collars" he makes. A "good collar" is an arrest for what is defined as a serious violation of the law that culminates in a conviction. Drug arrests qualify. They are among the easiest convictions, the most difficult to defend, and often lead to the longest prison terms as a result of mandatory sentences. But they are organizationally effective only if the person arrested is relatively powerless. Arrests of white male middle class offenders (on college campuses for example) are guaranteed to cause the organization and the arresting officers strain, as people with political influence and money hire attorneys for their defense. Arrests of poor black men, however, create only rewards for the organization and the officer as the cases are quickly processed through the courts, a guilty plea obtained and the suspect sentenced. Organizations reward role occupants whose behavior maximizes rewards and minimizes strains for the organization. In a class society, the powerless, the poor, and those who fit the public stereotype of "the criminal" are the human resources needed by law enforcement agencies to maximize rewards and minimize strains. It is not surprising, but sociologically predictable, then, that doubling the number of police officers in the last 10 years has tripled the number of people in prison and jail, filled these institutions with minor offenders, exacerbated the disproportionate imprisonment of minorities, and institutionalized racist beliefs that make being a young black man synonymous with being criminal.

SUMMARY AND CONCLUSIONS

. . . Reversing the process will prove to be more difficult than instituting it. Political leaders will have to show the kind of courage shown by Lyndon Johnson and Hubert Humphrey who defied the conservative platform's call for more police and harsher penalties with pleas for more public spending on schools and jobs. Law enforcement agencies will have to change their reward system to emphasize community policing and rewarding officers who do not have to make arrests in their communities, rather than rewarding those who do. And the media will have to assume some responsibility for educating rather than sensationalizing. Social scientists can play a critical role by conducting studies of law enforcement in the communities most affected and communicating the results to policymakers and the public. It is unlikely, however, that any of these changes will take place so long as we continue to criminalize drugs and provide an incentive for police officers and prosecutors to entrap and arrest people for the possession or sale of small amounts of drugs. The longer it takes, the more lives will be lost and the more the United States will move towards a society permanently divided by race and class into communities that are quasi police states patrolled by RDU-type police units in search of crime and communities where minor infractions of the law are treated, as they should be, as tolerable indiscretions.

NOTE

1. According to FBI statistics, approximately 10 percent of law enforcement personnel are now employed in specialized police units. In 1992 such specialized units accounted for 25 percent of police departments' budgets (Maguire, Pastore, and Flanagan, 1992).

REFERENCES

Anderson, Elijah, 1993. "Abolish welfare—then what?" The Washington Post, December 13:A23.

Austin, James, and John Irwin, 1989. Who Goes to Prison? San Francisco: The National Council on Crime and Delinquency.

Bureau of Justice Statistics, 1992a. "Drugs, crime and the criminal justice system." U.S. Department of Justice, Washington, D.C., NCJ 133652:28.

———. 1992b. "Criminal victimization in the United States: 1973–1990." U.S. Department of Justice, Washington, D.C.

———. 1994. "Drug offenders in federal prison." U.S. Department of Justice, Washington, D.C.

Chambliss, William J., 1991. Trading Textbooks for Prison Cells. Alexandria, Va.: National Center on Institutions and Alternatives.

Chambliss, William J., and Edward Sbarbaro, 1993. "Moral panics and racial oppression." Socio-Legal Bulletin, Melbourne, Australia.

Christie, Nils, 1993. Crime Control as Industry. London: Routledge.

Cohen, Stanley, 1980. Folk Devils and Moral Panics: The Creation of the Mods and Rockers: New York: St. Martins Press.

Gallup, George, 1993. The Gallup Poll: Public Opinion, 1935–1993. Wilmington, Del.: Scholarly Resources.

Maguire, Kathleen, and Timothy J. Flanagan, eds., 1990. Sourcebook of Criminal Justice Statistics 1990. Washington, D.C.: Bureau of Justice Statistics.

Maguire, Kathleen, Ann Pastore, and Timothy J. Flanagan, eds., 1993. Sourcebook of Criminal Justice Statistics. U.S. Department of Justice, Bureau of Justice Statistics. Washington, D.C.: USGPO, 1993.

Maurer, Mark, 1992. Young Black Men and the Criminal Justice System: A Growing National Problem. Washington, D.C. The Sentencing Project.

Media Monitor, 1994. 1993: The Year in Review: TV's Leading News Topics, Reporters, and Political Jokes. Washington, D.C.: Center for Media and Public Affairs. January/February.

Miller, Jerome, M., 1992. Search and Destroy: The Plight of African American Males in the Criminal Justice System. Alexandria, Va.: National Center on Institutions and Alternatives.

Statistical Abstracts of the United States, 1993. The National Data Book, Washington, D.C.: U.S. Department of Commerce.

Wilson, William Julius, 1987. The Truly Disadvantaged: The Inner City, the Underclass, and Public Policy. Chicago: University of Chicago Press.

———. 1993. The Ghetto Underclass: Social Science Perspectives. New York: Sage Publications.

15

Near Detroit, a Familiar Sting in Being a Black Driver

Robyn Meredith

Detroit, July 15—The yuppie couple were driving home through the suburb of Royal Oak after dinner and a movie when a police car behind them turned on its lights and siren.

"I pulled over," Dennis W. Archer Jr. said, recalling the incident on Memorial Day. "Completely surrounding us there are six police cars."

Despite politely asking why they had been stopped, Mr. Archer said, he and his date were ordered out of the car without explanation. As an officer aimed a shotgun at him, Mr. Archer said, he was patted down and then pushed into the back seat of a police cruiser, where he watched as his date was handcuffed.

After about 15 minutes, he said, the officers let them go, acknowledging, with little apology, that the couple were unlikely to have committed a nearby armed robbery minutes earlier. Mr. Archer's date works as a county prosecutor. Mr. Archer, 30, is a lawyer and the eldest son of Detroit's Mayor, Dennis W. Archer.

The officers were white. Mr. Archer and his date are black.

For Mayor Archer, there was a sad familiarity. When his son called, the Mayor said, "I had flashbacks to when I was stopped."

That was 15 years ago, when police officers in Detroit pulled him over.

"They had pulled guns and put me in the back seat," the Mayor said. They went through his Cadillac Seville, looking for evidence that he was the drug dealer they were looking for, he said. But when the police rifled through his briefcase, they learned he was president of the State Bar Association.

In stopping the Mayor's son, the Royal Oak police said, officers responded appropriately and followed normal procedures for an investigation of a felony, rather than a simple traffic stop. Three minutes before stopping Mr. Archer, the police had received a report that a gunman robbed a convenience store nearby, then drove off with another person in a dark blue Jeep. Mr. Archer's Jeep Grand Cherokee is black, and carried two people.

"This is not a case of stopping a black driver for the sake of stopping a black driver," said Comdr. Thomas Wightman of the Royal Oak Police Department.

But the Mayor's son believes that the police would have given better treatment to a white couple, and he plans to file a complaint with the police department on Monday.

Minority members around the country say it is so common for them to be stopped for what they feel are slender reasons that they have a name for an imaginary crime: D.W.B., driving while black.

Last month, President Clinton ordered Federal law-enforcement agencies to compile data on the race and ethnicity of those they stop and challenged state and local police to do the same. Mr. Clinton called the practice of stopping of drivers because of the color of their skin "morally indefensible."

In April, New Jersey officials admitted that state troopers had unfairly singled out minority drivers.

And in New York, where the police shooting of an unarmed black man who was approached for questioning led to weeks of protests, Deputy Mayor Rudy Washington recently told of his own experience in being harassed by the police.

Here in Detroit, a city that is 76 percent black, the police are long past the days when squad cars carrying burly white officers would pull up to street corners and beat up blacks. In the 1967 riots here, white officers opened fire on a black uniformed rookie officer, Isaiah McKinnon, who later became the city's police chief.

Detroit's police force has been well integrated, and for more than 25 years the city has been run by black mayors.

But blacks—rich, middle-class and poor alike—still tell of being followed by the police when they drive into the primarily white suburbs or of being otherwise harassed when they encounter suburban police.

A black executive with General Motors sent his nephew to shop in his exclusive neighborhood, only to soon have the police interrupt a party at his house to investigate whether the youngster had stolen a can of vegetables. The receipt was produced and the police left, but the executive said he was still shaken.

The recent stop was the worst, but not the first, for the Mayor's son.

"I have been stopped before for what has been, in my opinion, no apparent reason," Mr. Archer said. "You cannot come across anyone who is African-American who has not at some point felt that they have been either subtly or very directly discriminated against because of their race, myself included."

Mayor Archer said the incident made him feel that society had gone "back in time, as opposed to moving forward where we can put these issues behind us and have a society based on mutual respect."

He sat with his son in the Mayor's office, under a print of the famous Norman Rockwell painting of bygone days, when United States marshals were needed to escort a young black girl to a once-white school, past a wall where someone had scrawled a racial epithet and thrown tomatoes.

His son's traffic stop was a curt reminder, Mayor Archer said, "that we happen to be people of color."

"It doesn't matter what your name happens to be, what your title happens to be, whatever the case may be," the Mayor said. "Doesn't matter."

16

America's Iron Curtain: The Border Patrol State

Leslie Marmon Silko

I used to travel the highways of New Mexico and Arizona with a wonderful sensation of absolute freedom as I cruised down the open road and across the vast desert plateaus. On the Laguna Pueblo reservation, where I was raised, the people were patriotic despite the way the U.S. government had treated Native Americans. As proud citizens, we grew up believing the freedom to travel was our inalienable right, a right that some Native Americans had been denied in the early twentieth century. Our cousin, old Bill Pratt, used to ride his horse 300 miles overland from Laguna, New Mexico, to Prescott, Arizona, every summer to work as a fire lookout.

In school in the 1950s, we were taught that our right to travel from state to state without special papers or threat of detainment was a right that citizens under communist and totalitarian governments did not possess. That wide open highway told us we were U.S. citizens; we went free. . . .

Not so long ago, my companion Gus and I were driving south from Albuquerque, returning to Tucson after a book promotion for the paperback edition of my novel *Almanac of the Dead*. I had settled back and gone to sleep while Gus drove, but I was awakened when I felt the car slowing to a stop. It was nearly midnight on New Mexico State Road 26, a dark, lonely stretch of two-lane highway between Hatch and Deming. When I sat up, I saw the headlights and emergency flashers of six vehicles—Border Patrol cars and a van were blocking both lanes of the highway. Gus stopped the car and rolled down the window to ask what was wrong. But the closest Border Patrolman and his companion did not reply; instead, the first agent ordered us to "step out of the car." Gus asked why, but his question seemed to set them off. Two more Border Patrol agents immediately approached our car, and one of them snapped, "Are you looking for trouble?" as if he would relish it.

I will never forget that night beside the highway. There was an awful feeling of menace and violence straining to break loose. It was clear that the uniformed men would be only too happy to drag us out of the car if we did not speedily comply with their request (asking a question is tantamount to resistance, it seems). So we stepped out of the car and they motioned for us to stand on the shoulder of the road. The night was very dark, and no other traffic had come down the road since we had been stopped. All I could think about was a book I had read—*Nunca Más*—the official report of a human rights commission that investigated and certified more than 12,000 "disappearances" during Argentina's "dirty war" in the late 1970s.

The weird anger of these Border Patrolmen made me think about descriptions in the report of Argentine police and military officers who became addicted to interrogation, torture and the murder that followed. When the military and police ran out of political suspects to torture and kill, they resorted to the random abduction of citizens off the streets. I thought how easy it would be for the Border Patrol to shoot us and leave our bodies and car beside the highway, like so many bodies found in these parts and ascribed to "drug runners."

Two other Border Patrolmen stood by the white van. The one who had asked if we were looking for trouble ordered his partner to "get the dog," and from the back of the van another patrolman brought a small female German shepherd on a leash. The dog apparently did not heel well enough to suit him, and the handler jerked the leash. They opened the doors of our car and pulled the dog's head into it, but I saw immediately from the expression in her eyes that the dog hated them, and that she would not serve them. When she showed no interest in the inside of our car, they brought her around back to the trunk, near where we were standing. They half-dragged her up into the trunk, but still she did not indicate any stowed-away human beings or illegal drugs.

Their mood got uglier; the officers seemed outraged that the dog could not find any contraband, and they dragged her over to us and commanded her to sniff our legs and feet. To my relief, the strange violence the Border Patrol agents had focused on us now seemed shifted to the dog. I no longer felt so strongly that we would be murdered. We exchanged looks—the dog and I. She was afraid of what they might do, just as I was. The dog's handler jerked the leash sharply as she sniffed us, as if to make her perform better, but the dog refused to accuse us: She had an innate dignity that did not permit her to serve the murderous impulses of those men. I can't forget the expression in the dog's eyes; it was as if she were embarrassed to be associated with them. I had a small amount of medicinal marijuana in my purse that night, but she refused to expose me. I am not partial to dogs, but I will always remember the small German shepherd that night.

Unfortunately, what happened to me is an everyday occurrence here now. Since the 1980s, on top of greatly expanding border checkpoints, the Immigration and Naturalization Service and the Border Patrol have implemented policies that interfere with the rights of U.S. citizens to travel freely within our borders. I.N.S. agents now patrol all interstate highways and roads that lead to or from the U.S.-Mexico border in Texas, New Mexico, Arizona and California. Now, when you drive east from Tucson on Interstate 10 toward El Paso, you encounter an I.N.S. check station outside Las Cruces, New Mexico. When you drive north from Las Cruces up Interstate 25, two miles north of the town of Truth or Consequences, the highway is blocked with orange emergency barriers, and all traffic is diverted into a two-lane Border Patrol checkpoint—ninety-five miles north of the U.S.-Mexico border.

I was detained once at Truth or Consequences, despite my and my companion's Arizona driver's licenses. Two men, both Chicanos, were detained at the same time, despite the fact that they too presented ID and spoke English without the thick Texas accents of the Border Patrol agents. While we were stopped, we watched as other vehicles—whose occupants were white—were waved through the checkpoint. White people traveling with brown people, however, can expect to be stopped on suspicion they work with the sanctuary movement, which shelters refugees. White people who appear to be clergy, those who wear ethnic clothing or jewelry and women with very long hair or very short hair (they could be nuns) are also frequently detained; white men with beards or men with long hair are likely to be detained, too, because Border Patrol agents have "profiles" of "those sorts" of white people who may help political refugees. (Most of the political refugees from Guatemala and El Salvador are Native American or mestizo because the indigenous people of the Americas have continued to resist efforts by invaders to displace them from their ancestral lands.) Alleged increases in illegal immigration of people of Asian ancestry means that the Border Patrol now routinely detains anyone who appears to be Asian or part Asian, as well.

Once your car is diverted from the Interstate Highway into the checkpoint area, you are under the control of the Border Patrol, which in practical terms exercises a power that no highway patrol or city patrolman possesses: They are willing to detain anyone, for no apparent reason. Other law-enforcement officers need a shred of probable cause in order to detain someone. On the books, so does the Border Patrol; but on the road, it's another matter. They'll order you to stop your car and step out; then they'll ask you to open the trunk. If you ask why or request a search warrant, you'll be told that they'll have to have a dog sniff the car before they can request a search warrant, and the dog might not get there for two or three hours. The search warrant might require an hour or two past that. They make it clear that if you force them to obtain a search warrant for the car, they will make you submit to a strip search as well.

Traveling in the open, though, the sense of violation can be even worse. Never mind high-profile cases like that of former Border Patrol agent Michael Elmer, acquitted of murder by claiming self-defense, despite admitting that as an officer he shot an "illegal" immigrant in the back and then hid the body, which remained undiscovered until another Border Patrolman reported the event. (Last month, Elmer was convicted of reckless endangerment in a separate incident, for shooting at least ten rounds from his M-16 too close to a group of immigrants as they were crossing illegally into Nogales in March 1992.) Or that in El Paso, a high school football coach driving a vanload of his players in full uniform was pulled over on the free-way and a Border Patrol agent put a cocked revolver to his head. (The football coach was Mexican-American, as were most of the players in his van; the incident eventu-ally caused a federal judge to issue a restraining order against the Border Patrol.) We've a mountain of personal experiences like that which never make the newspapers. A history professor at U.C.L.A. told me she had been traveling by train from Los Angeles to Albuquerque twice a month doing research. On each of her trips, she had noticed that the Border Patrol agents were at the station in Albuquerque scru-tinizing the passengers. Since she is six feet tall and of Irish and German ancestry, she was not particularly concerned. Then one day when she stepped off the train in Albuquerque, two Border Patrolmen accosted her, wanting to know what she was doing, and why she was traveling between Los Angeles and Albuquerque twice a month. She presented identification and an explanation deemed "suitable" by the agents, and was allowed to go about her business.

Just the other day, I mentioned to a friend that I was writing this article and he told me about his 73-year-old father, who is half Chinese and had set out alone by car from Tucson to Albuquerque the week before. His father had become confused by road construction and missed a turnoff from Interstate 10 to Interstate 25; when he turned around and circled back, he missed the turnoff a second time. But when he looped back for yet another try, Border Patrol agents stopped him and forced him to open his trunk. After they satisfied themselves the he was not smuggling Chi-nese immigrants, they sent him on his way. He was so rattled by the event that he had to be driven home by his daughter.

This is the police state that has developed in the southwestern United States since the 1980s. No person, no citizen, is free to travel without the scrutiny of the Bor-der Patrol. In the city of South Tucson, where 80 percent of the respondents were Chicano or Mexicano, a joint research project by the University of Wisconsin and the University of Arizona recently concluded that one out of every five people there had been detained, mistreated verbally or nonverbally, or questioned by I.N.S. agents in the past two years.

Manifest Destiny may lack its old grandeur of theft and blood—"lock the door" is what it means now, with racism a trump card to be played again and again, shame-lessly, by both major political parties. "Immigration," like "street crime" and "wel-fare fraud," is a political euphemism that refers to people of color. Politicians and media people talk about "illegal aliens" to dehumanize and demonize undocumented immigrants, who are for the most part people of color. Even in the days of Spanish and Mexican rule, no attempts were made to interfere with the flow of people and goods from south to north and north to south. It is the U.S. government that has continually attempted to sever contact between the tribal people north of the bor-der and those to the south.[1]

Now that the "Iron Curtain" is gone, it is ironic that the U.S. government and its Border Patrol are constructing a steel wall ten feet high to span sections of the border with Mexico. While politicians and multinational corporations extol the virtues of NAFTA and "free trade" (in goods, not flesh), the ominous curtain is already up in a six-mile section at the border crossing at Mexicali; two miles are being erected but are not yet finished at Naco; and at Nogales, sixty miles south of Tucson, the steel wall has been all rubber-stamped and awaits construction likely to begin in March. Like the pathetic multimillion-dollar "antidrug" border surveillance balloons that were continually deflated by high winds and made only a couple of meager interceptions before they blew away, the fence along the border is a theatrical prop, a bit of pork for contractors. Border entrepreneurs have already used blowtorches to cut passageways through the fence to collect "tolls," and are doing a brisk business. Back in Washington, the I.N.S. announces a $300 million computer contract to modernize its record-keeping and Congress passes a crime bill that shunts $255 million to the I.N.S. for 1995, $181 million earmarked for border control, which is to include 700 new partners for the men who stopped Gus and me in our travels, and the history professor, and my friend's father, and as many as they could from South Tucson.

It is no use; borders haven't worked, and they won't work, not now, as the indigenous people of the Americas reassert their kinship and solidarity with one another. A mass migration is already under way; its roots are not simply economic. The Uto-Aztecan languages are spoken as far north as Taos Pueblo near the Colorado border, all the way south to Mexico City. Before the arrival of the Europeans, the indigenous communities throughout this region not only conducted commerce, the people shared cosmologies, and oral narratives about the Maize Mother, the Twin Brothers and their Grandmother, Spider Woman, as well as Quetzalcoatl the benevolent snake. The great human migration within the Americas cannot be stopped; human beings are natural forces of the Earth, just as rivers and winds are natural forces.

Deep down the issue is simple: The so-called "Indian Wars" from the days of Sitting Bull and Red Cloud have never really ended in the Americas. The Indian people of southern Mexico, of Guatemala and those left in El Salvador, too, are still fighting for their lives and for their land against the "cavalry" patrols sent out by the governments of those lands. The Americas are Indian country, and the "Indian problem" is not about to go away.

One evening at sundown, we were stopped in traffic at a railroad crossing in downtown Tucson while a freight train passed us, slowly gaining speed as it headed north to Phoenix. In the twilight I saw the most amazing sight: Dozens of human beings, mostly young men, were riding the train; everywhere, on flat cars, inside open boxcars, perched on top of boxcars, hanging off ladders on tank cars and between boxcars. I couldn't count fast enough, but I saw fifty or sixty people headed north. They were dark young men, Indian and mestizo; they were smiling and a few of them waved at us in our cars. I was reminded of the ancient story of Aztlán, told by the

Aztecs but known in other Uto-Aztecan communities as well. Aztlán is the beautiful land to the north, the origin place of the Aztec people. I don't remember how or why the people left Aztlán to journey farther south, but the old story says that one day, they will return.

NOTE

1. The Treaty of Guadalupe Hidalgo, signed in 1848, recognizes the right of the Tohano O'Odom (Papago) people to move freely across the U.S.-Mexico border without documents. A treaty with Canada guarantees similar rights to those of the Iroquois nation in traveling the U.S.-Canada border.

17

The Heartland's Raw Deal: How Meatpacking is Creating a New Immigrant Underclass

Marc Cooper

. . . In a sweeping regional arc from the Dakotas through Minnesota, Nebraska and Iowa, and down through Kansas into northern Texas and the foothills of the Missouri Ozarks, dozens of once lily-white heartland meatpacking communities have become the new homes to tens of thousands of impoverished Third World workers.

Putting the lie to the conventional wisdom undergirding our immigration policy, the arrival of these workers en masse is neither serendipitous nor the product of cunning smugglers. Rather, it is the direct result of a conscious survival strategy undertaken by a key U.S. industry, a plan developed and fully implemented only in the past few years.

Beef, pork, and poultry packers have been aggressively recruiting the most vulnerable of foreign workers to relocate to the U.S. plains in exchange for $6-an-hour jobs in the country's most dangerous industry. Since permanence is hardly a requirement for these jobs, the concepts of promotion and significant salary increase have as much as disappeared. That as many as half of these new immigrants lack legal residence seems no obstacle to an industry now thriving on a docile, disempowered work force with an astronomical turnover.

Staggering illness and injury rates—36 per 100 workers in meat—and stress caused by difficult, repetitive work often means employment for just a few months before a worker quits or the company forces him/her off the job. (Government safety inspections have dropped 43 percent overall since 1994, because of budget cuts and an increasingly pro-business slant at the Occupational Safety and Health Administration.) When disabled workers and their families remain in their new homes, the social cost of their survival is then passed by the company to the public. . . .

From "The Heartland's Raw Deal: How Meatpacking Is Creating a New Immigrant Underclass" by Marc Cooper in *The Nation* (3 March 1997). Reprinted with permission.

. . . Less than fifty yards from Iowa Beef Processor's (I.B.P.) shipping depot, we visit Lao women living in a series of railroad shacks in conditions so bad that they remind me of the scavengers I once saw living in wooden huts in Seoul. Their small rooms are overwhelmed with the medicinal reek of Ben-Gay and Tiger Balm, used in industrial quantities to quench the fire in fingers and elbows pushed to their limit by work on the slaughterhouse floor. . . .

LIFE UNDERGROUND

. . . Unlike the Lao, who are all legal residents, something like half the Latino workers and their families here are undocumented. Several workers tell me that valid Social Security cards—that belong to others—can be purchased for $300 to $500 and that the company does no checking. Other workers contend that I.B.P. management personnel moonlight in document-trafficking. That's a story the company denies.

I.B.P. openly admits that many of these Latinos—legal residents and otherwise—have come here recruited by the company, which has consistently used labor brokers to comb the border areas in south Texas and California to shuttle up new recruits at as much as $300 a head. A cursory look at a birth certificate or Social Security card was enough to satisfy the broker and the personnel department that the labor draftees were legal.

"The company loves to work with illegals," says 45-year-old Heriberto from inside his trailer, a few yards away from the scene of the December fire. "When you are illegal you can't talk back," he adds. Heriberto brings home $300 for a six-day, forty-eight-hour week. One paycheck goes for trailer rent. Another is sent back to relatives in Mexico. "You keep your head down and follow orders. We say you can't do nothing." Switching to Spanish, he says, "*Dices nada porque la planta es del gobierno*" (You say nothing because the plant is the government). Indeed. Though Latinos make up about a quarter of the I.B.P. work force and have the most dangerous jobs, Latino surnames show up on less than 5 percent of the worker comp claims filed between 1987 and 1995.

. . . There's a constant commerce of workers, relatives and friends between Storm Lake and Santa Rita. This human conveyor belt is powered by the grueling work regimen, which generates an astonishing worker turnover rate of more than 80 percent a year—a rate common to the entire industry. "Perfect for the company," says Heriberto. "Most workers leave before six months is up and the company has to start paying health insurance."

Meanwhile, in 1995 I.B.P. stripped off a juicy $257 million in profits on sales of $12 billion. Its C.E.O., Robert Peterson, made $1 million in salary and $5.2 million in bonuses that year. Storm Lake shows none of the blight that metastasized through the region after the eighties farm collapse. Its small and tidy downtown has no board-ups or vacancies. Four locally owned banks are thriving. The housing market is corset-tight. "You can't even rent," says Mayor Sandra Madsen. "We have two big payrolls, a stable downtown. Five years from now I think this town will realize we are all better off for the change we have gone through."

Perhaps. But for the moment, the dominant atmosphere is one of apartheid. "Race determines everything here," says an outreach worker to the Latino community. "Where you live, where you work, how much you earn, where you worship, even where you shop."

. . . When I stop to make a phone call from the local Conoco station, two locals overhear me speaking in Spanish. "Fuckin' Mexican should learn English," one says loudly to the other. The editor of the forward-looking *Storm Lake Times*, which has been a "pro-diversity" voice, jokes that the local good old boys like to call his paper "The Gook Times."

A lot of the local xenophobes had their big moment last May, when on a Friday afternoon seventeen armed Border Patrol officers—backed up by agents from the Immigration and Naturalization Service, units from local law enforcement and surveillance planes circling over the I.B.P. plant—staged an almost tragicomic raid on Storm Lake. In what amounted to a military occupation, agents spent two days going door to door in Little Mexico, setting up roadblocks and rousting suspects off the street in a sweep for illegals. A publicity-seeking U.S. Attorney even showed up to take credit for an operation he had little to do with. Prodded into action by the local police chief, who along with the I.N.S. had built up a database of some 600 suspected illegal aliens in town, the federal agents eventually arrested and deported a total of seventy-eight Latinos.

But when hundreds of other fearful workers—likely all undocumented or with false ID—failed to show up for work the next Monday and the pork began to spoil, I.B.P. management panicked. In a story corroborated by several sources, executives started calling community workers who have the confidence of their Latino clients. "I.B.P. told us to tell everyone to come back to work that afternoon," says a social worker. "It was O.K. now. The I.N.S. was gone and nobody was going to check anything."

Within a few weeks, say several workers, even some of those deported to Mexico were back on the job. "They just got some new ID," says one worker. "And the same gringos who turned them in hired them back like nothing had happened." After the raid was over an I.N.S. official met with the press and said I.B.P. had cooperated in the raid and would face no employer sanctions or fines.

'YOUR TIRED, YOUR POOR . . .'

. . . The bitter strike at Hormel's Austin, Minnesota, plant in 1985–86 (the subject of Barbara Kopple's Academy Award-winning documentary, *American Dream*) was the signal event in a labor counterrevolution that has convulsed and redrawn the face of U.S. meatpacking. And if you could boil that counterrevolution down into one slogan it would be: Death to Middle-Class Meatpackers!

Prior to the Reagan era, that's exactly what the meatpackers in Storm Lake were. The space now occupied by I.B.P. was the old Hygrade plant. The work force, unionized and virtually all white, was averaging $30,000 a year or more—some $51,000 in today's dollars. Refusing to reach agreement with its unions, Hygrade closed down in 1981.

After being enticed with $10 million in local tax subsidies, I.B.P. re-opened the plant a year later, offering $6 an hour. The pattern of de-unionization and ruralization was regional. One after another, meatpacking plants moved from the big cities, where they were close to labor, into the countryside, where they were near the animals and could save on transport costs. As supermarkets took on more specialty butchers, the processing plants needed more, but less-skilled, workers. Unions became anathema. The industry's hourly pay, including benefits, peaked at $19 in 1980. By 1992 it was below sixties levels at $12 an hour, and it has continued to fall. By 1995 unionization was half of what it was in 1963.

Where the new plants opened, labor was in relatively short supply. And even in Storm Lake, where hundreds of former Hygrade workers re-applied for the new jobs, I.B.P. hired back only thirty. "The company wanted to bar union-experienced workers from the shop floor," says Mary Grey. With just a few companies—I.B.P., Cargill, Con-Agra—dominating the field, competition was, no pun intended, cutthroat. Production lines were sped up; injury rates climbed. What was once a stable work force became frenetically mobile. . . .

WITH A WINK AND A HANDCUFF

Since 1992 the I.N.S. has arrested more than 1,000 meatpacking workers in the Midwest. This past summer, as part of a six-week regional sweep ordered by the Clinton Administration, 209 undocumented workers were detained in Iowa. The average pay for those arrested was $6.02 an hour. Now the four biggest meatpackers, including I.B.P. and Swift, have agreed to participate in an I.N.S. program that will use computers to check IDs.

Local Latino workers laugh it all off. "Everyone knows the company and the I.N.S. are in together on all this. They never make the company pay a fine, do they?" says Javier, an I.B.P. worker in Storm Lake who works under the ID he purchased in the name of a legal resident. "Everyone knows they are never going to arrest all of us. Who would do this shitty work for them? We know that every now and then the *migra* will come in and take a few away to keep the politicians happy. And then we won't see them again for another two years. That's how it works."

For more than a century now there's been a pattern of U.S. industries—one after another—actively recruiting Mexican labor while the rest of society turned a blind eye, says Fred Krissman, anthropologist at Washington State University. "You can go back to the 1920s and find all sorts of academic research in that period referring to Mexicans who could be brought here to work and then sent back home like homing pigeons to procreate." And there's always been that cognitive dissonance between the reality and the policy. "In 1954 during what was called Operation Wetback, a million Mexicans were randomly rounded up in the United States and deported," says Krissman. "At the same time we were bringing in 300,000 Mexicans in the Bracero program. We had trains running both ways on public money!"

The solution, he argues, is to dump current immigration policy and opt for the model of the European Union. When you have a system that frees the flow of capital across borders, you should move toward a transnationalization of labor, too. If you work in the United States you should have legal papers in the United States, and all such workers should be protected by serious enforcement of health and safety regulations on the books. This doesn't mean immigrant workers would suddenly make middle-class wages, but it would be the first step toward eliminating the employer abuses rained down on people with no legal standing. Most important, it would be a radical leap toward stabilizing these now-underground communities. At best, unions would have a better shot at organizing; at a minimum, individual workers would stand a better chance of raising their wages.

This is not a likely option when politicians from both parties struggle to outdo each other in cracking down on illegal aliens. . . .

Part Six

Structured Inequality—Acquiring Gender

18

Bodies that Matter:
On the Discursive Limits of "Sex"

Judith Butler

FROM CONSTRUCTION TO MATERIALIZATION

The relation between culture and nature presupposed by some models of gender "construction" implies a culture or an agency of the social which acts upon a nature, which is itself presupposed as a passive surface, outside the social and yet its necessary counterpart. One question that feminists have raised, then, is whether the discourse which figures the action of construction as a kind of imprinting or imposition is not tacitly masculinist, whereas the figure of the passive surface, awaiting that penetrating act whereby meaning is endowed, is not tacitly or—perhaps—quite obviously feminine. Is sex to gender as feminine is to masculine?[1]

Other feminist scholars have argued that the very concept of nature needs to be rethought, for the concept of nature has a history, and the figuring of nature as the blank and lifeless page, as that which is, as it were, always already dead, is decidedly modern, linked perhaps to the emergence of technological means of domination. Indeed, some have argued that a rethinking of "nature" as a set of dynamic interrelations suits both feminist and ecological aims (and has for some produced an otherwise unlikely alliance with the work of Gilles Deleuze). This rethinking also calls into question the model of construction whereby the social unilaterally acts on the natural and invests it with its parameters and its meanings. Indeed, as much as the radical distinction between sex and gender has been crucial to the de Beauvoirian version of feminism, it has come under criticism in more recent years for degrading the natural as that which is "before" intelligibility, in need of the mark, if not the mar, of the social to signify, to be known, to acquire value. This misses the point that nature has a history, and not merely a social one, but, also, that sex is positioned ambiguously in relation to that concept and its history. The concept of "sex" is itself troubled terrain, formed through a series of contestations over what ought to be decisive criteria for distinguishing between the two sexes; the concept of sex has a history that is covered over by the figure of the site or surface of inscription. Figured as such a site or surface, however, the natural is construed as that which is also without value; moreover, it assumes its value at the same time that it assumes its social character, that is, at the same time that nature relinquishes itself as the natural. According to this view, then, the social construction of the natural presupposes the cancellation of the natural by the social. Insofar as it relies on this construal, the sex/gender distinction founders along parallel lines; if gender is the social significance that sex assumes within a given culture—and for the sake of argument we will let "social" and "cultural" stand in any uneasy interchangeability—then what, if anything, is left of "sex" once it has assumed its social character as gender? At issue is the meaning of "assumption," where to be "assumed" is to be taken up into a more elevated sphere, as in "the Assumption of the Virgin." If gender consists of the social meanings that sex assumes, then sex does not *accrue* social meanings as additive properties but, rather, *is replaced by* the social meanings it takes on; sex is relinquished in the course of that assumption, and gender emerges, not as a term in a continued relationship of opposition to sex, but as the term which absorbs and displaces "sex," the mark of its full substantiation into gender or what, from a materialist point of view, might constitute a full *de*substantiation.

When the sex/gender distinction is joined with a notion of radical linguistic constructivism, the problem becomes even worse, for the "sex" which is referred to as prior to gender will itself be a postulation, a construction, offered within language, as that which is prior to language, prior to construction. But this sex posited as prior to construction will, by virtue of being posited, become the effect of that very positing, the construction of construction. If gender is the social construction of sex, and if there is no access to this "sex" except by means of its construction, then it appears not only that sex is absorbed by gender, but that "sex" becomes something like a fiction, perhaps a fantasy, retroactively installed at a prelinguistic site to which there is no direct access.

But is it right to claim that "sex" vanishes altogether, that it is a fiction over and against what is true, that it is a fantasy over and against what is reality? Or do these very oppositions need to be rethought such that if "sex" is a fiction, it is one within whose necessities we live, without which life itself would be unthinkable? And if "sex" is a fantasy, is it perhaps a phantasmatic field that constitutes the very terrain of cultural intelligibility? Would such a rethinking of such conventional oppositions entail a rethinking of "constructivism" in its usual sense?

The radical constructivist position has tended to produce the premise that both refutes and confirms its own enterprise. If such a theory cannot take account of sex as the site or surface on which it acts, then it ends up presuming sex as the unconstructed, and so concedes the limits of linguistic constructivism, inadvertently circumscribing that which remains unaccountable within the terms of construction. If, on the other hand, sex is a contrived premise, a fiction, then gender does not presume a sex which it acts upon, but rather, gender produces the misnomer of a prediscursive "sex," and the meaning of construction becomes that of linguistic monoism, whereby everything is only and always language. Then, what ensues is an exasperated debate which many of us have tired of hearing: Either (1) constructivism is reduced to a position of linguistic monism, whereby linguistic construction is understood to be generative and deterministic. Critics making that presumption can be heard to say, "If everything is discourse, what about the body?" or (2) when constructing is figuratively reduced to a verbal action which appears to presuppose a subject, critics working within such a presumption can be heard to say, "If gender is constructed, then who is doing the constructing?"; though, of course, (3) the most pertinent formulation of this question is the following: "If the subject is constructed, then who is constructing the subject?" In the first case, construction has taken the place of a godlike agency which not only causes but composes everything which is its object; it is the divine performative, bringing into being and exhaustively constituting that which it names, or, rather, it is that kind of transitive referring which names and inaugurates at once. For something to be constructed, according to this view of construction, is for it to be created and determined through that process.

In the second and third cases, the seductions of grammar appear to hold sway; the critic asks, Must there not be a human agent, a subject, if you will, who guides the course of construction? If the first version of constructivism presumes that construction operates deterministically, making a mockery of human agency, the second understands constructivism as presupposing a voluntarist subject who makes its gender through an instrumental action. A construction is understood in this latter case to be a kind of manipulable artifice, a conception that not only presupposes a subject, but rehabilitates precisely the voluntarist subject of humanism that constructivism has, on occasion, sought to put into question.

If gender is a construction, must there be an "I" or a "we" who enacts or performs that construction? How can there be an activity, a constructing, without presupposing an agent who precedes and performs that activity? How would we account for the motivation and direction of construction without such a subject? As a rejoinder, I would suggest that it takes a certain suspicion toward grammar to reconceive the matter in a different light. For if gender is constructed, it is not necessarily constructed by an "I" or a "we" who stands before that construction in any spatial or temporal sense of "before." Indeed, it is unclear that there can be an "I" or a "we" who has not been submitted, subjected to gender, where gendering is, among other things, the differentiating relations by which speaking subjects come into being. Subjected to gender, but subjectivated by gender, the "I" neither precedes nor follows the process of this gendering, but emerges only within and as the matrix of gender relations themselves.

This then returns us to the second objection, the one which claims that constructivism forecloses agency, preempts the agency of the subject, and finds itself presupposing the subject that it calls into question. To claim that the subject is itself produced in and as a gendered matrix of relations is not to do away with the subject, but only to ask after the conditions of its emergence and operation. The "activity" of this gendering cannot, strictly speaking, be a human act or expression, a willful appropriation, and it is certainly *not* a question of taking on a mask; it is the matrix through which all willing first becomes possible, its enabling cultural condition. In this sense, the matrix of gender relations is prior to the emergence of the "human." Consider the medical interpellation which (the recent emergence of the sonogram notwithstanding) shifts an infant from an "it" to a "she" or a "he," and in that naming, the girl is "girled," brought into the domain of language and kinship through the interpellation of gender. But that "girling" of the girl does not end there; on the contrary, that founding interpellation is reiterated by various authorities and throughout various intervals of time to reenforce or contest this naturalized effect. The naming is at once the setting of a boundary, and also the repeated inculcation of a norm.

Such attributions or interpellations contribute to that field of discourse and power that orchestrates, delimits, and sustains that which qualifies as "the human." We see this most clearly in the examples of those abjected beings who do not appear properly gendered; it is their very humanness that comes into question. Indeed, the construction of gender operates through *exclusionary* means, such that the human is not only produced over and against the inhuman, but through a set of foreclosures, radical erasures, that are, strictly speaking, refused the possibility of cultural articulation. Hence, it is not enough to claim that human subjects are constructed, for the construction of the human is a differential operation that produces the more and the less "human," the inhuman, the humanly unthinkable. These excluded sites come to bound the "human" as its constitutive outside, and to haunt those boundaries as the persistent possibility of their disruption and rearticulation. . . .[2]

There are defenders and critics of construction, who construe that position along structuralist lines. They often claim that there are structures that construct the subject, impersonal forces, such as Culture or Discourse or Power, where these terms occupy the grammatical site of the subject after the "human" has been dislodged from its place. In such a view, the grammatical and metaphysical place of the subject is retained even as the candidate that occupies that place appears to rotate. As a result, construction is still understood as a unilateral process initiated by a prior subject, fortifying that presumption of the metaphysics of the subject that where there is activity, there lurks behind it an initiating and willful subject. On such a view, discourse or language or the social becomes personified, and in the personification the metaphysics of the subject is reconsolidated.

In this second view, construction is not an activity, but an act, one which happens once and whose effects are firmly fixed. Thus, constructivism is reduced to determinism and implies the evacuation or displacement of human agency.

This view informs the misreading by which Foucault is criticized for "personifying" power: if power is misconstrued as a grammatical and metaphysical subject, and if that metaphysical site within humanist discourse has been the privileged site of the human, then power appears to have displaced the human as the origin of activity. But if Foucault's view of power is understood as the disruption and subversion of this grammar and metaphysics of the subject, if power orchestrates the formation and sustenance of subjects, then it cannot be accounted for in terms of the "subject" which is its effect. And here it would be no more right to claim that the term "construction" belongs at the grammatical site of subject, for construction is neither a subject nor its act, but a process of reiteration by which both "subjects" and "acts" come to appear at all. There is no power that acts, but only a reiterated acting that is power in its persistence and instability.

What I would propose in place of these conceptions of construction is a return to the notion of matter, not as site or surface, but as *a process of materialization that stabilizes over time to produce the effect of boundary, fixity, and surface we call matter*. That matter is always materialized has, I think, to be thought in relation to the productive and, indeed, materializing effects of regulatory power in the Foucaultian sense.[3] Thus, the question is no longer, How is gender constituted as and through a certain interpretation of sex? (a question that leaves the "matter" of sex untheorized), but rather, Through what regulatory norms is sex itself materialized? And how is it that treating the materiality of sex as a given presupposes and consolidates the normative conditions of its own emergence?

Crucially, then, construction is neither a single act nor a causal process initiated by a subject and culminating in a set of fixed effects. Construction not only takes place *in* time, but is itself a temporal process which operates through the reiteration of norms; sex is both produced and destabilized in the course of this reiteration.[4] As a sedimented effect of a reiterative or ritual practice, sex acquires its naturalized effect, and yet, it is also by virtue of this reiteration that gaps and fissures are opened up as the constitutive instabilities in such constructions, as that which escapes or exceeds the norm, as that which cannot be wholly defined or fixed by the repetitive labor of that norm. This instability is the *de*constituting possibility in the very process of repetition, the power that undoes the very effects by which "sex" is stabilized, the possibility to put the consolidation of the norms of "sex" into a potentially productive crisis.[5]

Certain formulations of the radical constructivist position appear almost compulsively to produce a moment of recurrent exasperation, for it seems that when the constructivist is construed as a linguistic idealist, the constructivist refutes the reality of bodies, the relevance of science, the alleged facts of birth, aging, illness, and death. The critic might also suspect the constructivist of a certain somatophobia and seek assurances that this abstracted theorist will admit that there are, minimally, sexually differentiated parts, activities, capacities, hormonal and chromosomal differences that can be conceded without reference to "construction." Although at this moment I want to offer an absolute reassurance to my interlocutor, some anxiety prevails.

To "concede" the undeniability of "sex" or its "materiality" is always to concede some version of "sex," some formation of "materiality." Is the discourse in and through which that concession occurs—and, yes, that concession invariably does occur—not itself formative of the very phenomenon that it concedes? To claim that discourse is formative is not to claim that it originates, causes, or exhaustively composes that which it concedes; rather, it is to claim that there is no reference to a pure body which is not at the same time a further formation of that body. In this sense, the linguistic capacity to refer to sexed bodies is not denied, but the very meaning of "referentiality" is altered. In philosophical terms, the constative claim is always to some degree performative.

In relation to sex, then, if one concedes the materiality of sex or of the body, does that very conceding operate—performatively—to materialize that sex? And further, how is it that the reiterated concession of that sex—one which need not take place in speech or writing but might be "signaled" in a much more inchoate way—constitutes the sedimentation and production of that material effect?

The moderate critic might concede that *some part* of "sex" is constructed, but some other is certainly not, and then, of course, find him or herself not only under some obligation to draw the line between what is and is not constructed, but to explain how it is that "sex" comes in parts whose differentiation is not a matter of construction. But as that line of demarcation between such ostensible parts gets drawn, the "unconstructed" becomes bounded once again through a signifying practice, and the very boundary which is meant to protect some part of sex from the taint of constructivism is now defined by the anti-constructivist's own construction. Is construction something which happens to a ready-made object, a pregiven thing, and does it happen *in degree*? Or are we perhaps referring on both sides of the debate to an inevitable practice of signification, of demarcating and delimiting that to which we then "refer," such that our "references" always presuppose—and often conceal—this prior delimitation? Indeed, to "refer" naively or directly to such an extra-discursive object will always require the prior delimitation of the extra-discursive. And insofar as the extra-discursive is delimited, it is formed by the very discourse from which it seeks to free itself. This delimitation, which often is enacted as an untheorized presupposition in any act of description, marks a boundary that includes and excludes, that decides, as it were, what will and will not be the stuff or the object to which we then refer. This marking off will have some normative force and, indeed, some violence, for it can construct only through erasing; it can bound a thing only through enforcing a certain criterion, a principle of selectivity.

What will and will not be included within the boundaries of "sex" will be set by a more or less tacit operation of exclusion. If we call into question the fixity of the structuralist law that divides and bounds the "sexes" by virtue of their dyadic differentiation within the heterosexual matrix, it will be from the exterior regions of that boundary (not from a "position," but from the discursive possibilities opened up by the constitutive outside of hegemonic positions), and it will constitute the disruptive return of the excluded from within the very logic of the heterosexual symbolic. . . .

NOTES

1. See Sherry Ortner, "Is Female to Male as Nature is to Culture?", in *Woman, Culture, and Society*, Michele Rosaldo and Louise Lamphere (Stanford: Stanford University Press, 1974) pp. 67–88.

2. For different but related approaches to this problematic of exclusion, abjection, and the creation of "the human," see Julia Kristeva, *Powers of Horror: An Essay on Abjection*, tr. Leon Roudiez (New York: Columbia University Press, 1982); John Fletcher and Andrew Benjamin, eds., *Abjection, Melancholia and Love: The Work of Julia Kristeva* (New York and London: Routledge, 1990); Jean-François Lyotard, *The Inhuman Reflections on Time*, tr. Geoffrey Bennington and Rachel Bowlby (Stanford: Stanford University Press, 1991).

3. Although Foucault distinguishes between juridical and productive models of power in *The History of Sexuality, Volume One*, tr. Robert Hurley (New York: Vintage, 1978), I have argued that the two models presuppose each other. The production of a subject—its subjection (*assujetissement*)—is one means of its regulation. See my "Sexual Inversions," in Domna Stanton, ed., *Discourses of Sexuality* (Ann Arbor: University of Michigan Press, 1992), pp. 344–361.

4. It is not simply a matter of construing performativity as a repetition of acts, as if "acts" remain intact and self-identical as they are repeated in time, and where "time" is understood as external to the "acts" themselves. On the contrary, an act is itself a repetition, a sedimentation, and congealment of the past which is precisely foreclosed in its act-like status. In this sense an "act" is always a provisional failure of memory. In what follows, I make use of the Lacanian notion that every act is to be construed as a repetition, the repetition of what cannot be recollected, of the irrecoverable, and is thus the haunting spectre of the subject's deconstitution. The Derridean notion of iterability, formulated in response to the theorization of speech acts by John Searle and J. L. Austin, also implies that every act is itself a recitation, the citing of a prior chain of acts which are implied in a present act and which perpetually drain any "present" act of its presentness.

5. The notion of temporality ought not to be construed as a simple succession of distinct "moments," all of which are equally distant from one another. Such a spatialized mapping of time substitutes a certain mathematical model for the kind of duration which resists such spatializing metaphors. Efforts to describe or name this temporal span tend to engage spatial mapping, as philosophers from Bergson through Heidegger have argued. Hence, it is important to underscore the effect of *sedimentation* that the temporality of construction implies. Here what are called "moments" are not distinct and equivalent units of time, for the "past" will be the accumulation and congealing of such "moments" to the point of their indistinguishability. But it will also consist of that which is refused from construction, the domains of the repressed, forgotten, and the irrecoverably foreclosed. That which is not included—exteriorized by boundary—as a phenomenal constituent of the sedimented effect called "construction" will be as crucial to its definition as that which is included; this exteriority is not distinguishable as a "moment." Indeed, the notion of the "moment" may well be nothing other than a retrospective fantasy of mathematical mastery imposed upon the interrupted durations of the past.

To argue that construction is fundamentally a matter of iteration is to make the temporal modality of "construction" into a priority. To the extent that such a theory requires a spatialization of time through the postulation of discrete and bounded moments, this temporal account of construction presupposes a spatialization of temporality itself, what one might, following Heidegger, understand as the reduction of temporality to time.

The Foucaultian emphasis on *convergent* relations of power (which might in a tentative way be contrasted with the Derridean emphasis on iterability) implies a mapping of power relations that in the course of a genealogical process form a constructed effect. The notion of convergence presupposes both motion and space; as a result, it appears to elude the paradox noted above in which the very account of temporality requires the spatialization of the "moment." On the other hand, Foucault's account of convergence does not fully theorize what is at work in the "movement" by which power and discourse are said to converge. In a sense, the "mapping" of power does not fully theorize temporality.

Significantly, the Derridean analysis of iterability is to be distinguished from simple repetition in which the distances between temporal "moments" are treated as uniform in their spatial extension. The "betweenness" that differentiates "moments" of time is not one that can, within Derridean terms, be spatialized or bounded as an identifiable object. It is the monthematizable différance which erodes and contests any and all claims to discrete identity, including the discrete identity of the "moment." What differentiates moments is not a spatially extended duration, for if it were, it would also count as a "moment," and so fail to account for what falls between moments. This "entre," that which is at once "between" and "outside," is something like non-thematizable space and non-thematizable time as they converge.

Foucault's language of construction includes terms like "augmentation," "proliferation," and "convergence," all of which presume a temporal domain not explicitly theorized. Part of the problem here is that whereas Foucault appears to want his account of genealogical effects to be historically specific, he would favor an account of genealogy over a philosophical account of temporality: In "The Subject and Power" (Hubert Dreyfus and Paul Rabinow, eds., *Michel Foucault: Beyond Structuralism and Hermeneutics* [Chicago: Northwestern University Press, 1983]), Foucault refers to "the diversity of . . . logical sequence" that characterizes power relations. He would doubtless reject the apparent linearity implied by models of iterability which link them with the linearity of older models of historical sequence. And yet, we do not receive a specification of "sequence": Is it the very notion of "sequence" that varies historically, or are there configurations of sequence that vary, with sequence itself remaining invariant? The specific social formation and figuration of temporality is in some ways unattended by both positions. Here one might consult the work of Pierre Bourdieu to understand the temporality of social construction.

19

Believing Is Seeing: Biology as Ideology

Judith Lorber

Until the eighteenth century, Western philosophers and scientists thought that there was one sex and that women's internal genitalia were the inverse of men's external genitalia: the womb and vagina were the penis and scrotum turned inside out (Laqueur 1990). . . .

In actuality, the basic bodily material *is* the same for females and males, and except for procreative hormones and organs, female and male human beings have similar bodies (Naftolin and Butz 1981). Furthermore, as has been known since the middle of the nineteenth century, male and female genitalia develop from the same fetal tissue, and so infants can be born with ambiguous genitalia (Money and Ehrhardt 1972). When they are, biology is used quite arbitrarily in sex assignment. Suzanne Kessler (1990) interviewed six medical specialists in pediatric intersexuality and found that whether an infant with XY chromosomes and anomalous genitalia was categorized as a boy or girl depended on the size of the penis—if a penis was very small, the child was categorized as a girl, and sex-change surgery was used to make an artificial vagina. In the late nineteenth century, the presence or absence of ovaries was the determining criterion of gender assignment for hermaphrodites because a woman who could not procreate was not a complete woman (Kessler 1990, 20).

Yet in Western societies, we see two discrete sexes and two distinguishable genders because our society is built on two classes of people, "women" and "men." Once the gender category is given, the attributes of the person are also gendered: Whatever a "woman" is has to be "female"; whatever a "man" is has to be "male." Analyzing the social processes that construct the categories we call "female and male,"

From "Believing is Seeing" by Judith Lorber in *Gender & Society* (1993): 568–81. Copyright © 1993 by Judith Lorber. Reprinted by permission of Sage Publications, Inc.

"women and men," and "homosexual and heterosexual" uncovers the ideology and power differentials congealed in these categories (Foucault 1978). This article will use two familiar areas of social life—sports and technological competence—to show how myriad physiological differences are transformed into similar-appearing, gendered social bodies. My perspective goes beyond accepted feminist views that gender is a cultural overlay that modifies physiological sex differences. That perspective assumes either that there are two fairly similar sexes distorted by social practices into two genders with purposefully different characteristics or that there are two sexes whose essential differences are rendered unequal by social practices. I am arguing that bodies differ in many ways physiologically, but they are completely transformed by social practices to fit into the salient categories of a society, the most pervasive of which are "female" and "male" and "women" and "men."

Neither sex nor gender are pure categories. Combinations of incongruous genes, genitalia, and hormonal input are ignored in sex categorization, just as combinations of incongruous physiology, identity, sexuality, appearance, and behavior are ignored in the social construction of gender statuses. Menstruation, lactation, and gestation do not demarcate women from men. Only some women are pregnant and then only some of the time; some women do not have a uterus or ovaries. Some women have stopped menstruating temporarily, others have reached menopause, and some have had hysterectomies. Some women breastfeed some of the time, but some men lactate (Jaggar 1983, 165fn). Menstruation, lactation, and gestation are individual experiences of womanhood (Levesque-Lopman 1988), but not determinants of the social category "woman," or even "female." Similarly, "men are not always sperm-producers, and in fact, not all sperm producers are men. A male-to-female transsexual, prior to surgery, can be socially a woman, though still potentially (or actually) capable of spermatogenesis" (Kessler and McKenna [1978] 1985, 2). . . .

In the Olympics, in cases of chromosomal ambiguity, women must undergo "a battery of gynecological and physical exams to see if she is 'female enough' to compete. Men are not tested" (Carlson 1991, 26). The purpose is not to categorize women and men accurately, but to make sure men don't enter women's competitions, where, it is felt, they will have the advantage of size and strength. This practice sounds fair only because it is assumed that all men are similar in size and strength and different from all women. Yet in Olympic boxing and wrestling matches, men are matched within weight classes. Some women might similarly successfully compete with some men in many sports. Women did not run in marathons until about twenty years ago. In twenty years of marathon competition, women have reduced their finish times by more than one-and-one-half hours; they are expected to run as fast as men in that race by 1998 and might catch up with men's running times in races of other lengths within the next 50 years because they are increasing their fastest speeds more rapidly than are men (Fausto-Sterling 1985, 213–18). . . .

WHAT SPORTS ILLUSTRATE

In professional and collegiate sports, physiological differences are invoked to justify women's secondary status, despite the clear evidence that gender status overrides physiological capabilities. Assumptions about women's physiology have influenced rules of competition; subsequent sports performances then validate how women and men are treated in sports competitions.

Gymnastic equipment is geared to slim, wiry, prepubescent girls and not to mature women; conversely, men's gymnastic equipment is tailored for muscular, mature men, not slim, wiry prepubescent boys. Boys could compete with girls, but are not allowed to; women gymnasts are left out entirely. Girl gymnasts are just that—little girls who will be disqualified as soon as they grow up (Vecsey 1990). Men gymnasts have men's status. In women's basketball, the size of the ball and rules for handling the ball change the style of play to "a slower, less intense, and less exciting modification of the 'regular' or men's game" (Watson 1987, 441). In the 1992 Winter Olympics, men figure skaters were required to complete three triple jumps in their required program; women figure skaters were forbidden to do more than *one*. These rules penalized artistic men skaters and athletic women skaters (Janofsky 1992). For the most part, Western sports are built on physically trained men's bodies. . . .

Organized sports are big businesses and, thus, who has access and at which level is a distributive or equity issue. The overall status of women and men athletes is an economic, political, and ideological issue that has less to do with individual physiological capabilities than with their cultural and social meaning and who defines and profits from them (Messner and Sabo 1990; Slatton and Birrell 1984). Twenty years after the passage of Title IX of the U.S. Civil Rights Act, which forbade gender inequality in any school receiving federal funds, the *goal* for collegiate sports in the next five years is 60 percent men, 40 percent women in sports participation, scholarships, and funding (Moran 1992). . . .

Assumptions about men's and women's bodies and their capacities are crafted in ways that make unequal access and distribution of rewards acceptable (Hudson 1978; Messner 1988). Media images of modern men athletes glorify their strength and power, even their violence (Hargreaves 1986). Media images of modern women athletes tend to focus on feminine beauty and grace (so they are not really athletes) or on their thin, small, wiry androgynous bodies (so they are not really women). In coverage of the Olympics,

> loving and detailed attention is paid to pixie-like gymnasts; special and extended coverage is given to graceful and dazzling figure skaters; the camera painstakingly records the fluid movements of swimmers and divers. And then, in a blinding flash of fragmented images, viewers see a few minutes of volleyball, basketball, speed skating, track and field, and alpine skiing, as television gives its nod to the mere existence of these events. (Boutilier and SanGiovanni 1983, 190).

Extraordinary feats by women athletes who were presented as mature adults might force sports organizers and audiences to rethink their stereotypes of women's capabilities, the way elves, mermaids, and ice queens do not. Sports, therefore, construct men's bodies to be powerful; women's bodies to be sexual. As Connell says,

> The meanings in the bodily sense of masculinity concern, above all else, the superiority of men to women, and the exaltation of hegemonic masculinity over other groups of men which is essential for the domination of women. (1987, 85)

. . . Given the association of sports with masculinity in the United States, women athletes have to manage a contradictory status. One study of women college basketball players found that although they "did athlete" on the court—"pushing, shoving, fouling, hard running, fast breaks, defense, obscenities and sweat" (Watson 1987, 441), they "did woman" off the court, using the locker room as their staging area: While it typically took fifteen minutes to prepare for the game, it took approximately fifteen minutes after the game to shower and remove the sweat of an athlete, *and* it took another thirty minutes to dress, apply make-up and style hair. It did not seem to matter whether the players were going out into the public or getting on a van for a long ride home. Average dressing time and rituals did not change. (Watson 1987, 443) . . .

. . . Such a redefinition of women's physicality affirms the ideological subtext of sports that physical strength is men's prerogative and justifies men's physical and sexual domination of women (Hargreaves 1986; Messner 1992, 164–72; Olson 1990; Theberge 1987; Willis 1982). . . .

DIRTY LITTLE SECRETS

As sports construct gendered bodies, technology constructs gendered skills. Meta-analyses of studies of gender differences in spatial and mathematical ability have found that men have a large advantage in ability to mentally rotate an image, a moderate advantage in a visual perception of horizontality and verticality and in mathematical performance, and a small advantage in ability to pick a figure out of a field (Hyde 1990). It could be argued that these advantages explain why, within the short space of time that computers have become ubiquitous in offices, schools, and homes, work on them and with them has been gendered: Men create, program, and market computers, make war and produce science and art with them; women microwire them in computer factories and enter data in computerized offices; boys play games, socialize, and commit crimes with computers; girls are rarely seen in computer clubs, camps, and classrooms. But women were hired as computer programmers in the 1940s because

> the work seemed to resemble simple clerical tasks. In fact, however, programming demanded complex skills in abstract logic, mathematics, electrical circuitry, and machin-

ery, all of which . . . women used to perform in their work. Once programming was recognized as "intellectually demanding," it became attractive to men. (Donato 1990, 170)

A woman mathematician and pioneer in data processing, Grace M. Hopper, was famous for her work on programming language (Perry and Greber 1990, 86). By the 1960s, programming was split into more and less skilled specialties, and the entry of women into the computer field in the 1970s and 1980s was confined to the lower-paid specialties. At each stage, employers invoked women's and men's purportedly natural capabilities for the jobs for which they were hired (Cockburn 1983, 1985; Donato 1990; Hartmann 1987; Hartmann, Kraut, and Tilly 1986; Kramer and Lehman 1990; Wright et al. 1987; Zimmerman 1983).

It is the taken-for-grantedness of such everyday gendered behavior that gives credence to the belief that the widespread differences in what women and men do must come from biology. To take one ordinarily unremarked scenario: In modern societies, if a man and woman who are a couple are in a car together, he is much more likely to take the wheel than she is, even if she is the more competent driver. Molly Haskell calls this taken-for-granted phenomenon "the dirty little secret of marriage: the husband-lousy-driver syndrome" (1989, 26). Men drive cars whether they are good drivers or not because men and machines are a "natural" combination (Scharff 1991). But the ability to drive gives one mobility; it is a form of social power. . . .

. . . I am not saying that physical differences between male and female bodies don't exist, but that these differences are socially meaningless until social practices transform them into social facts. West Point Military Academy's curriculum is designed to produce leaders, and physical competence is used as a significant measure of leadership ability (Yoder 1989). When women were accepted as West Point cadets, it became clear that the tests of physical competence, such as rapidly scaling an eight-foot wall, had been constructed for male physiques—pulling oneself up and over using upper-body strength. Rather than devise tests of physical competence for women, West Point provided boosters that mostly women used—but that lost them test points—in the case of the wall, a platform. Finally, the women themselves figured out how to use their bodies successfully. Janice Yoder describes this situation:

> I was observing this obstacle one day, when a woman approached the wall in the old prescribed way, got her fingertips grip, and did an unusual thing: she walked her dangling legs up the wall until she was in a position where both her hands and feet were atop the wall. She then simply pulled up her sagging bottom and went over. She solved the problem by capitalizing on one of women's physical assets: lower-body strength. (1989, 530)

In short, if West Point is going to measure leadership capability by physical strength, women's pelvises will do just as well as men's shoulders. . . .

THE PARADOX OF HUMAN NATURE

Gendered people do not emerge from physiology or hormones but from the exigencies of the social order, mostly from the need for a reliable division of the work of food production and the social (not physical) reproduction of new members. The moral imperatives of religion and cultural representations reinforce the boundary lines among genders and ensure that what is demanded, what is permitted, and what is tabooed for the people in each gender is well-known and followed by most. Political power, control of scarce resources, and, if necessary, violence uphold the gendered social order in the face of resistance and rebellion. Most people, however, voluntarily go along with their society's prescriptions for those of their gender status because the norms and expectations get built into their sense of worth and identity as a certain kind of human being and because they believe their society's way is the natural way. These beliefs emerge from the imagery that pervades the way we think, the way we see and hear and speak, the way we fantasize, and the way we feel. There is no core or bedrock human nature below these endlessly looping processes of the social production of sex and gender, self and other, identity and psyche, each of which is a "complex cultural construction" (Butler 1990, 36). The paradox of "human nature" is that it is *always* a manifestation of cultural meanings, social relationships, and power politics—"not biology, but culture, becomes destiny" (Butler 1990, 8).

. . . When we rely only on the conventional categories of sex and gender, we end up finding what we looked for—we see what we believe, whether it is that "females" and "males" are essentially different or that "women" and "men" are essentially the same.

REFERENCES

Birrell, Susan J., and Sheryl L. Cole. 1990. Double fault: Renée Richards and the construction and naturalization of difference. *Sociology of Sport Journal* 7:1–21.

Boutilier, Mary A., and Lucinda SanGiovanni. 1983. *The sporting woman.* Champaign, IL: Human Kinetics.

Butler, Judith. 1990. *Gender trouble: Feminism and the subversion of identity.* New York and London: Routledge & Kegan Paul.

Carlson, Alison. 1991. When is a woman not a woman? *Women's Sport and Fitness* March:24–29.

Cockburn, Cynthia. 1983. *Brothers: Male dominance and technological change.* London: Pluto.

———. 1985. *Machinery of dominance: Women, men and technical know-how.* London: Pluto.

Connell, R. W. 1987. *Gender and power.* Stanford, CA: Stanford University Press.

Donato, Katharine M. 1990. Programming for change? The growing demand for women systems analysts. In *Job queues, gender queues: Explaining women's inroads into male occupations*, written and edited by Barbara F. Reskin and Patricia A. Roos. Philadelphia: Temple University Press.

Fausto-Sterling, Anne. 1985. *Myths of gender: Biological theories about women and men.* New York: Basic Books.

Foucault, Michel. 1978. *The history of sexuality: An introduction.* Translated by Robert Hurley. New York: Pantheon.

Hargreaves, Jennifer A., ed. 1982. *Sport, culture, and ideology.* London: Routledge & Kegan Paul.

—————. 1986. Where's the virtue? Where's the grace? A discussion of the social production of gender relations in and through sport. *Theory, Culture, and Society* 3:109–21.

Hartmann, Heidi I., ed. 1987. *Computer chips and paper clips: Technology and women's employment.* Vol. 2. Washington, DC: National Academy Press.

Hartmann, Heidi I., Robert E. Kraut, and Louise A. Tilly, eds. 1986. *Computer chips and paper clips: Technology and women's employment.* Vol. 1. Washington, DC: National Academy Press.

Haskell, Molly. 1989. Hers: He drives me crazy. *New York Times Magazine,* 24 September, 26, 28.

Hudson, Jackie. 1978. Physical parameters used for female exclusion from law enforcement and athletics. In *Women and sport: From myth to reality,* edited by Carole A. Oglesby. Philadelphia: Lea and Febiger.

Hyde, Janet Shibley. 1990. Meta-analysis and the psychology of gender differences. *Signs: Journal of Women in Culture and Society* 16:55–73.

Jaggar, Alison M. 1983. *Feminist politics and human nature.* Totowa, NJ: Rowman & Allanheld.

Janofsky, Michael. 1992. Yamaguchi has the delicate and golden touch. *New York Times,* 22 February.

Kessler, Suzanne J. 1990. The medical construction of gender: Case management of intersexed infants. *Signs: Journal of Women in Culture and Society* 16:3–26.

Kessler, Suzanne J., and Wendy McKenna. [1978] 1985. *Gender: An ethnomethodological approach.* Chicago: University of Chicago Press.

Kolata, Gina. 1992. Track federation urges end to gene test for femaleness. *New York Times,* 12 February.

Kramer, Pamela E., and Sheila Lehman. 1990. Mismeasuring women: A critique of research on computer ability and avoidance. *Signs: Journal of Women in Culture and Society* 16:158–72.

Laqueur, Thomas. 1990. *Making sex: Body and gender from the Greeks to Freud.* Cambridge, MA: Harvard University Press.

Levesque-Lopman, Louise. 1988. *Claiming reality: Phenomenology and women's experience.* Totowa, NJ: Rowman & Littlefield.

Messner, Michael A. 1988. Sports and male domination: The female athlete as contested ideological terrain. *Sociology of Sport Journal* 5:197–211.

—————. 1992. *Power at play: Sports and the problem of masculinity.* Boston: Beacon Press.

Messner, Michael A., Margaret Carlisle Duncan, and Kerry Jensen. 1993. Separating the men from the girls: The gendered language of televised sports. *Gender & Society* 7:121–37.

Messner, Michael A., and Donald F. Sabo, eds. 1990. *Sport, men, and the gender order: Critical feminist perspectives.* Champaign, IL: Human Kinetics.

Money, John, and Anke A. Ehrhardt. 1972. *Man & woman, boy & girl.* Baltimore, MD: Johns Hopkins University Press.

Moran, Malcolm. 1992. Title IX: A 20-year search for equity. *New York Times* Sports Section, 21, 22, 23 June.

Naftolin, F., and E. Butz, eds. 1981. Sexual dimorphism. *Science* 211:1263–1324.

Olson, Wendy. 1990. Beyond Title IX: Toward an agenda for women and sports in the 1990s. *Yale Journal of Law and Feminism* 3:105–51.

Perry, Ruth, and Lisa Greber. 1990. Women and computers: An introduction. *Signs: Journal of Women in Culture and Society* 16:74–101.

Richards, Renée, with Jack Ames. 1983. *Second serve.* New York: Stein and Day.

Scharff, Virginia. 1991. *Taking the wheel: Women and the coming of the motor age.* New York: Free Press.

Slatton, Bonnie, and Susan Birrell. 1984. The politics of women's sport. *Arena Review* 8.

Theberge, Nancy. 1987. Sport and women's empowerment. *Women's Studies International Forum* 10:387–93.

Vecsey, George. 1990. Cathy Rigby, unlike Peter, did grow up. *New York Times* Sports Section, 19 December.

Watson, Tracey. 1987. Women athletes and athletic women: The dilemmas and contradictions of managing incongruent identities. *Sociological Inquiry* 57:431–46.

Willis, Paul. 1982. Women in sport in ideology. In *Sport, culture, and ideology,* edited by Jennifer A. Hargreaves. London: Routledge & Kegan Paul.

Wright, Barbara Drygulski et al., eds. 1987. *Women, work, and technology: Transformations.* Ann Arbor: University of Michigan Press.

Yoder, Janice D. 1989. Women at West Point: Lessons for token women in male-dominated occupations. In *Women: A feminist perspective,* edited by Jo Freeman, 4th ed. Palo Alto, CA: Mayfield.

Zimmerman, Jan, ed. 1983. *The technological woman: Interfacing with tomorrow.* New York: Praeger.

20

Towards Safer Societies: Punishment, Masculinities and Violence against Women

Laureen Snider

. . . Economic 'cushions' are under attack and income inequalities are increasing as nation states reduce deficits by eliminating social services, health care, minimum wages, worker protection laws and anything else that adds to the (corporate) cost of production. Removing social safety nets and public services is presented as necessary to allow developed countries (or the national and multinational corporations they shelter) to compete in cut-throat global markets. When capital, investment and jobs can easily be shifted from Birmingham to Bangladesh, they will go wherever the potential for short-term profits is highest, or so we are told. Currency speculators have become key players in this game of capital roulette. George Soros, for example, ex-Hungarian financier, acts as a 'global reality cop, pouncing on any government that overvalues or undervalues its currency' (Friedman 1995: A17). To appease investment-bankers and avert potentially disastrous runs on their currency, nation states have systematically begun campaigns to make their citizens less secure and more vulnerable, both psychologically and economically. Developed countries have entered a race to see who can create the most insecure, unhealthy and violence-prone population. The United States is ahead at the moment—but it had a head start, with fewer universal social programmes to dismantle—and Canada, New Zealand and the United Kingdom are catching up fast. . . . Public services are costly and inefficient; grants to poor people or provinces erode economic competitiveness and encourage dependence, according to right-wing think-tanks and politicians. But they also allow people to nourish their roots and remain in regions where they have traditions and histories, relatives and support networks. 'Subsidies' are important in creating less desperate people.

Psychological 'cushions', in the form of identification with values outside mass culture, are also under attack.[1] As many have pointed out, mass culture operates through consumerism, and consumerism works by creating and/or reinforcing personal and social insecurity. People with secure identities, independent of 'lifestyle', are harder for advertisers to manipulate, cannot be trusted to buy on cue, may fail to grasp that they are inadequate, inferior and socially irresponsible because they do not own the latest model cars, VCRs and Nikes. Consumerism has to create hierarchies and reinforce individual identities because if I have the fastest car or most fashionable clothes, you obviously do not. This is not a capitalist conspiracy, it is a natural correspondence of interests between privately owned media and capital. Like most ideologies, that of consumerism has a core of truth—many products do save labour, increase comfort levels and make life more pleasant. Add to this the socially created truths of consumerism, that not possessing certain 'things' leads other social actors to cast aspersions on your trustworthiness, thrift or credentials as a human being, and you have a very persuasive set of beliefs. But societies made up of people whose identities are solely dependent on purchased commodities are very vulnerable to capital's periodic cycles of contraction and expansion. Combining greater dependence with fewer social and economic supports leads inevitably to greater desperation, and some of this will emerge as increased interpersonal violence.

The content of mass culture is another factor linking desperation to violence. Without exploring the byzantine and endless debates over whether violent videos or television programmes directly incite aggressive acts or produce desensitization, the omnipresence of these messages—the fact that a high percentage of people's leisure time, daily routines and interactions with others revolve around violent events (be they fictional, news events or sports)—indicates that the messages have, at minimum, the power to monopolize human attention. Of course the actual effects of violent media will vary by individual, class, gender, values and role in the community. The food we consume also has different effects depending on body type, mood, age, gender, weight and level of nourishment. But if 'you are what you eat', you are even more totally what you direct your attention to, what you think about, and value. And modern cultural diets promote insensitization, the quick 30-minute fix, lists of winners and losers, the unambiguous black and white solution. Compromise means selling out, complexity is denied and violence, when used by 'people like us', is a good thing, the only way to surmount omnipresent forces of evil and incompetence.

When all this is added up—polarized politics, an increased focus on individualism at the expense of community, greater heterogeneity, decreased equality and the loss of older identities to mass consumerism—it appears to be a recipe for ever greater violence, deprivation, desperation and pain. It is hard to figure out modes of resistance, let alone transformation. . . .

BUILDING LESS VIOLENT COMMUNITIES AND FAMILIES

The focus here is on ways of building less violent families. While the difficulty of promoting micro and middle-level patterns at odds with macro-level forces cannot be underestimated, it is essential to examine the context of subordination and understand the ways in which domination and violence are rooted inside the individual, in the patterns of daily life (Giddens 1981; Smart 1992; Foucault 1982). Thus, even while macro-level institutions are reinforcing one set of social relations, other social relations are undermining class and patriarchy, resisting and refusing hegemonic ways of thinking and acting. Macro-level transformation cannot be effective 'if the agents upon whom [transformative politics] depends continue to be governed and defined by the very social contexts they are trying to transform' (Winter 1992; 812). The objective, then, is to examine how practices can be changed to foster subjectivities and identities which reject violent, dominator/dominated roles.

On a purely mechanistic level, attention must be paid to techniques and patterns of socialization. Child-rearing patterns based on rewards or the withdrawal of approval are more effective (that is, long-lasting and efficient) than those based on physical punishment. . . . Non-violent child-rearing techniques, then, produce better socialized individuals, but less violent people and families will result *only* if violent behaviours are targeted as guilt-producing behaviours, and prohibitions against violence are conveyed to miscreants by role models and significant others—teachers, employers, youth leaders and the like.

However, there is profound cultural resistance to wholesale and unqualified discouragement of individual aggression, particularly in the rearing of sons. Mothers as well as fathers, terrified of boys becoming 'wimps,' send contradictory messages about the acceptability of bullying and aggression. . . . To understand why some boys grow up embracing violent acts and identities, others eschew them, and the majority flounder in the middle, one must examine the relationship between micro-level patterns of control and systems of patriarchy. Literature on domestic assault tells us that many of the violent men who have been studied are frustrated individuals who see women as easy, weak and available targets. They are often jealous and insecure, they believe in traditional sex roles and deny, to themselves and others, that their assaults have serious effects on the victimized. Frequently they witnessed or experienced physical or sexual abuse as children. Such men tend to see women as objects whose duty is to make their men's lives easier, a duty women frequently fail to fulfil being 'by nature' unreliable, unfaithful, lazy, etc. Violence for them is instrumental as well as expressive, a method of resolving conflict, establishing dominance, and claiming male entitlement (Tifft and Markham 1991; Dobash and Dobash 1992, 1975; Dekeseredy and Hinch 1991; Ptacek 1988*a, b*; Stets 1988; Buchwald *et al.* 1993).

. . . Men construct masculinities in the same way that all identities are built, by choosing among the options they see as available and satisfying for 'people like them', people who share their class, race, neighbourhood, family and society as well as gender. In heterogeneous western societies a wide range of masculinities is available, offering much choice—and much confusion. However, the patriarchal man—silent, equipped with the latest $225 Reeboks, emotionally constipated and physically strong—is still the ideal, especially in mass culture. Hegemonic masculinities on this model are heavily promoted in dominant media and sport, and constitute the identities most visible, accessible and appealing, particularly to boys lacking alternative male role models. Peer groups of adolescent males, alienated from mainstream authority, use sport, rap and mass culture extensively to develop ideas of what it means to be a man in this class, race, region, culture and time. Frequently this means borrowing the most violent and misogynous components of mainstream identities on offer. The price of questioning hegemonic masculinities can be high, producing feelings of uncertainty about one's own masculinity, rejection by peers, or even physical attacks. Given dominant value-systems that glorify power as an end in itself, and the undeniable fact that force is useful in getting one's way (for it offers immediate gratification without the need to grovel, negotiate or compromise and, in sexual matters, without vulnerability or risk of rejection), it can be hard for those who buy in to understand why anyone would reject the entitlement offered by hegemonic masculinities. When you can partake of an identity that allows you, by the simple fact of gender, to see yourself as stronger and smarter than half the world, entitled by birthright to deference and power if not wealth, why would you question such beliefs? Dissident males, who by their very existence show that these identities are cultural creations supporting privilege rather than biosocial necessities, threaten the entire structure.

Class and ethnic differences must be figured into this equation because they mediate the appeal of certain masculinities. Poor black or hispanic men in marginalized underclasses, for example, may find identities based on possession of turf or defence of honour appealing, or those that celebrate individualistic and collective force as badges of status, perhaps because a block of contested cityscape, a muscular body and a gun are among the few resources they can claim in such environments (Polk 1994). For men in urban ghettos to claim identities where self-esteem or peer status depends on the successful attainment of professional credentials or higher degrees (as many reformers insist they should) would be psychological and cultural suicide. The economic and educational resources necessary to play this game are simply not available to the vast majority, however intelligent and industrious. The success of the handful who might make it would come at the psycho-social expense of the many who would not.

White working-class American men (and a small percentage of black men) have seen their relatively privileged positions, good wages and strong unions, disappear in recent decades. Some of them have turned to militia-style movements celebrating turf and force (the equivalent of ghetto youth identities but more rural and collective), and/or to nationalistic identities based on citizenship, claiming entitlement as citizens of the richest, best, most powerful nation in the world. Working-class European men, typically less marginalized than urban underclasses in the United States, and better protected from the vagaries of the global marketplace due to the psychological and economic cushions instituted in such states in the post-war period, have often used sport, particularly football (soccer to North Americans), to under-pin and reinforce concepts of manhood that contain notions of fair play in addi-tion to celebrating toughness, physicality and the ability to take life's reverses stoically—'like a man' (Williams and Taylor 1994).

For middle-class North American white men, born into settings where masculini-ties can be centered in occupational success and higher education, dominant mas-culinities show wide generational splits. Adolescent middle-class masculinity is of-ten premised on physical prowess, strength and sport (all linked to sexual success as a source of status), but with maturity job performance becomes paramount. In the merciless literally accurate language of the metaphor, occupational success 'separates the men from the boys'. Although phenomena such as the jobless recovery now threaten the economic prospects of the adult middle-class man, mainstream cultural goals of wealth, achievement and success through upward mobility were realistic goals for many decades. There was therefore less need, *as a class*, to cling to older mascu-linities stressing physical toughness, patriarchal notions based on the power of the male body. Men in this class were not so much learning to labour as learning to rule. This does not mean that middle or upper-class masculinities reject misogyny or vio-lence on either the personal or professional level (Godenzi 1994); the difference is often one of packaging more than substance. Levi (1994) points out that the City (the financial centre of London) is personalized by corporate executives and traders as a bitch goddess, a fickle female promising much but delivering little. Phrases such as 'the City is a place for men, not for boys' (Levi 1994; 241) (and, therefore, not for women at all) suggest a subculture where exchange markets are exclusive boys' clubs, and trading and deals are dominance games, competitions for personal as well as occupational power. The self images of urban currency traders reek of machismo— the cowboy mystique, the swaggering recklessness of the quintessential '25-year-olds in red suspenders', the 'bad boy' heroes such as Nick Leeson, the 28-year-old bond trader who single-handedly brought down Barings Bank, the power of a George Soros, who 'single-handedly broke the British pound' (Friedman 1995: A17). Such warrior power rivals that of earlier male heroes on the battlefields of Waterloo or the Plains of Abraham. Such identities celebrate dominance and patriarchy, but claims are based more on cerebral than physical power. This is hegemonic mascu-linity globalized. . . .

On the level of praxis and policy, any prescription for changing dominant mas-culinities and identities must be highly speculative: we simply do not understand the roots of these identities, their relation to biology, psychology, the social relations of capitalism or social practice. But the fact that traditional masculine identities are everywhere under attack is a source of hope for those who seek ameliorative social

change. It should, it *must* be possible to find ways of being manly that are not mi-
sogynous and do not require the repression of every human emotion except anger.
It should not be necessary to denigrate male sexuality or insist that it be denied to
address misogyny or assault, but it is essential to differentiate the sex drive from the
need to dominate. To understand the limits as well as the potential for change it is
useful to examine the decline and fall of traditional male spheres of action, male 'imperatives' to impregnate, provision and defend females and family groups (Gilmore
1990). These three have been central to male roles, male self-esteem and male identities, historically and cross-culturally, for thousands of years. There is no reason to
believe they are epiphenomena, mere social constructions that can be wiped out by
laws or political tinkering. Indeed it is more plausible to see the blockage and denial of 'maleness' symbolized by the denigration of these roles as fueling the male
rage that animates the late twentieth century. Right-wing, racist, militia-style social
movements and the reactionary, punishment-oriented political regimes which are
their psychological equivalents (both of which, surveys tell us, are supported by men
more than by women), are symptomatic. Male movements such as Promise Keepers and the Million Man March, although different from each other, represent other
attempts, by white and black men respectively, to struggle with these issues and reclaim male territory—in this case by redefining the responsibilities, distinctiveness
and privileges that defined masculinity in the past.

In less than one generation male prerogatives to impregnate, provide and defend
have been radically altered. Take the responsibility to provide for one's family: as we
have seen, technologies making many working-class jobs obsolete combined with
right-wing policies to accommodate capital's quest for higher profit margins have
destroyed union solidarity, wages and benefits, and abolished thousands of jobs. Since
few women occupied the well-paid unionized jobs in heavy industry or manufacturing that were the primary targets of this wave of downsizing, working-class men
were the main losers. In the 1990s downsizing spread up the class ladder; this time
men and women in middle management and public sectors took the hit. The ability to provide for oneself, let alone one's mates and children, was radically altered.
Government programmes, the economic cushions, softened the blow to an extent
in some European countries, but these are temporary measures at best. To make
matters worse, women sometimes found it easier to secure new jobs—they are typically better educated, more willing to accept low wage positions and are sometimes
viewed by employers as more reliable and less aggressive (positive traits in the job
market of the 1990s for many Mcjobs). In the middle classes, the success of feminism in securing equal opportunity, independence and promotion for women in
formerly male domains, while relieving economic stress for men lucky enough to
have partners with good jobs, added new stress to the pain of redundance and new
fuel to the fires of backlash (Faludi 1991).[2] In North America, women's wages rose
relative to men's as various equity programmes made hiring women (and some
minorities) beneficial, and their relative scarcity in many traditionally male professions such as science or engineering increased their market value. Thus in the 1990s,

just when large numbers of middle-class white men began experiencing intense marginalization for the first time, middle-class women began making real, though often exaggerated, gains.

The imperative to impregnate has become less necessary as well. Advances in technology threaten to make males redundant, with frozen sperm, artificial insemination and test-tube babies replacing humans. Patriarchy's historical monopoly over reproduction and hence over women has been challenged, and contraceptive pills, IUDs and legalized abortion have allowed many women, in the developed world at least, to control when, how and with whom they will reproduce. Backlash and resistance, as in laws requiring the consent of a partner or parent to procure an abortion, or 'voluntary chastity' movements, have been largely unsuccessful. The arrival of AIDS has made heterosexual promiscuity, always the prerogative of men more than women, literally life-threatening. Meanwhile overpopulation has rendered patriarchal structures that value men for the number of (male) offspring they can sire increasingly unfashionable, particularly in first-world countries where each new person consumes 17 times his or her share of the world's resources.

The need to defend oneself or one's mate against natural enemies (fire, flood and wild animals) has largely disappeared as well, particularly in developed and urbanized countries. But the desire for enemies is obvious: invented villains permeate popular culture, and heroes are pressed into service to ward off everything from godless communists, aliens and marauding rapists to killer hurricanes and runaway submarines. Unfortunately fulfilling the male imperative to defend in non-fictive realities runs up against state monopolies over the control of arms and the exercise of interpersonal violence. Thus we see the almost religious significance attached by militia movements to the 'right' to bear arms, or the more recent but equally intense reaction to the banning of handguns larger than .22 calibre following the Dunblane massacre in Britain (*Guardian Weekly*, 'Guns Go Abroad', 8 December 1996: 24). Public restrictions on private arsenals are essential, but they also benefit women as a group more than men as a group, since women are the more fearful and vulnerable sex. State social control deprives men of the right and obligation to display their (generally) superior physical strength and greater aggressive capacity, and another component of male identity disappears.

So what kind of remedies should progressive movements seek? No one would deny that many of these developments are positive. For people in urban industrialized societies to use violence to settle disputes unleashes cycles of escalating aggression and punishment, as life in many American cities today illustrates, where the wealthy barricade themselves inside armed enclosures and the poor kill each other off in the streets (or die in overheated tenements, too frightened to go outside or even open their windows, as in Chicago's 1995 heat wave). Only arms dealers and politicians who feed off fear benefit from this. And the answer is most certainly *not* to return to a time when female labour was even more underpaid and undervalued than it is now, or to sexual double standards that punished only women.

To my mind the evidence indicates that women, especially feminists, can play only minor roles in struggles to create and define less violent masculinities. The heavy misogyny found in male identity formation is too widespread, culturally and historically, to be wholly accidental. Blatant rejection of femininity and an exaggeration of male-female differences is a primary component of virtually every known male subculture (including those among gay men) (Jefferson 1994). Whether this is biologically or psychologically necessary is not known, nor is it particularly relevant from a utilitarian perspective. What matters is that, to have any appeal to rebellious adolescent males with much clearer ideas of what they reject than what they accept, alternate male identities must be *different* from female identities. It may turn out that the biosocial psychology of male humans, not to mention eons of evolution, make it important for boys to exaggerate gender differences in order to reject the mother-figure and distance themselves from the dependence of childhood. But there is no reason to suppose that the need to create identities that are distinctively different from women's implies a need to hate, devalue or dominate women. The latter are necessary components of patriarchy, not masculinity.

It also seems obvious that boys/men need roles, and therefore institutions and (sub) cultures, that allow them to be aggressive, risk-takers and adventurers (which does not mean that women should be denied such roles). There are few cultural or social spaces in developed societies where boys can be constructively adventurous or aggressive. Fantasy roles abound, from cyber-space to video games, but many of these exploit racism or homophobia rather than satisfying needs. With the disappearance of wild animals, frontiers and unexplored territory, the only adventurous legitimate *jobs* on offer are violent and destructive in nature (such as soldiers, police and/or criminals), or they are restricted to a privileged elite (space explorers today require doctorates in astrophysics). No wonder male police and prison guards cling so desperately to machismo images and subcultures, fighting academic and political directives which would replace warrior roles with service orientations (Heidensohn 1992; Reiner 1992). No wonder, too, that virtually all businesses and political organizations are gendered in ways that relegate women to secondary roles responsible for emotional scutwork, while men claim the adventurous, aggressive roles and the prestige, power and income such roles 'deserve' (Hochschild 1983). It is not functionality, capitalism, or the dictates of efficiency that require such subcultures or organizational divisions of labour.

Heterosexual women do have important parts to play in struggles to recast male identities. Too often women as mothers reward violence and toughness in their sons (and weakness in their daughters), or devalue emotionality and vulnerability in men with negative labels. Women as lovers and mates, particularly young women, cannot continue to respond erotically to machismo and reject men exploring alternate masculinities or those who have refused emotional castration. Feminism as a movement is well placed to problematize and consciousness raise around women's roles in reinforcing violent masculinities.

Because knowledge is a form of power, there are important tasks in this struggle for those in the academy as well. New male identities need to be wide-ranging, they will vary with class, ethnicity, orientation, religious identification, occupation and age (to name only a few factors), and they cannot be specified or prescribed in advance. They must be struggled for, forged by trial and error, and based in older masculinities and ways of being. But little is known about the structural and cultural forces forming masculinities and femininities, or about micro level processes which mediate the process of identity formation among individual men and women (Foucault 1982). Violence has historically been connected with dominance, and both with eroticism, but the roots and consequences of these links are unclear. We know little about the various agendas and interests animating struggles around masculinities today, and we have not adequately explored the social or political consequences of the different visions of male-female natures and relationships now vying for power. Some groups attempting to recast male and female identities, for example, take the partial, political and fragmented bits of biological knowledge we have about sex differences as facts, and argue for conservative policies on this basis (such as forcing women to stay home to bond with infants, or excluding them from higher education in mathematics because of alleged differences in left-right brain functions governing spatial abilities in men and women, for example). Naming the problems, specifying the implications and identifying the interest groups at play is a necessary first step to securing transformative changes and, even more crucial right now, to averting reactionary ones.[3] This is all part of the process of creating alternative models, of envisaging different ways of seeing to counter the dead weight of hegemony, for acceptance of the status quo rests heavily on notions that it constitutes the necessary and inevitable ordering of the world.

Directing greater attention to an 'ethics of care' might be a useful component of the process of constructing alternatives (Gilligan 1982; Smart 1989: 72–4; Kellough 1995). Kellough suggests that the intersecting values of capitalism and patriarchy have co-opted, through law, the common human urge to care for others and distorted it into a welfare/dependence frame. Women in particular are forced to choose between independence/autonomy and the obligation to care for others or nurture (Kellough 1995: 382–3). This is a false dichotomy because people must be nurtured (through socialization) in order to become autonomous, so caring and independence are intertwined not juxtaposed. Such a concept is useful insofar as it can be used as a counterbalance to voices advocating penalty and revenge, and a challenge to tyrannies of the binary. 'Using the need of human beings for the caring attention of others' (Kellough 1995: 383) as a tool to evaluate macro-level processes (laws, structures, policies and institutions) focuses attention on new concepts of human rights, concepts based in collectivist and dualistic rather than individualistic zero-sum terms. We know so little about the activities central to caring, or the institutions and implications of such an orientation, compared to those central to punishing. . . .[4]

NOTES

1. Earlier collective identities based in craft guilds have largely disappeared. Religion, a primary source of alternative value systems in many parts of the world, has been marginalized in much of Europe and Canada, and 'captured' by consumerism and capitalism in the United States (Bibby 1993). There has been talk about the potential of technology (the Net, for example) to recreate community and nourish alternate identities, but since it is still predominantly privileged classes, men, and increasingly commercial interests which are 'on line', it is unduly optimistic to see anything 'alternative' emerging here.

2. Jobs for married women are not new—all but the most privileged have worked outside the home since the dawn of the Industrial Revolution (except during the most intense periods of child-rearing), but their wages were kept low by a combination of sexism and glass ceilings, and their jobs were more likely to be seen, by women as well as men, as secondary.

3. The struggle for identity, the territory of internal or psychological change, is central to counter-hegemonic and ideological change. And it has not been claimed and politicized to the degree that structure-based change, now the apparently unchallengeable property of those who would make the world safe for profit maximization, has been. It may therefore be fertile soil politically, as well as essential knowledge.

4. Much caring labour, in the private sphere and in mainstream organizations ranging from airlines to government, is done by and expected from women rather than men (Hochschild 1983). However the consequences and implications this has for social policy, child-rearing, economic reform, and violence are unknown. Do male subcultures and identities lose the potential to express and develop caring identities because of the dominance of women in these spheres? Are women denied the chance to develop more instrumental abilities? With what consequences? The empirical and theoretical territory of caring needs to be explored as carefully as the terrain of penalty has been.

REFERENCES

Bibby, R. (1993), *Unknown Gods: The Ongoing Story of Religion in Canada*. Toronto: Soddart.
Buchwald, E., Fletcher, P. and Roth, M., eds. (1993), *Transforming a Rape Culture*. Minneapolis, MN: Milkweed Editions.
Dekeseredy, W. and Hinch, R. (1991), *Woman Abuse: Sociological Perspectives*. Toronto: Thompson Educational Publishing.
Dobash, R. E. and Dobash, R. (1975), *Violence Against Wives: A Case Against the Patriarchy*. New York: Free Press.
——— (1992), *Women, Violence and Social Change*. London: Routledge.
Faludi, S. (1991), *Backlash: The Undeclared War against American Women*. New York: Doubleday.
Foucault, M. (1982), 'The Subject and Power', in H. Dreyfus and P. Rabinow, eds., *Michel Foucault: Beyond Structuralism and Hermeneutics*, 194–230. Chicago: University of Chicago Press.
Friedman, T. (1995), 'Sorry, but this Group of Seven doesn't make the grade', *The Glove and Mail*, Tuesday, 30 May, A17 (reprinted from the *New York Times*).

Giddens, A. (1981), *The Class Structure of Advanced Societies*, 2nd ed. London: Hutchinson.

Gilligan, C. (1982), *In a Different Voice: Psychological Theory and Women's Development*. Cambridge: Harvard University Press.

Gilmore, T. (1990), *Manhood in the Making*. New Haven: Yale University Press.

Godenzi, A. (1994), 'What's the Big Deal?', in T. Newburn and E. Stanko, eds., *Just Boys Doing Business?*, 135–52. London: Routledge.

Heidensohn, F. (1992), *Women in Control*. Oxford: Oxford University Press.

Hochschild, A. R. (1983), *The Managed Heart: Commercialization of Human Feeling*. Berkeley: University of California Press.

Jefferson, T. (1994), 'Theorising Masculine Subjectivity', in T. Newburn and E. Stanko, eds., *Just Boys Doing Business?*, 10–32. London: Routledge.

Kellough, G. (1995), *The Abortion Controversy: A Study of Law, Culture and Social Change*. Toronto: University of Toronto Press.

Levi, M. 'Giving Creditors the Business: The Criminal Law in Inaction', *International Journal of the Sociology of Law*, 12: 321–33.

Ptacek, J. (1988*a*), 'How Men Who Batter Rationalize their Behaviour', in A. Horton and J. Williamson, eds., *Abuse and Religion*. Lexington, MA: Lexington Books.

—— (1988*b*), 'Why Do Men Batter Their Wives?', in K. Yllo and M. Bograd, eds., *Feminist Perspectives on Wife Abuse*. Newbury Park, CA: Sage.

Reiner, R. (1992), 'Police Research in the UK: A Critical Review', in M. Tonry and N. Morris, eds., *Modern Policing*. Chicago: University of Chicago Press.

Smart, C. (1989), *Feminism and the Power of Law*. London: Routledge.

—— (1992), 'The Woman of Legal Discourse', *Social and Legal Studies*, 1: 29–44.

Stets, J. E. (1988), *Domestic Violence and Control*. New York: Springer-Verlag.

Tifft, L. and Markham, L. (1991), 'Battering Women and Battering Central Americans', in Pepinsky and R. Quinney, eds., *Criminology as Peacemaking*, 114–53. Bloomington, IN: Indiana University Press.

Williams, J. and Taylor, R. (1994), 'Boys Keep Swinging: Masculinity and Football Culture in England', in T. Newburn and E. Stanko, eds., *Just Boys Doing Business? Men, Masculinities and Crime*, 214–34. London: Routledge.

Winter, S. (1992), 'Don't Trust Anyone Not Over the Sixties', *Law and Society Review*, 26/4 789–818.

21

Tomboys Yes, Janegirls Never

Barbara Arrighi

GENDER MESSAGES

The statements below comprise a collection of gendered directives assembled from various social and professional experiences, but primarily from classroom discussion when the topic was gender and masculinity. The name Billy is used here to demonstrate what a sustained barrage of gendered pointers would be like for one child to endure over time. Therefore, although Billy is fictitious, the comments are real. It is not out of the realm of possibilities that one child could hear most if not all of the following gender directives during childhood.

Immediate Family Members

Father to newborn Billy: "Little man, you take care of your mother while I'm gone."

Older brother to Billy: "Sissy, sissy, sissy. Billy is a sissy. Billy plays with dolls."

Older sister to Billy: "Billy is a sissy. Billy acts like a girl, looks like a girl, talks like a girl, walks like a girl."

Billy's father to no one in particular as Billy sits down to play the piano: "Oh, jeez, don't let him play the piano, the next thing he'll be walking around all limp-wristed."

Father to Billy: "Billy, give that doll back to your sister right now. I'm not raising no little fag."

Billy's father to Billy's mother: "How do you expect Billy to grow up and be a man when you're putting fingernail polish on him? I don't care if he is five years old. Before you know it, he'll be wearing your underwear."

Mother to Billy: "No, Billy, you can't play dress-up with your sister. Boys don't play dress-ups, just girls do."

Mother to Billy: "No, Billy, you can't get an ironing board for Christmas. That's just for girls. Are you a girl?"

Father to Billy's female cousin: "Oh, Lord, don't let Billy play with that ironing board. Billy, get away from that ironing board. What's wrong with you?"

Extended Family Messages

Uncle to nephew Billy: "Stop crying, Billy, boys don't cry."

Uncle to nephew Billy: "Billy, what are you gonna do with that ironing board? Why don't you go play football or something, boy?"

Gender Messages from the Educational System

Billy's teacher (a female) punishing Billy and another male student in the school cafeteria: "The two of you will walk around the cafeteria five times holding hands, repeating: We're girls; we're girls."

Billy's coach: "Aw, come on, Billy, you throw like a girl."

Billy's coach to Billy and Billy's teammates: "You played like a bunch of girls today."

Peers and Gender Messages

A male friend chiding Billy (who is hugging him): "Get away from me, you faggot."

A male friend teasing Billy about the amount of time he spends with his girlfriend: "Man, she has you pussy-whipped."

Billy's girlfriend to Billy when Billy failed to do an allotted number of sit-ups: "You sissy, don't be such a wimp."

Media

Message on a boy's tee shirt advertised in the local Sunday paper: You Play Like a Bunch of Girls.

The Enduring Impact of Gender Messages

Taken individually, the statements presented above seem harmless, but collectively, the impact of messages that demean behavior viewed as feminine can be defining for both boys and girls. Admonishing male children for what has been labeled cross-gender behavior effectively brings boys back into line. Perhaps more important, by chastising boys for engaging in female-identified behaviors, both girls and boys become cognizant of the second-class status of females in society.

Acting out cultural scripts of masculinity accords status, power, and privilege; therefore, young girl children generally do not receive cautionary messages when they engage in culturally defined boy typed play or act in a societally defined boy-typed manner; nor do they suffer loss of status. Young tomboys are subjected to far fewer negative reactions (until adolescence) than are Janegirls. The same is not true for boys who engage in culturally defined girl play (Macoby 1987). Because sanctions for behaviors perceived to be cross-gendered are more severe for boys, girls are more likely to imitate boys than vice versa (Bussey and Bandura 1992).

GENDERING IS AN INSIDIOUS PROCESS

What is remarkable about gendering is that males and females are more alike at birth than they are different, more alike than any other species. Within the first few moments of life, however, infants hear gendered words from mom, dad, doctor, and nurses. Newborn boys are busters or bouncing boys, while newborn girls are beautiful, delicate, petite. From infancy on, we experience gendered touches and gendered expectations. Acquiring gender is an insidious process, slow, subtle, unnoticed, until acquired behaviors appear natural, normal, appropriate. That said, by age five, compulsory masculinity has been established for the most part and God help the boy who is outside of the box (Nelson 1985).

A NETWORK OF SOCIALIZING AGENTS

Masculinity is not something that is simply transmitted from father to son. Everyone has a hand in the process, with family members at the top of the list. Laureen Snider notes in chapter 20 in this volume, "mothers as well as fathers, terrified of boys becoming 'wimps,' send contradictory messages about the acceptability of bullying and aggression."

The list doesn't stop with mom and dad; it includes siblings, extended kin, teachers, coaches, peers, and, of course, the media. What emerges is something akin to a network of gender police disallowing any semblance of societally defined feminine mannerisms or characteristics in boys and young men. It should come as no surprise, then, that frequently by adolescence males repress a range of emotions and actions lest they be associated with any and all things female and feminine (Bruch, Berko, and Haase 1998). In addition, by puberty, many young males have learned that the culturally correct, masculine way to relate with females is with the penis. Thus, one consequence of gendering that has implications for women and men is that some young boys are socialized to place a limited-use value on females.

No wonder young boys frequently refer to their female cohort with disdain - the "girls are yucky" syndrome. The need for self-protection causes boys to distance themselves from any activity that smacks of femininity. The fear of ostracism and alienation from those they revere (parents/teachers) and those they hold dear (peers) generally goes a long way toward constraining males from engaging in behavior that is seen as deviating from the norm of masculinity. After all, as social beings and conformists, what young boys would want to be considered odd men out? Individual gender transgressions, then, rather than dismantling gendered social structures, probably do more to strengthen gender-constructed boundaries. Boys will do whatever it takes to avoid being labeled a sissy. Analyzing within that context the gender statements given at the opening of this chapter offers insight into the overlapping systems of barrier-setting directives and actions that begin early in the lives of males and continue on into adulthood.

Looked at another way, children are socialized within a maze of linking, crosscutting, and/or interlocking social circles. If parents choose to raise their sons outside the bounds of our gender-typed culture—perhaps even androgynously—young boys will be exposed to many influences that are not consistent with their parents' way of thinking. For example, some parents might be slightly skittish but others might be outraged at the prospect of their young son coming home from a playmate's with painted nails and lips. The bottom line is that realistically, parents cannot control all socializing messages their children receive.

SCHOOL DAZE AND PEERS

Beyond the family's sphere of influence lie other important contributors to the acquisition of gender. The educational system plays a major role. For at least twelve years, children spend the greater part of their daily lives within the regimented environments of schools; the only other systems to rival the regimen are the military, prison, and perhaps religious life. No bastions of liberalism, schools are staffed, for the most part, by bureaucrats—administrators and teachers who are steeped in middle-class gendered values. The expectation is that girls will be nice, neat, quiet, obedient, helpful, cooperative, and cheerful. Boys, however, will be boys: assertive/aggressive, competitive, boisterous, messy, athletic, and even unruly at times. Those who refuse to conform are negatively sanctioned and even may be temporarily isolated from classmates until such time as their behavior conforms to the norm.

Teachers are not the only ones who play a crucial role in gendering children at school; students monitor each other for gender-appropriate behavior and sanction those children who transgress the norms, usually by ridicule or exclusion (who can forget cooties). School-related activities including recess, sports, and scouting separate students along gender lines that create, reinforce, and sustain gendered identities, gender boundaries, and a gendered system.

As children mature and become enmeshed in friendship groups at school and extracurricular activities, peer influence becomes paramount in providing gender guidelines, often overriding parental influence. Risman and Myers (1997) found that even in feminist households in which students espoused their parents' egalitarian views, the children did not adhere consistently to parental ideology. When family experiences conflicted with that of their friends, the influence of their friends prevailed.

CONFESSIONS OF A SMALL SAMPLE OF COLLEGE STUDENTS

How common are the admonishments listed at the beginning of this analysis? When students (a total of thirty-nine) in an introductory sociology class were asked anonymously if they had ever been referred to as a sissy, fag, or pussy, every male (twenty-one) answered yes. When asked if they had ever referred to a male using any of the three terms, all thirty-nine students indicated they had. While not a generalizable sample, the responses are indicative of a pattern that calls for further investigation.

What is particularly instructive and pertinent to the theme of this text is that all of the female students (eighteen) acknowledge that they too had used one or more of the terms to address males. The young women reported addressing younger brothers, older brothers, significant others, male friends, and classmates with these epithets. This is evidence of what Snider's argument suggests: that is, females as mothers (I would expand the circle to include friends, kin, wives, and lovers) contribute, perhaps unwittingly, to the perpetuation of machismo. More important, by chiding males who do not embody machismo or denigrating those males who act in a culturally defined feminine manner, women assist in the perpetuation of sexism. Simply put, by ridiculing behavior associated with that of their gender, women inadvertently and in subtle ways demean their own sex.

Even when used in a joking manner, the terms work to harness male behavior to narrow macho parameters. Thus, boys and men may feel compelled to separate themselves from all that is perceived in society as feminine and to embrace all that is defined in their culture as masculine. We have to ask ourselves: Is that what we want? Is that what society needs?

REFERENCES

Bruch, M. A., E. H. Berko, and R. F. Haase. 1998. Shyness, Masculine Ideology, Physical Attractiveness, and Emotional Inexpressiveness: Testing a Mediational Model of Men's Interpersonal Competence. *Journal of Counseling Psychology* 45: 84–97.

Bussey, K., and A. Bandura. 1992. Self-Regulatory Mechanisms Governing Gender Development. *Child Development* 63: 1236–50.

Macoby, E. E. 1987. The Varied Meanings of "Masculine" and "Feminine." In *Masculinity/Femininity: Basic Perspectives*, edited by J. M. Reinisch, L. A. Rosenblum, and S. A. Sanders, 227–39. New York: Oxford University Press.

Nelson, J. B. 1985. Male Sexuality and Masculine Spirituality. *Siecus Reports* 13: 1–4.

Risman, Barbara, and Kristen Myers. 1997. As the Twig Is Bent: Children Reared in Feminist Households. *Qualitative Sociology* 20: 229–52.

22

Hormonal Hurricanes:
Menstruation and Female Behavior

Anne Fausto-Sterling

. . . Is it possible that up to 100 percent of all menstruating women regularly experience emotional disturbance? Compared to whom? Are males the unstated standard of emotional stability? If there is but a single definition of what is normal and men fit that definition, then women with "female complaints" must by definition be either crazy or in need of medical attention. A double bind indeed.

Some scientists explicitly articulate the idea of the naturally abnormal female. Professor Frank Beach, a pioneer in the field of animal psychology and its relationship to sexuality, suggests the following evolutionary account of menstruation. In primitive hunter-gatherer societies adult women were either pregnant or lactating, and since life spans were so short they died well before menopause; low-fat diets made it likely that they did not ovulate every month; they thus experienced no more than ten menstrual cycles. Given current life expectancies as well as the widespread use of birth control, modern women may experience a total of four hundred menstrual cycles. He concludes from this reasoning that "civilization has given women a *physiologically abnormal status* which may have important implications for the interpretation of psychological responses to periodic fluctuations in the secretion of ovarian hormones"—that is, to menstruation (emphasis added).[1] Thus the first problem we face in evaluating the literature on the premenstrual syndrome is figuring out how to deal with the underlying assumption that women have "a physiologically abnormal status."

Researchers who believe in PMS hold a wide variety of viewpoints (none of them supported by scientific data) about the basis of the problem. For example, Dr. Katharina Dalton, the most militant promoter of PMS, says that it results from a relative end-of-the-cycle deficiency in the hormone progesterone. Others cite deficiencies in vitamin B-6, fluid retention, and low blood sugar as possible causes. Suggested treatments range from hormone injection to the use of lithium, diuretics, megadoses of vitamins, and control of sugar in the diet.[2] Although some of these treatments are harmless, others are not. Progesterone injection causes cancer in animals. What will it do to humans? And a recent issue of *The New England Journal of Medicine* contains a report that large doses of vitamin B-6 damage the nerves, causing a loss of feeling in one's fingers and toes.[3] The wide variety of PMS "causes" and "cures" offered by the experts is confusing to put it mildly. Just what *is* this syndrome that causes such controversy? How can a woman know if she has it?

With a case of the measles it's really quite simple. A fever and then spots serve as diagnostic signs. A woman said to have PMS, however, may or may not have any of a very large number of symptoms. Furthermore, PMS indicators such as headaches, depression, dizziness, loss or gain of appetite show up in everyone from time to time. Their mere presence cannot (as would measle spots) help one to diagnose the syndrome. In addition, whether any of these signals connote disease depends upon their severity. A slight headache may reflect nothing more than a lack of sleep, but repeated, severe headaches could indicate high blood pressure. As one researcher, Dr. Judith Abplanalp, succinctly puts it: "There is no one set of symptoms which is considered to be the hallmark of or standard criterion for defining the premenstrual syndrome."[4] Dr. Katharina Dalton agrees but feels one can diagnose PMS quite simply by applying the term to "any symptoms or complaints which regularly come just before or during early menstruation but are absent at other times of the cycle.[5] Dalton contrasts this with men suffering from potential PMS "symptoms," because, she says, they experience them randomly during the month while women with the same physical indications acknowledge them only during the premenstruum.

PMS research usually bases itself on an ideal, regular, twenty-eight-day menstrual cycle. Researchers eliminate as subjects for study women with infrequent, shorter, or longer cycles. As a result, published investigations look at a skewed segment of the overall population. Even for those women with a regular cycle, however, a methodological problem remains because few researchers define the premenstrual period in the same way. Some studies look only at the day or two preceding the menstrual flow, others look at the week preceding, while workers such as Dalton cite cases that begin two weeks before menstruation and continue for one week after. Since so few investigations use exactly the same definition, research publications on PMS are difficult to compare with one another.[6] On this score if no other, the literature offers little useful insight, extensive as it is.

Although rarely stated, the assumption is that there is but *one* PMS. Dalton defines the problem so broadly that she and others may well lump together several phenomena of very different origins, a possibility heightened by the fact that investigators rarely assess the severity of the symptoms. Two women, one suffering from a few low days and the other from suicidal depression, may both be diagnosed as having PMS. Yet their difficulties could easily have different origins and ought certainly to receive different treatments. When investigators try carefully to define PMS, the number of people qualifying for study decreases dramatically. In one case a group used ten criteria to define PMS only to find that no more than 20 percent of those who had volunteered for their research project met them.[7] In the absence of any clearly agreed upon definition(s) of PMS, examinations of the topic should at least state clearly the methodology used; this would enable comparison between publications, and allow us to begin to accumulate some knowledge about the issues at hand. At the moment the literature is filled with individual studies that permit neither replication or comparison with one another—an appropriate state, perhaps, for an art gallery but not for a field with pretensions to the scientific.

Despite the problems of method and definition, the conviction remains that PMS constitutes a widespread disorder, a conviction that fortifies and is fortified by the idea that women's reproductive function, so different from that of "normal" men, places them in a naturally diseased state. For those who believe that 90 percent of all women suffer from a disease called PMS, it becomes a reasonable research strategy to look at the normally functioning menstrual cycle for clues about the cause and possible treatment. There are, in fact, many theories but no credible evidence about the origins of PMS. . . . Some of the theories are ingenious and require a sophisticated knowledge of human physiology to comprehend. Nevertheless, the authors of one recent review quietly offer the following summary: "To date no one hypothesis has adequately explained the constellation of symptoms composing PMS.[8] In short, PMS is a disease in search of a definition and cause. . . .

If we continue to assume that menstruation is itself pathological, we cannot establish a baseline of health against which to define disease. If, instead, we accept in theory that a range of menstrual normality exists, we can then set about designing studies that define the healthy female reproductive cycle. Only when we have some feeling for *that* can we begin to help women who suffer from diseases of menstruation.

Many of those who reject the alarmist nature of the publicity surrounding PMS believe nevertheless that women undergo mood changes during the menstrual cycle. Indeed most Western women would agree. But do studies of large segments of our population support this generality? And if so, what causes these ups and downs? In trying to answer these questions we confront another piece of the medical model of human behavior, the belief that biology is primary, that hormonal changes cause behavioral ones, but not vice versa. Most researchers use such a linear, unicausal model without thinking about it. Their framework is so much a part of their belief system that they forget to question it. Nevertheless it is the model from which they work, and failure to recognize and work skeptically with it often results in poorly conceived research combined with implausible interpretations of data. Although the paradigm of biological causation has until very recently dominated menstrual cycle research, it now faces serious and intellectually stimulating challenge from feminist experts in the field.

LIFTING THE SHADOW: TOWARD AN UNDERSTANDING OF
MENSTRUATION AND BEHAVIOR

During the forty-five years that have elapsed since Benedek and Rubenstein published the first "modern" experimental study of mood and menstrual cycle,[9] countless additional studies have appeared. Why, then, is it possible for a scientist in 1981 to write the following?

> The question is still being debated. Are women's moods a function of their rhythmic reproductive physiology or not? Unfortunately the literature does not agree on the answer to the more basic questions: Do women experience cyclic mood fluctuations?[10]

In looking for answers, we encounter a research field filled with poorly designed studies. Inadequate sample sizes and measures, inappropriate choice of subjects, tests designed to obtain a desired outcome, and poor or nonexistent use of statistical analysis are but some of the problems. That so many scientists have been able for so long to do such poor research attests to both the unconscious social agendas of many of the researchers and to the theoretical inadequacy of the research framework used in the field as a whole. Once again we encounter the failure of a simple linear model of biological causation, and must struggle instead with a more complex conceptualization in which mind, body, and culture depend so inextricably on one another that allegedly straightforward studies, ones claiming to find single causes for cyclic behavior, must be looked upon with deep suspicion.

Over the years specific critiques of menstrual-cycle studies have accumulated. As early as 1877 physician and medical researcher Mary Putnam Jacobi pioneered menstrual-cycle research with the publication of her book *The Question of Rest for Women During Menstruation*. In this critical literature review she pointed out the relative novelty of the idea that women are *more* rather than *less* vulnerable at menstruation. In a thorough analysis of her own careful interviews with 268 women about their menstrual experiences, she presented results that have a ring of feminist modernity, suggesting that by no means do all women suffer menstrual pain and that among those who do are many who are otherwise in poor health or under stress, or who have insufficient exercise and education.[11]

Psychologist Mary Brown Parlee deserves the credit for breaking ground more recently with her analyses of the menstrual cycle. Her review article, "The Premenstrual Syndrome," published in 1973, systematically takes to task the research of the preceding thirty-five years and sets the stage for even more sophisticated theoretical and methodological analyses.[12] Parlee categorizes studies on premenstrual emotionality into four types: correlational, retrospective questionnaires, daily self-reports, and thematic analysis of word lists describing various feelings and moods.

Correlational studies. Through correlational studies, scientists look to see if particular phases of the menstrual cycle coincide with reported or observed behaviors.

Ideally investigators try to determine the phase of the menstrual cycle independently, using some reliable measure such as change in basal body temperature (an indication of ovulation) or beginning of the menstrual flow. Even these measures are imperfect, but Parlee points out that many studies don't even bother with independent confirmation of cycle phase. Properly done correlational studies also present problems. Early in their training, scientists learn that correlation gives no information about causation. As Parlee points out, most correlational studies seem to assume that when emotional changes correspond to changes in the menstrual cycle, hormones must be to blame. The model gives priority to biology by implication rather than by direct proof and leaves aside the idea that one's hormone biology might itself change under differing emotional conditions.

Retrospective questionnaires. Even today, one of the most widely used processes for studying premenstrual anxiety and depression is to ask women to fill out a form called the Menstrual Distress Questionnaire (abbreviated MDQ), on which they indicate which among a list of symptoms or moods they recall experiencing at different times of their menstrual cycle. Designed by a physician, Dr. Rudolf Moos, "to find the relationship between a woman's symptoms in different phases of her menstrual cycle," the questionnaire lists forty-seven "symptoms," only five of which—all found under the subheading "positive arousal"—have agreeable connotations.[13] . . . A rapid perusal alerts one to the fact that, starting out with the assumption of menstrual distress, one can design a test to prove one's point. Critics of this work recently designed a Menstrual Joy Questionnaire, which emphasizes positive feelings during the menstrual cycle.[14] The retrospective questionnaire holds additional problems, including the selective memory of the women completing it combined with their prior knowledge of the purpose of the study. Many women grow up with the expectation that they should feel bad just before their periods, and this belief can certainly predispose them to selectively remember feeling bad just before menstruation but not at other times of the month. As one researcher writes in a study on moods and menstruation in college students, "negative behavior exhibited premenstrually is perceived as evidence for the prevailing negative stereotype of female emotional behavior while positive behavior is ignored as something for which biology is irrelevant."[15]

The uncritical use of retrospective studies ignores the twin influences of negative cultural beliefs and outright ignorance about menstruation. A study of forty women at a Michigan clinic serving a poor, multiethnic clientele found patients to be "naive and misinformed about the true function of menstruation."[16] Most (63 percent) had no knowledge of menarche before they began to menstruate, while many thought that "cold" could enter the body during menstruation, "believing that a bath, a shampoo, a walk in the dew or rain might 'back up' menstrual flow and result in a stroke, insanity, or 'quick TB.'"[17]

A second type of investigation shows that middle-class children, presumably well educated about menstruation, still approach menarche with fixed ideas about what to expect. In one recent study most premenarcheal girls and boys of the same age believed menstruation to be a physically and emotionally disruptive event, while another found that 85 percent of the premenarcheal girls studied thought it inappropriate to discuss menstruation with boys.[18] Regardless of class or educational level, large numbers of women grow up with strong negative attitudes toward menstruation. It is obvious to many that these firm beliefs might affect answers not only to retrospective questionnaires but also the physiology of menstruation itself, yet possible effects are ignored in mainstream menstrual cycle research.

Daily self-reports. Some researchers overcome the problem of selective memory on retrospective forms by using daily self-reports. With this method groups of women keep daily menstrual calendars on which they record their moods and the first day of menstruation. Until very recently, however, such studies have not been "blind"— the subject always knew that she was part of an attempt to correlate mood and menstrual phase.

Thematic analysis. In the fourth type of study reviewed by Parlee, researchers ask women to speak in unstructured fashion about daily life experiences. The interviewers then analyze the language content, scoring for indications of hostility and anxiety. By performing such analyses over the course of one or more menstrual cycles, investigators hope to correlate emotional changes with physiological ones. Although with this approach, the subject may be unaware of the study's purpose, the analyst isn't. In other words, this too is a "sighted" study with all the pitfalls of subjective analysis. The most reliable studies employ double blinds, in which neither the experimental subject nor the person gathering and categorizing the results knows the true purpose of the study. The few studies of premenstrual emotional changes done in this way fail to show cyclical mood alterations.[19]

Parlee's report merely scratches the surface, beneath which lies so huge a number of methodological problems that the thoughtful menstrual-cycle researcher risks paralysis in dealing with them, while they simply overwhelm the unwary layperson. . . .

How is it that so many different and seemingly obvious things could be wrong with the bulk of menstrual-cycle research? The answer, hidden within the walls of the research structure, is usually plastered over with clever techniques and detailed measurements. Why, for instance, do researchers looking at women's hormone cycles and mood changes fail to mention the monthly cycle of testosterone?[20] The answer, I suggest, is that testosterone is seen as a male hormone, hence "normal," and thus not an obvious subject for inquiry when looking at the "abnormalities" of menstrual mood changes. How, too, can so many highly trained researchers fail even to discuss the problem of double-blind experimentation? The answer lies in their belief in biological primacy. One need worry about double blinds only if one remains conscious of the fact that thoughts, mind-sets, and emotions can affect one's physiology. Of course most women know this perfectly well, since overexcitement, exhaustion, travel, illness, and stress can alter the timing of one's period, change the number and intensity of premenstrual signals, and influence the presence or absence of the menstrual flow and its degree of discomfort; these are all variations in the physiological expression of the monthly cycle, influenced by one's emotional state.

Dr. Randi Koeske, author of the most up-to-date analyses of menstrual-cycle theory,[21] paints in clear detail the consequences of reliance on "a normative 'disease-model' framework" for the menstrual cycle, a framework that gives precedence to biological variables (which researchers view as representing the "real" underlying cause of behavior), while relegating social-cognitive variables to secondary positions.[22] It is a theoretical approach that emphasizes technical measurement even when it is devoid of meaning and focuses on "context-free factors inside the organism," as if the organism existed separately from its environment; at the same time the normative disease-model framework views "changeableness, emotionality, and rhythmicity" as either "inherently unhealthy" or as changes from norms (usually based on men) about how often and to what degree rhythmic variations are "appropriate." Such a viewpoint allows researchers to ignore the historical and cultural contexts of their work and, as Koeske so nicely puts it, reduces them to "capturing brief snapshots of time, rather than allowing processes to unfold in context."[23]

Despite such insights, it is not yet time to write the ending to the saga of menstrual-cycle research. One can look forward to new illumination of this subject. A younger generation of scientists has begun to take fresh research initiatives, forging different theoretical approaches and using them to make their way toward better designed, more informative studies of the menstrual cycle. One of the most pleasurable aspects of reading the work of these scientists is that it stems from a full respect for women. A close second is the intellectual challenge encountered in considering complex, contextual research that precludes the reduction of human behavior to some simple biological variable. "The *real* alternative to biomedicine," Koeske writes, "is a system of health research . . . which finds a way to reintegrate the whole person from the jigsaw of parts created by modern scientific medicine. The strength of the feminist perspective is the recognition that the parts biomedicine currently recognizes cannot be reassembled into a whole."[24] The challenge presented to menstrual-cycle researchers is to find the missing pieces and light the way toward integration.

Koeske suggests several steps in that direction which, if followed inventively, will help deepen our understanding of the problem. These include:

1. Start with clearly stated and testable hypotheses, rather than creating a hypothesis after collecting the data.
2. Use more than one method to test the hypothesis, rather than relying solely on one highly modish approach.
3. Listen carefully to what women actually say about their bodies, lives, and perceptions, and treat their views as data, rather than restricting their choice of feelings in order to construct an "objective" measurement.
4. Beware (especially feminists) of replacing a biologically reductive theory with a socially reductive one.[25]

Like the merits of Mom and apple pie, Koeske's cautions may seem self-evident. When applied to actual research problems, however, they bring interesting results. Some examples follow.

1. Dr. Alice Rossi introduced "the social week" into her studies and found that both men and women experienced cyclical changes during this period. They tended to feel down on Tuesdays and happiest on weekends.[26]

2. Dr. Koeske bases some of her recent work on attribution theory, which tries to understand how people interpret their experiences. In one set of studies she asked students presented with made-up "case studies" that included menstrual-cycle information to interpret the behaviors of hypothetical "patients." Her findings bore out her hypothesis that only hostile or angry behaviors during the premenstruum were attributed to biology; the students believed that positive behaviors during the same period stemmed from individual personality traits or some external positive situation.[27]

3. Dr. Alice Dan, another member of the "new wave" of menstrual-cycle researchers, took up a point first made by Parlee—that we have yet to use two different measures to show the same menstrually related mood changes. In her study Dan compared self-reports of menstrual changes with analysis of open-ended conversations held at different times during the menstrual cycle. Her finding that the two independent assessments disagreed with one another raises some important questions, both about the validity of past studies and the interpretation of present ones. She considers reasonable the "suggestion that we stop measuring 'mood' changes over the menstrual cycle until we have developed a better understanding of what we are measuring."[28]

4. Dr. Sharon Golub found that premenstrually related increases in anxiety were far smaller than the heightened anxiety experienced by students subjected to the stress of an examination. In general she found premenstrually related mood changes to be of small magnitude, concluding that "the premenstrual hormonal changes appear to impose little psychological burden," and are often so slight that women "are sometimes not even aware of them."[29]

One of the lessons of so much critical analysis of menstrual-cycle research is that there is no such thing as a perfect study. The examples just cited may best be thought of as pilot projects. Through them, researchers will learn how to design good studies, how to validate the methods they use, and how to state their hypotheses explicitly and in testable fashion.

Change *does* loom on the horizon. But it will come not from proponents of the medical model of menstruation, from those who suggest that women take hormones, diuretics, or tranquilizers to control their unruly bodies. . . . As Dr. Koeske puts it: "Who knows? With a little luck and a lot of hard work, the only thing that may turn out to be unusual or uninterpretable about female premenstrual emotionality is the fact that no one understood it before."[30] And understanding, I believe, will come from the type of research undertaken by the feminist biologists and social scientists of today.

NOTES

1. Frank A. Beach, Preface to chapter 10, in *Human Sexuality in Four Perspectives* (Baltimore: Johns Hopkins University Press, 1977), 271.

2. Rosenthal, "Insights into the Premenstrual Syndromes."

3. Herbert Schaumberg et al., "Sensory Neuropathy from Pyridoxine Abuse," *New England Journal of Medicine* 309[1983]: 446–48.

4. Judith Abplanalp, "Premenstrual Syndrome: A Selective Review," *Women and Health* 8(1983): 110.

5. Katharina Dalton, *Once a Month*, 12.

6. J. Abplanalp, R. F. Haskett, and R. M. Rose, "The Premenstrual Syndrome," *Advances in Psychoneuroendocrinology* 3(1980):327–47; and Judith Abplanalp, "Premenstrual Syndrome: A Selective Review," *Women and Health* 8(1983).

7. Abplanalp, "Premenstrual Syndrome: A Selective Review."

8. Robert L. Reid and S. S. Yen, "Premenstrual Syndrome," *American Journal of Obstetrics and Gynecology* 139(1981) 97.

9. T. Benedek and B. B. Rubenstein, "The Correlations between Ovarian Activity and Psychodynamic Processes: I. The Ovulative Phase," *Psychosomatic Medicine* 1(1939):245–70; and T. Benedek and B. B. Rubenstein, "The Correlations between Ovarian Activity and Psychodynamic Processes: II. The Menstrual Phase, *Psychosomatic Medicine* 1(1939):461–85.

10. Janet R. Swanby, "A Longitudinal Study of Daily Mood Self Reports and their Relationship to the Menstrual Cycle," in *The Menstrual Cycle*, vol. 2, ed. P. Komnenich et al., (New York: Springer, 1981), 94.

11. Mary Putnam Jacobi, *The Question of Rest for Women During Menstruation* (New York: G. P. Putnam's Sons, 1877).

12. Mary Brown Parlee, "The Premenstrual Syndrome," *Psychological Bulletin* 80(1973):454–65.

13. Rudolf Moos, "Typology of Menstrual Cycle Symptoms," *American Journal of Obstetrics and Gynecology* 103(1969):390–402.

14. J. Delaney, M. J. Lupton, and E. Doth, *The Curse: A Cultural History of Menstruation* (New York: Dutton, 1976).

15. Randi Koeske, "Premenstrual Emotionality: Is Biology Destiny?," *Women and Health*, 1(1976):12.

16. Loudell Snow and Shirley M. Johnson, "Myths about Menstruation: Victims of Our Own Folklore," *International Journal of Women's Studies* 1(1978):70.

17. Ibid.

18. This study was reviewed by Sharon Golub, ed., "Lifting the Curse of Menstruation," *Women and Health* 8 (1983).

19. J. Brooks, D. N. Ruble, and A. E. Clark, "College Women's Attitudes and Expectations Concerning Menstrual-Related Changes," *Psychosomatic Medicine* 39 (1977):288–98; and D. Ruble, "Premenstrual Symptoms: A Reinterpretation," *Science* 197(1977):291–92.

20. H. Persky, "Reproductive Hormones, Moods and the Menstrual Cycle," in *Sex Differences in Behavior*, ed. R. C. Friedman, R. M. Richart, and R. L. Vande Wiele (Huntington, N.Y.: Krieger, 1974), 455–66; W. P. Collins and J. R. Newton, "The Ovarian Cycle," in *Biochemistry of Women: Clinical Concepts*, ed. A. S. Curry and J. V. Hewitt (Boca Raton, Fla.: CRC Press, 1974).

21. Randi Koeske, "Premenstrual Emotionality: Is Biology Destiny?"; "Lifting the Curse of Menstruation: Toward a Feminist Perspective on the Menstrual Cycle," *Women and Health* 8(1983); 1–16; and "Theoretical Perspectives on Menstrual Cycle Research," in *The Menstrual Cycle,* vol. 1, ed. A. Dan, E. Graham, and C. P. Beecher (New York: Springer, 1980), 8–24.

22. Koeske, "Theoretical Perspectives on Menstrual Cycle Research."

23. Koeske, "Lifting the Curse of Menstruation," 6.

24. Ibid., 13.

25. Koeske, "Theoretical Perspectives on Menstrual Cycle Research."

26. Alice Rossi and P. Rossi, "Body Time and Social Time: Mood Patterns by Menstrual Cycle Phase and Day of the Week," *Social Science Research* 6(1977):273–308.

27. Koeske, "Theoretical Perspectives on Menstrual Cycle Research."

28. Alice Dan, "Free-Associative versus Self Report Measures of Emotional Change over the Menstrual Cycle," in *The Menstrual Cycle,* vol. 1, ed. Dan, Graham, and Beecher, 119.

29. Sharon Golub, "Premenstrual Changes in Mood, Personality and Cognitive Function," in *The Menstrual Cycle,* vol. 1, ed. Dan, Graham, and Beecher, 244.

30. Koeske, "Theoretical Perspectives on Menstrual Cycle Research," 24.

Part Seven

Corporate Gatekeeping: Fitting In

23

Talking from 9 to 5: How Women's and Men's Conversational Styles Affect Who Gets Heard, Who Gets Credit, and What Gets Done at Work

Deborah Tannen

. . . There are many ways that women entering the world of work are entering "the men's house," to use the phrase coined by Captain Carol Barkalow as the title of her book about her military career. The very language spoken is often based on metaphors from sports or from the military, terms that are just idioms to many women, not references to worlds they have either inhabited or observed with much alacrity. Such expressions as "stick to your guns," "under the gun," "calling the shots," "an uphill battle," "a level playing field," "a judgment call," "start the ball rolling," "a curve-ball," "the ball's in their court," "batting a thousand," "struck out," "getting flak," "the whole nine yards," "in the ballpark," and "deep-six it" are part of our everyday vocabulary. . . .

Although there is evidence that women do adapt their styles to those of men when they find themselves in interaction with men, they rarely adopt men's styles whole-hog. And it is well that they don't, because men and women who model their behavior on someone of the other gender often get a very different reaction than their role models get. In a workplace situation, it is frequently a man who has been the model, while a woman who tries to behave like him is distressed to find that the reaction she gets is very different.

A dramatic example of this phenomenon happened to Captain Carol Barkalow. One of the first women to attend West Point, Captain Barkalow rose to the position of company commander at Fort Lee in Virginia. In her attempt to make herself more like a male commanding officer, she took up bodybuilding. What better way to challenge the unfair assumption that women are not as strong as men, not strong enough to lead their unit? She did so well that she won second place in a bodybuilding competition.

Two months before Captain Barkalow was to take her command, news of her triumph was published in the post newspaper, along with the standard championship photograph in which she posed standing beside her trophy, clad in a bikini designed to show off the muscles she had worked so hard to develop. And this photograph very nearly cost her the command and her career. In the words of the brigade commander, "She had become the masturbatory fantasy of every goddamned male noncommissioned officer in the company." Her attempt to enhance her image in a male domain—the strength of her muscles—was interpreted sexually because a photograph of a woman posing in a bikini, even though the pose she struck was designed to look powerful rather than seductive, brought to mind an image not of fitness and strength but of a pinup. . . .

THE GLASS CEILING AS A WALL OF WORDS

Here is a brief explanation of how conversational-style differences play a role in installing a glass ceiling. When decisions are made about promotion to management positions, the qualities sought are a high level of competence, decisiveness, and ability to lead. If it is men, or mostly men, who are making the decisions about promotions—as it usually is—they are likely to misinterpret women's ways of talking as showing indecisiveness, inability to assume authority, and even incompetence. . . . For example, a woman who feels it is crucial to preserve the appearance of consensus when making decisions because she feels anything else would appear bossy and arrogant begins by asking those around her for their opinions. This can be interpreted by her bosses as evidence that she doesn't know what she thinks should be done, that she is trying to get others to make decisions for her. . . .

Public speaking is frightening for almost everyone. But standing up in front of a large group of people, commanding attention, and talking authoritatively are extensions of the socialization most boys have been forced to endure, as boys in groups tend to vie for center stage, challenge the boys who get it, and deflect the challenges of others. Many of the ways women have learned to be likable and feminine are liabilities when it comes to public presentations. Most girls' groups penalize a girl who stands out or calls attention to herself in an obvious way.

A woman who works as a trainer for business people coming to the United States realized that a disproportionate amount of the criticism she and her colleagues delivered to the trainees was directed at women, especially in the nebulous category of "professional presence." They found themselves telling women, more often than men, that they did not speak loudly enough, did not project their voices, should stop cocking their heads to one side, should try to lower the pitch of their voices. A few women were told that their way of dressing was too sexy, their manner too flirtatious, if they wanted to be taken seriously in the American business environment.

In a sense, they were appearing too "feminine." But there were also women who were told that they were too challenging and abrasive. They launched into questions without a lead-in or hedges; they asked too many insistent questions; they did not tilt their heads at all or seemed to be tilting them in challenging ways. Although the trainers did not think of it in these terms, you could say that these women were not "feminine" enough.

In at least one case, a particular trainee had to be told that she was coming across as both too flirtatious and too confrontational. In wondering why such a large percentage of women in her program (a small one to start with) had the basic skills down cold, yet seemed to be undermining their own effectiveness by their nonverbal behavior, the trainer concluded that they had a very fine line to walk: The range of behaviors considered acceptable for them was extremely narrow. And, perhaps most important, the American professional business culture in which they were learning to fit was not only American but also American male.

All of the factors mentioned by the trainer indicate that making presentations is a prime example of an activity in which behavior expected of women is at odds with what is expected of an effective professional. In fact, the very act of standing up in front of a group talking about ideas is something that was unthinkable for women not so long ago. The nineteenth-century abolitionist Abby Kelley was reviled as a "Jezebel" and "fornicator" because of her public speaking. Because she was physically attractive, men saw her as a dangerous seductress.

Once a woman (or man) does make public presentations, she (or he) is open to challenge or even attack. Many women have been told they cave in too quickly rather than stand their ground. Being able to deal effectively with public challenges is not something that comes easily to many women (or men). . . .

THE DRAGON LADY

When I heard the same remark twice in one week about two different women, I knew there was something going on. "Before I came to work for Ann," a man who reports to her told me, "everybody warned me to watch out. They called her the dragon lady. But I don't know what they were talking about. I've always found her great to work with." A few days later, a woman at another company commented about the woman she works for, "I've heard people call Marie the dragon lady. But I've never seen anything to justify that. She's the best boss I've ever worked for." I wondered, Why the dragon lady? Not only was there nothing dragonlike about either Ann or Marie, but they were as different from one another as could be, in age, temperament, and personal style. The only thing they had in common was the "lady" part. Being women highly placed in their organizations seems to have caused people to look at them through conventional images of women in positions of authority. Our culture gives us a whole menagerie of stereotypical images of women: schoolmarm, head nurse, headmistress, doting mother, cruel stepmother, dragon lady, catwoman, witch, bitch.

An article about President Clinton's health czar, Kristine M. Gebbie, began by saying she didn't look like a czar, then went on to say she had the air of a head nurse. Although there is nothing inherently negative about being head nurse, the image this term evokes in our culture is decidedly negative: In the tradition of Ken Kesey's Nurse Ratched, the villain in his novel *One Flew Over the Cuckoo's Nest*, it suggests a woman who is arbitrarily authoritarian, life-killingly humorless, and stiffly unfeminine. . . . The writer explains, "There is something at once no-nonsense and fussy about her—her erect posture, her precise and proper answers, her tendency to correct an interviewer's questions." Hmmm. Shouldn't a czar stand erect and have a no-nonsense manner? Shouldn't a czar give precise and proper answers? Correcting an interviewer's questions seems a good way to maintain control when being interviewed. But all these qualities took on a very different effect because they were found in a woman.

"Presto!" a newspaper announced in large type, summarizing an accompanying story. "A stuffy schoolmarm is a contender." I began reading the article and learned that an Illinois gubernatorial candidate named Dawn Clark Netsch had won the Democratic nomination after she managed "to alter her image to a down-to-earth contender from that of a stuffy schoolmarm." But further down, I was surprised to read that the "bookish" candidate, who had previously "talked too much" and sounded "like some kind of egghead," had been a law professor at Northwestern University for eighteen years. This seemed to explain why she might be "bookish," talk a lot, and be denigrated by some as an egghead. But none of these qualities is suggested by "schoolmarm," which has different connotations entirely: stuffy, yes, but a strict disciplinarian rather than bookish, and small-minded rather than an egghead. Forced to choose between a professional image, appropriate to the qualities the paper attributed to her as well as to her profession, and "schoolmarm," suggested by her gender, the newspaper went for the gender.

THE IMAGE OF AUTHORITY

. . . Femaleness is associated with softeners, mitigation, and politeness, whereas maleness is associated with authority. This means that women who want to sound authoritative must risk sounding male. (It also means that men who want to sound polite must risk sounding female.)

Realizing that the very image of authority is associated with masculinity makes it easier to understand the images of professional women in our society. . . .

When I asked people for their impressions of the men and women they worked with and for, I noticed a pattern: When they commented on women in managerial positions—but never when they commented on men—people often said, "She's abrasive," or, just as often, "She's not abrasive," "not aggressive," or "has a soft touch." It is one thing to describe how you think someone is—"abrasive," "aggressive," and so on. But why would people mention what someone is not? It makes sense only against the expectation that the person would be that way. So it seems that when a woman is in a high position, there is an expectation that she will be unfeminine, negative, or worse. When she isn't, it is perceived as worth mentioning. And these prevalent images ambush professional women as they seek to maintain their careers as well as their personal lives—and their femininity.

. . . Individuals in positions of authority are judged by how they enact that authority. This poses a particular challenge for women. The ways women are expected to talk—and many (not all) women do talk—are at odds with images of authority. Women are expected to hedge their beliefs as opinions, to seek opinions and advice from others, to be "polite" in their requests. If a woman talks this way, she is seen as lacking in authority. But if she talks with certainty, makes bold statements of fact rather than hedged statements of opinion, interrupts others, goes on at length, and speaks in a declamatory and aggressive manner, she will be disliked. Our language is rich in words to describe such unwomanly women—words that have been hurled at many prominent women in positions of authority such as Jeane Kirkpatrick, Geraldine Ferraro, and Margaret Thatcher, as well as innumerable women in offices, factories, and studios around the country. Looking closely at how women in positions of authority use language to do their jobs—and how others respond to them— sheds light on our images of women as well as our understanding of authority. . . .

When I talked to people about their work lives, I asked them, among other things, what they think management is all about, and what makes a good manager or a poor one. When I put this question to women in positions of authority, one of the most frequent statements they offered to explain what makes them good managers is that they do *not* act like an authority figure—insofar as an authority figure is thought to be authoritarian. They told me that they don't lord it over subordinates, don't act as though they are better than those who report to them. I began to wonder why women in authority are so concerned not to appear authoritarian—not to appear as if they think they are superior or are putting themselves in a one-up position, even though that is exactly the position they are in.

CREATING AUTHORITY AS A PROFESSOR

. . . Linguist Elisabeth Kuhn examined the way male and female university professors established their authority, and she came to conclusions comparable to Smith's for student preachers. Kuhn noticed that the American women professors she taped avoided giving their students direct orders at the beginning of the term. Instead, they spoke of "the requirements" of the course, as if these were handed down directly from the institution, and then told the students how they could fulfill the requirements. This is how three different women professors introduced their syllabi—written outlines of the courses:

"We are going to talk about the requirements."

"I also tell you what the course requirements are, since I'm sure you're interested in that. Um, there is going to be a midterm and a final. Okay?"

"Now, let me say a little bit about the requirements for the course. I think if you look on the bottom of the second page, the cues are all there. . . . There are two papers, the first paper, ah, let's see, is due it's back here [while looking at her sheet] at the beginning."

Kuhn contrasts this with the male professors in her study who also handed out lists of requirements in the form of syllabi but made it explicit that the syllabi set forth decisions they personally had made:

"I have two midterms and a final. And I added this first midterm rather early to get you going on reading, uh, discussions, so that you will not fall behind."

"I want you to read NN's XX. But I have not assigned a textbook for you to go out and buy because I assumed either you have a copy of XX which will include the NN, or you will be delighted to go out and provide yourself with it. . . . I'm gonna ask you to do one midterm, which will primarily be a reading check to make sure that you're with it."

. . . The women professors used impersonal statements like, "There is going to be a midterm and a final," and "There are two papers," to avoid stating directly that they had devised and imposed the requirements. By using personal statements such as "I'm gonna ask you to do one midterm," the men professors called attention to their authority by going "on record" as the ones setting the requirements for the course.

In all these studies, women were found to downplay their authority while exercising it. It seems that creating their demeanor in a position of authority is yet another conversational ritual growing out of the goal of keeping everyone on an equal footing, at least insofar as appearances are concerned. This doesn't mean that women or men who speak this way really think everyone is equal; it means they have to do a certain amount of conversational work to make sure they maintain the proper demeanor—to fit their sense of what makes a good person, which entails not seeming to parade their higher status. If they have to tell others what to do, give information, and correct errors—all of which they will have to do on the job, especially if they are in a position of authority—they will expend effort to assure others that they are not pulling rank, not trying to capitalize on or rub in their one-up position. In contrast, since men's characteristic rituals have grown out of the assumption that all relationships are inherently hierarchical, it is not surprising that many of them either see less reason to downplay their authority or see more reason to call attention to it—to ward off inevitable challenges.

Choices of ways of speaking that highlight or downplay authority are not deliberate decisions that are thought through with each utterance but are rather habitual phrasings learned over time that become automatic, seemingly self-evidently appropriate ways to say what you mean.

I cannot emphasize enough that the appearance of equality I am referring to is ritual, not literal. I am not implying that individual women doubt their superior position in the hierarchy. . . .

Another liability for women in authority is that if they do not talk in ways that highlight the power of their position, they are more vulnerable to challenges to it. Like many conversation rituals common among women, talking as if "we're all equals" but still expecting to receive the respect appropriate to the higher-status position depends on the participation of the other person to respect that position. The president of a women's college had a long and difficult meeting with a student who protested her choice of commencement speaker. Finally, the president said, "What it comes down to is that you don't accept my right to make this decision, after considering your point of view and everyone else's." The student thought about it and agreed. "When I see you on campus after hours dressed informally, I forget about your position," she said. "If you were an older white man, it would be easier." In addition to dressing informally when she went to her office evenings and weekends, the president probably also spoke in ways that did not continually create a stance of authority, and this no doubt contributed to the student's forgetting the power of her position. . . .

. . . When people told me about men who had "strictly business" or "no-nonsense" styles, they simply said, "He's a strictly business type," or they referred to his profession: "He's a typical accountant." But when they were commenting on the same style in a woman, I frequently heard, "She's got a pseudomasculine style." Because this style was expected of and associated with men, women who adopted it were seen not as trying to be efficient, competent, and businesslike, but as trying to be like men.

One man I interviewed mentioned the same characteristic—directness—in talking about three people in his company. But it was a complaint in the case of the two women and a compliment when applied to the man. About one woman he said:

> Well, her style was very direct. I think very direct and abrupt. Because that was one of the criticisms I had of her . . . was a, somewhat of a lack of tact. Because she could make statements which were right, but not tactfully made. And she tended to upset—or ruffle some feathers.

. . . And yet, in telling me why he particularly admired a man he worked with, he mentioned the same quality—directness:

> And I had a great deal of admiration for him. I think he's direct, he's aggressive, he's very intelligent. . . . On the other hand, he does carry a big hammer! And if he needs to, he'll use it and you'll get squashed!

I have no way of knowing whether the people this man was referring to really did talk in the same way. No doubt there were many aspects of their styles and personalities that were different. But it is clear that the quality of directness made a different impression on him when it was used by the man and by the two women.

Another facet of this dynamic is that individuals within a culture may be punished by others if they do not conform to expectations for their sex. Anne Statham notes in her study of male and female managers that individuals of both sexes who departed from the norms for their own sex were viewed negatively by subordinates of the same sex. A male manager whose style approximated those of the women was seen as "fairly meek" and "weak" by men who worked for him, though he was highly praised by women subordinates. A woman manager whose style was more like those of the men in the study was criticized for neglect by a woman who reported to her (she "never shows any personal interest in me . . . she has only asked me to lunch once") and by her secretary for having "superior airs." The woman herself felt that women subordinates resisted accepting decisions she made independently.

Similar findings were uncovered by Susan Schick Case in a study of men and women managers talking together in groups of ten at a management school. Case concluded that two of the most influential members of the groups were a woman and a man whose styles combined ways of speaking expected of the two sexes. (She gauged influence by who talked more, how much, to whom, about what, and in what way.) The ways the particularly influential man spoke included hesitating, using rising intonation at the end of statements; mitigating statements with qualifiers; expressing feelings, and talking about himself. He also used "masculine traits" like swearing and joking. The particularly influential woman's style included using complex sentences, slang, resisting interruptions, and talking to the group as a whole. Her style also had many feminine aspects: She did not swear, did not talk "about competition, aggression, taking charge or one-upmanship," and her talk was often personal; Case found her to be the most supportive group member linguistically, but the only woman in the group who never said "mm-hmm." Case further describes her style in this way:

> She contributed 83% of all female usage of interruptions and all the incidents of disallowing interruption. That is not to say that she always disallowed interruptions. But the times she allowed interruptions accounted for only 18% of the female total. Although very assertive, her style was not confrontative, thus placing her in the bottom quartile in arguing, confronting, and attacking. She stated her own ideas, but also built on others' utterances and asked questions to elicit ideas, both female traits.

All in all, Case's description sounds quite appealing. So it comes as a surprise to learn that this woman was widely disliked and provoked openly hostile comments from others in the group whom Case describes as "male group members with prototypical male-style speech." Here are some of the things they said about her:

"You're playing the role of a man in the group. There's an issue of competition."

"Castrating bitch."

The men whose speech combined male and female traits, including the one Case singled out as being one of the most influential group members, did not, apparently, elicit the anger that this woman did, but neither were they pleased with the receptions they got. One man whose speech Case calls "balanced" measured in the middle in terms of influence, but he was the least influential of the men. . . .

. . . I have heard from many women in positions of authority who say the assertiveness required on the job causes problems at home. An attorney told me that she finds herself questioning her mother in a way that her mother protests, "You're not a lawyer now." Her husband too at times reminds her, "You're home now." One woman said that her husband told her, "Go out, come back in, and try saying that a different way. I'm not your secretary." Another woman told me that her husband became angry because instead of waiting on the sidewalk while he hailed a cab, she stepped into the street and raised her own arm, as she had come to do automatically when she needed to hail a cab in the course of her work. A third woman told of a similar experience: She and her husband arrived at an expensive restaurant for dinner. As usual, she had made the reservations. (This was no problem.) But as they approached the maître d', it was she who gave their name and helped the maître d' locate it on his list by pointing to it. By the time they were seated, her husband was livid. "Don't you ever do that again," he seethed. "You are the only woman in this whole restaurant who did that!"

In the case of the last example, I had to ask for clarification, to be sure I understood what exactly had angered the woman's husband. (It was that she took charge, dealing with the maître d' herself rather than hanging back and letting him do it.) But if women and men are to relate to each other as equals, shouldn't they be following the same norms in talking to each other? . . .

In considering these examples, I wondered why these women's husbands felt their wives were trying to dominate them, when the women did the very things that the men themselves wanted to do? . . .

WHAT'S A WOMAN TO DO?

. . . Our expectations for how a person in authority should behave are at odds with our expectations for how a woman should behave. If a woman talks in ways expected of women, she is more likely to be liked than respected. If she talks in ways expected of men, she is more likely to be respected than liked. It is particularly ironic that the risk of losing likability is greater for women in authority, since evidence indicates that so many women care so much about whether or not they are liked.

24

Women in the Power Elite

Richard L. Zweigenhaft and G. William Domhoff

. . . In 1962, Felice Schwartz founded Catalyst, a nonprofit agency specializing in women's job issues. Over the years, Catalyst developed a dual mission: to assist women in business and the professions to achieve their maximum potential, and to help employers capitalize on the abilities of their female employees.[1] In 1977, responding to requests from some major corporations, Catalyst began its Corporate Board Resource. This program was designed to draw on Catalyst's database of women of achievement "to help board chairmen carefully select and recruit female directors."[2] By the late 1970s, then, Catalyst was systematically monitoring the progress of women on boards and simultaneously working with boards to increase the presence of women.

Using a slightly broader sample than *Fortune* did in 1973 and 1978—one that included all directors of the top 1,300 companies, not just those who had earned $40,000 or more that year—Catalyst found that in 1977 there were 46 women on boards. By 1984, that figure had climbed to 367, 2.3 percent of all directors in the study.[3]

. . . By the mid-1990s the number of women on boards had climbed steadily, and there were indications that the trend was continuing. Fifty-eight percent of the Fortune 1,000 companies had at least one woman on their boards in 1994, and 20 percent had at least two; all of the ten most profitable companies had at least one woman director, and five of the ten had two or more. A few boards had more than three women.[4]

In 1995 *Fortune* published a new version of its list, one that merged the companies that had formerly been on the Fortune 500 and Service 500 lists. Catalyst's 1995

From *Diversity in the Power Elite* by Richard L. Zweigenhaft and G. William Domhoff (New Haven: Yale University Press, 1998), pp. 43–58. Copyright © 1998 by Richard Zweigenhaft and G. William Domhoff. Reprinted with permission.

report was based only on the Fortune 500, not the entire 1000, and it then recreated lists for 1994 and 1993 by looking at old data only for those companies that still appeared on the 1995 list. (Some had been bumped off by Fortune Service 500 companies formerly on the Service 500 list.) Because larger companies are more likely than smaller companies to include women on their boards, this had the effect of slightly increasing the percentage in the Catalyst report. The share of seats held by women on Fortune 500 companies rose from 6.2 percent to 6.3 percent for the revised analysis based on 1993, and from 6.9 percent to 8.7 percent for the revised analysis based on 1994; for 1995, the figure was up to 9.5 percent. In 1996, Catalyst's annual report indicated that for the first time the figure exceeded 10 percent, though the rate of increase had declined.[5]

In October 1996, Catalyst published a study based on a census of the 1995 annual reports and proxy statements of the five hundred largest companies. Although 9.5 percent of the corporate directors were women, only 1.9 percent of the top five earners at these companies—and only 2.4 percent of those holding the titles of chairman, chief executive, vice chairman, president, chief operating officer, or executive vice president—were women. In the words of Wellington, "the numbers are pathetic" and the picture remains "dismal."[6]

. . . Who are these women, and how did they come to be corporate directors? Do they come from similar or different backgrounds from the white, Protestant, American-born sons of businessmen and professionals who constituted the corporate elite in 1956? What role do they play on the corporate boards—are they tokens, or have they assumed positions of importance equal to those of their male counterparts on their boards?

Three studies help answer these questions. The first was performed in 1977 by Burson-Marsteller, a public relations and advertising firm, for a client. The second is a 1986 Ph.D. dissertation by Beth Ghiloni. The third and most recent study was done by Catalyst in 1991. Although their methods and samples differed, together these studies suggest some patterns and some changes over time in the characteristics of women on corporate boards.

The Burson-Marsteller study was based on interviews with women who sat on the boards of Fortune 500 companies, the fifty largest banks, or the fifty largest retail organizations. After eliminating those who had been on those boards for less than a year and those who were the wives or daughters of company founders, the researchers contacted seventy-five women, thirty-one of whom agreed to be interviewed. These women were highly educated. Thirty-nine percent held Ph.D.'s and another 16 percent held law degrees. Only 16 percent had not attained an undergraduate degree. As might be predicted from their level of academic achievement, many had risen to the top of their fields in education and law, but few had attained leadership roles in corporations before being asked to join a corporate board. The study included no information about marital status, race, or class background.[7]

As part of her dissertation, Ghiloni studied the backgrounds of women who sat on Fortune 1000 boards in 1983. She identified 338 women occupying 508 directorships (figures that are similar to the Catalyst data for that period). She, too, found that women directors were "an exceptionally well-educated group": 53 percent held postgraduate degrees (27 percent had Ph.D.'s and the others had M.A.'s, M.B.A.'s, law degrees, or M.D.'s). These women directors, she noted, were more highly educated than male directors; in a comparable study of male directors, Michael Useem and Jerome Karabel found that 44 percent held postgraduate degrees.[8]

Ghiloni did not estimate the percentage of female board members who were from upper-middle-class backgrounds, but she did estimate the percentage who were from the upper class. Using attendance at exclusive prep schools, listing in the *Social Register*, or membership in an exclusive club as evidence of membership in the social upper class, and using ownership of large amounts of stock in a *Fortune*-level firm as evidence of membership in the economic upper class, she concluded that 33 percent of her sample were from either the economic or the social upper class or both. This figure is similar to overall findings for samples of predominantly male directors for 1963 by Domhoff and for 1970 by Dye.[9]

. . . The Catalyst study was based on a questionnaire sent in the summer of 1991 to all 394 female directors of Fortune 500 and Fortune Service 500 companies. The response rate was 41 percent, or 162 surveys. When possible, the researchers also drew on information available in annual reports and proxy statements.

The average age of the women directors in 1991 was fifty-six, a bit younger than that of the men who sat on boards that year (average age, fifty-nine). Eighty-five percent had been married; 9 percent were divorced and 6 percent widowed. Almost three-fourths (74 percent) had children, with the older directors having had more children. The racial makeup of the women directors was similar to that found in Ghiloni's study: 90 percent were white, 6 percent were African American, and 3 percent were Hispanic.[10]

The women surveyed in 1991, like those surveyed in 1977 and 1983, were highly educated. One-fourth had attended women's colleges, and all but "one or two" of the women's schools they attended were seven sister schools. Catalyst did not report the number with Ph.D.'s or law degrees but did indicate that the "area of significant experience" for 16 percent of the respondents was law, and that 49 percent were primarily involved with education. Cross-tabulations looking at age and work experience indicated that the older directors were much more likely to have had their major work experience in academia, and the younger directors were much more likely to have had their major work experience in corporations or in companies they had founded.

THE PRESSURE TO ASSIMILATE

. . . Rosabeth Moss Kanter has suggested that the need to reduce uncertainty in large and impersonal institutions leads to the strong emphasis on conformity in behavior and homogeneity in background. "It is the uncertainty quotient," she wrote, "that causes management to become so socially restricting; to develop tight inner circles excluding social strangers; to keep control in the hands of socially homogenous peers; to stress conformity and insist upon a diffuse, unbounded loyalty; and to prefer ease of communication and thus social certainty over the strains of dealing with people who are 'different.'"[11]

A few years after Kanter's book appeared, when we interviewed black and white Jewish and Gentile men and women who had M.B.A.'s from Harvard and were in (or had been in) the corporate world, this theme emerged again and again. Notably, the Jewish women we interviewed agreed that being a woman posed more of a hurdle than being Jewish. A number of them, however, explained that this did not mean that their Jewishness was completely without significance. As one put it, "It's not irrelevant. It's part of the total package. Ultimately, in the fishbowl-type environment you're in, they scrutinize you carefully. It's part of the question of whether you fit the mold. Are you like me or not? If too much doesn't fit, it impacts you negatively." Another explained, "It's the whole package. I heard second hand from someone as to how I would be perceived as a pushy Jewish broad who went and got an M.B.A. Both elements, being Jewish and being a woman, together with having the M.B.A., were combined to create a stereotype. I had to work against that stereotype from the first day." Another summed the situation up by saying, "Anything that makes you different is more likely to be a factor at senior levels because it's so much more homogeneous there."[12]

. . . When the report was issued by the Federal Glass Ceiling Commission in 1995, comments by the white male managers who had been interviewed and surveyed supported the earlier claims that upper management was willing to accept women and minorities only if they were not too different. As one manager explained, "What's important is comfort, chemistry, relationships, and collaborations. That's what makes a shop work. When we find minorities and women who think like we do, we snatch them up."[13]

. . . Similarly, when the editors of *Executive Female* magazine surveyed the top fifty women in line-management positions (in sales, marketing, production, and general management with a direct impact on the company's bottom line), they asked them why more women had not made it to the "upper reaches of corporate America." The most frequently identified problem was the "comfort factor"—that the men atop their corporations wanted others around them with whom they were comfortable, and that generally meant other men similar to themselves. One of the other most frequently identified problems, not unrelated to the comfort factor, was the exclusion from "the social networks—the clubs, the golf course—where the informal networking that is so important to moving up the ladder often takes place."[14]

. . . Whether or not playing golf is necessary to fit in, it is clear that women who make it into the corporate elite must assimilate sufficiently into the predominantly male culture to make it into the comfort zone. As Kathleen Jamieson points out, however, this, can place them in a double bind. On the one hand, women in the corporate world are expected to be competitive and tough-minded—but not too competitive or tough-minded, or they risk being called ballbusters. On the other hand, women in the corporate world are expected to be feminine enough to be seen as attractive and caring—but not too feminine, lest their appearance and behavior be seen as inappropriate or as an indication that they are tender-minded.[15]

... Indeed, it is not unusual to discover that women executives have athletic interests formerly held only by men and that they are described in terms formerly applied to men. Consider the following description in *USA Today* of Judy Lewent when she was named chief financial officer of Merck and Company (number 59 on the 1995 *Fortune* list): "Judy C. Lewent plays tennis like a pro, swims like a shark and performs her job as chief financial officer of Merck & Co. with military precision. Her boss, senior VP Francis H. Spiegel, Jr., says, 'She would have been a hell of a Marine. She's lean, mean and determined. . . . Her idea of a perfect vacation: two hours of tennis each day followed by 50 to 60 laps in the pool and an hour's walk on the beach. Competitiveness seems to define her life.'"[16]

... Aside from wanting their companies to appear diverse (especially if they cater to a diverse clientele) and wanting to mollify their female relatives, is there something more that drives corporations to include women in higher management and on their boards? We think there is. It has to do with the use of women to create a "buffer zone."

As part of his analysis of the transition from a pure patriarchal system, in which all power is held by males, to modern capitalism, Michael Mann proposes that "a kind of compromise between patriarchy and a more gendered stratification hierarchy has emerged," both in the households and in the marketplace. In this compromise, women now occupy buffer zones between the men of their own class and the men in the classes below. This phenomenon appears at every point in the class hierarchy. Women who are part-time and unskilled manual laborers in low-income jobs, for example, serve as a buffer between the mostly male unemployed below them and the mostly male skilled manual workers above them. Secretaries and other white-collar women interact with the blue-collar workers who do maintenance jobs and deliver packages for the male managers. Women are the nurses and paralegals for physicians and lawyers. And women in the higher reaches function as a buffer between "capital and all labour" by serving as volunteers, fund raisers, and board members for a wide range of charitable and social service organizations.[17]

Drawing on this analysis, we conclude that the men who run America's corporations have women in higher management and on their boards not only to present a corporate image of diversity, and not only to deflect criticism from their wives, daughters, and granddaughters, but to provide a valuable buffer between the men who control the corporation and the corporation's labor force (and the general public). It is not surprising, therefore, that in its 1996 study of the top corporate officers at Fortune 500 companies, Catalyst found that only 28 percent of the women officers who held the titles of executive vice president, senior vice president or vice president had positions with operational responsibility for profit and loss. Instead, many had been channeled into positions specializing in such areas as labor relations and public relations.[18] It is in these jobs especially that women are used as effective buffers. Because these staff jobs seldom lead to positions in top management, Ghiloni concluded her study of the velvet ghetto of public affairs in a top-50 corporation by noting that "women can play an increasingly important role in the corporation and still not gain power."[19]

Long before women joined corporate boards or were employed in personnel and public relations, women of the upper class interceded in the social system in ways that smoothed out the hard-edged, profit-oriented impact of a business-driven economy. In the Progressive Era, some upper-class women argued for protective labor legislation, maximum hours, and more respectful treatment of labor. They came to call themselves volunteers as they took a hand in running health, cultural, and social welfare agencies that added a humane, socially concerned dimension to their lives of wealth and privilege. First in nonprofit institutions, and now in corporations, we see the intersection of gender and class in a way that serves the power elite by providing a buffer zone between the wealthy few and the rest of society.[20]

NOTES

1. Felice Schwartz has shown the ability to help found programs that have real and lasting power. In 1947, just two years after graduating from Smith College, Schwartz founded the National Scholarship Service and Fund for Negro Students (NSSFNS). She left NSSFNS in 1952 but remained on the board for twenty years. NSSFNS was a forerunner and partial model for other programs that provide scholarships for young black students, including the A Better Chance Program. Phone interview by Richard Zweigenhaft with Felice Schwartz, August 7, 1986.

2. "Women on Corporate Boards: The Challenge of Change," Catalyst, 1993, p. 4.

3. "You've Come a Long Way, Baby—But Not as Far as You Thought," *Business Week*, October 1, 1984, p. 126.

4. The following boards had three or more women: American Electric Power, Avon, Baxter International, Central Fidelity banks, Dayton Hudson, Federal National Mortgage Association, Gannett, Great Atlantic and Pacific Tea, Hasbro, Hershey Foods, Johnson & Johnson, Knight-Ridder, Kroger, Levi Strauss, Long Island Lighting, Longview Fibre, New York Times, Ogden, Principal Mutual Life Insurance, Rochester Community Savings Bank, Rubbermaid, Stanhome, Student Loan Marketing Association, TIAA, U.S. West.

5. See "1995 Catalyst Census: Female Board Directors of the *Fortune 500*," Catalyst; Judith H. Dobrzynski, "Women Pass Milestone in the Board Room," *New York Times*, December 12, 1996.

6. "Catalyst Census of Women Corporate Officers and Top Earners as of February 28, 1996," Catalyst, 1996, pp. 6–9. For the quotations by Sheila Wellington, see Judith H. Dobrzynski, "Study Finds New Women in 5 Highest Company Jobs," *New York Times*, October 18, 1996.

7. Burson-Marstellar, *Study of Women Directors* (New York, 1977), cited in "Women on Corporate Boards," Catalyst, 65.

8. Beth W. Ghiloni, "New Women of Power: An Examination of the Ruling Class Model of Domination," Ph.D. diss., University of California, Santa Cruz, 1986, pp. 137–141. See Michael Useem and Jerome Karabel, "Pathways to Top Corporate Management," *American Sociological Review* 51(1986), 184–199.

9. Ghiloni, "New Women of Power," 122–136; G. William Domhoff, *Who Rules America?* (Englewood Cliffs, N.J.: Prentice-Hall, 1967), 51, 57; Thomas R. Dye, *Who's Running America? The Carter Years*, 2d ed. (Englewood Cliffs, N.J.: Prentice Hall, 1979), 169–170.

10. "Women on Corporate Boards," Catalyst, 12–20.

11. Rosabeth Moss Kanter, *Men and Women of the Corporation* (New York: Basic, 1977), 49.

12. Richard L. Zweigenhaft, *Who Gets to the Top? Executive Suite Discrimination in the Eighties* (New York: Institute of Human Relations, 1984), 17.

13. *Good for Business: Making Full Use of the Nation's Human Capital* (Washington, D.C.: U.S. Government Printing Office, 1995), 28.

14. Basia Hellwic, "Executive Female's Breakthrough 50," *Executive Female*, September–October 1992, p. 46.

15. Kathleen Hall Jamieson, *Beyond the Double Bind: Women and Leadership* (New York: Oxford University Press, 1995), 120–145.

16. Julia Lawlor, "Cracks in 'Glass Ceiling,'" *USA Today*, June 1, 1990.

17. Michael Mann, "A Crisis in Stratification Theory? Persons, Households/Families/Lineages, Genders, Classes, and Nations," in Rosemary Crompton and Michael Mann, eds., *Gender and Stratification* (London: Polity, 1986), 47. See also Peta Tancred-Sheriff, "Gender, Sexuality, and the Labour Process," in Jeff Hearn, Deborah L. Sheppard, Peta Tancred-Sheriff, and Gibson Burrell, eds., *The Sexuality of Organization* (London: Sage, 1989), 45–55. Tancred-Sheriff suggests that women in corporations use "implicit sexuality" as a form of "adjunct control" that serves to "facilitate the operation of the capitalist enterprise" (53).

18. "Catalyst Census of Women Corporate Officers and Top Earners," 8.

19. Beth W. Ghiloni, "The Velvet Ghetto: Women, Power, and the Corporation," in G. William Domhoff and Thomas R. Dye, eds., *Power Elites and Organizations* (Beverly Hills, Calif.: Sage, 1987), 21–36.

20. See G. William Domhoff, *The Higher Circles* (New York: Random House, 1970), 35; Susan Ostrander, *Women of the Upper Class* (Philadelphia: Temple University Press, 1984).

25

Women above the Glass Ceiling: Perceptions on Corporate Mobility and Strategies for Success

Sally Ann Davies-Netzley

. . . The number of women who have attained elite positions in corporate offices and boardrooms in the United States remains considerably low. Women comprise roughly 4 percent of directors and 2 percent of corporate officers in Fortune 500 companies (Von Glinow and Krzyczkowska-Mercer 1988). More progress has been made in corporate boardrooms. In the mid-1970s, only 13 percent of the 1,350 major corporations in the United States had a female director on their board. By 1985, that figure rose to 41 percent (*The Wall Street Journal* 1986).

Some scholars interpret these gains as dismal progress for women and emphasize the lack of substantial numbers of women at the top. Others characterize women in elite corporate positions as token workers who are less integrated in the large, influential central circles of power (Kanter [1977] 1993; Moore 1988). While we can point to a limited number of studies discussing elite women as "outsiders on the inside," there is a lack of research focusing on women's experiences in elite corporate positions and their perspectives on corporate mobility and success. . . .

This study builds on the existing literature on women in management in several ways. First, I question the extent to which men and women in elite corporate positions offer similar perspectives on corporate success and mobility. Second, I examine how women presidents and CEOs respond to a work situation that, ideologically, has been associated with masculinity and continues to be characterized by mostly men. What strategies do women use to succeed in their elite positions above the corporate glass ceiling?

METHODOLOGY

In the fall of 1995 and 1996, I interviewed men and women who occupy elite corporate positions in Southern California. I considered those in elite positions to be
at the top of the corporate hierarchy. Consequently, I limited my sample to individuals who hold the title of president or chief officer. Participants were selected from
a wide range of industries: a midsize law firm, a private university, a local bank, and
one of the largest local hospitals. The financial and advertising companies have been
reported among the top 25 of their industries in terms of employees and revenues,
which ranged from $250,000 to $500,000. The bio- and high-technology firms had
revenues exceeding 1 million annually, and some ranked in the top 10 of their industries. . . .

Most interviews were conducted face-to-face in the offices of the informants and
lasted about one hour. Questions were open-ended and focused on the respondents'
social origins, education, career path, business and social affiliations, characteriza-
tion of social networks, and factors assisting them in their rise to the top and their
ability to successfully function in their position. Respondents also were asked to
characterize their views concerning social relationships between people in elite positions and the extent to which gender was a significant factor in influencing an
individual's success.

Sixteen informants were interviewed. Nine were white women, and seven were
white men. Considering the small size of my sample and that most corporate CEOs
and presidents are white, it is not surprising that snowball sampling produced an
all-white sample. An obvious drawback of this sample is that it does not allow for
direct comparisons to men and women of color. The median age was 52 for men
and 50 for women. In addition, all of the interviewees had earned bachelor's degrees.
Six of the men and five of the women had degrees beyond the bachelor's level. The
median years in current position was eight for men and seven for women. Six of
the men and five of the women were presently married. All of the men and five of
the women had children.[1]

IDEOLOGY AT WORK: ELITE MEN'S PERSPECTIVES

. . . When discussing what it takes to make it to the top, the men primarily attribute
their success and elite status to their own individual qualities.[2] These men uphold
the dominant stratification ideology in the United States by emphasizing that success and economic reward come from individual talent and effort.

Overall, the men ranked hard work as the most important element for success.
Douglas Strickland, president of a biotechnology corporation, comments, "Everyone in the game is smart enough. It takes hard work." In thinking about what is
most important in achieving and maintaining a top position, Strickland notes, "Hard
work is first, timing/luck, cold honest appraisal, and good, useful ideas."

Strickland mentions luck as the second factor in achieving success. Four other men also mention luck as one factor in success, but they always place luck after individual effort. For instance, Steven Putnam, a law firm partner, notes, "I think luck has something to do with it, but I don't think luck is a major factor." He continues, "It's a matter of some internal drive people develop." For Putnam, this inner drive, possessed by some but not all individuals, is important for a successful career. Similarly, Matthew Gilbert, president of a scientific institute, and John Holden, CEO of a private university, emphasize the importance of an individual's inner qualities, particularly leadership skills, in becoming successful.

The men highlight competitive qualities needed to succeed in business, and several drew parallels between being a corporate elite and an athlete. For instance, Holden makes the connection between sports and the business world:

> I don't think you'll find a successful CEO that doesn't thrive on competition. . . . To use a sports analogy, think of the person who wants the ball at the last of the game. A lot of people who don't want the ball say, "What if I miss?" I think competitors say, "What if I make it?"

Likewise, Strickland uses a football analogy, comparing a president of a company to a quarterback: "The quarterback has got to do his job, even though he knows that within a split second of throwing the football, he's going to get creamed."

These men define their success in terms of performance and winning, dominant values of organized sports. The analogy they draw between business and organized sports is significant, because sports are an important organizing institution for the embodiment of masculinity and represent "a practice through which men's separation from and power over women is embodied and naturalized" (Messner 1989, 73). These elite men discuss the qualities needed to function in business and sports, such as competitiveness, but they do not acknowledge the male-dominated nature of these institutions.

When thinking about their own success and what it takes to make it to the top, all of the men downplay the importance of an "old boys' network" or peer similarities among men and underscore the significance of individual qualities. A good example of undermining the importance of all-male, elite networks is provided by Strickland. He initially denies the existence of an old boys' network but acknowledges that many boardrooms are occupied primarily by men: "Oftentimes I'll go to a meeting and it will be all white men in the room." Still, he undermines the assertion that gender plays an important role: "But I know these men and they don't give a damn. If there's a woman in there who can give them an edge, then get in there." For Strickland, the old boys' network does not explain success: "It isn't an old boys' network—but it is, it's an old boy network of 'successful' people, it has nothing to do with men and women, or black and white."

. . . In addition to asking the men about success, I also asked for their thoughts on the paucity of women at the top. Assumptions inherent in patriarchal gender ideology were used by the men to explain why women are underrepresented in elite positions. Three men felt that women's lack of necessary skills and know-how had prevented them from attaining elite positions. James Olson, president of a financial institution, describes the recent addition of the first woman to the bank's board: "We talked about having a woman in the past but had been unable to settle on someone who we thought could make a major contribution." According to Olson, until recently, many women did not have the skills to contribute meaningfully at the board level.

. . . Family conflict also was suggested by four of the men as the most significant reason why few women are at the top. These men equate women primarily with the homemaker role, asserting that because women's family responsibilities are paramount, they are often unable to commit the time needed in an elite position. Gilbert comments,

> No matter how much you want to fight it, there is this underlying thing for women that they always have to be the wife, the mother. The male, well, they're supposed to be the father and husband, but that doesn't mean quite the time commitment.

He states that married women do not perform as well because they can't commit the time that male counterparts can. Norton also argues that there is still conflict between work and home for women in senior positions that require 12- to 14-hour workdays. These four men view single women without children as better suited to corporate elite positions than wives and mothers. And while they felt it was problematic for women at the top to have families, they did not view their own family responsibilities as a hindrance for their work in elite positions.

Five men in the sample had wives who stayed at home for most of their children's school-age years. The two men with wives working in the paid workforce relied more heavily on paid child care. All of the men (all have children) state that they have sacrificed family time for work; however, they all underscore the benefits of an elite position for their families: private school attendance, a "nice home in a nice area," and recreational opportunities. Although it appears that men in the United States have shifted their attitudes toward the provider role in a more egalitarian direction (Wilkie 1993), the men in my sample typify primary breadwinning men who view their parental contribution in terms of income and financial support.

SUCCESS FROM THE STANDPOINT OF ELITE WOMEN

Unlike the men who describe moving up the ladder quickly or growing with the company, all of the women offered examples of experiencing gender discrimination in their corporate careers—whether it be in the form of comments from men colleagues questioning their ability to have a career and family or feeling left out of informal networking opportunities. To advance their careers, five of the women talked of fleeing larger corporations, working in smaller firms, networking in the local corporate community, and then moving into higher positions in more established corporations. The act of leaving large corporations and moving to "smaller, more hospitable organization(s)" is a common response among professional women experiencing workplace discrimination (Rosener 1995, 113). This is illustrated by Marie Johnson, president of a consulting company, who left a lucrative position in a large company because her advancement opportunities were blocked. She explains,

> I told my boss that I wanted to be more involved with customers. I wanted to take the next step. He said to me that he didn't think that women with children could do "marketing." I decided at that point to move on.

Likewise, advertising president Jennifer Anderson recalls gender discrimination in her previous place of business.

> I've been in meetings where men haven't listened to leadership from a woman. But women are needed and should be valued. You have to prove yourself more as a woman. There's a kind of silent hostility out there toward women in business. I think there's this anger that men have to share "what belongs to them" with women.

Having experienced workplace discrimination and glass ceilings, the women's perspectives on corporate mobility contrast considerably with those of men peers. An immediate difference emerges in the role played by hard work. In contrast to men, all of the women assert that hard work alone, or even intelligence or talent, is not enough to succeed, and that opportunities are often blocked to individuals who are not white males. All of the women assert that external barriers exist to hinder a hardworking woman from achieving upward corporate mobility. Tracy Newton, CEO of a biotechnology company, illustrates this point: "Some people feel it's just hard work, do a good job, and you'll get promoted. That might be true to a certain point and that point is wherever the glass ceiling is."

This is not to say that the women did not acknowledge individual qualities as factors for success. Overall, the women agreed that an individual's inner drive, high self-esteem, and communication skills are important for success. They also felt that women were just as capable as men in displaying such qualities. Ultimately, however, the women emphasize that corporate mobility to the top does not depend primarily on individual-level variables such as inner drive or work ethic. Their views on corporate mobility and success are different from the men's.

Male-Dominated Networks

Whereas the men legitimize their positions through the ideology of individualism, all the women I spoke with explain their success by referring to social-structural variables. They emphasize social networks as most significant for success at elite levels and argue that the existence of an old boys' network continues to make it more difficult for women to succeed. They assert that success depends largely on how entrenched male networks are and how willing elite men are to accept the women into the networks.

Most of the women talk of experiencing old boys' networks within more established corporations when attempting to make their way up the corporate ladder. Newton describes the corporate atmosphere of a former workplace: "It was a male dominated culture with a good old boys' network. The only women they wanted at the top were the ones they placed there as tokens." Newton also adds that if women want to reach senior positions, they need to network with men in power positions. Newton argues, "The power is still in the males 50-plus years old. If you want to reach the top, those are the people you have to network with."

Even after having reached an elite corporate position, all of the women still consider themselves outsiders to a system that accommodates men. They speak of encountering an old boys' network composed of elites from other companies, which at times makes it difficult to function. Marsha Wagner, president of a manufacturing company, exemplifies this point: "Fund-raising is tougher for women in business because they don't have the network of 'good old boys' to put in money." Joan Miller, a former CEO who sits on several boards of directors, comments, "There is an old boys' network, and I have no doubt that there probably are opportunities (I've) missed, there probably are certain positions that I never could be in." Even though Miller and Wagner have obtained top corporate positions, they still feel excluded from business opportunities because of the existing old boys' network. This echoes the sentiments of Nancy Harrison, president of a high-technology corporation, who still does not consider herself "part of the group."

> The people at the top of this indu]stry are still mostly men. I try not to let it bother me. I think they respect me as a professional, but I don't feel like I'm part of the group. I don't feel like I belong.

Likewise, Carrie Hughes, president of an investment corporation, describes feeling like an outsider after becoming a newly appointed board member:

> It doesn't occur to some men that a woman would be there to contribute to the board. There was this one incident when this board member thought I was part of the hotel staff and tried to pick me up. I introduced myself and he immediately backed off.

Such statements reinforce Moore's (1988) findings that even after reaching elite positions, women are still "outsiders on the inside" and often feel invisible or excluded from informal relationships and networks of all-men colleagues. Some of these women do believe, however, that it is only a matter of time before women are integrated into elite circles. Wagner states, "The network will break down. Younger men are different. They respect your leadership more." Hughes adds, "The weight of the numbers in business are now such that they won't be able to use excuses for much longer."

Peer Similarities

. . . These women also note that the rapport between elite men often hinders women's pathways to success. Feeling like outsiders, they recognize that the nature of the relationships developed between elite males is fundamentally different from that between men and women in elite positions. Katherine Frost, president of a scientific corporation, made this point:

> There is definitely a different rapport between men. It's subtle, but they can say to each other. "Hey, could you wait a minute, I'd like to talk over some ideas with you after the meeting." With me, I think there's the hesitation of, well, she might think I'm coming on to her.

WOMEN'S SURVIVAL STRATEGIES AT THE TOP

. . . Earning advanced degrees and credentials (higher than those of most men) appears to be a way that women compete with men for elite positions. Three of the women purposefully returned to school to increase their credentials and make themselves more competitive for top positions. Hughes asserts, "I got an MBA in marketing 10 years after my MA in communication because it was apparent that I wasn't going to go higher in the corporate world without it." Master's degrees in business and law degrees are most closely related to entry into elite positions (Ward, Orazem, and Schmidt 1992). A total of five women in my sample had graduate degrees but mentioned difficulties during their graduate programs with being taken seriously by male faculty. Miller talks of one dissertation committee member: "He thought they shouldn't waste graduate positions on women because they would just marry, have children, and not be as professional."

The women also emphasize the need to develop similarities with male peers to be successful. Rather than highlighting hard work, the women talk primarily of strategies they use for fitting in: altering appearance to fit the proper business attire and changing speech and behaviors to conform to situations with other elites. Forst notes, "There are certain ways of acting in these meetings, I mean for business investors or advisory meetings, I pull my hair back, wear a suit, don't act giggly . . . because you need to fit in." When meeting with other elites, Frost puts on a calculated performance. She modifies her appearance, wears her hair differently, and dresses differently, because she knows that this is the expected way to look and behave. Likewise, this conscious modification spills over into social situations with other corporate elites. Hughes discusses avoiding some country club activities with male peers. She jokes, "It's too tough to be taken seriously when you're wearing a tennis skirt!"

These modifications are predictably influenced by gendered expectations. For instance, one man I interviewed, Douglas Strickland, comments on appropriate behavior in board meetings: "If you're going to be a frilly little sweetheart and have people open your doors . . . that isn't what it's about. I mean it has its place." Encountering such kinds of attitudes, the women attempt to downplay their own feminine qualities to fit in. Newton makes this point: "I talk sports, politics, read the *Wall Street Journal.* I talk what the guys do. I have to. My belief is 'when in Rome, do as the Romans do.'" Newton consciously brings up topics she feels will be of interest to other male elites, topics she would not otherwise discuss outside these circles. Hughes also talks of "speaking 'their' language in board meetings." And Miller also notes, "There certainly is an old boys' network, but "I've also found that you can enter it, I think, so long as you are sort of, not the word, asexual, but if you don't act like a female."

. . . Finally, I questioned what strategies these women use to survive in such an elite position and reconcile their family lives. Two women made a conscious decision not to have children with such a demanding career. Hughes emphasizes that with her busy travel schedule and 12-hour days, she could not devote the time necessary to raising children. "My career goals have definitely influenced my decision not to have children. I think for me, I just don't think it would be fair to have children and this kind of schedule." . . .

Five of the women in my sample have children, two with school-age children, three with adult children. They all acknowledge that work and family have conflicted at some point in their careers. . . .

Miller also discusses balancing the responsibilities of having a child and working in a high-power position. "It's had a lot of inconveniences," she states. "But," she continues, "it's never impossible because (my husband and I have) always been able to work it out."

While these women comment on work and family conflicts, they also are quick to suggest that they can juggle such responsibilities. As with all working parents, they talk of methods for reconciling work and family such as day care facilities and modifying schedules with partners to accommodate child care. They also are able to pay for live-in help, something most other American families cannot afford. . . .

CONCLUSIONS

Most of the top executive positions and directorships in corporate America continue to be held by white men of upper- or upper-middle-class origin. In recent years, however, there has been an increase of women, particularly white upper-middle- to upper-class women, in top corporate positions. Most studies of women at the top have addressed their numbers in the leadership of the entire nation, using survey data to examine their gains within major national corporations and the U.S. government (Dye 1995; Moore 1988). This study provides a unique, detailed look at men and women who comprise part of a local community-based elite, how they think about corporate mobility, and women's strategies for success at the top. . . .

My finding that men are less sensitive to external barriers facing women and minorities is supported by a recent survey of 325 men CEOs conducted by Catalyst (Townsend 1996). Eighty-two percent cited a lack of general management experience as the reason women are held back from corporate leadership (Townsend 1996). In contrast, among the 461 women in vice president or higher positions, male stereotyping of women was the number-one cited obstacle to women's advancement, with exclusion from informal ("old boy") networks the next most serious deterrent

(Townsend 1996). This article also reveals strategies women use in maintaining their elite positions, such as displaying cultural capital in the form of advanced degrees or in modification of appearance and speech. . . .

This study has revealed perspectives of white men and women in top corporate positions; future work must assess explicitly and directly the dynamics of gender, race, and class for moving above the glass ceiling. Women's work experiences are not only affected by gender but also by race, ethnicity, nationality, and class. It is little surprise that women privileged within race and class hierarchies in the United States are moving up the corporate ladder. Understanding their perceptions of corporate mobility, and those of both women and men in ethnic minorities, continues to be crucial for revealing how outsiders climb the corporate ladder and break through the glass ceiling.

NOTES

1. All names of the interviewees and some biographical details have been changed.

2. Social psychologists also have found that American men in achievement situations tend to internalize and take credit for their successes, illustrated by male college students when passing an exam (Sweeney, Moreland, and Gruber 1982). For social psychologists, socialization is an important explanation for this internal attributional style among men. Contradictory evidence has been found with respect to women's attributions of success (Deaux 1976; Wiley, Crittenden, and Birg 1979). In response to the social psychology literature, I argue that it is important to keep in mind that attributional patterns are based on men's and women's social experiences and responsive to social context and cultural ideology.

REFERENCES

Dye, Thomas. 1995. *Who's running America? The Clinton years.* Englewood Cliffs, NJ: Prentice Hall.

Kanter, Rosabeth Moss. (1977) 1993. *Men and women of the corporation.* New York: Basic Books.

Messner, Michael. 1989. Masculinities and athletic careers. *Gender & Society* 3:71–88.

Moore, Gwen. 1988. Women in elite positions: Insiders or outsiders? *Sociological Forum* 3:566–85.

Rosener, Judy B. 1995. *America's competitive secret: Utilizing women as a management strategy.* New York: Oxford University Press.

Townsend, Bickley. 1996. Room at the top for women. *American Demographics* 18(July)7: 28–37.

Von Glinow, M. A., and A. Krzyczkowska-Mercer. 1988. Women in corporate America: A caste of thousands. *New Management* 6:36–42.

The Wall Street Journal. 1986. The board game: More women are becoming directors but it's still a token situation, 24 March, section 4, 290.

Wilkie, Jane Riblett. 1993. Changes in U.S. men's attitudes toward the family provider role, 1972–1989. *Gender & Society* 7:261–79.

26

What Do Men Want?

Michael S. Kimmel

Freud's famous cry of resignation—"Women, what do they want?"—has been a feminist touchstone for nearly a century. By contrast, the good doctor and countless other social commentators always assumed they knew what men wanted, especially in the realm of work. After all, a man's profession and his ability to bring home a paycheck have traditionally defined who that man was. With wives to manage the domestic scene, working men of the past had little reason to question a system designed by and for them. . . .

Not all men want the same thing, of course. Some still resist efforts to change the old rules for masculine behavior. But in the professional ranks, a new organization man has indeed emerged, one who wants to be an involved father with no loss of income, prestige, and corporate support—and no diminished sense of manhood. Like working women, we want it all. Yet in today's insecure corporate world, we're even less sure of how to get it.

Few 1990s men fit the traditional picture of distant father, patriarchal husband, and work-obsessed breadwinner; fewer still have dropped out of the working world completely into full-time daddydom and househusbandhood. Rather than a suburban conformist or high-flying single yuppie, today's organization man carries a briefcase while pushing a baby carriage.

Given that most American men grew up believing in the traditional symbols of manhood—wealth, power, status—there are clear emotional and financial costs involved in making other choices. Since many companies still deem dedication to career the sole marker of professional success, the new organization man may believe he has to hide his participation at home. Instead of taking advantage of his company's formal parental-leave policies, for instance, he's more likely to use sick days to watch over a new baby. Even if his boss knows this man is caring for a child and not really sick, the time off is viewed as an exception rather than a threat to the status quo.

With the costs of redefining the male role, however, come the benefits that are driving men to change: as a number of the books reviewed here will show, men who call themselves involved fathers often report that their lives are more meaningful. Some have chosen careers that provide more intrinsic satisfaction, like social work or teaching. Other involved fathers build a sense of who they are outside of work, essentially opting for less demanding jobs or "daddy tracks" that allow for more time with their kids.

But what about those who want both a challenging career and involved fatherhood? Not surprisingly, the compromises made by the new organization man bear a striking resemblance to those of the new organization woman. Because the male experience has been viewed as the norm, many more research studies have been conducted on women's efforts to balance work and family. Yet even if the evidence supporting the changing needs of corporate men is primarily anecdotal, based as it is on interviews and clinical case studies, companies would do well to consider what the new breed of organization man says he wants. . . .

WHO WAS THE OLD ORGANIZATION MAN?

. . . During the high-flying 1980s, the image of the career-oriented professional took a back seat to that of the greedy Wall-Streeter popularized by Hollywood. But Hanan's new organization man, having cut his teeth on the political and social movements of the 1960s, was by no means amoral or uncommitted to community. Rather, this man believed in the importance of questioning authority and "that intelligent, consistent dialogue can accelerate institutional change." He fully expected to have more than one career and was most excited by entrepreneurial opportunities within his corporation, such as subsidized start-ups of new businesses. These "corporateurs" didn't necessarily want to start their own companies, but they certainly wanted "to share in the personal benefits of leadership." . . .

In *The Male Ego*, psychiatrist Willard Gaylin discusses the current erosion of American manhood in three roles: protector, procreator, and, especially, provider. He notes that "nothing is more important to a man's pride, self-respect, status, and manhood than work. Nothing. Sexual impotence, like sudden loss of ambulation or physical strength, may shatter his self-confidence. But . . . pride is built on work and achievement, and the success that accrues from that work. Yet today men often seem confused and contradictory in their attitudes about work."

Gaylin accurately captures the ambivalence and frustration of many men. He says, for example, that "I have never met a man—among my patients or friends—who in his heart of hearts considers himself a success." He satirizes the executive's need for "little pink roses," those pink message slips that tell a man that he's wanted. But when that chairman of the board or CEO finally retires, he suddenly learns he's lost all value. "He becomes a non-person," in Gaylin's words, shocked and overwhelmed by the fact that "he never was someone to be cherished for his own sake but only as an instrument of power and a conduit of goods."

Such strong words sound a bit sweeping; but they do resonate emotionally with the experiences of men who have recently lost their jobs. Indeed, depression is often the result, and as a number of recent studies show, the rate of various forms of depressive illness is on the rise for American men.[1] Gaylin describes self-loathing as one of the hallmarks of depression, a state in which a man tells himself, "I am not dependable; I am a fragile reed. Indeed, I must depend on you." As Gaylin indicates, a man's success is often defined by those around him rather than his own sense of how well he's done. Consider, then, the shaky ground that men are on once they've been laid off. No longer able to provide for their families (or perhaps even themselves), they've lost both their own sense of purpose and their value in society's eyes.

. . . Few of the "well-functioning" 80 executives sociologist Robert S. Weiss chose to interview for *Staying the Course*, his insightful if overly celebratory 1990 study, defined themselves by vaulting ambition; most seemed to be content with a kind of grounded stability—being what they called good fathers, good providers, good men. But all of them reported stress and irritability; half had trouble sleeping; most had few close friends, choosing instead to compartmentalize their lives to get through the day.

While they claimed to be devoted fathers and husbands, none of these executives shared housework or child care equally with their wives. Most continued to see their children in economic terms, as "a commitment, an investment, an obligation." Weiss's executives clearly demonstrate how twentieth-century fathers have come to nurture through financial support, a notion that still underpins the prevailing definition of manhood, especially in the corporate arena.

Yet that hasn't always been the case. Historian Robert L. Griswold's impressive 1993 book *Fatherhood in America* charts how involved fatherhood has waxed and waned throughout U.S. history. Some middle class eighteenth- and nineteenth-century fathers, for instance, were deeply involved in their children's lives—or at least in the education of their sons. In the early nineteenth century, advice manuals to parents about how to raise their children were addressed primarily to fathers, not mothers.

Although these fathers didn't shoulder domestic responsibilities as their wives did, they were sources of intellectual support. Affectionate bonds were especially strong between fathers and sons; before and during the Civil War, for example, letters from sons were primarily addressed to fathers. But after the war, letters written home were increasingly directed to mothers, as fathers became more remote, enveloped by the rise of the modern corporation and the financial rewards of American Big Business.

But now the terms have changed again, Griswold argues. The economic need for the two-income couple and women's desires to enter or remain in the labor force bring men face-to-face with their children in unprecedented ways. . . .

. . . Just because so many U.S. women now work doesn't mean that women as a whole care less about nurturing family intimacy. Women not only want both work and family but seem to need both. A number of researchers have discovered that, contrary to conventional wisdom, women who are both employees and mothers often have better self-esteem and experience less stress than those who spend all their time at home with children.[2] But ironically, the very fact of women in the workplace has thrown men's lives into disarray. Now men too face some painful choices. . . .

It's not that men don't say they want to change. A 1989 *New York Times* article is typical of the many work-family surveys conducted in recent years: in it, two-fifths of the fathers interviewed said they would quit their jobs if they could spend more time with their children.[3] But the desire to change is often more rhetorical than real; few men would actually switch places with their nonworking wives if given the opportunity.

. . . But for most men who say they're involved fathers, a sense of domestic purpose begins in the nursery, not in the kitchen or laundry room. Men "make use of various employer policies to accommodate their work role to their family obligations to a far greater degree than is generally realized," reports psychologist Joseph H. Pleck in Jane C. Hood's *Men, Work, and Family*, a useful collection of cutting-edge empirical research on men's shifting priorities on the job and on the domestic front.

As Pleck notes, however, in the absence of corporate or peer-group support, men often do so through less formal channels. For example, a man may take vacation or sick leave to attend to births and the rigors of a young baby. This professional may tell his boss that he's having some tests run and will be in the hospital for a week—wink, wink. Even committed family men may steer clear of parental-leave policies that are essentially intended by top management for women. In addition, while many more men use a company's options for flexible scheduling than paternity leave, they often say it's for another reason besides child care.

Such dissembling is one indication of how little the conception of success on the job has changed—and why men still avoid the domestic responsibilities many say they want. . . .

RESISTANCE TO CHANGE: CORPORATE INFLEXIBILITY

The definition of masculinity has proved remarkably inelastic—or, depending on your perspective, amazingly resilient—under its current siege. Except for a few involved fathers, it binds men as tightly as ever to success in the public sphere, in the world of other men, as the markers of manhood and success. "I'm not secure enough, I guess, to stay home and be a househusband," confesses one man, himself an involved father, to Kathleen Gerson.

The traditional definitions of masculinity leave today's new man stranded without social support or a set of viable options. But the real problem, Gerson argues, is institutional. It's corporate inflexibility that reinforces rigid gender definitions. In this, company policies toward family leave exemplify the unconscious assumptions top managers make about what men want—or are supposed to want. A 1989 survey, cited in Joseph Pleck's chapter of *Men, Work, and Family,* found that only 1% of U.S. male employees had access to paid paternity leave, while another 18% had access to unpaid leave. Nine of ten companies made no attempts to inform employees that such leaves were available to new fathers. As a result, we currently have "more reasons to be optimistic about men's desire to nurture children than their opportunity to do so," claims Gerson. . . .

In the United States, men now work alongside an increasing number of female colleagues, which has dramatically altered the traditionally all-male arena of the corporation. Such a shift in the workplace has helped to change some old prejudices; but it has also produced a new tension between the sexes, as some men complain that women are competing for "their" jobs. Gerson's breadwinners, for example, resent women's entry into the workplace, holding fast to the solace of the all-male public arena before it was "invaded" by women. In this context, sexual harassment will continue to be a significant problem for working women. Such harassment is a way for men to remind women that they are, after all, "just" women who happen to be in the workplace but don't really belong there.

The cause of such bitterness and uncertainty, however, lies not in the supposed new power of women but in the rapid changes taking place in today's corporations. In fact, the Corporate America originally designed by men doesn't work anymore for most of us. The tension and low morale now found in many large companies reflect the clash between the need for organizational change and the old ideology. On the one hand, companies furiously restructure and reengineer work to match a new information economy and more diverse labor force; on the other hand, the perceived costs of being an involved father—loss of income, male comradeship, and manhood—remain real because the traditional view of what makes a professional successful hasn't changed. . . .

NOTES

1. Cross-National Collaborative Group, "The Changing Rate of Major Depression: Cross-National Comparisons," *Journal of the American Medical Association*, December 2, 1992, pp. 3098–3105; Gerald L. Klerman and Myrna M. Weissman, "Increasing Rates of Depression," JAMA, April 21, 1989, pp. 2229–2235; and Priya J. Wickramaratne, Myrna M. Weissman, Philip J. Leap, and Theodore R. Holford, "Age, Period, and Cohort Effects on the Risk of Major Depression: Results for Five United States Communities," *Journal of Clinical Epidemiology*, Vol. 42, No. 4, 1989, pp. 333–343.

2. See Faye J. Crosby's *Juggling: The Unexpected Advantages of Balancing Career and Home for Women and Their Families* (New York: Free Press, 1991) for an overview of the research

done on women, work, and family. Among the many pioneering researchers Crosby cites are Rosalind Barnett and Grace Baruch.

3. Lisa Belkin, "Bars to Equality of Sexes Seen as Eroding, Slowly," *New York Times*, August 20, 1989, p. A1, A26.

Part Eight

Women's Equality:
Progress and Resistance

27

Women against Women: American Anti-Suffragism, 1880–1920

Jane Jerome Camhi

. . . Although the origins of feminism in general and suffragism in particular can be traced back to the first decades of the nineteenth century, the antisuffrage movement did not surface until the last two decades of the century. Beginning in the 1880s and gathering momentum through the 1890s, the antisuffrage movement reached its peak of power and influence between 1895 and 1907. Nevertheless, it retained sufficient force in 1919 and 1920 to offer substantial opposition to suffrage efforts to ratify the federal woman suffrage amendment. At its height the movement encompassed more than 25 state associations, some having numerous city and local branches, and a national association.[1]

The movement was organized, led, and staffed by women who went to lengths inconsistent with their goals in order to prevent the extension of suffrage to women. Common to all antisuffragists was the belief that the entry of women into public life (which was considered the inevitable consequence of the ballot) would bring in its wake disaster not only for women themselves but for all of society. Despite this belief, the antisuffragists were so intent on resisting the coming of woman suffrage that they leaped midstream into the battle, adopting all of the techniques they were so eager for womankind to avoid, including campaigning and even lobbying.

The women who led this movement were usually members of the social aristocracy. They were, for the most part, urban, wealthy, native born, Republican, and Protestant—members of established families either by birth or marriage, or both. They claimed to be favorably disposed to the gradual improvements in the status of women that had taken place over the century and, in this sense, did not consider themselves unsympathetic to women's rights as such. Nevertheless, on one issue they

From *Women against Women: American Anti-Suffragism, 1880–1920* by Jane Jerome Camhi (Brooklyn: Carlson Publishing Inc., 1994). Reprinted with permission.

remained unanimously and steadfastly opposed—the granting of suffrage to women. . . .

The opponents of woman suffrage employed a wide variety of arguments in their efforts to influence the public to resist any extension of the elective franchise to women. The arguments, however, had two things in common. First, they were almost all predictive—intimating, if not explicitly detailing, the evil consequences that would ensue if woman suffrage were enacted. Second, they were usually imputative; that is, the arguments were presented in such a way that the suffrage question emerged as a mere symbol of what was assumed to be the real issue, the threat of the spread of feminist ideas. Most antisuffragists did not consciously intend to confuse the issue. If anything, their rhetoric belied the confusion in their own minds. However, whether conscious or not, it was one of the antisuffragists' most effective weapons.[2]

Obfuscating the issue by causing the advocates of suffrage to appear as feminists played upon contemporary uncertainties regarding the changing role of women. As a result, many who might not have taken issue with the justice or expedience of extending suffrage to women found themselves forced to take a stand either for or against what was made to appear to be two opposing value systems. The result was that the question of woman suffrage, which had over the years come to assume a symbolic significance for those in the suffrage movement, also began to assume a symbolic significance in the minds of the uncommitted and the unsure.

WOMAN'S SPECIAL ROLE

A primary assumption of the Antis was that the family was the basic nexus, the self-governing unit upon which the state was built. Therefore, as a microcosm of the state, every well-regulated family had to have one head, for if authority were divided the outcome would be domestic anarchy.[3] To be preserved as a unit the family must be represented in the state by the voting power of its head, the man of the family.[4] The notion that there should be one head of the family and that this head should be the man even influenced the Antis' position on child custody. The Antis were in accord with the laws giving custody of children to the father in cases of disagreement and argued against granting equal custody to each parent. . . .

If woman's work in the home were always properly performed, declared the Antis, "there would be far fewer bosses, ringsters and grafters in the world at large." Even more extravagant was their contention that when woman fails to perform the work nature has assigned her she "leaves the world depleted by just so much of moral strength and all the best educators and scientists declare, lowers the entire race in its affectional, social and moral achievements."[5]

The distinctive genius of woman, it was argued, did not lie in her logical or executive abilities, but in her sensibilities, which made her irreplaceable in the home where her influence over the lives of those around here was much greater than any she could possibly wield as a voter, where she would count as only one man.[6] . . .

PRIVILEGE AND POWER

The Antis argued that if women voted they would lose the power to mold the citizens of the future. Antisuffrage campaign material often included posters depicting the evil effects of woman suffrage on the domestic scene. In the antisuffrage litany, motherhood and participation in public life were always presented as mutually exclusive. . . .

The business of state, on the other hand, was not only man's work but also his highest prerogative. To make and execute the laws of the country was equated with manhood. Therefore, men who favored the ballot for women "lowered their own dignity in the State and belittled their own importance as the true makers and enforcers of law."[7] From the lofty perspective of female Antis, governing was the one activity that "makes him a man, a being worthy to stand upon an equality with woman."[8]

Primaries, caucuses, conventions, courts, and legislatures were all involved in the simple casting of a ballot. These were man's work, however, and gave to man the inalienable quality that distinguished him from a mere brute. In other words, if politics were taken away, little would remain. Man's power to rule was what evened the balance between the sexes. Without it, man would be shorn of his manhood and the balance between the sexes destroyed. "What woman wants a man whose power of law-giving is no more than equal to her own?" She has her great gift from God to serve as mother of men, "the exemplar and expounder of all noble, moral and spiritual gifts." His birthright is equally inalienable. If he robs himself of it, "what would become of that mutual homage and respect which is the natural bond between the sexes? No, let him keep for himself something by which we may still reverence him, the horns of Moses, his manly power of law-giving!"[9]

. . . On the one hand, taking their cues from the suffragists, who devoted most of their energies to foreseeing changes in the female role, the Antis, like the suffragists, did not really question the basic patriarchal norms that expected the male to be provider, authority, stoic, protector, or lawmaker. On the other hand, since in the Antis' view all of these roles depended primarily on the male's greater physical strength, and since they believed that governments operated by rule of force, the question of how man could harness this brute force and yet not lose his manhood was crucial. By employing it to enforce the dictates of a civilized state, man's brute strength was transmitted into a special social virtue. Man the animal became man the governor. . . .

. . . It undoubtedly worked to the advantage of the Antis, both in terms of morale and practical politics, to underscore the fact that the main opponents of woman suffrage were women and to urge that if women really wanted to vote, they would have it. For one thing, it enabled them to depict suffrage as the "only woman's movement which has been met by the organized opposition of women."[10] For another, it enabled them to claim that the weight of public opinion was on their side rather than just the self-interested forces that the suffragists consistently defined as the enemy.

> ... *chief opponents of woman suffrage are* not the special interests nor those men who
> take a narrow and prejudiced view of woman's relation to the state, but those *women*
> who have grave doubts whether their duty lies in service to the state by the ballot, or
> by a fulfillment of present responsibilities which bear no relation to the ballot.[11]

It was inevitable that politicians and legislators reluctant to advance the cause of
woman suffrage would find it to their advantage to stress the fact that women themselves were opposed to woman suffrage.

Although the Antis billed themselves as representing the "silent majority" of
American women, they were certainly not representative. They came from families
that had both money and power, and therefore they could not be construed as a cross
section of society. As members of a native-born monied class, they shared all the
prejudices of those who felt they had something to lose by the changes taking place
in American society. They resented the immigrant and distrusted the poor and feared
the swelling of the ranks of the electorate by what they regarded as an illiterate and
ignorant vote. It was only natural that these class prejudices were reflected in their
views concerning the types of women they felt ought *not* to vote and thus became
part of their rationale for resisting the extension of suffrage.

Taking their cue perhaps from Catherine Beecher, who had classified women into
five categories, the Antis were fond of visualizing womanhood as consisting of set
types. Although these varied somewhat as to particulars, for the most part they constituted three basic categories—the better class, the indifferent, and the degenerate.
It was only natural that the Antis considered themselves, and were in fact, a representative segment of the first category.[12] This was the handful of women who carried on church, philanthropic, and reform work when they were not devoting themselves to their domestic tasks. The Antis felt that this kind of woman was capable
of developing an interest in and an understanding of political questions but was
usually too preoccupied with her primary tasks to take the time to cast her ballot.[13]

The indifferent women constituted the vast majority and included the following
subgroups—women of the shopkeeper, clerk, artisan, and prosperous laborer class;
wage-earning women; immigrant women, and black women. The first sort were
assumed to be overburdened with domestic duties and uninterested in questions
outside of their limited sphere.[14] The working women were thought to be exposed
to political affairs, but deemed uninterested in questions outside of their own narrow interests.[15] The Antis could not place immigrant women as a group or black
women as a race in the third category reserved for what was variously designated
the evil, wrongminded, corrupt, and sordid women.[16] But they did cast them at the
bottom of the heap of the indifferent. The Antis feared that the ignorance of immigrant women would make them subject to manipulation by their men, who would
have no compunctions about selling not only their own votes, but those of their wives
and daughters as well.[17] Sometimes, however, they were not too careful in distinguishing between the illiterate and the vicious.

> We must think of the tens of thousands of illiterate and vicious women in New York
> City, and just as carefully of the scores of thousands of ignorant negresses at the

South. . . . Are we prepared to throw into political life all the women good and bad, intelligent and unintelligent, of the whole U.S., including the swarms which belong to Europe but have been adopted here?. . . . Surely the well-trained, educated, intelligent boys of New York City, even though they be not more than ten years old, would make better voters than vicious tramps or stupid foreigners all but wholly ignorant of the English language.[18]

The third kind of woman—the degenerate—consisted of two general types, both considered beyond the pale of respectability and believed to far outnumber the first category of good women.[19] These were the prostitutes, manipulated by bosses, pimps, and saloon keepers, and who, it was feared, would vote because private (and sinister) interests would see to it that they did.[20] The following excerpt reflects this kind of thinking. Printed and reprinted by the Antis, this article appeared in the *San Francisco Examiner* the day after an election in which women voted.

McDonough Brothers had several automobiles busy all day long hauling Barbary coast dance hall girls and the inmates of houses on Commercial street to the different booths, and always the women were supplied with a marked sample ballot.[21]

. . . Arguing that the best women would remain at home, Senator Morgan of Alabama, in an 1887 Senate debate on woman suffrage, complained

The effect would be to drive the ladies of the land, as they are termed, the well-bred and well-educated women, the women of nice sensibilities, within their home circles, there to remain, while the ruder of that sex would thrust themselves out on the hustings and at the ballot-box, and fight their way to the polls through Negroes and others who are not the best of company even at the polls, to say nothing of the disgrace of association with them. You would paralyze one-third at least of the women of this land by the very vulgarity of the overture made to them that they should go struggling to the polls in order to vote in common with the herd of men.[22]

The degenerate women, argued the Antis, were powerless without the vote, but once enfranchised, the ballot would become a weapon they would use against reform measures because they would want to ensure that their way of life was not interfered with.[23] Whether they went to the polls on their own behalf or because they were forced to, a higher percent of this sort of woman than of respectable women would vote, they predicted.

Apathetic, ignorant, sordid women—poor or rich—as things now stand, are at worst a negative evil. But such women, with votes, become potential reinforcements to the forces of vice, and those forces are always prompt in rallying their re-enforcements.[24]

The other kind of degenerate or wrong-minded women were those who would devote their lives to public affairs, seeking conspicuous offices and "playing the role of bosses among the ignorant of their sex."[25] They would "employ the distinctive power of their sex in caucuses, in jury-boxes, and in legislative and congressional committees; thus adding another to the many deteriorating influences of public life." Thus the best of women would shun political life and the most unprincipled would have the field to themselves.[26]

Tallying up the score, the Antis felt that if women were enfranchised, the influence (and the interests) of the "better class of women" would be nullified. Woman suffrage would destroy the indirect power of the informed woman since the vote would give equal power to the uninformed. . . .

Perhaps what most irritated the traditional type of woman was not that women were actually out there on platforms agitating for change but that they were willing to consider their own cause—that of women—as a priority. This went against the grain of womanly self-denial. What was admired in the male sex as initiative, independence, and self-esteem was looked upon in women as selfish and self-serving, bold and unwomanly. A short article in the January 1912 issue of *The Anti-Suffragist* singled out the dropping of the husbands' names on the visiting card or address of married women as the "most noticeable social innovation of the suffragists" and condemned it as "an assertion of separate and individual interests and bank account." . . .

As if woman suffrage by itself were not sufficiently worthy of contempt, the Antis often embellished its horror by equating it with any one of the so-called radical isms. If not actually equated with feminism, bolshevism, or socialism, then it was the necessary harbinger of these and similar horrors. In the charged atmosphere of the years surrounding World War I, the Antis consciously resorted to a campaign designed to discredit the suffragists by playing upon popular fears of bolshevism and social revolution. . . .

. . . In 1887 the Senate had witnessed a debate on woman suffrage in which various southern senators, reacting against a "wholesale and indiscriminate extension of the electorate," zeroed in especially on the black woman. According to Senator Beck of Kentucky, one mistake had already been made, when the ignorant "colored men of the South" had been enfranchised. It was going to take years not only to dispel their ignorance but also to turn them into intelligent voters. The colored woman, he argued, was even more ignorant, never having had the advantages of communication with the outside world.

> No one perhaps in a hundred of them can read or write. . . . Take them from their washtubs and their household work and they are absolutely ignorant of the new duties of voting citizens. . . . Why, sir, a rich corporation or a body of men of wealth could buy them up for fifty cents a piece, and they would vote, without knowing what they were doing, for the side that paid most.[27]

During the battle over ratification, the Antis would continue to exploit southern prejudice by identifying women suffrage with racial equality. In a leaflet entitled "That Deadly Parallel," they quoted the Fifteenth Amendment and the proposed woman suffrage amendment in parallel columns in order to link woman suffrage with Negro suffrage. Another leaflet warned that woman suffrage meant reopening the Negro question, the loss of states' rights, and all the reconstruction horrors with "female carpet-baggers as bad as their male prototypes."[28]

. . . Judge Joseph C. Higgins, president of the Tennessee Constitutional League, told the press that if the legislature ratified, the league "would be constrained to go into the courts and inhibit the Secretary of State from certifying."[29] On August 12, the Senate and House committees on constitutional amendments held a joint hearing. Both suffragists and Antis spoke. Charlotte Rowe of New York, a lawyer and an active Anti, explained the attitude of the Antis.

> We feel that if you men are good enough to work for us, die for us, live for us, you are good enough to vote for us . . . to give woman the ballot is only to break up the home and the beginning of socialism.[30]

. . . Viola Klein, although primarily a sociologist, has also been concerned with how women as members of an "out-group" have internalized society's attitudes toward them. By "out-group," Klein means that women are distinguished from the dominant (male) strata by virtue of their physical characteristics, historical tradition, and social role. Furthermore, as in the case of other groups in a similar position, women have been subjected to preconceived opinions and collective judgments instead of being treated on their own merits. The general effect of this stereotyping is to inhibit the development of individualism, resulting in an "incalculable amount of restrictions, discouragement, ill-feeling and frustration."[31] . . .

It is difficult to say to just what extent a vulnerable sense of self-esteem may have contributed to the psychological makeup of an Anti, yet there is evidence that this was at least a contributing factor. Antisuffrage journalist Richard Barry, after interviewing Josephine Daskam Dodge Bacon, quoted her in "Why Women Oppose Woman's Suffrage."

> No, I do not believe in woman suffrage. Why? Because a woman can no more do a man's work that a man can do a woman's. There has never been a first-class woman writer, statesman, general or executive. I write second-class stuff myself. All women writers are second-class the minute you compare their work with that of the best *workmen*. But while there have been no really great women writers . . . no really great generals . . . no really great painters . . . there *have* been a large number of good mothers.
>
> And while women have repeatedly been great mothers I defy you to mention a man who has ever been a really first-class mother.
>
> Therefore, I conclude it is possible for women to achieve greatness as mothers and in no other way, and I do not believe Nature intended us to enter a field of effort where the laws of our being declare us outsiders.[32]

Mrs. Richard Watson Gilder, president of the New York State Association Opposed to Woman Suffrage, in a letter signed only H. de K. G., spoke of the "unable worm," houseless and weak, which is soon destroyed. Woman without the art of homemaking, she felt, was not only vulnerable, she was nothing.[33]

Apparently some Antis believed that it was a fairly general phenomenon that women did not have faith in other women. Mrs. Augustine H. Parker, an antisuffrage essayist, contended that because most women "are unconvinced by the feminists' protestations, few women care to be represented by other women." This was only natural, she thought, since "women do not, as a rule, employ other women to take care of their business affairs." As evidence she pointed to the fact that one half of the stock of the Pennsylvania Railroad was owned by women who could have elected several women directors if they wished, and yet the board was composed entirely of men.[34]

What at first may seem a strictly fanciful model for understanding the Antis emerges from Albert Memmi's study of colonialism, *The Colonizer and the Colonized*. Racism serves the same function in colonialism as sexism does in a patriarchal system. That is, in the same way that "racism sums up and symbolizes the fundamental relation which unites colonialist and colonized," sexism functions to unite male and female. The analogy is even more striking if one looks at the three major ideological components that according to Memmi constitute colonial racism: a gulf between the culture of the colonialist and the colonized; exploitation of these differences for the benefit of the colonialist; and the use of these supposed differences as standards of fact.[35]

The colonialist stresses those things that keep him separate, just as does the male in a patriarchy. And once the behavioral feature that characterizes the colonialist (or male) and contrasts him with the colonized (or female) has been isolated, this gap must be kept from being filled.

> The colonialist removes the factor from history, time, and therefore possible evolution. What is actually a sociological point becomes labeled as being biological or, preferably metaphysical. It is attached to the colonized's basic nature.

If the colonizer (colonialist) wants to be the master, it is not enough for him to be so in fact, "he must also believe in its legitimacy." Furthermore, in order for that legitimacy to be complete, it is not enough for the colonized to be a slave, "he must also accept his role."[36] In the history of the relationship between the sexes, women until quite recently also have accepted their role, thus helping to legitimize the condition of male supremacy.

One of the devices that maintain the subordination of women and prevent the formation of a shared community of interest between the sexes is the prevalence of stereotypes that conform to mankind's needs. So, too, in the cases of the colonizer and the colonized. Another similarity is that the traits ascribed to the weaker are in both cases often incompatible with one another. Both women and colonized are simultaneously regarded as inferior and wicked, lazy and backward, without desires (frigid) and gluttonous (insatiable).

> The humanity of the colonized, rejected by the colonizer, becomes opaque. It is useless, he asserts, to try to forecast the colonized's actions ("They are unpredictable!"

"With them, you never know"). It seems to him that strange and disturbing impulsiveness controls the colonized. The colonized must indeed be very strange if he remains so mysterious after years of living with the colonizer.[37]

Another mark of the colonized's depersonalization is the "mark of the plural." Just as Viola Klein pointed out in the case of women as an out-group, the colonized does not exist as an individual. Neither women nor colonized are free to choose between being colonized or not being colonized.

One of the most compelling similarities between the plight of the colonized and that of all women is that they have been removed from history and from the community. As Memmi indicates, "Colonization usurps any free role in either war or peace." The colonizer "pushed the colonized out of the historical and social, cultural and technical current."[38] While Memmi feels that the colonizer did so in order to subdue and exploit, and it is certainly not clear that male domination involved such vindictive motives, nevertheless the dynamics in both situations were such that the success of the one depended on the failure of the other. If one looks at the culture, society, and technology of both women and colonized, one sees how seriously damaged they are. And the same holds true of women as of the colonized—one has no idea what they would have been without colonization (or subjection), but one can see what has happened to both as a result.

There are also remarkable similarities between the *experiences suffered* by the colonized and by women in general. For many women, as for the colonized, their first ambition was to assimilate, to "become equal to that splendid model and resemble him to the point of disappearing in him." Memmi points out that when the colonized rebelled, the rebels were laughed at because of their insistence on wearing khaki uniforms. They hoped to be considered soldiers, and by this tactic, "They laid claim to and wore the dress of history."[39] By the same token, women suffered ridicule when they first expressed belief in their autonomy by donning the female facsimile of male dress, namely bloomers.[40]

Considered incapable of governing, both women and colonized were kept away from power. And in both cases, long absence from autonomous government resulted in the loss of interest in and feeling for the control and skills that it requires.

As a result of colonization, says Memmi, the colonized almost never experiences nationality and citizenship, except privately. This social and historic mutilation (the absence of self-assurance or pride of citizenship) is perpetuated by the educational system where references to the community and nation are always in terms of the colonizing nation.[41] In what schools or textbooks could American women have derived any pride of citizenship in learning about the history of their country? Everything takes place outside of the experience of the oppressed. They are nonentities or exist only with reference to others. Neither women nor the colonized recognize that they had a past. They have no history, no leaders, no heroes.

Faced with little hope of changing this situation, says Memmi, the only alternative is to live isolated from one's age. The young colonized will fall back on traditional values. This usually results in an internal catastrophe.

He will remain glued to that family which offers him warmth and tenderness but which simultaneously absorbs, clutches and emasculates him.[42]

In the historical experience of women, the Antis emerge as the young women who fall back on traditional values, with one important difference from the colonized. As domesticity engulfed them and removed them from the mainstream of civilization, they attempted to find comfort in the only way of life they ever knew by postulating that it was the highest kind of life for all women. Instinctively they rebelled against assimilation, against becoming "equal" to the male model and resembling man to the point of disappearing in him. This would have deprived them of what was uniquely their own. Psychologically wedded to the system, they sought to secure their way of life by enveloping it in a self-perpetuating mystique. . . .

Memmi argues that the colonial condition cannot be changed except by doing away with the colonial relationship. The relationship demands that there be both the colonizer and the colonized; therefore, if one or the other is eliminated the basic relationship is altered. Assimilation and colonization are contradictory, for if all the colonized were assimilated, the colonizers would have no one left to exploit. On the other hand, when assimilation does occur, the colonized is even further removed from being in touch with his culture. . . .

According to Memmi, in order for recovery of self to occur, a conscious rejection of assimilation is necessary. If imitating the colonizer requires self-denial, then it would seem as if rejection of the colonizer is the "indispensable prelude to self-discovery." Memmi treats the two as mutually exclusive. "After having been rejected for so long by the colonizer, the day has come when it is the colonized who must refuse the colonizer."[43] So, too, the Anti had to "refuse" the male.

And just as the colonized, excluded from the universality common to all men, begins to assert his differences, the Anti also had to assert hers. Both ran the same risks. By taking up the challenge of exclusion, the colonized and the Antis accepted being separate and different, *but* their individuality was that which was limited and defined by the colonizer. Thus both the colonized and the Antis drew pride from their differences, but they were differences that had been formulated by the dominant group. Therefore, rejection of the colonizer's values and system was based on the conviction that everything that belonged to the colonizer was *not* appropriate for the colonized. According to Memmi, this is just what the colonizer has always told the colonized. Therefore, the rebellious colonized takes the first step toward liberation by accepting and glorifying an image of himself that emphasizes the apparent differences between himself and the colonizer. . . .

Both Antis and suffragists had benefited from advances in women's rights such as higher education, access to the professions, and control over their property; therefore, there was hardly any difference between them regarding the desirability of women's rights—in all areas, that is, except the vote. But, according to Kraditor, the significance of the latter for the feminists was that it represented *autonomy*, the desire to be recognized in economic, political, and social realms as individuals in their own right. It was this, rather than a redefinition of woman's proper sphere, that loomed as the feminist objective and served to differentiate feminists and suffragists from Antis. . . .

. . . But Antis and suffragists were "social feminists"—urban upper- and middle-class women whose social worlds often overlapped through their activities as club-women. Thus, in addition to the fact that these social justice activities became the principal justification for feminism, most of the organization Antis were also clubwomen.

. . . Now one has to take into account the fact that often both Antis and suffragists shared a similar worldview and possibly even a similar experience. In many cases it was only their solutions that differed. Furthermore, this approach enables one to view both suffragism and antisuffragism simply as variations of a new and growing trend toward activism among women. Looked at this way, Antis and suffragists had more in common with each other than with the aggregate of women in general. In any event, it becomes necessary to delineate more flexible denominators in dealing with women's behavior in groups than simply saying that some were pro and some were anti; this must be done so that the commonality of shared experience is not obscured by the differences that divided them.

> Women have been the only subordinated group that has belonged to the same families as its rulers. The ambiguous status of well-to-do women, as both ruler and ruled, generated contradictions and ambiguities in both feminists' and antifeminists' attitudes toward women.[44]

NOTES

1. It is virtually impossible to arrive at an accurate number of state associations. In the last issue of *The Woman's Protest* (February 1918), the Antis claimed 25 state associations serving their purpose. Nevertheless, it is doubtful that all of these states had fully constituted statewide organizations such as those of Massachusetts or even New York. Many of them were probably no more than committees. Furthermore, the list omits the Tennessee chapter, which became one of the more active state groups. Until further work is done on each state association, one can only estimate the extent of the antisuffrage organization.

2. Some individuals deliberately exploited the relationship between suffragism and feminism, arguing that the ballot for women would lead inevitably to the latter. The Men's League Opposed to Women Suffrage, "Brief Argument against Woman Suffrage" (Philadelphia 1913) MHS.

3. James McGrigor Allan, *Woman Suffrage Wrong in Principle, and Practice* (London: Remington and Co., 1890), p. 23; Mrs. A. J. George, "Suffrage Fallacies," *Anti-Suffrage Essays by Massachusetts Women* (The Forum Publications of Boston, 1916), p. 29.

4. Mrs. Herbert Lyman, "The Anti-Suffrage Ideal," *Anti-Suffrage Essays by Massachusetts Women*, pp. 118–22; Goldwin Smith, "Woman Suffrage," *Essays on Questions of the Day* (New York: Macmillan & Co., 1894), pp. 183–218.

5. Illinois Association Opposed to Woman Suffrage, *Fifteenth Annual Report*, December 1911. Other statements reflecting these and similar sentiments include the following: "If men are doing poorly—it is due to the women who trained them. We need better voters, not more voters." Alice N. George, "Woman's Rights vs. Woman Suffrage" (New York: National Association Opposed to Woman Suffrage, 1913), p. 8.

> If women had conquered their own part of life perfectly, one might wish to see them thus leave it and go forth to set the world to rights. But on the contrary, never were domestic conditions so badly attended to. Until woman settles the servant question, how can she ask to run the government? (Emily Bissell, "A Talk to Women on the Suffrage Question" [New York State Association Opposed to Woman Suffrage, 1909], p. 5.)

6. The Reverend Charles H. Parkhurst, "The Inadvisability of Women Suffrage," Supplement to the *Annals of the American Academy of Political and Social Science* 35 (May 1910), pp. 36–37.

7. Elizabeth Jackson, "Suffrage and the School Teacher," *Anti-Suffrage Essays by Massachusetts Women*, p. 86.

8. Illinois Association Opposed to Woman Suffrage, *Fifth Annual Report*, 1901.

9. Letter to Editor, Chicago *Record-Herald*, May 17, 1911.

10. George, "Suffrage Fallacies," p. 28; Man-Suffrage Association, *The Case Against Woman Suffrage* (New York, 1915), p. 6.

11. George, "Woman's Rights vs. Woman Suffrage," p. 3 (my italics).

12. Margaret C. Robinson, "Woman Suffrage in Relation to Patroiotic Service" (Public Interest League of Massachusetts, Sophia Smith Collection, Smith College), pp. 99, 102.

13. Ibid; M. G. van Rensselaer, "Should We Ask for the Suffrage?," p. 47.

14. Rensselaer, "Should We Ask for the Suffrage?," Massachusetts Association Opposed to the Further Extension of Suffrage to Women (n.d.), p. 47.

15. Ibid., p. 49.

16. Robinson, "Woman Suffrage a Menace to Social Reform"; Catharine Esther Beecher, *Woman's Profession as Mother and Educator* (Philadelphia: G. Maclean, 1872), p. 11; Bissell, "A Talk to Women on the Suffrage Question"; Lilly Rice Foxcroft, "Why Are Women Opposing Woman Suffrage?" *Wellesley Alumnac Quarterly* (April 1917); Rensselaer, "Should We Ask for the Suffrage?,"p. 52.

17. Rensselaer, "Should We Ask for the Suffrage?,"p. 50.

18. Ibid., pp. 9, 10, 14.

19. The Antis feared that if women were given the vote, the larger number of degenerate or wrong-minded women would vote against the reform measure of "good" women, who would have only a few ballots to cast. Robinson, "Woman Suffrage a Menace to Social Reform," p. 106.

20. Rensselaer, "Should We Ask for the Suffrage?," p. 52.

21. The article from which this excerpt was taken was printed in the Cambridge *Chronicle* (October 16, 1915). It was republished by the Women's Anti-Suffrage Association of Massachusetts and excerpted by Robinson in "Woman Suffrage a Menace to Social Reform," p. 107.

22. Quoted in Carrie Chapman Catt and Nettie Rogers Shuler, *Woman Suffrage and Politics* (New York: Charles Scribner's Sons, 1923), p. 233.

23. Robinson, "Woman Suffrage a Menace to Social Reform," p. 106.

24. Foxcroft, "Why Are Women Opposing Woman Suffrage?," p. 4.

25. Rensselaer, "Should We Ask for the Suffrage?," p. 52.

26. Beecher, *Woman's Profession*, p. 11. Beecher's choice of words is very revealing. If by "distinctive power of their sex" she means sexuality or even feminine wiles, why is this assume to be such a deleterious influence on public life? She does not explain. Others certainly shared their feelings, yet none of the female Antis addressed herself to just how this evil influence would operate. Does this perhaps reflect the fear that women free to engage in public life might use their sexual attractiveness to allure other women's husbands? We have only the male reaction of historian and antisuffragist Francis Parkman, who felt that their sex would give women a political advantage. Women would be free to be aggressive and even attack the men, while the latter, out of chivalry, would be unable to be forthright and fight back. Man-Suffrage Association, "Some of the Reasons Against Woman Suffrage," n.d., reprinted by MAOFESW, *Why Women Do Not Want the Ballot*, vol. 1, no. 7.

27. Burrill (no first name given), "Some Practical Aspects of the Question," Anti-Suffrage Essays by Massachusetts Women (n.d.), pp. 43–52.

28. It is difficult to understand how the Antis failed to regard this situation as anything but obvious tokenism. Perhaps from the vantage point of that period, however, this did represent an advance for women.

29. A Tennessee constitutional league had been formed to oppose ratification as a violation of the state constitution, but it was not nearly as active as the Southern Women's Rejection League. A. Elizabeth Taylor, *The Woman Suffrage Movement in Tennessee* (New York: Bookman, 1957).

30. *Nashville Tennessean*, August 13, 1920, cited ibid.

31. Viola Klein, *The Feminine Character*: History of an Idealogy (London: K. Paul, Trench, Trubner, 1946), pp. 4, 5.

32. Richard Barry, "Why Women Oppose Woman's Suffrage," *Pearson's Magazine* (February/March 1910), pp. 326–27.

33. Mrs. Richard Watson Gilder, "A Letter on Woman Suffrage," (Massachusetts Association Opposed to the Further Extension of Suffrage to Women, 1894), p. 11.

34. Mrs. Augustin H. Parker, "Are Suffragists Sincere Reformers?," *Anti-Suffrage Essays by Massachusetts Women*, p. 83.

35. Albert Memmi, *The Colonizer and the Colonized* (New York: The Orion Press, 1965), pp. 70–71.

36. Ibid., pp. 71, 89.

37. Ibid., p. 85.

38. Ibid., pp. 91, 114. Kate Millett points out that "In terms of industry and production, the situation of women is in many ways comparable both to colonial and to pre-industrial peoples. Although they achieved their first economic autonomy in the industrial revolution and now constitute a large and underpaid factory population, women do not participate directly in technology or in production." Even when they do participate in production of commodities, they do not "own or control or even comprehend the process in which they participate." Furthermore, women's distance from technology "is sufficiently great that it is doubtful that (in the absence of males) they could replace or repair such machines on any significant scale. If knowledge is power, power is also knowledge, and a large factor in their subordinate position is the fairly systematic ignorance patriarchy imposes upon women." *Sexual Politics* (Garden City, N.Y.: Doubleday & Company, Inc., 1970), pp. 41–42.

39. Memmi, *Colonizer and Colonized*, pp. 116, 95.

40. Mary Wollstonecraft, writing in 1792, was concerned about the fact that masculine virtues seemed excessively valuable to early feminists. Women resemble soldiers, she wrote, in that, "They both acquire manners before morals and a knowledge of life before they have, from reflection, any acquaintance with the grand ideal outline of human nature." *A Vindication of the Rights of Woman* (New York: W. W. Norton & Company, Inc., 1967), p. 40.

41. Memmi, *Colonizer and Colonized*, p. 96.

42. Ibid., p. 99.

43. Ibid., p. 128.

44. Eileen S. Kraditor, *Up from the Pedestal: Selected Writings in the History of American Feminism* (Chicago: Quadrangle Books, 1968), p. 10.

28

Where the Girls Are: Growing Up Female with the Mass Media

Susan J. Douglas

. . . I was not yet in college in the spring and summer of 1968; I wasn't a member of any of the various oppositional political groups that organized against and did battle with government authorities. I was, like the vast majority of young people, still only a spectator. Yet spectatorship in 1968—even in the confines of your own home—was a politicizing activity.

Just think about what we saw in this one year. In January, Dr. Spock, who had helped our mothers raise us, was indicted for "aiding and abetting" draft evasion. In February, we watched the Tet Offensive on TV, which suggested that maybe Vietnam wasn't going to be the Sunday football game rout the president and the Pentagon had assured us it would. On March 12, Eugene McCarthy won the New Hampshire primary, and four days later, Bobby Kennedy declared his candidacy for president. Just two weeks after this, in what I thought would be yet another lie-filled address to the nation, Lyndon Johnson stunned us all by announcing that he was stepping down from the presidency when his term expired. The elation I felt over this blockbuster development lasted exactly four days until, at 6:00 P.M. on April 4—just in time for the nightly news—Martin Luther King was assassinated.

Less than three weeks after this disaster, on April 23, somewhere between 800 and 1,000 students at Columbia barricaded themselves inside campus buildings to protest the university's ties to the Pentagon and its ongoing appropriation of poor, residential neighborhoods in upper Manhattan. The takeover ended the next week when 1,000 cops stormed the buildings, arresting 700 college kids and injuring at least 150 of them. And it was only five weeks later that we watched those sickening images of Bobby Kennedy lying on the floor of the Ambassador Hotel in Los Angeles, his wife cradling his bloody head in her lap. . . .

The public activism of young people was one of the biggest ongoing stories of 1968. After all, between January and June of that year alone, there were 221 major demonstrations at 101 colleges and universities involving some 39,000 students.[1] Public demonstrations were automatically newsworthy because they provided news organizations with provocative pictures, they represented conflict, and they sometimes produced arrests and violence, two of the news media's yardsticks for determining whether an event merited coverage. But precisely because of such criteria, and the news media's ingrained preference for covering events rather than explaining underlying causes or processes, their desire to identify leaders and spokesmen even in groups that refuse to have them, and their insistence that there are two sides— no more, no less—to every news story, such coverage was a mixed blessing for the young people of the New Left. It would prove to be a mixed blessing for feminists as well.

When feminists staged their own demonstrations, they encountered not just deeply entrenched journalistic conventions but also the most recently established routines and biases shaping the coverage of social movements and demonstrations. By the time of the Miss America demonstration, certain precedents in the press coverage of dissent were well-established. The news media cast the protests of young people as simultaneously dangerous and ineffectual, deeply subversive yet of little consequence. Solemn references to "Communist elements" and constant reliance on two incendiary images—burning draft cards with Vietcong flags—were intermixed with dismissive comments like this wrap-up from CBS's Bruce Morton: "Most people have doubts that U.S. foreign policy can be changed on the streets."[2] *The New York Times* and CBS, by turns, emphasized the extremism of antiwar demonstrators yet ridiculed their beards and blue jeans as signs that they were nothing more than naive, style-over-substance poseurs. The "other side" the media gave time to were often ultraright-wing types, as if there was some equivalence between their politics and those of kids trying to stop the war.[3]

News organizations habitually minimized the movement's numbers, its effectiveness, and its motivations, and acted as if it was as far from mainstream America as Joseph Stalin. Reporters were used to dealing with leaders and spokesmen—that's what the government trotted out—and when deeply nonhierarchical organizations like SDS refused to name someone as "head," the media anointed leaders on their own, which was deeply divisive to the internal operations of SDS. The important precedent was that the news media routinely divided the antiwar movement into what Todd Gitlin termed "legitimate main acts and illegitimate sideshows," meaning the moderate, conciliatory positions worth listening to and all the rest that the news media indicated were not.[4] . . .

The treatment of the Miss America protest made it clear that the media coverage of the women's movement would be strikingly similar to that of the antiwar movement. But where women were involved, there were some extra, important touches. How feminists used, or failed to use, their faces and their bodies, and the extent to which their faces and bodies conformed to those in a Max Factor ad, were central features of the coverage. If these girls were out on the streets and swinging bras around, why, they must be closet exhibitionists, narcissists, or simply hysterical, and language that suggested witchcraft or secret cults resonated darkly with the magical powers of sitcom characters. The media also paid inordinate attention to the way feminists violated physical and social boundaries, and suggested that, by doing so, they were making spectacles of themselves, just as Beatles fans had done a few years earlier. Feminists were cast as unfeminine, unappealing women who were denouncing the importance of the male gaze, yet who secretly coveted that gaze for themselves by protesting in public. These poor girls, it was suggested, sought to get through political flamboyance what they were unable to get through physical attractiveness.

It was not just what was said to or about women in the media that was important; news stories and TV shows were structured so that feminism was positioned as deviant. The standards by which something was judged newsworthy were, in fact, deeply masculine. The emphases on conflict in the public sphere, on crime, on dramatic public events rather than behind-the-scenes processes, on the individual rather than the group, and on competition rather than cooperation all biased the news toward masculine public enterprise. The public sphere was defined, visually and rhetorically, as the place where men make history. The news also exploited the highly emotional as spectacle while denigrating overly emotional commentary about events as not objective and therefore invalid. Because of these journalistic conventions, the only places any female had in the news were as victim, hysteric, sex object, or wife of a prominent man. In other words, the desire to make news, and the act of doing so, two impulses considered perfectly natural in men, rendered feminists as deviant, no longer feminine but not quite masculine either. The overwhelmingly dismissive coverage of the women's movement that followed was in many ways inevitable.

These biases, of course, were reinforced by the structures of the news organizations themselves, which were rigidly hierarchical and male-dominated. In the late 1960s, women journalists were confined to writing about spring hats and thirty-one new ways to cook squash, or they were researchers for male reporters, and they were rarely seen on television except as weather girls. Women trying to break out of these confines faced enormous pressures to conform to how the boys did things, and they also faced editors and publishers deeply hostile to the women's movement.

Perhaps one reason that the Miss America demonstration is not remembered as frequently as it should be is that it happened amidst the swirl of so many shocking events in 1968. Yet retrospectives today on the late 1960s seem all too eager to show young girls smoking pot and dancing partially clad at love-ins while they completely ignore Atlantic City in September. But anyone who cares about the sick proliferations of the anorexic body as the ideal for all women, or who is tired of the constant equation between crow's-feet and female worthlessness, should keep the memory of this protest alive and well, for us and for future generations. Robin Morgan and her organization, the New York Radical Women, took direct aim at what they called "the degrading mindless-boob-girlie symbol" so prevalent in the media and decried the "ludicrous 'beauty' standards we ourselves are conditioned to take seriously." They also attacked "the unbeatable madonna-whore combination" and the mixed messages women had been socialized to internalize. "To win approval, we must be both sexy and wholesome, delicate but able to cope, demure yet titillatingly bitchy. . . . Miss America and *Playboy*'s centerfolds are sisters over the skin."[5] . . .

The New York Time's coverage of the protest in Atlantic City indicated how the women's movement would be framed by the news media over the next five years, and some female journalists were just as dismissive as their male counterparts. *Times* reporter Charlotte Curtis, emphasizing what she saw as these women's desperate need for attention, observed, "Television and news photographers were allowed and even encouraged to photograph the pickets, and the women . . . escalated their activities when the cameramen arrived." . . .

Throughout the article, the demonstrators were made to appear ridiculous, frivolous, and hypocritical. All the women's charges about sexism in the United States were placed in quotation marks, suggesting that these were merely the deluded hallucinations of a few ugly, angry women rather than a fact of life. The demonstrators' rhetoric was cast as highly inflated and thus absurd, and their complaints about female oppression seen as representing a wacky, self-seeking, publicity-hungry fringe of distinctly unrepresentative women. So the women who were protesting the public exhibition of women's bodies were themselves cast as nothing more than needy exhibitionists. The contrast was stark: Miss America contestants, beautiful, docile, and compliant, who eagerly sought out and competed for the male gaze, deserved their day in the public spotlight; the demonstrators, unruly, rebellious, excessive, who attacked the institutionalization of male voyeurism, did not.

In this way the protesters played into—as some of them feared they would—the media's love of conflict, especially among women, and the image of feminists as hostile to other women began to crystallize. Yet even as these early feminist activists despaired over their new image as storm troopers jealous of pretty women, they quickly saw another immediate result of this dismissive coverage: it promoted female solidarity. In the aftermath of the Atlantic City protest, New York Radical Women was flooded with new members, and other feminist organizations were founded around the country.[6]

One year later, *Newsweek* would describe the Miss America demonstration as one in which 150 women "gathered in front of Convention Hall and burned their brassieres," even though no bra burning had occurred in Atlantic City.[7] But bra burning had become the news peg for media coverage of the women's movement, a metaphor that trivialized feminists and titillated the audience at the same time. For the press, burning bras was a natural segue from burning draft cards. It fit into the dominant media frame about women's liberation and equated the women's movement with exhibitionism and narcissism, as if women who unstrapped their breasts were unleashing their sexuality in a way that was unseemly, laughable, and politically inconsequential, yet dangerous. Women who threw their bras away may have said they were challenging sexism, but the media, with a wink, hinted that these women's motives were not at all political but rather personal: to be trendy, and to attract men.

Even for those of us who didn't recognize it at the time, 1968 was a turning point. All the prefeminist glimmerings in girl group music, Beatlemania, perky teens, and women with magical powers, the exhortations to make something of ourselves and change the world, and the image of the political woman we first saw in Joan Baez and Mary Travers—these shards started coming together and magnified one another during 1968. The acceptance by millions of us of some version of feminist ideology was a fitful process during which we began questioning, rethinking, and revising our sense of what it meant—or ought to mean—to be an American woman. Baby boomers' sense of being part of something bigger would begin to shape not just a social identity but a political identity, and one with political consequences. The process began accelerating in 1968 as many of us developed a deep antipathy and contempt for the status quo and an inflated sense of our mission to reject it. And then, for a brief moment on the TV screen, there were these women, charging that what completely undergirded that hideous status quo was the subordination and objectification of women. . . .

So where are we now, in the era of "I'm not a feminist, but . . . "? We are an overlay of imprints, bearing, in some way or another, the fossilized remains of *Queen for a Day, Sputnik,* the Sexual Revolution, the Chiffons, Beatlemania, perkiness, the women's movement, the catfights, *Charlie's Angels,* and buns of steel. We have learned to be masochistic and narcissistic, feisty and compliant, eager to please and eager to irritate and shock, independent and dependent, assertive and conciliatory. We have learned to wear a hundred masks, and to live with the fact that our inner selves are fragmented, some of the pieces validated by the mass media, others eternally ignored. All our lives, we have watched women from Beatles fans to Anita Hill and Hillary Rodham Clinton breaching barricades and crossing boundaries they weren't supposed to: we have seen how stepping out of line has been punished and how effective— and utterly futile—such punishments have been. Certain women are demonized, but they, and others emboldened by their actions, come back for more. We have grown up with these ever discrepant representations of women, and related to them all our lives, and while we have shaped them, they have had more power to shape us. We have grown up and continue to live with media images not of our making, so, on some level, we will always feel like outsiders looking in at a culture that regards us as unknowable, mysterious, laughable, other. But we are insiders too, having been formed by this very same culture, our desires researched to the hilt and then sold back to us in a warped, yet still recognizable fashion. We stand on the border, looking out and looking in, feeling simultaneously included and excluded, wooed as consumers yet rejected as people.

One of the major traits that defines womanhood in the 1990s is our daily war with all those media which we love and hate and which, after all these years, don't know what to do about us or for us, although they seem to have a better grip on what to do to us. It is easy for many of us to understand what an advertiser or a TV producer wants us to take away from this ad or that show, but that doesn't mean that women always, in fact, buy into and accept those meanings. We are fed up with ads that tell us we're too old, too fat, and too marked up in some way, but we feel, nonetheless, too old, too fat, and too marked up. We are tired of blockbuster movies that glorify beefy, rippled men who speak monosyllabically and carry extremely well-endowed sticks, but we go to them anyway, nursing our fury and enjoying our catharsis. We get the bends as we escape into the schizophrenic landscape of *Glamour* or *Vogue*, in which editorials, advice columns, and articles urge us to be assertive, strong, no-nonsense feminists while the fashion and beauty layouts insist that we be passive, anorexic spectacles whose only function is to attract men and who should spend our leisure time mastering the art of the pedicure. We throw half-eaten bagels at Saturday morning kids' shows and commercials that train our daughters to be giggling, air-headed Valley Girls, but we go ahead and buy them Glitter Ken and the Fisher-Price toy kitchen on the theory that we played with Barbie and we came out OK—well, sort of. We think that news programs must be getting less sexist because there are now famous women newscasters like Connie Chung, Diane Sawyer, and Nina Totenberg, but we also see how so-called women's issues are either sensationalized (have one more drink and you'll die of breast cancer) or trivialized (so what if a woman has to drive 300 miles to get an abortion, or a sixteen-year-old has to get permission to do so from a father she never sees?), while women's voices about major areas of national policy are ignored. Most of all, the constant erasure of the contradictions that define our lives makes us crazy, since all the media, completely confused and conflicted about what to do about women, subtly acknowledge those contradictions while either pretending they don't exist or insisting they can be resolved, especially with a purchase or two. . . .

This is what it has come to. On the one hand, few women want to take on the baggage of the feminist stereotype. On the other hand, they embrace much of what feminism has made possible for them—which they also learned about, initially, from the media—and are uninterested in returning to the days of woman as doormat. Since the 1960s, legitimation of feminism in the mass media and backlash against it have smacked against each other with the force and chaos of billiard balls colliding. Individual women, too often isolated by the pressures of juggling work, relationships, kids, and trying to see a movie once a year, are left on their own to arrange the balls nearty in some psychic rack that makes sense for them, if only momentarily.

What the mass media don't convey, and can't convey, is that feminism is an ongoing project, a process, undertaken on a daily basis by millions of women of all ages, classes, ethnic and racial backgrounds, and sexual preferences. Feminism is constantly being reinvented, and reinvented through determination and compromise, so that women try, as best they can, to have love and support as well as power and autonomy. As they do so, they have certainly taken note, with Susan Faludi's help, of a backlash filled with wishful thinking pronouncements about the "death" of feminism and the heralding of a new "postfeminist" age.[8] . . .

The news media, for their part, are today a schizophrenic mess about feminism, and there is a powerful reverberation between their schizophrenia and our own. They continue to cover feminism and describe feminists as if the movement is monolithic and feminists are all alike. At the same time, in their stories and their hiring practices, we see that in the news media (as elsewhere) feminism is many things to many women; that there is not one feminism but many; and that there are beautiful, amiable women who claim feminism and shrill, mean-spirited ones who condemn it. . . .

. . . Women's voices are rarely heard on the news. Feminism is still kept in ideological purdah. Female "experts" are interviewed for the nightly news when the topic is abortion, child care, or affirmative action; but when the topic is war, foreign policy, the environment, or national purpose, female voices, and feminist voices in particular, are ignored. A recent study revealed that in 1988 only 10.3 percent of the guests on *Nightline* were female, and of the twenty most frequent guests, none were women. Another study from 1990 found that the ten individuals who appeared most frequently as analysts on the CBS, ABC, and NBC nightly news were all men, and some of them appeared as many as fifty-eight times in a single year.[9] Betty Friedan's Women, Men and Media Project found that the percentage of female correspondents was only 15 percent in 1989, and that there were some nights when you could watch the news and see no women reporters at all. Of the one hundred most frequently seen correspondents on TV, only eight were women. Diane Sawyer and Connie Chung remain exceptions, and they represent a very small and privileged class of women. More to the point, they are gorgeous. . . .

Thanks to the women's movement, my consciousness as a woman and as a mother was very different from my mother's. I was aware of our country's pathological schizophrenia about mothers and children: revere them in imagery, revile them in public policy. But this wasn't my own lonely observation; unlike my mother, I could read, hear, and see other women, in a variety of places, articulating these same criticisms. I also had the language, as well as the sense of obligation, to dissect the media's role in sustaining this hypocrisy. . . .

Nowhere is the gap between image and reality wider than the one separating the smiling, serene, financially comfortable, and perfectly coiffed media mom from her frazzled, exhausted, sputum-covered, real-life counterpart. Everywhere I turned, as I read child-care books, watched TV, or went shopping for baby paraphernalia, I found myself navigating the powerful crosscurrents of middle-class motherhood. Like all the other messages surrounding us—about sex, about assertiveness, about women in politics, and about independence—the messages about motherhood and babies crash into each other like tidal waves. Shooting these ideological rapids on a daily basis, while also taking care of a baby, can produce a certain astringency in the new mom's worldview. And I found myself getting more astringent as I took inventory of the completely unrealistic images of motherhood we imbibed. Here was my love-hate relationship with the mass media writ large.

In the early months of my daughter's life, I watched more TV than usual, but with a more jaundiced eye. Yet even my old standbys let me down. On *L. A. Law*,

Ann Kelsey and Stuart Markowitz, who had been trying unsuccessfully to have a baby, adopted an infant girl. . . .

Motherhood had virtually no impact on this woman's life or work, while those of us sitting at home in our sputum-covered bathrobes and ratty slippers were wondering how we were going to survive the next day at work on no sleep. This baby, like most media babies, was a trouble-free, ecstasy-producing, attractive little acquisition; if you "get" one, it will make you feel real good, look great in a rocking chair, and make you fall in love with your spouse all over again. Now, while babies are, at times, an indescribable joy, caring for them makes you feel like you've been tortured in an especially sadistic sleep-deprivation experiment. The feel-good images are a complete lie, and you know it. But they burrow into you, forcing you to castigate yourself for not being serene enough, organized enough, or spontaneous enough as a mother.

At the same time that this little fantasy world was beaming out from dramatic television, the concept of the "mommy track" was getting bandied about in the news media, promoted by huge cover stories in the newsmagazines and major stories on TV. According to this proposal, mothers should be on a separate—and unequal— career track that gives them more flexible hours in exchange for no promotions, no challenging assignments, less autonomy, and no raises.

Talk about getting the bends! On the one hand, we had the TV supermoms, size-six women with perfectly applied makeup who could do anything and apparently didn't need any sleep. On the other hand, we got a recognition that motherhood might be just a tad demanding, but acknowledged only in the age-old blame-the-victim solution of the mommy track. Between these two extremes were millions of us, the real mothers of America, with no place to stand. We were either supposed to act as if children don't hamper our ability to be overachieving workaholics and we can do everything we did before plus raise a baby or two or acquiesce to second-class citizenship, acknowledging that being a mother is so debilitating that we're only capable of having dead-end, place-holding jobs while men, including fathers, and women without kids step on our backs to get the next promotion. Either way, the real-life mother is humiliated, especially if she has a job, as opposed to a "career," in which the whole notion of advancement or a "track" is patently absurd. Meanwhile, there is no recognition that fatherhood might be exhausting too, and that new fathers are also operating under a completely different set of circumstances. In the supermom fantasies of TV and the mommy track proposals of corporate America, what remains enshrined is our country's craven, hypercompetitive yuppie work ethic. Babies and parents are supposed to work around these increasingly preposterous norms of what constitutes adequate job performance.

These contradictions surrounding motherhood and children differ from what our mothers confronted, but they have their roots firmly and deeply in the 1950s. For even now, no matter what you do, you can't ever be good enough as a mother. If you don't work, you're a bad mom, and if you do work, you're a bad mom. Then there's all the advice that comes at us from *Working Mother, Parents, Newsweek,* the nightly news, *20/20*, and *Oprah*. Let your baby cry herself to sleep; never let your baby cry. Don't be too rigid, but don't be too permissive. Don't ever spank your child; an occasional swat on the butt is good for a kid. Encourage your child to learn, but don't push her to learn. Be her friend; never be her friend. Rein her in; cut her some slack. The tightrope walks are endless. Once again we find ourselves under surveillance, not only as sex objects, or as workers, but as mothers. And on all sides of us are voices with megaphones, yelling completely opposite things to us as we figure out whether we have time to do a wash or will simply have to turn the kid's underwear inside out tomorrow.

And here, again, we feel the pull between sisterhood and competitive individualism. At 4:00 A.M., when it seemed like everyone in the world except my daughter and I was asleep, I felt myself part of that transhistorical and transcultural group called mothers, the ones who get up, no matter what, listening to the soft snorings of others, while tending to the needs of a child. Now this may sound overly romantic and sentimental, but I didn't expect to feel such a powerful bond with other women across space and time. . . .

This is why Roseanne Barr, now Arnold, became the top female sitcom star in America in the early 1990s. Despite the incredibly hostile treatment she has gotten in the press—because she's four things TV women are not supposed to be, working-class, loudmouthed, overweight, and a feminist—Roseanne became a success because her mission was simple and welcome: to take the schmaltz and hypocrisy out of media images of motherhood. Her famous line from her stand-up routine—"If the kids are alive at five, hey, I've done my job"—spoke to millions of women who love their children more than anything in the world but who also find motherhood wearing, boring, and, at times, infuriating. She spoke to women who had seen through June Cleaver and Donna Reed years ago, and were struggling to see through the supermom image now. Roseanne also took aim at the class biases around media images of motherhood: that good mothers looked like those svelte, smiling, beauty queen moms in Gerber ads or the moms in white muslin on the beach pitching Calvin Klein perfume. Most moms are not corporate attorneys, Roseanne insisted, nor do they fit into a size six, carry a briefcase, or smile most of the time. They are waitresses, or work in factories, or in tiny office cubicles, or in other dead-end jobs, and they don't have $700 suits or nannies. . . .

Both the news and entertainment media have had enormous power to set the agenda about how people consider, react to, and accept women's changing roles and aspirations. Frequently, and without obvious collusion, the various media have managed to settle on what becomes the prevailing common sense about women's place in the world. Having that common sense repeated and reenacted in sitcoms, movies, and newscasts has a powerful effect on women's self-perceptions and on men's perceptions of them. To point out that these dominant images are perforated with rifts and contradictions that have sometimes emboldened women does not undercut their basic power.[10] The media have helped instigate change for women while using a host of metaphors—women with magical powers, the catfight, the choked-off female voice—to contain and blunt that change.

So, for us, the question about whether the mass media lead social change or lag behind it sets up a false dichotomy, for we have seen and felt them do both at the same time. Yet sometimes the mass media lag much more than they lead, and today we live in an especially conservative media environment, in which ownership of media outlets is increasingly concentrated in the hands of fewer megacorporations and the voices of those not smack dab in the moderate political center are vilified or silenced. Images of scores of women in satin teddies and garter belts hopping in and out of bed with whomever is handy suggest, to some, an overly "liberal" media when such images are, in fact, deeply reactionary. And one of the most persistently conservative elements we women face is the story, the narrative, which continues to be structured around boys taking action, girls waiting for the boys, and girls rescued by the boys. In these stories, someone, usually the girl, is a victim, and someone else, usually the boy, is an actor in the world, while we feel ourselves to be both active agents and ongoing victims of stories we never wrote and images we never drew. . . .

The only advice I have for women today is to purchase two things: extra slippers, for throwing at the TV set, and extra stationary, for writing letters to soda companies telling them we'll never buy their swill again and will organize boycotts if they keep pitting Cindy Crawford against older women and keep pitting us against one another. We can also reclaim the word *feminist* from the trash heap it's been relegated to by the media and remind them and ourselves that a woman who says, "I'm not a feminist, but . . ." is, in fact, a feminist. I agree with Susan Faludi, who said, "All women are feminists. It's just a matter of time and encouragement."[11] And despite their best efforts to keep *feminism* a dirty word and women under control, the media will continue, often inadvertently, to play a critical role in providing that encouragement. They are still our worst enemy and our best ally in our ongoing struggle for equality, respect, power, and love.

NOTES

1. Rita Lang Kleinfelder, *When We Were Young: A Baby-Boomer Yearbook* (New York: Prentice Hall, 1993), p. 472.

2. Todd Gitlin, *The Whole World Is Watching* (Berkeley: University of California Press, 1980), p. 121.

3. See ibid., pp. 47–52 and pp. 90–94.

4. Ibid., p. 6.

5. "No more Miss America!" in Robin Morgan, ed., *Sisterhood is Powerful* (New York: Vintage, 1970), pp. 521–524.

6. Echols, *Daring to Be Bad*, pp. 98–99.

7. "The Big Letdown," *Newsweek*, September 1, 1969, pp. 49–50.

8. Susan Faludi, *Backlash: The Undeclared War Against American Women* (New York: Crown, 1991), pp. 76–77.

9. Susan Douglas, "The Representation of Women in the News Media," EXTRA!, March–April 1991, p. 2.

10. Justin Lewis, *The Ideological Octopus* (New York: Routledge, 1991), pp. 203–205.

11. Ruth Conniff, "An Interview with Susan Faludi," *Progressive*, June 1993, p. 35.

29

Mating, Marriage, and the Marketplace: A Survey of College Students' Attitudes and Expectations

Barbara A. Arrighi

Those of you reading this text have experienced the economic recession, corporate mergers, and massive layoffs of the late twentieth century. In your lifetime you have undoubtedly acquired some familiarity with terms like merger mania, corporate downsizing, corporate rightsizing, bull markets, bear markets, day trading, e-commerce, and the NASDAQ. Politically, you have lived through the country's shift from democratic liberalism to an embracing of Reagonomics, a turn toward Clinton's democratic conservatism, with compassionate conservatism ushering in the twenty-first century.

You have come of age in the midst of the continuing fallout of the liberalized sexual mores of the 1960s. The culture has bequeathed to you spiraling divorce rates, increased remarriage rates, destigmatization of and an increasing occurrence of cohabitation, legalization of abortion, premarital sex as normative, higher rates of out-of-wedlock births (even as birth control has become more accessible and more reliable), and an increasing proportion of wives and mothers as full-time, year-round workers. In general, though many young women have not embraced feminism as a social or political ideology, they have practiced its tenets: higher levels of education for women, delayed first marriage, fewer children, and a sustained commitment to the workplace.

You have been subjected to televised discussions, debates, and even U.S. Senate hearings about formerly taboo subjects like domestic violence, sexual harassment, the health risks of unprotected sex, and the unforgettable, tortured definition of sex by a sitting president. All of this has played out, synchronized to the beat of successive political and religious calls for a return to family values.

Within an environment of changing sexual mores and lifestyle patterns, what can be gleaned about the future from this generation's attitudes and expectations concerning mating, marriage, and the marketplace? This study provides a descriptive analysis of a sample of members of the cohort born in the late 1970s and early 1980s and their views on these issues, all within the context of a culture in flux.

SEX-ROLE ATTITUDES AND EGALITARIANISM

Research indicates that attitudes and education are linked, and that values change with increased education (Ross 1987). For example, there is evidence that those with higher levels of education are more accepting of equality between the sexes. In marital relationships, husbands' level of education is a predictor of their willingness to share household tasks (Farkas 1976). Furthermore, there is evidence that husbands with twelve or more years of education do more housework than those with fewer years of education (Presser 1994).

Societal definitions of what women and men should be emerge within the process of doing gender (West and Zimmerman 1987); that is, designations of appropriately masculine or feminine behavior are constructed within institutional contexts. Thus, they are socially constructed as well as structured in family systems and educational systems, to name just two. Gendered role performances reinforce and legitimate existing gender-patterned behaviors that are interwoven into our institutions and thus our social relationships.

As an institution, the family provides the initial and perhaps most enduring inculcation of gender. For example, at birth males and females are more alike than different; however, because of the institutionalized gender expectations of significant others, the gender division—a mere seam at birth—becomes a chasm by young adulthood. The structure of gendering means the similarities between females and males are denied (Rubin 1975). The patterns of gender behavior and power relations in one's family of origin influences the gender development of a child as well as the gender organization of family life when two people marry. In analyzing the data in this study, I am interested in determining to what extent college students in the sample give gendered responses concerning mating, marriage, and the marketplace.

METHODS

A convenience sample of 354 students completed surveys in four sections of introductory sociology courses during the fall semester of 1997. One hundred thirty-three respondents were males and 221 were females. The majority of students were freshmen between 17 and 21 years of age. What we learn about these students cannot be generalized to other college-age women and men, but the findings can provide a sense of the direction future research should take.

RESULTS

The attitudes and expectations of the young women and men in the sample converged on many issues, especially those relating to marriage and family. The most notable gender differences emerged on workplace issues.

GENDER AND MATING

Traditionally, women were to remain virginal until marriage (no matter how late they wed; men, however, were expected, even encouraged, to become experienced sexual partners. Indeed, the prevailing thinking until the 1960s was that women were void of any "carnal motivation" (Collins and Coltrane 1991; Cott 1978). Even today the messages about appropriate sexual behavior for women are ambiguous at best. In light of this, it is instructive that almost half of the college males (46 percent) expressed a centuries-old preference to marry a virgin, and that about a third of young women in the sample responded that they, like the young men in the sample, would prefer to marry a virgin.

The student responses could reflect the religious influence of the larger community in which the university is situated. Located along the northern edge of the Bible Belt, the university is also in an area that is heavily Catholic. Virgin Mary sightings, attracting hundreds of faithful, have been reported in the last few years at a Catholic church located not far from the university.

However, something other than religious dogma could be motivating the responses. For example, fear of deadly sexually transmitted diseases could be informing their responses. Then again, women's responses might be nothing more than a desire for equity concerning the sexual behavior of their partner. Simply put, if men prefer virgins, women can too.

While a substantial proportion of college men surveyed expressed a traditional preference for a virgin, the expectations of many appeared grounded in contemporary sexual mores. Almost half of the men (44 percent) and more than half of the women (51 percent) stated that they do not expect to marry a virgin. However, if national data are accurate, a substantial proportion of students in the sample are going to be disappointed, because virgins appear to be an endangered species. At the turn of twentieth century, less than 25 percent of women reportedly had engaged in premarital sex, but by the late 1980s the proportion had increased to 66 percent (Family Planning Perspectives 1985). The shift for men went from 66 percent in the 1920s who reported having engaged in premarital sexual activity to about 95 percent in the 1980s (Collins and Coltrane 1991). Clearly, the expectations of students surveyed do not reflect the national shift toward premarital sexual activity.

STUDENTS AND A DOUBLE STANDARI

Both male and female students in the sample thought a double s
cerning sexual behavior. For example, a majority of the men (68 pe
(85 percent) disagreed with the statement: "Today a woman can
tive as a man and it will not reflect negatively on her." The finding suggests that the
students in this sample would think the 66 percent of young women in the national
sample (noted above) who reportedly engage in premarital sex do so at risk to their
reputation. While both groups of students in this sample agree that being sexually
active is problematic for women, the young men appear to welcome the idea of
women taking the lead in a relationship. More than half of the college men surveyed
disagreed with the statement: "In relationships, it is best for the man to pursue the
woman." However, less than half (45 percent) of women in the sample were willing
to forgo tradition and take on the role of the pursuer. No doubt their hesitancy was
related to their awareness of the resiliency of the double standard.

GENDER, MARRIAGE, AND HOUSEWORK

The issue of who should be the pursuer may be debatable, but most survey respondents seemed prepared to follow the traditional path of marriage and family. The
overwhelming majority of students expect to marry (87 percent of men and 93 percent of women) and raise a family (86 percent of males and 89 percent of females).

How couples set up their households has been central to research examining equality within the family. Prevailing cultural norms define men by their ability to provide for their families (Bernard 1981). Within that context many, if not most, men
view paid work as the arena in which their success will be measured and the family
as a separate institution that provides a "haven in a heartless world" (Lasch 1977).
Being a provider is steeped in gender and confirms men's masculine identity (Bernard 1981).

Because being a homemaker, like being a provider, is steeped in gender too, men
who engage in housework do not fit the cultural definition of masculinity (Bernard
1981). Men might resist sharing household tasks because "real" men wouldn't do
them (Fowlkes 1980). Even at that, the work and family literature has reported that
men and women support the notion of men contributing to household labor, especially when wives are employed outside the home (Pleck 1993; Thompson and
Walker 1989).

Though there is consensus that men should share housework with their significant others, the research consistently has found that men typically do no more than
a third of household labor. Yet in a departure from tradition, the expectation of the
majority of this sample of college students is that they will share household tasks
equally (men 77 percent, women 88 percent). It should be noted that in the face of

, seemingly egalitarian view, almost half of the male respondents indicated that some household tasks were better suited to women! That 40 percent of women agreed with the men sheds some light on why the proportion of housework completed by men has not changed dramatically. Could it be that some women resist giving up tasks that they think display being a woman? Should future research shift the focus from why men do not do more to why women will not do less? Are men reluctant to take on work that they feel best displays being a woman? Is it that men are reluctant to take on more than a third of household work, or is it more that too many women resist giving up the home as their primary responsibility, possibly even acting as gatekeepers for men sharing housework?

Indeed, two-thirds of the sample agreed with the statement: "There are natural differences between men and women and we shouldn't try to change things." The responses to the survey statements are at the core of the gender perspective's argument about gender displays. Although being a man or woman socially is not the inevitable outgrowth of biological features, it is made invisible through gendering and thus comes to be viewed as natural (Ferree 1990; Gerson and Peiss 1985). The college sample's responses align with a 1993 Gallup Poll (Newport 1993) in which 56 percent of men and 73 percent of women agreed that "not including purely physical differences, men and women are basically different." If the dominant thinking of both sexes is that women and men are innately different, appeals by a minority of women and men for equality between the sexes will be resisted by the majority.

STUDENTS' VIEWS ABOUT CHILD CARE

Although the men surveyed believed there are some tasks for which women are better suited, there was ambivalence concerning child care. Half of the male respondents (and 69 percent of women) believed that women are not automatically better caretakers of children than men. The students' responses concerning child care correspond with prior research that suggests that, of all the household duties, men are more likely to assist with child care than with other tasks. As we forge a new century, some foresee the increasing expectation for fathers to become equal coparents (Doherty, Kouneski, and Erickson 1998; Pleck and Pleck 1997). Men can even find child care rewarding (Gerson 1993).

STUDENT ATTITUDES ABOUT WORK AND FAMILY

Should wives stay home? Not according to a majority of the students surveyed. Overall, two-thirds disagreed with the statement: "It is better for the family if the wife stays home and the husband goes to work." Nationally, well over half of women with school-aged children are in the workplace, and student responses are consistent with that data. It is possible that for many of the students their own childhood experiences included having a working mom. Unfortunately, that information about students in the sample is unavailable in these data.

Despite reports indicating that 48 percent of employed married women provide half or more of family income (Families and Work Institute 1995), they tend to be thought of as supplemental rather than co-providers (Ferree 1990). Research has suggested that even in the face of harsh economic reality, many couples think the provision of family income should be the husband's sole responsibility (Vannoy-Hiller and Philliber 1989). And cross-cultural research supports the notion that the bread-winner status is attached to the man, not the woman. What does our sample think?

Not only do the men surveyed not object to the prospect of working wives, they report not being threatened by the prospect of their mates earning more than they do. Seventy percent of the men and 65 percent of the women do not think that it is better for the family if the husband earns more than the wife.

GENDER AND THE WORKPLACE

The young college men have thus far presented somewhat egalitarian attitudes and expectations concerning mating and family matters; they appear to draw the line, however, when it comes to the workplace. Seventy-three percent of the men think that "There are some jobs in the workplace that are better suited for men than for women." If, as Bernard and others suggest, men view paid work as the arena in which their success is measured and their manhood is defined, within that context their response makes sense. Their thinking here provides further evidence that the students subscribe to the natural difference argument. More than half (57 percent) of the young women in the sample agreed with the men, which is alarming and indicates the complexity of the issue of resistance to full integration of women in the workplace. Is the glass ceiling being held in place with the help of some women?

Although these data are not generalizable, the students' responses are consistent with the results of a 1993 Gallup Poll cited above (Newport 1993), in which the majority of both sexes concurred with the notion that men and women are basically different. Taken together, it is a conundrum for women. Can equality between the sexes be achieved if difference is the paradigm?

STUDENTS AND AFFIRMATIVE ACTION

It is instructive that although the women surveyed did not seem to consider "his and her jobs" problematic, at least 41 percent of women did not agree with this statement: "Affirmative Action is no longer needed to help women get ahead." While not a majority, it is nearly double the 24 percent of college men who disagreed. The findings correspond with a 1995 Gallup Poll that found only 43 percent of women and 38 percent of men approved of Affirmative Action for women. Thompson's

(1991) argument that women and men typically compare their situations with others of the same sex rather than with those of the opposite sex may be appropriate here in explaining men's lack of support for Affirmative Action and women's lukewarm support.

Thirty-nine percent of women and 35 percent of men responded "don't know" to the above statement about Affirmative Action. Their response could reflect their inexperience with and/or lack of knowledge of Affirmative Action issues in the workplace. It is worth noting that, though support for the Affirmative Action statement above was minimal, 72 percent of the college women and 50 percent of the young men disagreed with this statement: "If women and men have the same qualifications and do the same job, they are paid the same wage." Interestingly, students surveyed are cognizant that inequality exists in the workplace, but their lack of endorsement for Affirmative Action indicates they do not support a policy to change it. As noted above, if male identity and financial well-being are attached to the marketplace, men's self-interested stance on Affirmative Action is logical.

But what can be said of women's lack of support for Affirmative Action? It could be that inequality that has the potential to lead to conflict is suppressed or denied by those who are victimized by it. It could be that women are a colonized group and do not fully grasp their subordination. It could be too, as Ferree (1990) argues, that rather than look at the structure of inequality we try to resolve it "by invoking supposed differences in the characters of men and women" (876). It is less disruptive, less messy, less risky to blame the individual rather than to take on the daunting task of structurally addressing issues of inequality. It allows the status quo to remain intact.

CONCLUSION

If education liberalizes attitudes, some of the responses from this sample of college students point to an egalitarian perspective, especially about issues concerning home life and children. It appears that for the most part the students expect to share household tasks and child care as some have predicted will happen in the twenty-first century.

If this group of college students has its way, however, the workplace will remain divided into his and hers. A gender perspective is at work here. The men clearly do not favor Affirmative Action to ameliorate job segregation, and women are not much more enthusiastic. Furthermore, while endorsing equality in the home, a sizable proportion of the college women seem to accept a segregated status for women and men at work. If this sample is in any way representative of the next generation of workers, equality in the workplace will continue to elude us.

The study has provided a snapshot of college students' attitudes concerning work and family issues. While it provides some insights, the findings are not generalizable. Longitudinal research is needed so that we can understand the process by which students form their attitudes and the extent to which students' attitudes about family and work can predict their behaviors.

The direction of future research should be threefold. One should focus on explaining men's role in the household division of labor as well as men's gate-keeping function in the workplace. A second should focus on women as gatekeepers in the home—that is, to what extent are women resistant to men's encroachment on their turf? Finally, the third focus of the analysis should examine women's role in perpetuating workplace job segregation.

REFERENCES

Bernard, Jessie. 1981. The Good Provider Role: Its Rise and Fall. *American Psychologist* 36: 1–12.

Collins, Randall, and Scott Coltrane. 1991. *Sociology of Marriage and the Family: Gender, Love, and Property*. Chicago: Nelson Hall.

Cott, Nancy F. 1978. Passionlessness: An Interpretation of Victorian Sexual Ideology 1790–1850. *Signs* 4: 219–36.

Doherty, William J., Edward F. Kouneski, and Martha F. Erickson. 1998. Responsible Fathering: An Overview and Conceptual Framework. *Journal of Marriage and the Family* 60, 277–92.

Families and Work Institute. 1995. *Women: The New Providers*. Benton Harbor, Mich.: Whirlpool Foundation.

Family Planning Perspectives. 1985. Recently Wed Women More Likely to Have Had Premarital Sex. 17 (September/October): 142.

Farkas, George. 1976. Education, Wage Rates, and the Division of Labor between Husband and Wife. *Journal of Marriage and the Family* 38: 473–83.

Ferree, Myra Marx. 1990. Beyond Separate Spheres: Feminism and Family Research. *Journal of Marriage and the Family* 38: 473–83.

Fowlkes, Martha. 1980. *Behind Every Successful Man*. New York: Columbia University Press.

Gerson, Kathleen. 1993. *No Man's Land*. New York: Basic Books.

Gerson, Judith, and Kathy Peiss. 1985. Boundaries, Negotiations, Consciousness: Reconceptualizing Gender Relations. *Social Problems* 32: 317–31.

Lasch, Christopher. 1977. *Haven in a Heartless World*. New York: Basic Books.

Moore, David W. 1995. Americans Today Are Dubious about Affirmative Action. *The Gallup Monthly Poll* (March): 36–38.

Newport, Frank. 1993. Americans Now More Likely to Say: Women Have It Harder than Men. *The Gallup Monthly Poll* (October): 11–13.

Pleck, Joseph. 1993. Are 'Family-Supportive' Employer Policies Relevant to Men? In *Men, Work and Family*, edited by Jane C. Hood, 217–37. Newbury Park, Calif.: Sage.

Pleck, E. H., and J. H. Pleck. 1997. Fatherhood Ideals in the United States: Historical Dimensions. In *The Role of the Father in Child Development*, 3rd ed., edited by M. E. Lamb. New York: Wiley.

Presser, Harriet. 1994. Employment Schedules among Dual-Earner Spouses and the Division of Household Labor by Gender. *American Sociological Review* 59: 348–64.

Ross, Catherine E. 1987. The Division of Labor at Home. *Social Forces* 65: 816–33.

Rubin, Gayle. 1975. The Traffic in Women: Notes on the 'Political Economy' of Sex. In *Toward an Anthropology of Women,* edited by R. Reiter. New York: Monthly Review Press.

Thompson, Linda. 1991. Family Work: Women's Sense of Fairness. *Journal of Family Issues* 12: 181–96.

Thompson, Linda, and Alexis J. Walker. 1989. Gender in Families: Women and Men in Marriage, Work and Parenthood. *Journal of Marriage and the Family* 51: 41–57.

Vannoy-Hiller, Dana, and William W. Philliber. 1989. *Equal Partners: Successful Women in Marriage.* Newbury Park, Calif.: Sage.

West, Candace, and Don H. Zimmerman. 1987. Doing Gender. *Gender and Society* 1: 125–51.

Part Nine

Aging: Devalued Women *and* Men

30

Jane Fonda, Barbara Bush and Other Aging Bodies: Femininity and the Limits of Resistance

Myra Dinnerstein and Rose Weitz

. . . Part of the problem women face in resisting cultural definitions of femininity is that these definitions influence us in ways that we do not fully recognize. While many women are aware of the barrage of messages from the media about appropriate feminine appearance, few realize how insidiously these notions have entered our individual psyches or think to question their legitimacy. Newspaper articles might report on studies showing that a high proportion of ten-year-old girls diet and that an epidemic of anorexia and bulimia has swept the country, but few women respond to this evidence of the dire consequences of preoccupation with body size by changing their own attitudes and behaviors. . . .

Our analysis of Fonda and Bush joins this discussion by highlighting the interplay between agency and social control in the reactions of heterosexual white women to their aging appearance, demonstrating how Fonda and Bush simultaneously have attempted to resist the dominant discourse on aging and have been constrained by it. Their experiences delineate the difficulties of resistance and underscore the struggle required to establish oppositional discourses.

For this article, we draw on all articles written about Bush and Fonda in women's magazines (including fashion magazines) indexed in the *Readers' Guide to Periodical Literature* beginning in 1977, when Fonda turned forty.[1] Expectations about women's aging bodies are well articulated in these magazines, making them a useful source of data. . . .

Because of the nature of our data, our findings refer only to white, heterosexual, economically privileged women. As others have noted, previous research provides relatively little information about the attitudes of working class women, lesbians, or women of color toward their bodies (Thomas 1989; Thomas and James 1988, 524; Smith, Burlew, and Lundgren 1991, 269; Rothblum, in press). We would add that previous research provides even less information about their views toward the *aging* body. . . .

AGING FEMALE BODIES: A BRIEF HISTORY

What constitutes a culturally appropriate appearance for aging women has changed considerably over time (Banner 1983; Schwartz 1986; Seid 1989). Until the mid-twentieth century, American society expected older women to have what was termed a "mature figure" and to wear "mature" fashions. Beginning in the 1950s, however, this demarcation between youthful and aging appearances began to break down. The emphasis on youth accelerated in the 1960s and early 1970s, as both medical and fashion experts, bolstered by the highly visible youth culture, declared the youthful, slim body the standard for all (Seid 1989, 116–123, 175–76). By the late 1970s, as the baby boomers who had fostered the youth culture aged, the struggle to maintain a youthful appearance had fostered a nationwide fitness craze. . . .

The increased cultural focus since the 1970s on controlling women's bodies has led several critics to label it a "backlash" to the rising power and visibility of women. These commentators suggest that keeping women involved with controlling their bodies diverts their energies from striving to achieve more control in the public arena (Bordo 1989, 14, Bordo 1990, 105; Faludi 1991, 203–204; Wolf 1991, 9–12). An analysis of Jane Fonda, who both rode the wave of the new fitness craze and helped to create it and who promotes women's control of the body as a form of "liberation," illuminates the contradictions of preoccupation with the body.

MANAGING THE AGING BODY

Jane Fonda: Relentlessly Improved

. . . Ever since she turned forty, Fonda has garnered particular attention and admiration as a woman who has aged yet retained her beauty. With each successive year, the women's magazines have marked Jane Fonda's chronological aging by announcing her age and marveling at how well and specifically, how young she looks (e.g., Davis 1990, 165; Andersen 1989, 112). . . .

In the 1980s, as Fonda emerged as an exercise guru, she at first extolled the virtues of intervening only minimally in the aging process. At age 47, writing about aging skin and cosmetic surgery in *Women Coming of Age* (1984, 71), her book on midlife, she advised, "The course I prefer: making peace with the growing numbers of fine (and some not so fine) lines you see on your face. . . . Wrinkles are part of who we are, of where we've been. Not to have wrinkles means never having laughed or cried or expressed passion, never having squinted into the sun or felt the bite of winter's wind—never having fully lived!" . . .

Despite this rhetoric, however, most of Fonda's pronouncements even during these years centered on changing and controlling rather than accepting the body. Yet in these statements as well, Fonda used feminist rhetoric such as "freedom" and "liberation" to frame this bodily control as a form of resistance to traditional expectations of female emotional and physical weakness. Bodily control, she has argued, "gives me a sense of freedom" (Kaplan 1987, 417), for "discipline is freedom" (*Mademoiselle* 1980, 38). Similarly, she has described herself as "liberated" from the cultural pressures that led her to engage in binge/purge eating until age 35.

. . . Fonda sees exercise as a means toward mental health: "Exercise does a tremendous amount for emotional and mental stability. . . . That is what satisfies me most . . ., the people who come up after a week or two of classes and say, 'Hey, I'm not depressed anymore'" (*Harper's Bazaar* 1980, 82).

Given the prevailing discourse on femininity and on aging, it is not surprising that Fonda and her admirers have characterized her as feminist. In a culture which characterizes women as weak, Fonda's goal of strengthening the body offers an alternative to fragile womanhood. It also disputes the idea that the aging body is a run-down machine (Martin 1987, 40–46).

. . . What Fonda and her admirers have overlooked, however, in their litany of the benefits of exercise, is the contrast between the obsessive and punitive self-control and self-surveillance implicit in the exercise and beauty regimens she advocates and the liberation she claims to derive from them. In the same quote in which she encourages women to accept wrinkles, for example, she also urges "doing your best through nutrition, exercise, proper cleansing, moisturizing, sleep, and healthy living habits to avoid aggravated and premature wrinkles" (Fonda 1984, 71). This lengthy list of tasks suggests the level of work needed to age "properly" and not "prematurely."

. . . In one interviewer's words, Fonda is "an exercise addict, like few others" (Levin 1987, 28). Her language of war, struggle, and labor indicates the amount of effort and self-surveillance she devotes to bodily control: "I have a constant weight problem. . . . It's just a constant struggle." (*Mademoiselle* 1980, 40). Similarly: "I constantly fight against weight, and I don't necessarily have a good figure. I have to work for it, and I do work for it" (Harrison 1978, 40). . . .

It seems, then, that Fonda's desire for a culturally appropriate body has tyrannized rather than liberated her. Fonda's life demonstrates that maintaining an "acceptable" body requires constant vigilance. As feminist critics have pointed out, such constant demands for self-surveillance keep women in line (Faludi 1991; Wolf 1991).

. . . Bodily control signifies self-control, and hence moral superiority. This belief, which permeates the health and fitness movement, has been labeled a "new asceticism" or "new Puritanism" (Turner 1984; Kilwein 1989, 9–10). If in the past individuals disciplined the body to control their passions and submit to God, nowadays individuals discipline the body to extend their lives and increase their pleasures (Turner 1984, 156, 161–163, 172). . . .

In Fonda's secularized world, personal "salvation" (of the character and body, if not the soul) is possible through self-abnegation—denying oneself food and exercising even to the point of pain (cf., Bordo 1990, 83). She has waxed lyrical about the physical benefits of denying herself food: "Going to bed on an empty stomach and waking up hungry is the greatest thing you can do for yourself. If you go to bed hungry and wake up hungry, you've got unbelievable energy" (*Mademoiselle* 1980), 40). . . .

A similar disempowerment results from Fonda's stance on sexuality. Fonda appears to be rescuing aging women from their usual portrayal as asexual by arguing that is possible for aging women to remain active, sexual beings. "I think," she says, "that when you're healthy, no matter what age you are, you have more sexual stamina and desire and flexibility and the things that go into an active sex life" (Orth 1984, 416). In Fonda's worldview, however, a woman can retain sexuality only by retaining a youthful body. No alternative vision of aging sexuality is presented or considered. All that remains is the impossible goal of remaining young.

An emphasis on youth is not the only drawback to Fonda's ideal of femininity. Despite her emphasis on fitness, Fonda has not created a new and liberating model of femininity so much as she has adopted a model that unrealistically combines stereotypical masculine and feminine elements. Fonda began her fitness quest by arguing for the virtues of a muscled and virtually fat-free body. When asked why she added bodybuilding exercises, Fonda remarked "I didn't have any muscles. I like to see muscle, I like to see sinews, and after taking this class, I could see definition in my arms, shoulders, and back. There's no fat anywhere, not anywhere" (*Mademoiselle* 1980, 38). This near-fatless ideal corresponds to an archetypal male body. More recently, as her relationship with Hayden faded, Fonda additionally has strived to achieve the archetypal female hallmark—large breasts—by submitting to cosmetic surgery (Andersen 1990, 327–28; Ball 1992, 97). Since her marriage to cable television owner Ted Turner in 1991, she is now, one magazine writer notes, "playing the part of the glamorous wife—blond, bejeweled and dressed to kill" (Messina 1993, 65).

Fonda's body thus has come to symbolize the duality of current femininity: tight muscles but with large breasts.[4] The desire for a more masculine body, Bordo argues, appeals to some women because it symbolizes power in the public arena and a revolt against maternity and restrictive definitions of femininity (Bordo 1990, 105). Simultaneously, the inflated breasts serve as a reminder that a woman's body is there for male desires. Mainstream American culture idealizes women who are both supermen (in their muscles) and superwomen (in their breasts). These women, their bodies suggest, won't be dependent but will continue to seek the "male gaze" to affirm themselves. Fonda's enthusiastic embrace of this dual-function body represents not resistance but submission to the demands of femininity.

Fonda's use of cosmetic surgery (which did not end with her breast implants) suggests that the value she places on having a culturally acceptable body overrides any philosophical commitment to achieving a fit body through hard work. As one magazine asked rhetorically, "Doesn't cosmetic surgery contradict everything she advocates?" (Messina 1993, 65). As Fonda now argues, "If you're trying to buy yourself a few years, especially if you're in the business of looks the way an actress is, then why not?. . . . What the hell is the big deal, as long it's done carefully and with thought?" (Ball 1992, 97). In making these decisions, Fonda turns her body into a commodity that can be used, in her words, to "buy" her a few years.

The image of Fonda passively lying on a table while receiving breast implants appears to contradict her active and aggressive advocacy of exercise as a means of achieving self-improvement. Yet all her efforts are really of one piece, aimed at maintaining a youthful and culturally acceptable appearance. . . .

Not surprisingly, as purveyors of the prevailing discourse on femininity, women's magazines uphold Fonda's body as a standard to which women should aspire. Many of the writers demonstrate both the wish to imitate her and their despair of ever doing so by their barely disguised envy—"her enviable long legs" (Farr 1980, 39), "her enviable body" (Glasser and Decatur 1982, 22), a body that is "frighteningly firm" (Jong 1984, 35). As one writer acknowledged, "most of us would be pleased to look at 34 the way she looks at 54, especially in Lycra" (Ball 1992, 96). By continuing to run layouts featuring her exercises (e.g., *Redbook* 1990; Messina, 1993) the magazines offer hope to their readers that they too can look like her. There is little acknowledgement that Fonda's body represents an unrealistic goal for most aging women.

BARBARA BUSH: RESOLUTELY "NATURAL"

In contrast to Jane Fonda, Barbara Bush at least appears to resist and reject the cultural ideal of femininity that valorizes youthfulness. Bush's white hair and wrinkles seem to challenge the prevailing feminine ideal and signal her rejection of technological "fixes" for aging (Morgan 1991, 28).

Even more than Fonda, Bush frames her appearance as resistance to cultural strictures about women's bodies. In Bush's worldview, her unwillingness to change her appearance beyond dressing well, using light makeup, and exercising regularly and moderately underscores her interest in focusing on what she considers important rather than frivolous and narcissistic concerns. She thus draws on a spiritual tradition that disregards the body and looks to the state of the soul for moral value (Turner 1984, 164). . . .

Bush appears to counterpose the value of "naturalness" against the contrivances of anti-aging technology. "What you see is what you get" (*Vogue* 1988, 442) is one of her favorite self-descriptions, implying that her relative lack of artifice in appearance means that she stands revealed for who she is without the "disguises" of cosmetics, plastic surgery, or even a diet-improved shape. One writer quotes her remark that all she owes to the public is "to look nice and have a clean mind and a clean head of hair" (Adams 1988, 151).

. . . Despite Bush's rhetoric, however, a close reading of her interviews reveals the great efforts she makes to meet standards of feminine attractiveness and to show herself as reasonably concerned about her appearance. In doing so she reveals her exquisite awareness of the demands of femininity and of her need at least partially to comply. She wears contact lenses and her well-known three strands of false pearls because, she says, she's "too vain" to wear glasses and needs to cover her "sagging neck" (Avery 1989, 191). Moreover, although she does not engage in the kind of obsessive exercising Fonda prefers, Bush regularly walks and rides a stationary bicycle to maintain her weight (Avery 1989, 192).

Bush also pays attention to her wardrobe, wearing fashionable designer clothes. As Judith Viorst astutely noted, "though Barbara Bush seems to define herself publicly as a slightly schlumpy Everywoman, she is considerably more than that. . . . Her grooming, from well-coiffed white hair to well-shod toe, is what anyone would call 'impeccable'" (Viorst 1991, 40), an observation repeated by other magazine writers (*Vogue* 1998, 444; Cook 1990, 230). As one points out, "Her hairdresser attends her regularly, sometimes as often as three times a day" (McClellan 1992, 191).

Bush's use of self-deprecating humor further indicates her felt need to explain her deviation from cultural expectations. Self-deprecating humor, in which individuals mock themselves for not meeting social expectations, allows individuals both to demonstrate their commitment to those expectations and to frame their deviations as humorous rather than serious flaws (Coser 1960; Goffman 1963, 100–101; Ungar 1984; Haig 1988; Koller 1988; Walker 1988). As a result, such humor, which is most common among relatively powerless groups, "is ingratiating rather than aggressive; it acknowledges the opinion of the dominant culture—[and] even appears to confirm it."[3] . . .

It seems, then, that Bush, like many women, uses self-deprecating humor to try to turn her departures from appearance norms into an unimportant, humorous matter.[4] At least one reporter has recognized this, describing her humor as "a preemptive strike" (Cook 1990, 230), in which Bush makes comments about her appearance before interviewers can. Thus, Bush is not, despite her protests, rejecting femininity standards, but is acknowledging their power and her failure to meet them.

Bush's statements about her sexuality also reveal the limits of her resistance. In her self-descriptions, she often desexualizes herself, referring to herself not merely as a grandmother but as "everybody's grandmother." She uses this exceptional status to place herself outside the bounds of femininity. "I mean," she says, "kissing me is like kissing your grandmother" (Reed 1989, 314).

Bush's depiction of herself as outside the definition of normative femininity does not help to construct a positive, alternative model of female aging. Rather, she has escaped the bonds of cultural standards only by forfeiting claims to sexuality—a high price to pay. Thus her model is a bleak one, which denies the sensual possibilities of the aging female body. . . .

To "normalize" Bush's appearance, the magazines, like Bush, have stressed her grandmotherly qualities, labeling her "every American's favorite grandmother" (Mower 1992) and an honorific grandmother of us all. They have focused on her work with children and her role as the matriarch of the large Bush clan (Reed 1989, 314). In this role as super-grandmother, the magazines allow Bush to remain outside the normal discipline of femininity, a disembodied maternal archetype. . . .

Despite these efforts to normalize Bush's appearance, the magazines continue to demonstrate considerable ambivalence toward her looks. For example, in an article published in *Ladies Home Journal* (Avery 1989), the author praises Bush for her apparent acceptance of aging but suggests that other women should hesitate before adopting Bush as a role model, citing the numerous studies that show that attractive women do better in the job market. The writer concludes with the admonition that even "exceptional women" like Bush need to recognize the benefits of attractiveness, and predicts that "perhaps after she's had a year or two squarely in the public eye, we'll begin to notice subtle changes—a wrinkle smoothed here, a pound or two dieted off there." Bush, in other words, will see the light and conform to cultural standards of femininity.

The author and magazine reveal their real attitudes in two full-length pictures of Bush which dominate the article's first two pages (Avery 1989, 120–121). On the first page is the actual Barbara Bush. Attached to various parts of her in balloon-like fashion are boxes advising her how to deal with her wrinkles, her clothes, and her shape. On the opposite page stands a re-touched Bush with all the suggestions put into practice: slimmer, with fluffed out hair, wrinkles surgically removed, wearing cosmetics, and fashionable clothes. It is the ultimate make-over! This desire to change Bush so that she fits in with prevailing notions of femininity is a frequent theme in women's magazines.

WOMEN'S POWER AND WOMEN'S BODIES

The treatment of Jane Fonda and Barbara Bush by women's magazines explicates the discourse on femininity and illustrates the difficulties women face in resisting cultural dictates regarding their aging bodies. Women's magazines praise Fonda only because she conforms to cultural ideals. The magazines' more ambivalent attitude toward Bush reflects their consternation and ultimate disapproval of those who do not appear to comply with appearance norms, even when such individuals in various ways acknowledge their deviance.

Women do not have to be film stars or political wives to feel the pressures imposed by cultural definitions of femininity. Those pressures are everywhere, and it is the rare woman who can evade them. . . .

The pressures to conform to cultural standards of femininity disempower women in insidious ways—insidious because we have internalized them in ways we are hardly aware of and at costs we have not calculated. Cultural standards encourage women's sense of inadequacy and promote frantic use of expensive, time-consuming and sometimes dangerous technologies in a futile effort to check aging and increase one's "femininity." Furthermore, such a focus on the body as a privatistic concern turns people away from focusing on social issues (Stein 1982, 176–177). This is particularly relevant during this current period of backlash to the feminist movement in which many women now find it easier to focus on their individual selves than to continue struggling for the social betterment of women. As Fonda herself admits about exercising, "in a world that is increasingly out of control, it's something you can control" (Ball 1992, 143). Thus an emphasis on the self diverts women from resisting current power relations.

The successes of the feminist movement have depended on the movement's ability to question received "wisdom" about women and to expose both the cultural construction and harmfulness of that "wisdom." Feminists have challenged pay inequities, inadequate child care arrangements, restrictions on reproductive freedom, and a host of other problems. But the issue of obsessiveness about body size and appearance is a virtually untouched arena for concerted feminist political action, despite the pioneering work of such individuals and groups as Orbach (1982), Wolf (1991), Bordo (1989, 1990, 1991), Faludi (1991), and the fat acceptance and anti-diet movements (Millman 1980; Kano 1989; Hirschmann and Munter 1988). Their efforts to help women accept their bodies and abandon perpetual dieting have failed to affect large numbers of women, despite the increasing medical evidence that body, shape stems largely from genetic factors and that frequent dieting is unhealthy and does not necessarily result in a leaner body[5] and despite increasing coverage of this evidence in popular magazines (e.g., Brownell 1988; *Good Housekeeping* 1993; Kaufman 1992; Seligmann 1992).

NOTES

1. Bush does not appear to any extent in the magazines until the late 1980s when her husband begins his presidential campaign.

2. We are grateful to Susan Bordo for this suggestion.

3. In contrast, other forms of humor typically serve as demonstrations of aggression and of power (e.g., Coser 1960; Fine 1983; Zillman 1983; Ungar 1984, Haig 1988: Koller 1988; Walker 1988).

4. Bush's self-deprecating humor cannot be dismissed simply as "ice breakers," designed to put reporters as their ease, for self-deprecating humor is rarely used in this way. Moreover, Bush uses self-deprecating humor not at the beginning of interviews, but scattered throughout whenever the subject of her body appears.

5. See, for example, Brownell (1991, 307–308), Brownell and Wadden (1992, 507–508), Dulloo and Girardier (1990, 418–419), Rodin, Radke Sharpe, Rebuffe-Serive and Greenwood (1990, 307), and Wadden, Barlett, Letizia, Foster, Stundkard, and Conill (1992, 206).

REFERENCES

Adams, Cindy. 1988. "Talking with the New First Lady." *Ladies Home Journal*, October.

Andersen, Christopher. 1990. *Citizen Jane*. New York: Henry Holt.

Andersen, Christopher P. 1989. "Jane Fonda: I'm Stronger Than Ever." *Ladies Home Journal*, October.

Avery, Caryl S. 1989. "How Good Should You Look?" *Ladies Home Journal*, June.

Bachrach, Judy. 1989. "Feel the Burn." *Savvy Woman,* October.

Ball, Aimee Lee. 1992. "How Does Jane Do It?" *McCall's*, March.

Ballaster, Ros, Margaret Beetham, Elizabeth Frazer and Sandra Hebron. 1991. *Women's Worlds: Ideology, Femininity and the Woman's Magazine*. London: Macmillan.

Banner, Lois W. 1983. *American Beauty*. New York: Alfred A. Knopf.

Bordo, Susan. 1989. "The Body and the Reproduction of Femininity: A Feminist Appropriation of Foucault." In *Gender/Body/Knowledge*, ed. Alison M. Jaggar and Susan R. Bordo, 13–33. New Brunswick, New Jersey: Rutgers University Press.

———. 1990. "Reading the Slender Body." In *Body/Politics: Women and the Discourses of Science*, ed. Mary Jacobs, Evelyn Fox Keller, and Sally Shuttleworth, 83–112. New York: Routledge.

———. 1991. "'Material Girl'. The Effacements of Postmodern Culture." In *The Female Body*, ed. Laurence Goldstein, 653–677. Ann Arbor: The University of Michigan Press.

Brownell, Kelly D. 1988. "Yo Yo Dieting." *Psychology Today* 22 (January): 20–23.

———. 1991. "Personal Responsibility and Control Over Our Bodies." *Health Psychology* 10(5): 303–310.

Cook, Alison. 1990. "At Home with Barbara Bush" *Ladies Home Journal*, March.

Coser, Rose Loeb. 1960. "Laughter Among Colleagues." *Psychiatry* 23:81–95.

Davis, Sally Ogle. 1993. "Hollywood Marriages: The Good, The Bad and The Disasters." *Ladies Home Journal,* March.

Dulloo, Abdul G., and Lucien Girardier. 1990. "Adaptive Changes in Energy Expenditure During Refeeding Following Low Calorie Intake: Evidence for a Specific Metabolic Component Favoring Fat Storage." *American Journal of Clinical Nutrition* 52: 415–420.

Farr, Louise. 1980. "Jane Fonda." *Ladies Home Journal*, April.

Faludi, Susan. 1991. *Backlash: The Undeclared War Against American Women*. New York: Crown.

Fine, Gary Alan. 1983. "Sociological Approaches to the Study of Humor." *In Handbok of Human Research*, Vol. 1, ed. Paul Z. McGhee and Jeffrey H. Goldstein, 138–157. New York: Springer-Verlag.

Fonda, Jane. 1984. *Women Coming of Age*. New York: Simon and Schuster.

Glasser, Dorothy Ann and Stephen Decatur. 1982. "Jane Fonda." *Ladies Home Journal*, February.

Goffman, Erving. 1963. *Stigma. Notes on the Management of Spoiled Identity*. Englewood Clifs, NJ: Prentice-Hall.

Good Housekeeping 1993. "I Was a Yo Yo Dieter." February.

Haig, Robin A. 1988. *Anatomy of Humor*. Springfield, IL: Charles C. Thomas.

Harper's Bazaar. 1980. "The California Workout." January.

Harrison, Barbara Grizzuti. 1978. "Jane Fonda: Trying To Be Everywoman." *Ladies Home Journal*, April.

Hirschmann, Jane R. and Carol H. Munter. 1988. *Overcoming Overeating*. New York: Ballantine.

Jong, Erica. 1984. "Jane Fonda," *Ladies Home Journal*, April.

Kano, Susan. 1989. *Making Peace with Food*. New York: Harper and Row.

Kaplan, Janice. 1987. "The Fitness Queen." *Vogue*, November.

Kaufman, Pamela. 1992. "Rethinking Diets." *Vogue,* March.

Kilwein, John H. 1989. "No Pain, No Gain: A Puritan Legacy." *Health Education Quarterly* 16(Spring):9–12.

Koller, Marvin R. 1988. *Humor and Society: Explorations in the Sociology of Humor.* Houston: Cap and Gown Press.

Levin, Susanna. 1987. "Jane Fonda. From Barbarella to Barbells." *Women's Sports and Fitness,* December.

Mademoiselle. 1980. "Fitness." March.

Martin, Emily. 1987. *The Woman in the Body.* Boston: Beacon Press.

McClellan, Diana. 1992. "Barbara Bush: The Final Battle." *Ladies Home Journal,* October.

Millman, Marcia. 1980. *Such a Pretty Face.* New York: Norton.

Messina, Andrea. 1993. "Fonda's Workouts That Work." *Family Circle,* January 12.

Morgan, Kathryn Pauly. 1991. "Women and the Knife: Cosmetic Surgery and the Colonization of Women's Bodies." *Hypatia* 6(3):25–53.

Mower, Joan. 1992. "What Kind of First Lady Do We Really Want?" *McCall's,* September.

Orbach, Susie. 1982. *Fat Is a Feminist Issue.* New York: Berkley.

Orth, Maureen. 1984. "Fonda. Driving Passions." *Vogue,* February.

Redbook. 1990. "Relax with Jane Fonda." March.

Reed, Julia. 1989. "The Natural." *Vogue,* August.

Rodin, Judith, Norean Radke Sharpe, Marielle Rebuffe-Serive, and M. R. C. Greenwood. 1990. "Weight Cycling and Fat Distribution" *International Journal of Obesity* 14:303–310.

Rothblum, Esther D. In press. "Lesbians and Physical Appearance: Which Model Applies?" *Contemporary Perspectives in Lesbian and Gay Psychology.*

Schwartz, Hillel. 1986. *Never Satisfied: A Cultural History of Diets, Fantasies and Fat.* New York: The Free Press.

Seid, Roberta Pollack. 1989. *Never Too Thin.* New York: Prentice-Hall.

Seligmann, Jean. 1992. "Let Them Eat Cake." *Newsweek,* August.

Smith, Lori R., Ann Kathleen Burlew, and David C. Lundgren. 1991. "Black Consciousness, Self Esteem, and Satisfaction with Physical Appearance Among African-American Female College Students." *Journal of Black Studies* 22(2): 269–283.

Stein, Howard F. 1982. "Neo Darwinism and Survival Through Fitness in Reagan's America." *The Journal of Psychohistory* 10(2):163–187.

Thomas, Veronica G. 1989. "Body Image Satisfaction Among Black Women." *The Journal of Social Psychology* 129(1):107–112.

———— and Michelle D. James. 1988. "Body Image, Dieting Tendencies, and Sex Role Traits in Urban Black Women." *Sex Roles* 18(9/10). 523–529.

Turner, Bryan S. 1984. *The Body and Society: Explorations in Social Theory.* New York: Basil Blackwell.

Ungar, Sheldon. 1984. "Self Mockery: An Alternative Form of Self-Presentation." *Symbolic Interaction* 7(1): 121–133.

Viorst, Judith. 1991. "It's Time to Bring Back the Family." *Redbook,* May.

Vogue. 1988. "Winning Style: Kitty Dukakis and Barbara Bush on First Lady Dressing." November.

Wadden, T. A., S. Bartlett, K. A. Letizia, G. D. Foster, A. J. Stankard, and A. Conill. 1992. "Relationship of Dieting History to Resting Metabolic Rate, Body Composition, Eating Behavior, and Subsquent Weight Loss." *American Journal of Clinical Nutrition* 56(1 Supplement:203s–208s)

Walker, Nancy A. 1988. *A Very Serious Thing: Women's Humor and American Culture*. Minneapolis: University of Minnesota.

Wolf, Naomi. 1991. *The Beauty Myth*. New York: William Morrow.

Zillman, Dolf. 1983 "Disparagement Humor." In *Handbook of Humor Research*, Vol. 1, eds. Paul E. McGhee and Jeffrey H. Goldstein, 85–108. New York: Springer-Verlag.

31

The Aging Woman in Popular Film: Underrepresented, Unattractive, Unfriendly, and Unintelligent

Doris G. Bazzini, William D. McIntosh, Stephen M. Smith, Sabrina Cook and Caleigh Harris

. . . Because one of the central media messages concerning women is that women's primary value lies in their appearance, it seems plausible that sexist and ageist stereotypes may interact. That is, the tendency for the media to exhibit more negative depictions of people as they age may be more pronounced for aging women than for aging men.

There is little research that directly compares ageist depictions of men and women in the media. Palmore (1971) studied jokes about the elderly and found that, relative to old men, there were three times as many negative jokes about old women. Further, depictions of women over 40 were found to be almost totally absent from advertising, where physically attractive people are routinely utilized to add appeal to a product (Unger & Crawford, 1992). Davis and Davis found that television not only portrays fewer older female characters, but depicts them as much less useful than their male counterparts (Bell, 1992). . . .

Markson and Taylor (1993) found a particularly striking bias in the ages of Academy Award nominees and winners for actors and actresses from 1927 through 1990. The sample was comprised of 1,169 actresses and actors who had been nominated in four acting categories: Best Actress, Best Actor, Best Supporting Actress, and Best Supporting Actor). In the 63 years of awards for Best Actress/Actor, only 27% of female award winners were over the age of 39, as compared to 67% of male winners. Across decades, the age difference between male and female winners was typically around 10 years. For example, in the 1930s, the average age of award-winning actresses was 32 and for winning actors it was 40. Among Oscar winners for supporting roles, women were, on the average, seven years younger than men. . . .

It has been argued that movies are one of the clearest and most accessible representations of the past, present and future of our society (Haskell, 1974). In the present research, we sought to gain a clearer understanding of how women have been represented in film. Markson and Taylor (1993) have demonstrated that in Hollywood women are honored primarily when they are young and beautiful; we sought to clarify and extend these findings in a number of ways.

First, are younger women simply more likely than their older counterparts to be recognized with high honors for their acting, or is it the case that older women are also less likely to be *depicted* in film? We predicted that there would be a greater discrepancy between the number of older (i.e., over 35) male and female characters in popular film than among younger male and female characters. Segments of the population that are underrepresented in the media tend to be those that are considered less valued or desirable (e.g., Weigel, Loomis, & Soja, 1980), thus it is likely that older women are underrepresented in film.

In addition to being underrepresented in film, it is possible that, when older women *are* represented, they are depicted as possessing negative characteristics. If, indeed, one message conveyed by popular film is that women are valued primarily for youth and beauty, another way to communicate this message is to link age with negative traits for female characters. If men are valued for characteristics other than youth, there should be little relationship between a male character's age and the positivity with which he is depicted. Specifically, we expected to find the following in observing the characters in popular film from the past 5 decades:

1) Age would be more negatively related to personality characteristics for women than for men. Specifically, older women would be associated with: (a) more unfriendliness, (b) lower intelligence, (c) less "goodness" and (d) less physical attractiveness than older men.

2) As both men and women age, they would be depicted as engaging in less romantic and sexual activity, but this decline would be more pronounced for women.

3) In general, wealth increases with age. We expected to find a positive relationship between wealth and age, but more so for men than for women, because wealth is a positive quality often associated with intelligence and competence.

4) The "just world phenomenon" (Lerner, 1980) suggests that people tend to believe that good things happen to good people, and bad things happen to bad people. If women are indeed depicted more negatively with age than are men, we expected that greater age would be related to more negative outcomes at a film's end for women that for men.

The study involved viewing a total of 100 movies, 20 from each decade spanning the 1940s through the 1980s. The movies were randomly selected from a list of the top 20 grossing movies of each year from each decade. Independent raters judged all of the significant characters in each film in terms of how they were depicted across the following dimensions: attractiveness, friendliness, goodness, intelligence, socioeconomic status, romantic activity, attractiveness, and outcome at film's end. The raters also estimated the age of each character. The relationship between age, personality characteristics, and various outcome measures was examined.

METHOD

Raters

The ratings were completed by 12 people (7 males and 5 females). Raters ranged in age from 28 to 60. Each rater was provided with both written and verbal instructions on how to carry out the ratings before viewing a film.

Movie Characters

Overall, 829 characters were rated across 100 movies. Of the total, 253 were deemed "central" characters (pivotal to the movie's storyline), 281 were deemed "secondary" characters (important to the plot, but not essential), and 295 were deemed "peripheral" characters (superficial to the movie's plot).

Procedure

Movie Selection. We chose to examine trends in gender and age across 5 decades: the 1940s to the 1980s. In order to choose movies that were representative of the decade from which they were chosen, movies were randomly selected from a list of the top 20 grossing movies of each year. For a given decade, 20 movies were randomly selected from 200 possible movies (20 of the yearly, top-grossing movies x 10 years within a decade), resulting in 1,000 films in the *initial* pool. Only theater box office sales at the time of the movie's first release counted toward its gross. So, for example, Alfred Hitchcock classics, such as *Vertigo*, still play in movie theaters from time to time, but this additional revenue was not counted in determining the top grossing movies of each decade. Overall, 100 movies were selected for the study (*n* = 20 movies for each of the five decades). Two movies that were selected, *Who Framed Roger Rabbit* (1988) and *An American Tail* (1986) were rejected because the main characters were animated, and thus meaningful ratings of age could not be made. Two movies were randomly selected from those remaining on the list (*Heartbreak Ridge*, 1986 and *When Harry Met Sally*, 1989) to replace them. The genres of the movies selected were classified (by film critics) as follows: 28% were comedies, 24% were dramas, 14% were action/adventure, 13% were musicals, 6% were suspense, 5% were children/family, 4% were western, and 3% were science fiction/fantasy.

Rating Procedure. In order to optimize the reliability of ratings, each movie was rated by at least three people (*M* = 3.38 raters per movie).

Characters in each film were rated on the following dimensions:

1. Age. Raters estimated the age of each character. The instructions given were to estimate the age of the character being portrayed, rather than the age of the actor or actress performing. On occasion, an actor or actress may play a role that is not congruent with his or her age, such as when a thirty-year-old current box-office favorite is cast in the role of a high school student.

2. Goodness. Raters assessed the character's moral virtue on a scale ranging from 0 (Extremely immoral, i.e., total sleaze) to 10 (extremely moral, i.e., saintly).

3. Socioeconomic Status. SES was rated on a scale ranging from 0 (extremely poor, lower class) to 10 (extremely rich, upper class).

4. Intelligence. The character's intelligence was assessed on a scale ranging from 0 (extremely unintelligent) to 10 (extremely intelligent).

5. Friendly. Raters assessed each character's friendliness on a scale ranging from 0 (extremely unfriendly) to 10 (extremely friendly).

6. Romantic activity. A character's real or implied romantic and/or sexual activity during the film was rated on a scale ranging from 0 (totally inactive) to 10 (extremely active). . . .

7. Physical Attractiveness. Ratings of physical attractiveness were based on a 10-point scale ranging from 0 (extremely unattractive) to 10 (extremely attractive). . . .

8. Outcome. The positivity of a character's outcome at film's end was rated on a scale of 0 (extremely negative; e.g., died) to 10 (extremely positive; e.g., struck it rich and lived happily ever after). . . .

DISCUSSION

Although the motion picture industry is referenced frequently as both instigator and perpetuator of stereotypes directed against women, few studies have systematically examined the content of motion pictures produced with regard to how depictions of males and females compare (see also Markson & Taylor, 1993). The current study was one such investigation. We were interested in examining male and female character portrayals in popular films spanning five decades (the 1940s through the 1980s). We predicted that Hollywood would perpetuate already existing female stereotypes in two ways: (1) by underrepresenting older women in film and (2) by consistently depicting more negative images of older women than of older men.

We found that, compared to men, women of all ages were underrepresented. However, this was particularly the case for women over the age of 35. Eighty percent of characters over the age of 35 were male, whereas only 20% were female. The discrepancy between male and female characters under the age of 35 was much less pronounced, with 46% of these characters being women and 54% being men.) These results are consistent with the observation across media that a female who shows signs of age cannot successfully endorse (and ultimately sell) a product—be it lingerie, cosmetics, or a feature film. Even when a well-known older woman is photographed for a magazine, her image is altered such that her 60-year-old face looks more like that of a 45-year old (Wolf, 1991).

Our study also extends the work of Markson and Taylor (1993), demonstrating that one of the reasons for the severe underrepresentation of older Academy-Award-winning females is that few portrayals of older women occur in movies. That is, the current study lends empirical support to Markson and Taylor's suggestion that few older women appear in film. It is not simply that the work of older female actresses is not honored in film; rather, they are rarely seen in film.

We found ageist stereotypes, in general, to be prevalent across the films of five decades. That is, for the most part, older individuals of both genders were portrayed as less friendly, having less romantic activity, and as enjoying fewer positive outcomes than younger characters at a movie's conclusion. In light of such a finding, it is not surprising that when college students were asked to evaluate photos of the same man taken at age 25, 52, and 73, he was evaluated most negatively (in terms of intelligence, activity level, attractiveness, and competence) at the oldest age (Levin, 1988).

However, older females were cast in a particularly negative light. As compared to males, older females were perceived as less friendly, less intelligent, less good, possessing less wealth, and being less attractive. Such beliefs may be linked to a cultural "what is beautiful is good" stereotype (Dion, Berscheid, & Walster, 1972). Because beauty is a more salient feature in judgments about women than about men (Unger & Crawford, 1992), perhaps as a female ages there is a greater tendency to ascribe more negative traits to her.

Of course, it is possible that Hollywood was less the culprit of such negative stereotypes about women than were our raters, given that ratings of a character's friendliness, intelligence, goodness, etc., are subjective perceptions rather than fact. Although it is possible that our raters were operating on preconceived stereotypes of older women, the high interrater reliabilities that we obtained argue otherwise. With interrater reliabilities all above .76 (with most greater than .85), we would assert that the movies provided raters with unambiguous, easily observable information concerning characters' traits. If the raters' judgments were strongly driven by their own biases, we would expect that individual differences between the raters would result in more variability across raters (particularly in light of the age differences among our raters).

It is also interesting to note the age differences that emerged between male and female leading (central) characters. With the exception of the 1970s, leading women were at least 6 years younger than leading men (in some cases 10 years younger), once again reaffirming that as men age they are presented as remaining a vital part of society. Youthfulness (and with it attractiveness) continues to be the attribute which affords women the most opportunities.

Looking across the different decades, we found no strong pattern to suggest that age was related to more negative characteristics for women than for men for any given decade. It might be expected that the relationship between gender and ageism would decline with time, because in the past there was less awareness of the inappropriateness of perpetuating negative stereotypes of people based on their age or gender, whereas more recently much attention has been devoted to these issues (Bell, 1992). However, this pattern was not reflected in the data, suggesting that Hollywood has not attempted to adjust its depictions of people in order to be more sensitive to the perpetuation of negative age stereotypes.

To the extent that the depiction of people in movies reflects an accurate view of cultural standards, our findings suggest that women face an increasingly problematic dilemma. Even if a woman possesses beauty when she is young, she will ultimately be unable to maintain that beauty. This is a dilemma because traditionally women have not been encouraged to develop traits that improve with age, such as wisdom and intellectual competence (Stoddard, 1983), but have learned that physical beauty is the quality which affords them the most power and esteem in our culture. Perhaps media images of aging women help to explain why therapists have recently found a "depletion syndrome" prevalent in older women, characterized by feelings of worthlessness, no interest in things, a sense of hopelessness, and thoughts of death (Newmann, Engel, & Jensen, 1990). Because representation in the media signifies social existence, and underrepresentation signifies inexistence (Gerbner as cited in Tuchman, 1979), the media's failure to portray aging female characters reinforces an unattainable cultural standard that perpetuates women's struggle to fight aging at all cost.

Of course, it remains to be seen whether depictions of women have changed in the films of the 1990s. Evidence suggests that women are increasingly entering into formerly male-dominated professions (Unger & Crawford, 1992) and acquiring greater positions of power in society. Future research should investigate whether popular film has maintained the double standard regarding depictions of male and female characters in the current decade, or whether it has portrayed women and men more equitably.

REFERENCES

Bell, J. (1992). In search of a discourse on aging: The elderly on television. *The Gerontologist, 32*, 79–80.

Dion, K., Berscheid, E., & Walster (Hatfield), E. (1972). What is beautiful is good. *Journal of Personality and Social Psychology, 24*, 285–290.

Haskell, M. (1974). *From reverence to rape: The treatment of women in the movies.* New York: Holt Rinehart and Winston.

Lerner, M. J. (1980). *The belief in a just world: A fundamental decision.* New York: Plenum.

Levin, W. C. (1988). Age stereotyping: College student evaluations. *Research on Aging, 10*, 134–148.

Markson, E. W., & Taylor, C. A. (1993). Real versus reel world: Older women and the academy awards. *Women and Therapy, 14*, 157–172.

Motion Picture Almanac. (1996). New York: Quigley Publishing Co., Inc.

Newmann, J. P., Engel, R. J., & Jensen, J. (1990). Depressive symptom patterns among older women. *Psychology of Aging, 5*, 101–118.

Palmore, E. (1971). Attitudes toward aging as shown by humor. *The Gerontologist, 11*, 181–186.

Stoddard, K. M. (1983). *Saints and shrews: women and aging in American popular film.* Westport, Connecticut: Greenwood Press.

Tuchman, G. (1979). Women's depiction by the mass media. *Signs, 4*, 528–542.

Unger, R., & Crawford, M. (1992). *Women and gender: A feminist psychology.* New York: McGraw-Hill.

Weigel, R. H., Loomis, J. S., & Soja, M. J. (1980). Race relations on prime time television. *Journal of Personality and Social Psychology, 39*, 884–893.

Wolf, N. (1991). *The beauty myth: how images of beauty are used against women.* New York: Doubleday.

32

Older Men as Invisible Men in Contemporary Society

Edward H. Thompson

. . . There are already nearly 13 million men age 65 and older. The minority among elders, and especially the minority among the very elderly, 13 million older men is still a sizable population. It is greater than the number of all undergraduates enrolled full-time in 4-year colleges in 1992 (U.S. Department of Education, 1992), greater than the number of children living in single-parent families in 1980 (Thompson & Gongla, 1983; U.S. Bureau of the Census, 1992), nearly 20 times greater than the number of physicians practicing medicine in 1993 (Roback, Randolph, & Seidman, 1993) and 10 times the number of people incarcerated in correctional institutions in 1990 (U.S. Bureau of the Census, 1993). Mainstream journals and opinion makers have made us much more familiar with these folks, however smaller their population size.

REASONS FOR VISIBILITY

Older men have remained invisible for reasons besides their smaller number. For one, gerontologists have not encouraged the distinction between the concepts of "sex" and "gender." *Gender* is often accepted as if synonymous with *sex*, serving fundamentally as a categorical construct for grouping the aged. Consequently, the literature introduces us to older biological males by virtue of describing a sex difference in aging. However, what surely distinguishes older biological males, as a group, is their cohort-specific, gendered social lives. As much as research has treated all men as if

they were genderless (Kimmel & Messner, 1992), fewer researchers have paid attention to the masculinities that older men encounter or those they disclose.

Another reason for older invisibility is that aging and ageism do not affect men
and women equally. From a political economy perspective, it is true that older men
have a more comfortable, privileged life compared to older women of the same generation. Consequently, when gender is taken into consideration, elderly women have
a much higher profile in gerontological research because the view of aging places
women in double jeopardy relative to older men (Sontag, 1972) and because sociological research on "advantaged" groups has traditionally attracted less sustained attention than studies of the disadvantaged (Berger, 1963). In this frame, the perni-
cious concept of "the aged" is synonymous with a disadvantaged group and thus more
synonymous with the providence of older women than older men.

Similarly, the organizations, interest groups, industries, professional societies, and
political bodies that make up "the aging enterprise" and serve the elderly in one capacity or another (Estes, 1979, 1993) also furnish ideas about aging and images of
elder men. These are elaborately constructed images pressed into public consciousness, and the images that aging enterprise has fabricated are just that—"constructed."
To illustrate, for two decades the medical-industrial complex has profited handsomely
by medicalizing elderly men's lives more than meeting elderly men's and women's
needs. Cardiac catheterization laboratories, fourth- and fifth-generation ventricular
pacemakers, arthroscopic surgical technology, and cardiac bypass surgery all derive
great profit by "servicing" the elderly male population's health problems and yield
much greater profit for the enterprise than would programming to raise the standard of living and health status of all elders. The socially constructed image of elderly men—former breadwinners and national leaders—as "old" and by definition
in poor health fuels compassion and, of course, greater profit than the image of most
elderly men (and women) as having poor access to health and medical care services.
This "compassionate ageism" (Binstock, 1983) is also sexist. It has medicalized elderly men's lives and their perceived well-being, perhaps more than elderly women's.
One unintended consequence, for example, of the "compassion" and profiteering is
that older men's nonmedical needs become frivolous. The everyday needs of healthy
elder males, as well as elder men's need for services other than medical interventions,
become remote concerns when compared to the life-and-death emphasis.

In much the same way that gerontologists have inadvertently homogenized elders
to make older men genderless, scholars working in the field of gender studies have
not paid much notice to men in late life. Older men's masculinities are couched as
an invisible part of the dynamics of hegemony or, more simply, ignored. Whether
in the research traditions or contemporary theorizing "about men," age is truncated.
To illustrate, Daniel Levinson and his colleagues (1978) discuss men's late adulthood
in their landmark *The Seasons of a Man's Life* in just seven pages (pages 33–39) and
characterize this age in "discontinuous" imagery, as if aging is a negation of masculinity: "A primary developmental task of late adulthood is to find a new balance of
involvement with society and with the self. A man in this era is experiencing more

fully the process of dying and he should have the possibility of choosing more freely his mode of living" (p. 36). The widely praised second edition of *Men's Lives* that Kimmel and Messner organized for gender scholars has not one article among the 56 that directly probes older men's masculinities. At this point in the development of gender studies, the masculinities of older men have been subordinated to the concerted effort to understand middle-aged and younger men's lives, who are, as Ortega y Gasset (1958) suggests, "the dominant" group. Even when a life course perspective is recognized (e.g., Connell, 1992; Segal, 1990), the theoretical discourse on masculinities has concentrated on social practices of young to middle-aged men and, by default, marginalized the masculinities of elderly men. But, meta-theoretically, has the marginalization of older men in the scholarship on gender contributed to the preservation of conventional discourses on masculinity? Failing to acknowledge elderly men as a distinct group of men may have homogenized not only adulthood but also theory on masculinity.

One can see, with retrospective clarity, how these four initiatives have helped conceal older men's lives. My interest is to examine them collectively in greater detail. The task is to advance the conceptual and theoretical underpinnings for a more long-term discussion of older men as men and as elders. . . .

SOCIALLY CONSTRUCTED IMAGES OF AGED MEN

Visualize the image. The men hold themselves upright and proud—these middle-aged men whose time of life is shifting from "early" to "middle adulthood" and who are perhaps at a peak in their impact on the world outside the home. They are the "dominant" generation, as Ortega y Gasset defined the age 45–60. They make their ideas and aims the pivotal ones in every sector of society: business, politics, religion, science. But soon they take up wearing bifocals, their skin wrinkles more, their hair turns silvery, they become grandparents, they stoop, and they embrace the season of life that Levinson and his colleagues (1978) call "late adulthood" and, for some, "late, late adulthood."

In the popular culture men in late adulthood no longer occupy center stage. Their generation is no longer the dominant one: It has been displaced by a younger, "Pepsi" generation. Men in late life are classed as "senior" or "old." They become "socially opaque" (Green, 1993). They are presumed to have completed the major part—perhaps all—of their life work. The older man sees himself living in his shadow or death's (Levinson et al., 1978). Writing in *Esquire*, novelist Thomas Morgan (1987, p. 162) describes a memory of his father's 60th birthday: "I do not remember his exact words, only that he seemed to be telling me he was conceding at sixty, perhaps welcoming at sixty that he need not be a part of the future. . . . As it happened, he worked ten more years, but lived, I'm sorry to say, as though it were all an anticlimax."

Television commercials, newspaper presentations, and magazine advertisements fully impart this image, too. No longer in control, wealthy, and urbane, old men are pictured as living neither in the city nor the suburbs but in a small rural town or in the country, near the pasture. Homes are smaller, more plain, without gadgets and machines. Bodies are not virile, rather pleasantly plump. Checked flannel shirts have replaced the dark blue suit. As part of the "grandparent" generation, advertisements will show that the older man's soft lap cat has replaced the younger man's spirited black Labrador retriever. Lemonade is now the drink of choice (Bucholz & Bynum, 1982; Ferraro, 1992; Kaiser & Chandler, 1988; Powell & Williamson, 1985; Swayne & Greco, 1987). Such images seem inflated to the point of parody. Perhaps, as Wernick (1987, p. 283) would maintain, when advertisers and other opinion makers become interested in speaking to and about older men, the more conventional construction of masculinity as a symbolic term will have weakened, and we can expect a disappearance of what one might call the *metaphorical* old man.

Until then, it seems that the constructed images of older men leave these elders with two strikes against them. First is the prejudice within public (and professional) attitudes regarding "old age" in general (Butler, 1969; Walsh & Connor, 1979). Elders—in particular, elderly men—are thought to suffer significant losses: Their occupational role, their livelihood and community of co-workers, their health and independence, and their masculinity are commonly thought to be displaced by aging. The traditional discourses of masculinity and aging separate adult men into two categories: old and all others. The older man is depicted in a yo-yo fashion, with both positive and negative content (Hummert, 1990). He is portrayed as interactively and psychologically involved in more expressive and caring roles within the family. He is also, by default, contrasted with an image of the younger, justly preoccupied father and husband whose primary concern is with productive labor and power management. The underlying core values in the discourse extol youth, independence, and economic productiveness and an aversion to aging and anything feminine (Cole, 1986; Fischer, 1978; Green, 1993, p. 53).

By displacing elder men from the mainstream, one result of contemporary cultural coding is the oppression of older men. As Fischer (1978) observed when he reviewed American cultural documents and chronicled the development of a "cult of youth" from 1770 to 1970, the definition of elder men as oppressors provided a symbol for all other echelons among men to unite against gerontocracy.

The second strike is older men's perceived genderlessness. Ask people to complete the sentence "An old man . . ." and then listen to ungendered ageism and his feminization. Older men are depicted as sedentary, resting on a park bench, passing time, asexual. Images of older men basically portray diminished masculinity (Kite, Deaux, & Miele, 1991; Puglisi & Jackson, 1980–81; Silverman, 1977). To many people, aging is a negation of masculinity, and thus older men become effeminate over time. Given this cultural assumption, older men are used, however unwittingly. The degendered imagery of the older man keeps afloat a masculinity and a discourse that sustains younger men. The conventional discourse describes gender in simply binary terms, wherein aging diminishes men's masculinity and, by default, heightens their femininity over time. Framed this way, images of age-specific and cohort-specific masculinities never rise to a threshold of public consciousness. Rather, the social construction maintains that "old men" are not men at all.

DISCOURSES IN THE ACADEMY

As the size of elderly female population increased between 1930 and 1990, the importance of gender and aging commanded greater and greater attention among academics and policy makers (Haug, Ford, & Sheafor, 1985; Herzog, Holden, & Seltzer, 1989; Lesnoff-Caravaglia, 1984; Markson, 1985; Matthews, 1979; also see Coyle, 1989). Ironically, as older women's lives and their profound needs gained visibility, older men became more marginal and invisible. In fact, being elderly appears in some quarters to have become synonymous with being female. For example, in *Gender and Later Life*, Arber and Ginn (1991, p. vii) state, "Later life is primarily an experience of women." Their first chapter is powerfully titled "The Feminization of Later Life," because the demographics of aging show that elderly women outnumber elderly men in later life, especially as age advances. The message that is constructed, however, goes beyond making note of a sex differential in longevity. Rather, as women's experience in later life is brought to the foreground, older men's fade from attention. Arber and Ginn's otherwise very fine work makes "later life" as synonymous with women as "gender" has become.

Homogenizing elders—as reflected by mid-century discourses on "the aged" or the new academic discourse on feminization—was once said to be akin to "tabloid thinking" (Binstock 1983, p. 140). Homogenizing sets the stage to ignore individual differences and to think about "the elderly" only at the collective level as disadvantaged individuals beset by common problems. Kalish (1979) warned that this construction was a form of "new ageism." The new discourse of feminization of the aged goes beyond the devaluation of diversity (Butler, 1969) to thwart discussion of the ways in which the population of older men is itself devalued and the ways in which men's personal experiences of age are challenged by cultural double binds and structurally induced conflicts about masculinities—conflicts such as about their work ethic and their diminished social significance as men, or their relative social opaqueness as individuals versus a collective.

Although the core value behind older men's invisibility is academics' "compassionate ageism" for older women (Binstock, 1983), knowledge production in gerontological studies currently makes for blind spots and a lack of understanding of older men. As Cook (1992, p. 293) warned in an editorial in *The Gerontologist*, "If we want the public and the media to abandon the oversimplifying generalities they often make about age and aging and look instead at the diversity among older people, then gerontologists must stop asking attitudinal and factual questions about 'the elderly' as if they were a homogeneous group."

In the sociologies of the life course and family life, elderly men were not often studied as men but served as the referent point to better understand late-life families, elderly women's lives as caregivers, or younger men. Small wonder than that as much as "wives' sociology" once informed us about family life (Safilios-Rochschild, 1969), there is a "midlife sociology" that has tried to theorize about older men's lives. To illustrate, role-theory sociologies directed attention to the rolelessness of late life. Retired men were envisioned outside the "normal" work spaces, and, by default, they were invading their wives' space—the family home (see literature review in Brubaker, 1990). This early sociological discourse of older men defined their lives as a period of indispensable disengagement from former, power-brokering statuses. Older men were portrayed as obsolete currency in a culture that cherishes power; in disengagement terms, the spotlight was on younger men's welfare. Later discourses of activity theory similarly emphasized the core values of a masculinity that best fits younger employed men's lives. Neither did these theoretical accounts reveal much about older men as a group or about subgroup and individual differences.

Logically, the diversity among young and middle-aged men does not disappear at age 65, 70, or 75, when older men leave the workplace to take up more assiduously their semipublic and private social worlds. Their gendered lives continue. Their relationships with institutions, women, other men, and children press on. Dannefer (1988) pointed out that as men grow older, their accumulated decisions about life course options produce increased differentiation among them. But in what ways? Do age and gender interact to affect older men's thoughts, feelings, behaviors, and relations with others? Do the two interact to affect men as a group?

REFERENCES

Arber, S., & Ginn, J. (1991). *Gender and later life: A sociological analysis of resources and constraints.* London: Sage.

Berger, P. L. (1963). *Invitation to sociology: A humanistic perspective.* New York: Anchor.

Binstock, R. H. (1983). The aged as scapegoat. *The Gerontologist, 23,* 136–143.

Brubaker, T. H. (1990). Families in later life: A burgeoning research area. *Journal of Marriage and the Family, 52,* 959–981.

Buchholz, M., & Bynum, J. E. (1982). Newspaper presentations of America's aged: A content analysis of image and role. *The Gerontologist, 22,* 83–88.

Butler, R. N. (1969). Age-ism: Another form of bigotry. *The Gerontologist, 9,* 243–246.

Cole, T. R. (1986). "Putting off the old": Middle class morality, antebellum Protestantism, and the origins of ageism. In D. van Tassel & P. N. Stearns (Eds.), *Old age in a bureaucratic society* (pp. 49–65). Westport, CT: Greenwood Press.

Connell, R. W. (1992). A very straight gay: Masculinity, homosexual experience, and the dynamics of gender. *American Sociological Review, 57,* 735–751.

Cook, F. L. (1992). Ageism: Rhetoric and reality. *The Gerontologist, 32,* 292–293.

Coyle, J. M. (1989). *Women and aging: A selected, annotated bibliography.* Westport, CA: Greenwood Press.

Dannefer, D. (1988). Differential gerontology and the stratified life course: Conceptual and methodological issues. In G. L. Maddox & M. P. Lawton (Eds.), *Annual review of gerontology and geriatrics* (Vol. 8, pp. 3–36). New York: Springer.

Estes, C. L. (1979). *The aging enterprise.* San Francisco: Jossey-Bass.

Estes, C. L. (1993). The aging enterprise revisited. *The Gerontologist, 33,* 292–298.

Ferraro, K. F. (1992). Cohort changes in images of older adults, 1974–1981. *The Gerontologist, 32,* 296–304.

Fischer, D. H. (1978). *Growing old in America* (expanded ed.) New York: Oxford University Press.

Green, B. S. (1993). *Gerontology and the construction of older age: A study in discourse analysis.* Hawthorne, NY: Aldine.

Haug, M., Ford, A. B., & Sheafor, M. (1985). *The physical and mental health of aged women.* New York: Springer.

Herzog, A. R., Holden, K. C., & Seltzer, M. M. (1989). *Health and economic status of older women.* Amityville, NY: Baywood.

Hummert, M. L. (1990). Multiple stereotypes of elderly and young adults: A comparison of structure and evaluation. *Psychology and Aging, 5,* 182–193.

Kaiser, S. B., & Chandler, J. L. (1988). Audience responses to appearance codes: Old-age imagery in the media. *The Gerontologist, 28,* 692–699.

Kalish, R. A. (1979). The new ageism and the failure models: A polemic. *The Gerontologist, 19,* 398–402.

Kimmel, M. S., & Messner, M. A. (1992). *Men's lives* (2nd ed.). New York: Macmillan.

Kite, M. E., Deaux, K., & Miele, M. (1991). Stereotypes of young and old: Does age outweigh gender? *Psychology and Aging, 6,* 19–27.

Lesnoff-Caravaglia, G. (1984). *The world of the older woman: Conflicts and resolutions.* New York: Human Sciences Press.

Levinson, D. J., Darrow, C. N., Klein, E. B., Levinson, M. H., & McKee, B. (1978). *The seasons of a man's life.* New York: Knopf.

Markson, E. W. (1985). *Older women: Issues and prospects.* Lexington, MA: Lexington Books.

Matthews, S. H. (1979). *The social world of old women: Management of self-identity.* Beverly Hills, CA: Sage.

Morgan, T. B. (1987, May). What does a sixty-year-old man see when he looks in the mirror? *Esquire,* pp. 161–167.

Ortega y Gasset, J. (1958). *Man and crisis.* New York: Norton.

Powell, L., & Williamson, J. B. (1985). The mass media and the aged. *Social Policy, 16,* 38–49.

Puglisi, J. T., & Jackson, D. W. (1980–81). Sex role identity and self esteem in adulthood. *International Journal of Aging and Human Development, 12,* 129–138.

Roback, G., Randolph, L., & Seidman, B. (1993). *Physician characteristics and distribution in the United States,* Chicago: American Medical Association.

Safilios-Rochschild, C. (1969). Family sociology or wives' family sociology? A cross-cultural examination of decision-making. *Journal of Marriage and the Family, 31,* 290–301.

Segal, L. (1990). *Slow motion: Changing masculinities, changing men.* New Brunswick, NJ: Rutgers University Press.

Silverman, M. (1977). The old man as woman: Detecting stereotypes of aged men with a femininity scale. *Perceptual and Motor Skills, 44,* 336–338.

Sontag, S. (1972). The double standard of aging. *Saturday Review, 55*(39), 29–38.

Swayne, L. E., & Greco, A. J. (1987). The portrayal of older Americans in television commercials. *Journal of Advertising, 16*(1), 47–54.

Thompson, E. H., & Gongla, P. A. (1983). Single parent families: In the mainstream of American society. In E. D. Macklin & R. H. Rubin (Eds.), *Contemporary families and alternative lifestyles: Handbook on research and theory.* Beverly Hills, CA: Sage.

U.S. Bureau of the Census. (1992). *Marital status and living arrangements: March 1992.* Current Population Reports, Series P20, No. 468. Washington, DC: Government Printing Office.

U.S. Bureau of the Census. (1993). *Statistical abstracts of the United States, 1992.* Washington, DC: Government Printing Office.

U.S. Department of Education. (1992). *Projections of education statistics to 2003.* Washington, DC: Government Printing Office.

Walsh, R. P., & Connor, C. L. (1979). Old men and young women: How objectively are their skills assessed? *Journal of Gerontology, 34,* 561–568.

Wernick, A. (1987). From voyeur to narcissist: Imaging men in contemporary advertising. In M. Kaufman (Ed.), *Beyond patriarchy: Essays by men on pleasure, power, and change* (pp. 277–297). Toronto: Oxford University Press.

Part Ten

The Price of Deviance

33

The Unruly Woman: Gender and the Genres of Laughter

Kathleen Rowe

. . . Since Freud, few people question laughter's entanglements with aggression. Both spring from the unconscious, and both are, to varying degrees, taboo for women. The notion of "angry young women films" like the "angry young men" films popular in the 1950s and 1960s has itself been laughable, at least until *Thelma and Louise*, Ridley Scott's 1991 take on the buddy movie/road movie, shocked, moved, and polarized audiences on the issue of women's violence against men. Women's anger more often remains unspoken, as Julia Lesage writes, repressed beneath "all of women's depression—all our compulsive smiling, ego-tending, and sacrifice; all our psychosomatic illness, and all our passivity" ("Women's Rage" 421). Because women lack acceptable aesthetic or social structures through which to express or even "think" anger, it rarely erupts into the violence or transgressive laughter of *A Question of Silence* or *Thelma and Louise*. In melodrama and film noir, for example, women's anger appears as insanity or perversity, including grotesque images of lesbianism. Even art by women has rarely contained direct expressions of women's rage. What's needed are "self-conscious, collectively supported, and politically clear articulations of our anger and rage," in Lesage's words—articulations that cannot be made in the mode of "nice girls" ("Women's Rage" 420, 427). That is, women must be willing to offend and to be offensive, to look beyond the doomed suffering women of melodrama and the evil ones of film noir.

I would like to suggest that those structures for expressing women's anger do exist—in the genres of laughter, and, at least in rudimentary form, in the structure of narrative itself. . . .

From *The Unruly Woman: Gender and the Genres of Laughter* by Kathleen Rowe (Austin: University of Texas Press, 1995). Excerpts from chapter 2 were first published as "Roseanne: Unruly Woman as Domestic Goddess" in *Screen* 31, no. 4 (1990): 408–19. Reprinted with permission.

All narrative forms contain the potential to represent transformation and change, but it is the genres of laughter that most fully employ the motifs of liminality. From romance to satire to the grotesque, these genres are built on transgression and inversion, disguise and masquerade, sexual reversals, the deflation of ideals, and the leveling of hierarchies. It is to these motifs, which are also the motifs of the carnivalesque, that B. Rudy Rich refers when she advocates the feminist potential of the "Medusan film," a type of film about sexuality and humor.[1] She argues that comedy should not be overlooked as a weapon of great political power, which women should cultivate for "its revolutionary potential as a deflator of the patriarchal order and an extraordinary leveler and reinventor of dramatic structure" (353).[2]

The name "Medusan" is borrowed from Hélène Cixous's "The Laugh of the Medusa," an essay that might well have inspired *A Question of Silence*. Medusa, of course, is a mythological woman whose story bears important implications for theories of sexuality, spectacle, and cinema. When Medusa boasted of her beauty to Athena, Athena became jealous and changed Medusa and her sisters into monsters with fangs for teeth, snakes for hair, and staring eyes that could transform people into stone. Perseus killed her by looking at her reflection in his mirrorlike shield and then beheading her. The blood from her left side was fatally poisonous, and that from her right could restore life to the dead. Medusa remains an evocative symbol in contemporary culture, appearing, for instance, as an evil woman who threatens an androgynous male hero and the furry creatures who follow him in *Captain EO*, a Michael Jackson video shown in the early 1990s in Disneyland.[3] One could say that among the many things Medusa embodies is extreme ambivalence toward women—toward their bodies, their beauty, their celebration of self, and their blood.

Whereas for Freud, Medusa incarnates male fears of castration, Cixous uses her to mock those theories built on such notions of female lack. In the most widely quoted passage from the essay, she writes that what Perseus averted his eyes from was not a deadly monster but a woman without the deformities "male" theories attempt to inflict on her: "You have only to look at the Medusa straight on to see her. And she is not deadly. She's beautiful and she's laughing" (255). While underscoring yet another failure, like that of Bakhtin, to "hear" women's laughter, this rewriting of Medusa's story exemplifies the kind of creative destruction Bakhtin associates with the grotesque.

Feminist film theory has yet to pursue fully the implications of Medusa's power both to draw Perseus's gaze as spectacle and to fix her own gaze, her "staring eyes," on him.[4] By using her power to draw his gaze, she can halt his quest for his Oedipal patrimony, robbing him, in fact, of his own eyes. From Cixous's perspective, that power becomes deadly only because of Perseus's refusal to meet her gaze. A more courageous meeting of her gaze would allow Perseus to apprehend not petrifying monstrosity but beauty: "You have only to look at the Medusa straight on . . . " As long as men avert their eyes from her, fearing the sight of her *and* her gaze, "woman" can be only a phantasm of castration for them, deadly and grotesque. And more important, as long as women do not look at *each other* straight on, they can see only distorted reflections of themselves. . . .

Medusa, like Bakhtin's grinning pregnant hags, contains some of the earliest out-lines of the unruly woman, an ambivalent figure of female outrageousness and trans-gression with roots in the narrative forms of comedy and the social practices of car-nival. The unruly woman represents a special kind of excess differing from that of the femme fatale (the daughters of Eve and Helen) or the madonna (the daughters of Mary), whose laughter, if it ever occurred, no longer rings in the myths still cir-culating around them. Like Medusa, the unruly woman laughs. Like Roseanne Arnold, she is not a "nice girl." She *is* willing to offend and be offensive. As with the heroines of the romantic film comedy, from Ellie in *It Happened One Night* (1934) to Loretta in *Moonstruck* (1987), her sexuality is neither evil and uncontrol-lable like that of the femme fatale, nor sanctified and denied like that of the virgin/madonna. Associated with both beauty and monstrosity, the unruly woman dwells close to the grotesque. But while mythology taints and dooms Medusa, the unruly woman often enjoys a reprieve from those fates that so often seem inevitable to women under patriarchy, because her home is comedy and the carnivalesque, the realm of inversion and fantasy where, for a time at least, the ordinary world can be stood on its head.

. . . The figure of the unruly woman contains much potential for feminist appro-priation, for rethinking how women are constructed as gendered subjects in the lan-guage of spectacle and the visual. The parodic excesses of the unruly woman and the comedic conventions surrounding her provide a space to "act out" the "dilem-mas of femininity," in Mary Russo's words (225), to make not only "fantastic" and "incredible" but also laughable those tropes of femininity valorized by melodrama. Russo asks in what sense women can produce and make spectacles of themselves *for* themselves. The unruly woman points to new ways of thinking about visibility as power. Masquerade concerns itself not only with a woman's ability to look, after all, but also with her ability to affect the terms on which she is seen.

Such a sense of spectacle differs from the one that shaped early feminist film theory. Granting that visual pleasure and power are inextricably bound, this position would see that relation as more historically determined, its terms as more mutable. It would argue that visual power flows in multiple directions and that the position of spec-tacle isn't necessarily one of weakness. Because public power is predicated largely on visibility, men have long understood the need to secure their power not only by look-ing but by being seen, or rather, by fashioning—as subject, as author, as artist—a spectacle of themselves. . . .

. . . The topos of the unruly woman . . . reverberates whenever women disrupt the norms of femininity and the social hierarchy of male over female through excess and outrageousness. Historian Natalie Davis does not provide an inventory of qualities asso-ciated with female unruliness but instead a wide-ranging collection of examples of "women on top" and a powerful theoretical framework for understanding them.[5] . . .

1. The unruly woman creates disorder by dominating, or trying to dominate, men. She is unable or unwilling to confine herself to her proper place.
2. Her body is excessive or fat, suggesting her unwillingness or inability to con-trol her physical appetites.

3. Her speech is excessive, in quantity, content, or tone.
4. She makes jokes, or laughs herself.
5. She may be androgynous or hermaphroditic, drawing attention to the social construction of gender.
6. She may be old or a masculinized crone, for old women who refuse to become invisible in our culture are often considered grotesque.
7. Her behavior is associated with looseness and occasionally whorishness, but her sexuality is less narrowly and negatively defined than is that of the femme fatale. She may be pregnant.
8. She is associated with dirt, liminality (thresholds, borders, or margins), and taboo, rendering her above all a figure of ambivalence.

These are some of the tropes or signifiers of female unruliness. Ideology holds that the "well-adjusted" woman has what Hélène Cixous has described as "divine composure" (246). She is silent, static, invisible—"composed" and "divinely" apart from the hurly-burly of life, process, and social power. Such is not the case with the unruly woman. Through her body, her speech, and her laughter, especially in the public sphere, she creates a disruptive spectacle of herself. The tropes of unruliness are often coded with misogyny. However, they are also a source of potential power, especially when they are recoded or reframed to expose what that composure conceals. Ultimately, the unruly woman can be seen as prototype of woman as subject—transgressive above all when she lays claim to her own desire. . . .

In July 1990, Roseanne Barr Arnold, star of the top-rated ABC sitcom *Roseanne*, was invited to sing the national anthem at a double-header between the Cincinnati Reds and the San Diego Padres. Tom Werner, coproducer of the TV show and owner of the Padres, thought that the fat and noisy comedian would give a boost to his losing team. It was Working Women's Night at the San Diego stadium, and Arnold was nationally known for her depiction of working-class family life in *Roseanne*. With thirty thousand fans in the stands, Arnold screeched out the song, grabbed her crotch, spit on the ground, and made an obscene gesture to the booing crowd. Werner had been right; the team won its next two games. But the performance, intended as a parody of baseball rituals, unleased a firestorm in the press. CNN broadcast the story with interviews of outraged "people on the street." In one segment, baseball fans drove a steamroller over a boom box containing a tape of her voice. Angry calls flooded the switchboards at ABC. On national television, President George Bush called her performance "disgraceful." Arnold received threats on her life.

The incident boosted media coverage of the already controversial Arnold from the tabloids to the establishment press and from the gossip columns to Page One. Headlines joked about "the fat lady singing" or the "Barr-mangled banner," while the tabloid *Star* more graphically exclaimed "Barrf!" and then listed "Her 10 most gross moments." From sports writers to political commentators, all felt compelled to say something about the incident. William C. Rhoden wrote in the *New York Times*: "Barr is merely the symptom of the excess of greed in American sports. . . .

One gets what one pays for" (B9). Opera singer Robert Merrill, who had sung the anthem at Yankee Stadium for eighteen years, spoke of "this woman, who obviously has no taste at all. . . . It was like, 'Here I am, and to hell with you.' . . . I almost upchucked my dinner. . . . I don't know if I've ever felt so angry" (quoted in Georgatos A4). Perhaps the most virulent reaction was that of conservative columnist George Will. Leading his column with quotations from five news stories about children killed or critically injured that summer by gunfire in New York City, he linked Arnold's performance not only to the horrors of American cities in decay but to the sneak attack on the nation by the Japanese at Pearl Harbor. What seemed to distress him most was that, in his view, she was feeding the nation's fatal appetite for "slob television." First paraphrasing the American epic poet Walt Whitman ("I hear American bullets singing"), he then lamented the "alabaster cities" of "America the Beautiful" which no longer "gleam, undimmed by human tears!" (A15).

Obviously Arnold had struck a nerve. Other singers have been criticized for their highly stylized renditions of "The Star Spangled Banner"—among them Jose Feliciano, Bobby McFerrin, Marvin Gaye, and Willie Nelson. And one could argue that Arnold, as a comedian, was doing nothing more than they had, shaping the performance according to her own comedic artistry. But none provoked a reaction comparable to this one. Arnold jested about it—"I must be the greatest singer. My voice can stop a fucking nation." . . .

In other words, as Will insists, there are indeed limits or barriers, especially for women who behave as Arnold does. His description of her as a "star and a slob" only dimly suggests the powerful and contradictory status she has achieved by whining, wisecracking, munching, mooning, screeching, and spitting her way into the national consciousness. If it is dangerous "to be a woman, period," it is especially so to be an *unruly* woman, and Arnold's performance in San Diego that summer confirmed her status as such.

Women rarely have the opportunity to claim the kind of public space that Arnold did that day, and her experience offers abundant lessons about the relation between social power and public visibility. Invisibility helps constrain women's social power; as long as women are not seen in the public sphere, they do not exist. Arnold heightened her visibility by forcing herself from one—less visible—category of popular discourse into another usually unavailable to women—from "soft news" to "hard news." Soft news includes gossip, the tabloids, *People* magazine, lifestyle and entertainment sections of the newspaper, hard news covers events clearly in the public sphere and appears on the front pages and op-ed pages of newspapers and at the beginning of newscasts. If sports is not exactly hard news, it's not soft either, because of its particular status in masculine culture. When Arnold walked into that stadium, she made herself the subject of hard news, subject to those voices that had never touched her when she was safely contained in a place marked "sitcom" or "HBO Comedy Special," or in the feminized discourse of gossip columns and tabloids.

Implicit in the unruly woman's heightened visibility is her potential to bring about a process Erving Goffman describes as "breaking frame." Goffman suggests that social life is an "endless negotiation" about which cultural frame should surround, and thereby give meaning to, various events and bits of behavior. He argues that the meaning of a social situation can be radically altered by changing the frame in which it is perceived and that frames are most vulnerable at their margins. Because she is dangerously situated in the margins of social life, the unruly woman enjoys heightened "frame-busting" power.

Arnold entered a space that day already defined as liminal or sacred in patriarchal culture. Baseball is not merely a game, something that is played, but a collective, public, and masculine ritual, a quasi-religious reaffirmation of patriarchy, patriotism, and the myth of our nation's Edenic history. Unlike football, its rival in the national mythology of sports (at least until the rise of basketball in the past twenty years), baseball, with its grace and decorum, is the game of choice for intellectuals and the upwardly mobile. It is George Will's favorite sport. Free of the narrative constraints of her television series, Arnold staged a joke that reframed that ritual event and turned it into something else—a carnivalized moment of leveling, mockery, and inversion. By exceeding the limits of play tolerated on that diamond, parodying the gestures of the Boys of Summer, and singing the national anthem less than reverentially—in effect, by being who she was, a comedian, joke-maker, and unruly woman—she violated the space of that ritual and, indeed, the national airwaves that had been given over to its celebration. What might have been a harmless spoof of the tropes of masculinity and patriotism became a threat to the sanctity of all American institutions, invoking that "perilous realm of possibility," in Victor Turner's words where "anything *may* go'" (41).

According to Turner, at times of dramatic social change, sacred symbols—such as baseball, the national anthem, and the flag—burst into the public arena to mobilize people to defend their cultures. In the summer of 1990, the U.S. government was laying the groundwork for its showdown with Saddam Hussein and preparing to deploy sixty thousand troops in Kuwait. Flag-burning had become a controversial issue, with proposals in Congress for a constitutional ban against it. Arnold's performance made her vulnerable to the official voices of masculine authority, the voices of news and government from George Will to George Bush, which projected onto her all perceived threats to the dominant culture. Indeed, Will's near loss of control over his own rhetoric exposed his column's subtext—the range of repressed fears this disorderly fat woman released about racial threats to the nation's "alabaster" cities, about mass culture with its "slob" values encroaching on the tidy domain of those who know Walt Whitman's poetry well enough to paraphrase it.[6]

Not only in this incident but throughout her career Arnold has used the semiotics of unruliness to break frame, to disrupt, to expose the gap between, on the one hand, the New Left and the women's movement of the late 1960s and early 1970s, and on the other hand, the realities of working-class family life two decades later. On one level, of course, Arnold's joke backfired. On another and more important one, however, it succeeded as a powerful demonstration of the disruptive power of the unruly woman. Even as fans were booing her in the stadium, others were cheering.[7] As Arnold's career has unfolded, her fat, unruly body—and her noisy, angry, funny persona—have shape-shifted into forms that might appear less transgressive than the ones that first defined her. . . .

The cover of the December 1990 issue of *Vanity Fair*—headlined "Roseanne on Top"—shows Arnold holding the wrists of her husband Tom Arnold to pin him beneath her. Her mouth is open in what appears to be a laugh. She is wearing a low-cut red dress, a strawberry-blonde wig, diamonds, and a white fox fur, a look that parodically recalls the blonde bombshells and gold diggers of early classical Hollywood film. The photograph, a medium shot, centers on Arnold's massive cleavage. Tom Arnold's face, looking at the camera and registering little emotion, is upside down.

The words and images of the cover suggest that Arnold wields power in multiple dimensions—power over men, financial power, celebrity power, sexual power. These words and images also acknowledge that she has achieved that power by cultivating a particular persona defined by gender inversion. . . .

. . . Arnold's success has not generated universal enthusiasm, as the national-anthem incident made clear. Nor was that incident an isolated event, but merely the most provocative in a series of episodes that included dropping her pants at other public events, cracking jokes about menstruation on national television, and generally, "making a spectacle of herself." Many people find Arnold's persona deeply offensive and controversy has followed her up almost every run of the ladder to success. She and her series have been trashed by the tabloids, snubbed by the Emmies, and condescended to by media critics.[8] At the same time, her fans have been loyal and numerous enough to propel her to, and sustain, her success. In a *People* magazine poll, readers voted her their favorite female television star and the one most likely to have a flourishing career in the year 2000. The August 1989 issue of *Esquire*, on its favorite (and least favorite) women, concisely displayed this ambivalence, or difficulty in placing her, by running two stories by two men, side by side—one called "Roseanne—Yea," and the other, "Roseanne—Nay."

While this ambivalence cuts across media and class lines, the supermarket tabloids have perhaps played the largest role in creating and popularizing Arnold's unruly persona. The tabloids are the carnivalesque of the popular print media, giving heightened representations of the kinds of "weirdness or disjunction" their readers experience in everyday life (Fiske 114). They are popular with the same demographic group targeted by Arnold's show, women aged 18–34, or, as comedian Alan King more colorfully describes them, "the hopeless underclass of the female sex. The polyester-clad, overweight occupants of the slow track. Fast-food waitresses, factory workers, housewives—members of the invisible pink-collar army. The despised, the jilted, the underpaid." "In other words," as Arnold replies, "the coolest people" (both quoted in O'Connor B27). Arnold shares with the tabloids a taste for the self-consciously excessive, vulgar, and sensational. Both Arnold and the tabloids carnivalize, invert, and mock the norms of bourgeois taste. . . .

. . . As sociologist Jack Leven said in the article, "Here's this abrasive, aggressive, stubborn, wealthy person who happens to be a woman. If Donald Trump behaved in the same way, people would overlook it or might even admire it" (51). . . .

Arnold hardly fared better among more sophisticated commentators. In an early review of *Roseanne*, Elvis Mitchell noted in the *Village Voice* how "startled" he was to see "this kind of arrogance so early in the run of a TV series" (47). He criticized the general lack of "class" or "taste" in television viewers and reviewers, describing her show as the "1040 EZ, low-income, no deductions" version of *The Cosby Show*. And according to Joyce Maynard, Exeter- and Yale-educated author of the syndicated column "Domestic Affairs," Arnold was "obnoxious and insulting to the average American wife/mother and homemaker" (C1.). Both commentators displayed certain recurring problems in contemporary cultural criticism—the left's difficulties with gender, and middle-class feminism's with class. While Mitchell appreciated the "tastelessness" of *Married With Children,* finding the show a hip send-up of working-class family life, *Roseanne,* with its strong female character and feminist content, was "arrogant." Maynard's difficulty in understanding Arnold's appeal began with her unthinking assurance that she could speak for the "average American wife/mother and homemaker," despite the class privileges that she enjoys.[9]

One explanation for the contradictions that have characterized Arnold's reception in U.S. culture lies in the phenomenon of stardom itself. As Dyer has explained (*Stars*), people become stars because their images play on—and magically resolve—ideological contradictions of their times. In Arnold's case, her copious body could be seen as a site which makes visible, and reconciles, the conflicts women experience in a culture that says consume (food) but look as if you don't. Or it makes visible the conflict any member of the working class might experience in a culture that says consume (goods—conspicuously and lavishly) but don't expect a job that provides you with the means to do so. This explanation is apt, but it doesn't fully explain the extreme ambivalence that has marked Arnold's career from its outset.

Such an explanation, I believe, would locate Arnold in the historical and theoretical context of female unruliness. In an article on the op-ed page of the *New York Times* ("What Am I, a Zoo?"), Arnold describes her own awareness of the carnivalesque heterogeneity of her image by enumerating the groups she has been associated with—the regular housewife, the mother, the postfeminist, the "Little Guy," fat people, the "Queen of Tabloid America," the "body politic," sex, "angry womankind herself," "the notorious and sensationalistic La Luna madness of an ovulating Abzugian woman run wild"—and so on. . . .

Arnold's unruliness is more clearly paradigmatic than syntagmatic, less visible in the stories her series dramatizes than in the image cultivated around her body: Roseanne Arnold-the-person who tattooed her buttocks and mooned her fans, Roseanne Connor-the-character for whom farting and nose-picking are as much a reality as dirty dishes and obnoxious boy bosses. It is Arnold's *fatness*, however, and the *looseness* or lack of personal restraint her fatness implies, that most powerfully define her and convey her opposition to middle-class and feminine standards of decorum and beauty. Indeed, the very appearance of a 200-plus-pound woman on a weekly prime-time sitcom is significant. More than anything, I believe, her fatness is the source of the hostility directed against her. Even if a fat woman says or does nothing, her very appearance, especially in public space, can give offense. Fatness has carried more positive implications for women in other historical periods and among other ethnic and racial groups, but in white, late-twentieth-century America, it signifies a disturbing unresponsiveness to social control.

As Michel Foucault has shown, social groups exercise control over their members by inscribing standards of beauty and perfection, of social and sexual "normalcy," on their bodies. At the same time, the body serves as a vehicle for communication from subject to social world—a nonverbal communication that is often hidden by the social privileging of speech (Douglas, *Implicit Meanings* 87). Body language conveys the individual's relation to the social group along a continuum of control, from strong to weak, from total relaxation to total self-control. Among the socially powerful, relaxation signifies "ease." Among those deemed in need of social control, it signifies "looseness" or "sloppiness." The body that "refuses to be aestheticized," that does not control its "grotesque, offensive, dirty aspects," can thus communicate resistance to social discipline (Fiske 97). George Will could find no better way to express his reaction to Arnold's rebelliousness than by describing her as a "slob."

Arnold's body epitomizes the grotesque body Bakhtin described, an affinity that is clear from the first paragraph of *Roseanne: My Life as a Woman* (Barr), where her description of her "gargantuan appetites" even as a newborn baby brings to mind Bakhtin's study of Rabelais. Arnold compounds her fatness with a looseness of body language and speech. She sprawls, slouches, and flops on furniture: her speech—even apart from its content—is loose, its enunciation and grammar "sloppy," and its tone and volume "excessive."

In twentieth-century U.S. culture, these qualities have long lost the positive charges they might have carried in the cultures Bakhtin described. Our culture stigmatizes all fat people by psychologizing or moralizing their obesity.[10] For *women*, body size and bearing are governed by especially far-reaching standards of normalization and asetheticization, which forbid both looseness and fatness. Women of ill-repute, whether fat or thin, are described as "loose," their bodies, especially their sexuality, seen as out of control. Similarly, fat women are seen as having "let themselves go." To protect themselves against the threat of rape, violence, come-ons, and offensive male vulgarity, poor women, especially women of color, may assume a bearing that is "stiff" and "ladylike." Anita Hill displayed extreme dignity and reserve during the 1991 Senate hearings on the appointment of Supreme Court Justice Clarence Thomas, although that bearing did not protect her from sexual innuendoes by men or charges of "aloofness" by women.

The cult of thinness is among the most insidious means of disciplining the female body in contemporary U.S. culture. Because a woman's social well-being is largely dependent on her appearance, heavy women suffer more than heavy men from the culture's tendency to stigmatize fat people. Comedians make fat jokes about Arnold but they usually spare John Goodman, the equally fat actor who plays her husband on her sitcom. While other cultures have considered round and fleshy women as sensuous and feminine, our culture considers them unfeminine, rebellious, and sexually deviant, either undersexed or oversexed. In her studies of women's relation to food (*Fat is a Feminist Issue* and *Hunger Strike*), Susie Orbach has described anorexia as the "metaphor of our times," an expression of the extreme contradictions women experience when they are socialized to tend to the needs of others but deny their own. Femininity is gauged by how little space women take up; women who are too fat or move too loosely appropriate too much space, obtruding upon proper boundaries (Henley 38). It is no coincidence, Orbach writes, that since the 1960s, when women accelerated their demands for more space in the public world, the female body ideal has become smaller and ever more unattainable. At the same time, the incidence of anorexia has sharply increased. The anorectic takes the imperative to deny her desire and "aestheticize" her body beyond healthful limits, her emaciated form becoming a grotesque exposure of the norms that seek to control women's appetites in all areas of their lives.

The transgressive, round female body is also the maternal body, and maternity ties women to the process of generation and aging. As a result, the figure of the grotesque old woman often bears a masculinist culture's projected fears of aging and death. While Arnold is hardly an old woman and the media do not attempt to portray her as such, fatness and age are closely related because both foreground the materiality of the body. . . .

Women are expected to keep not only their bodies but their utterances unobtrusive. As Henley notes, voices in any culture that are not meant to be heard are perceived as loud, when they do speak, regardless of their decibel level. The description of feminists as "shrill"—with voices that are too loud and too high-pitched—quickly became a cliché in accounts of the women's movement. Dominant cultures characterize minorities among them as loud—Americans in Europe, Japanese in the United States. In white U.S. culture, the voices of blacks are characterized as not only "loud" but "unclear," "slurred," and "lazy"—in other words, loose. Farting, belching, and nose-picking convey a similar failure—or refusal—to restrain the body. While boys and men can make controlled use of such "uncontrollable" bodily functions to rebel against authority, such as avenue of revolt is generally not available to women. But, as Henley suggests, "if it should ever come into women's repertoire, it will carry great power, since it directly undermines the sacredness of women's bodies" (91).

Expanding that repertoire of revolt is entirely consistent with Arnold's professed mission. She writes of wanting "to break every social norm . . . and see that it is laughed at. I chuckle with glee if I know I have offended someone, because the people I intend to insult offend me horribly" (Barr, *Roseanne* 50). Arnold describes how Matt Williams, the producer she eventually fired from her show, tried to get *her* fired: "He compiled a list of every offensive thing I did. And I do offensive things. . . . That's who I am. That's my act. So Matt was in his office making a list of how gross I was, how many times I farted and belched—taking it to the network to show I was out of control" (quoted in Jerome 85–86). Of course she was out of control—*his* control.

By being fat, loud, and ever willing to "do offensive things," the star persona "Roseanne Arnold" displays, above all, a supreme ease with her body—an ease which triggers much of the unease surrounding her because it diminishes the power of others to control her. Pierre Bourdieu describes such a manner as an "indifference to the objectifying gaze of others which neutralizes its power . . . [and] appropriates its appropriation" (208). It marks her rebellion against not only the codes of gender but those of class, for a culture's norms of beauty or the "legitimate" body—fit and trim—are accepted across class boundaries while the ability to achieve them is not. Ease with one's body is the prerogative of the upper classes. For the working classes, the body is more likely to be a source of embarrassment, timidity, and alienation. . . .

. . . Growing up as a Jew in Utah among relatives who remained haunted by memories of the Holocaust taught her about marginality and fear. She learned about madness and institutionalization at the age of sixteen when she spent eight months in a mental hospital because of nightmares and other symptoms of psychological trauma she experienced after being hit by a car. Like other labels of deviancy, madness is often attached to the unruly woman, and it is a leitmotif in Arnold's autobiography and the tabloid talk about her. . . .

. . . What finally convinced her to cast her lot with comedy was "the thought of a woman, any woman, standing up and saying NO . . . a huge, cosmic NO." She explains, "The first time I went on stage, I felt *myself* say it, and I felt chilled and free and redeemed" (Barr, *Roseanne* 152). This "no" draws on laughter's power to negate. It refuses the affirmation men often like to attribute to women, as in Molly Bloom's famous, unconditional, rhapsodic "yes" at the end of James Joyce's *Ulysses*. . . .

Arnold discovered her stance (or attitude, if you will) when she realized that she could take up the issue of female oppression by adopting its very language. Helen Andelin's *Fascinating Womanhood* (1965) was one of the most popular femininity manuals for the women of her mother's generation. Part of a movement that exalted homemaking as a form of self-expression, the book taught women to manipulate men by becoming "domestic goddesses." Yet, Arnold discovered, such terms might also be used for "self-definition, rebellion, truth-telling" for telling a truth that in her case is both angry and affirmative (Barr, *Roseanne* 172). So she built her act and her success by exposing those "tropes of femininity" stylized and valorized, as Mary Ann Doane explains in *The Desire to Desire*, in the women's melodrama. Arnold attacked the ideology of "true womanhood"—how to be the perfect wife and mother—by cultivating the opposite, an image of the unruly woman. Appropriating Andelin's words but to very different ends, she called this figure the "Domestic Goddess."

It is no accident that a tradition of funny, angry women is hard to find, for the closeness between laughter and anger produces deep constraints on how women may express or participate in both. These constraints are illuminated by Freud's theory of wit (*Jokes and Their Relation to the Unconscious*), which points to the importance of gender in much comedy and laughter. For Freud, joke work arises from the unconscious much as dream work does. It has three related forms—the joke itself, the comic, and the humorous—which all release energy otherwise spent in repression. . . .

In Freud's account, the joke in its basic form requires three parties—two men and a woman. The first man initiates the joke to release an aggressive impulse, originally sexual, toward the woman. He forces her to participate in the joke through her embarrassment, her acknowledgement that she understands its content. (Such was the case when Anita Hill was made to repeat Clarence Thomas's remarks to her about pubic hair on a Coke bottle.) Through its cleverness, the joke veils and makes socially acceptable its underlying aggression. The joke does not exist until the laughter of the second man confirms it; the woman, as the joke's passive butt, thus enables the formation of a bond between the two men. According to Freud, the replacement of an actual woman by a symbolic substitute marks the advance of civilization, as does the joke's evolution from smut to content that is less overtly sexual.[11]

Freud's account of the joke suggests why so much laughter is directed *at* women and why so much comedy is misogynistic. It also explains why women so often feel alienated from many traditions of comedy, whether the slapstick of early silent film or the routines of standup comedians from Andrew Dice Clay to Eddie Murphy. For this reason, standup comedy—highly dependent on the dynamics of joke making—has, until the 1960s, been an unfriendly place for female performers. Until then, women rarely appeared in a comic act without a male partner. Even after the sixties, women who succeeded as standup comedians tended, in a sense, to occupy the "male" position by directing their jokes at themselves in self-deprecating barbs, or at other women. Much of the humor of Phyllis Diller and Joan Rivers falls into this category.

Freud's analysis explains how precariously the unruly woman is poised between serving as a target of hostile laughter herself and hurling that laughter back at its sources. It also gives yet another explanation for the furor Arnold provoked in San Diego. Not only did she violate the space of baseball, but she encroached on another sacred masculine territory—that of the joke-maker. Arnold "made" a joke, and a tendentious one, containing a thinly veiled message of aggression. Refusing to play the passive victim herself, she forced men into that role. As in her standup routine, she used the social pressure mobilized by the joke to force men to assume a perspective, even if only briefly, they ordinarily would not—to laugh at their symbols of masculine pride. In order to laugh, men had to adopt the double perspective that characterizes women's lives, experiencing the joke as both subject and object, as butt and complicitous second party. For many, obviously, that was impossible.

NOTES

1. See "In the Name of Feminist Film Criticism." An example of such a film is Jacques Rivette's *Celine and Julie Go Boating* (1974), which was almost universally denounced by male critics for its "silliness" but has become a favorite of feminists. Pitting a new kind of comedy against the genre of melodrama, the film suggests a seemingly unending capacity for prolonging the middle section of narrative with its invention, liminality, and play. See also Lesage's "*Celine and Julie Go Boating:* Subversive Fantasy."

2. Rich warns against an overemphasis on form or "signifying practices" in judging a film's feminist potential. Her call for "a bit of phenomenology" about the existence and experience of the female spectator remains as cogent today as when she made it in 1978. Comedy's potential for feminism has long been recognized as well by Patricia Mellencamp, whose persuasive and witty work on the subject began with articles on the Marx Brothers ("Jokes and Their Relation to the Marx Brothers"), Lucille Ball, and Gracie Allen and has

continued through her recent books on the avant-garde, television, and the discourses of scandal.

3. Medusa retains even greater currency in the avant-garde. Her story is rewritten, feminized, and conflated with that of Eve in Monique Wittig's *Les Guérillères* (see Suleiman 132). Her face appears on the cover of a recent book about female performance artists (Juno and Vale, *Angry Women*). Suleiman describes the laughing Medusa as a "trope for women's autonomous subjectivity and for the necessary irreverence of women's writing—and rewriting" (168).

4. De Lauretis makes a provocative move in this direction when, in the context of a "politics of the unconscious," she rewrites the Medusa story so that Medusa is not sleeping but is awake when Perseus slays her (*Alice Doesn't* 134–136). By doing so, she points to the fact that our culture demands that women be "asleep" whenever it asks us to identify with the images of dead women it parades before us and when it privileges "aesthetic" standards at the expense of any other kind of identification. I take a similar position in relation to high cultural modes of criticism in "Romanticism, Sexuality, and the Canon."

5. That framework is based on the notion of sexual inversion, which I will discuss in more detail later in this chapter. I substitute *gender inversion* for *sexual inversion*, to avoid any ambiguity that might arise from the latter's associations with homosexuality in psychoanalytic discourse. While the list that follows is my own, it is largely indebted to Davis, as is this entire study. Like Mary Russo's, her work has made immeasurable contributions to my own.

6. As Arnold herself noted, the reaction to her performance, not the performance itself, carried the more alarming message. As for Bush, she says, he "should have been paying attention to Kuwait" (quoted in Hirschberg 224).

7. Later that year, the incident appeared in an episode of the courtroom drama series, *L.A. Law*, where it was rewritten as a conflict between a sympathetically portrayed, heavy black male blues singer and a team owner, whose stuffiness was shown to be un-American.

8. In July 1991, she beat four male competitors—Dan Quayle, Saddam Hussein, U.S. Senator Jesse Helms, and developer Donald Trump—to win the first annual "Sitting Duck" award given by the National Society of Newspaper Columnists ("People" 2A).

9. After being deluged with letters from her readers, Maynard later acknowledged that she had felt threatened by a woman who discarded so many of the super-woman expectations that she had placed on herself. Subsequently Maynard described the breakup of her own marriage and ended her column. Arnold has criticized the middle-class biases of popular U.S. feminism: "I feel bad when I read *Ms.* magazine and they have a whole article about, like Tracey Ullman and Carol Burnett and Bette Midler, and don't mention me—I mean, as a woman who did the first show about how women really live. And then I go, it's classism. It's even more insidious that any sort of sexism. . . . Because I'm of a working-class background. I mean, I get every kind of ism that there is. And they're all ugly" (quoted in Hirschberg 231).

10. Marcia Millman writes that fat people arouse "horror, loathing, speculation, repugnance, and avoidance" (71). In the working class, fatness becomes a sign of a failure to achieve upward mobility. She also notes that some men hold a secret attraction to fat women.

11. Other studies confirm this scenario. As Mary Douglas suggests, people tend to direct jokes "downward," toward groups that are lower in social power (*Implicit Meanings* 95). Or, as lesbian comedian Kate Clinton writes, "Male penile humor—the ultimate in stand-up comedy—is based on the hierarchical power structure of the put-down" (quoted in Pershing 224). Studies of the socialization of women (McGhee) show that in mixed company,

women look to men for permission to laugh. Girls learn early in their lives that their role is not to "make" jokes themselves, to be comic artists, but to smile or laugh at the jokes men make, often at women's expense. Joke making is considered unfeminine.

REFERENCES

Andelin, Helen. *Fascinating Womanhood.* Santa Barbara, Calif.: Pacific Press, 1965.

Arnold, Roseanne. Interview with Kathleen Rowe. June 20, 1991.

———. See also Barr, Roseanne.

Bakhtin, Mikhail. *The Dialogic Imagination.* Edited by Michael Holquist. Translated by Caryl Emerson and Michael Holquist. Austin: University of Texas Press, 1981.

———. *Rabelais and His World.* Translated by Helene Iswolsky. Bloomington: Indiana University Press, 1984.

Barr, Roseanne. *Roseanne: My Life as a Woman.* New York: Harper and Row, 1989.

———. See also Arnold, Roseanne.

———. "What Am I, a Zoo?" *New York Times* (national ed.), July 31, 1989: I15.

Bourdieu, Pierre, *Distinction: A Social Critique of the Judgement of Taste.* Translated by Richard Nice. Cambridge, Mass.: Harvard University Press, 1984.

Cixous, Hélène. "The Laugh of the Medusa." Translated by Keith Cohen and Paula Cohen. In *New French Feminisms,* edited by Elaine Marks and Isabelle de Courtivron, pp. 245–264. Brighton: Harvester, 1980. Originally published as "Le Rire de la Méduse." *L'Arc* 61 (1975): 39–54.

Davis, Natalie Zemon. *Society and Culture in Early Modern France.* Stanford, Calif.: Stanford University Press, 1975.

de Lauretis, Teresa. *Alice Doesn't: Feminism, Semiotics, Cinema.* Bloomington: Indiana University Press, 1984.

Doane, Mary Ann. *The Desire to Desire: The Woman's Film of the 1940s.* Bloomington: Indiana University Press, 1987.

Douglas, Mary. *Implicit Meanings: Essays in Anthropology.* Boston: Routledge & Kegan Paul, 1975.

Dyer, Richard. *Heavenly Bodies: Film Stars and Society.* New York: St. Martin's Press, 1986.

Fiske, John. *Understanding Popular Culture.* Boston: Unwin Hyman, 1989.

Foucault, Michel. *Discipline and Punish: The Birth of the Prison.* Translated by Alan Sheridan. New York: Random House, 1979.

Freud, Sigmund. *Jokes and Their Relation to the Unconscious.* Translated by James Strachey. New York: W. W. Norton, 1960.

Georgatos, Dennis. "When the Fat Lady Sings. . . . Some San Diego Padre Fans Are Glad When It's Over." *Eugene* [Oregon] *Register-Guard* July 27, 1991: A1, A4.

Goffman, Erving. *Frame Analysis: An Essay on the Organization of Experience.* Boston: Northeastern University Press, 1986.

Henley, Nancy M. *Body Politics: Power, Sex and Non-Verbal Communication.* Englewood Cliffs, N.J.: Prentice-Hall, 1977.

Hirschberg, Lynn. "Don't Hate Me Because I'm Beautiful." *Vanity Fair* December 1990: 182–186+.

Jerome, Jim. "Roseanne Unchained." *People* October 9, 1989: 84–98.

Juno, Andrea, and V. Vale, eds. *Angry Women.* San Francisco: Re/search Publications, 1991.

Lesage, Julia. "*Celine and Julie Go Boating:* Subversive Fantasy." *Jump Cut* 24–25 (19): 37–43.

————. "Women's Rage." In *Marxism and the Interpretation of Culture,* edited by Cary Nelson and Lawrence Grossberg. Chicago: University of Illinois Press, 1988. 419–428.

Maynard, Joyce. "Domestic Affairs." *The Oregonian.* February 11, 1989: C1.

McGhee, Paul E. "The Role of Laughter and Humor in Growing Up Female." In *Becoming Female: Perspectives on Development,* edited by Clair B. Kopp, pp. 183–206. New York: Plenum Press, 1979.

Mellencamp, Patricia. *High Anxiety: Catastrophe, Scandal, Age & Comedy.* Bloomington: Indiana University Press, 1992.

————. *Indiscretion: Avant-Garde Film, Video, & Feminism.* Bloomington, Indiana University Press, 1990.

————. "Jokes and Their Relation to the Marx Brothers." In *Cinema and Language,* edited by Stephen Heath and Patricia Mellencamp, pp. 63–78. Frederick, Md.: University Publications of America, 1983.

————. "Situation Comedy, Feminism and Freud: Discourses of Gracie and Lucy." In *Studies in Entertainment,* edited by Tania Modleski, pp. 80–95. Bloomington: Indiana University Press, 1986.

Millman, Marcia. *Such a Pretty Face: Being Fat in America.* New York: W. W. Norton, 1980.

Mitchell, Elvis. "Smug Trafficking." *The Village Voice* April 25, 1989: 47–48.

O'Connor, John J. "By Any Name, Roseanne is Roseanne is Roseanne." *New York Times* August 18, 1991: B1, B27.

Orbach, Susie. *Fat is a Feminist Issue II.* London: Arrow, 1982.

————. *Hunger Strike: The Anorectic's Struggle as a Metaphor for Our Age.* New York: W. W. Norton, 1986.

"People." *Eugene* [Oregon] *Register-Guard* July 1, 1991: A2.

Pershing, Linda. "There's a Joker in the Menstrual Hut: A Performance Analysis of Comedian Kate Clinton." In *Women's Comic Visions,* edited by June Sochen, pp. 193–236. Detroit: Wayne State University Press, 1991.

Rhoden, William C. "Sports of the Times: In the Land of the Free." *New York Times* (national ed.), July 31, 1990: B9.

Rich, B. Ruby. "In the Name of Feminist Film Criticism." In *Movies and Methods II,* edited by Bill Nichols, pp. 340–358. Berkeley: University of California Press, 1985. (Originally published in *Jump Cut* 19 [1978].)

Rowe, Kathleen K. "Romanticism, Sexuality, and the Canon." *Journal of Film and Video* 42.1 (1990): 49–65.

Russo, Mary. "Female Grotesques: Carnival and Theory." In *Feminist Studies, Critical Studies,* edited by Teresa de Lauretis, pp. 213–229. Bloomington: University of Indiana Press, 1986.

Suleiman, Susan Rubin. *Subversive Intent: Gender, Politics, and the Avante-Garde.* Cambridge, Mass.: Harvard University Press, 1990.

Turner, Victor. "Frame, Flow and Reflection: Ritual and Drama as Public Liminality." In *Performance in Postmodern Culture,* edited by Michel Benamou and Charles Caramello, pp. 33–55. Milwaukee: University of Wisconsin-Milwaukee Press, 1977.

Waters, Harry F., with Steven Waldman, Daniel Glick, and Kim Fararo. "Rhymes With Rich: A Queen on Trial." *Newsweek* August 21, 1989: 46–51.

Will, George. "Cities Gleam with Gunfire." Syndicated column in *Eugene* [Oregon] *Register-Guard* August 1, 1990: A15.

34

Too Old, Too Ugly, and Not Deferential to Men

Christine Craft

When someone draws a railroad track down one side of your face, you'd better learn to turn the other cheek. I watched in the mirror as Lynn Wilford drew a shorter, more petite track on the left side. She was determined to neutralize the asymmetry of my bone structure, no matter what it took. Emphasizing the word "contouring" with a mock French accent, she whipped out yet another weapon in the battle against reality. Actually, she held two of them, white grease pencils, one in each hand. Pressed for time, she pulled and tugged at my skin, applying twin reverse panda circles around each eye.

Daubing a sponge caked with rancid makeup in some water, she applied two of the thickest coats of pancake I had ever endured. It was literally difficult to speak without cracking this mask. Never had anyone, even at CBS, piled this pore-clogging guck on my face with such overstatement. Then it was time for the cheek color. Have you ever seen anyone blush in triangles? Evidently such unnatural geometry was necessary for a credible news anchor. The ones Lynn chose for me were equidistant, and in a shade best described as screaming vermillion. The next step was to paint dark brown lines down each side of my turned-up nose to make it seem more aquiline. As she dusted on mounds of powder, I found it difficult to catch my breath without inhaling gusts of beige-tone particulate matter.

Moving right along, she came to her favorite area, the eyes. With a changing palette of mauve, lilac, violet, aubergine, and just plain purple, she begin creating a dubious orbital maquillage that began just above the lash line and continued up, up, and beyond the eyebrow. It would have looked terrific on rockers Annie Lennox of the Eurythmics or Cyndi Lauper. It did not look terrific on me, aging, all-American, "natural" type that I was. Just to make her statement perfectly clear, she blackened and enlarged my eyebrows to Victor Mature proportions. That left the lips, but not for long: two-tone lipliner, drawing the pout on permanently, eliminating any semblance of normal expression I might still have managed to muster. Voilà! I was done, and Lynn was gone, off to Tulsa where she would work more of her special breed of magic on another anchorclone, willing or not.

I climbed the steps from studio to newsroom feeling like a zombie. The first person who saw me coming was my friend, Phil French, the chief cameraman with whom I had driven across Kansas. A crazy cowboy with a flair for candor, Phil wasted no words. "Oh, my God, what have they done to you now? You look like a Kabuki doll." . . .

If my presentation seemed a little stilted that night, no doubt it was in part due to the fact that even Scott had a hard time looking in my direction. By now, the lipstick had found its way onto my teeth. The eyeshadow had worked down into my left contact lens. My pores were screaming. This I could not endure. The newscast ended none too soon. A red-faced Ridge told me to take off the makeup for the eleven o'clock news. Upstairs in the lobby, the switchboard operator told me they'd been swamped by calls from Kansas Citians asking why I had "all that crap" on. Some of those phone calls had apparently even made it to the sixth-floor executive suites. Intercepted there by the redoubtable R. Kent Replogle, they were translated into an executive order. Lynn's makeup job on me had been positively embarrassing. I was to do my own again, sort of. Media Associates would send some charts I could follow in applying the cosmetics. . . .

When I returned after the dinner break, I found a fat manila envelope in my mailbox. Attached to it was a handwritten note from Ridge Shannon stating that the contents were important reading. I thought it might be a standards and practices manual for the newsroom. Instead, I found *Dress for Success*, the men's edition. . . .

By about the sixth month, I had agreed to wear clothes a Macy's buyer selected for me. They would be altered, checked for color on camera, and purchased through an advertising trade with the station. I had not gone to Kansas City to fail, and even though this new requirement was not in the spirit of our original negotiations, I was determined to be a good sport. I spent endless hours in Macy's trying on combinations of polyester bowed blouses and blazers. It was the Kansas City schoolteacher look, and if they provided it, I would wear it. Though I refused to wear some of the items offered by my "fashion consultant," Maureen Shauvers, generally the clothes were just boring, clonish, and bland. Tapes were made in the studio of various outfits. I tried on one blouse with four jackets, two jackets with twelve blouses. On the air, I wore the clothes preselected by Macy's and Media Associates. The Texas firm looked at all the tapes, and the women in the office there decided which outfits best promoted credibility. There I was, a California woman, dressed for the Kansas City television news viewers by the steno pool in Texas. It was quite a cross-cultural experience, a real bit of America. Polyester has always made my skin crawl. . . .

The next day I was removed from my anchor job. I had come in early to listen to a veteran's narrative I was using for a series on Agent Orange. All smiles, Ridge motioned for me to step into his office for a moment. As he closed the door, his expression changed. He told me to sit down, that what he was about to tell me was "nothing personal." Holding up a thick ring-bound report, he thumbed the pages in front of my face. "We've just gotten our research back. Never in the history of Media Associates has reaction to someone been so negative. The people of Kansas City are apparently more provincial than even we had thought. They don't like you because you are too old, too unattractive, and not sufficiently deferential to men. I know it's silly, but you don't hide your intelligence to make the guys look smarter. For example, people don't like that you know the difference between the American and the National League." He emitted a nervous laugh. Did he expect me to be amused by such news? "I'm removing you from the anchor desk effective immediately. Oh, you can stay on and earn the rest of your contracted salary as a reporter, but when the people of Kansas City see your face, they turn the dial."

I was shocked, stunned, amazed, and horrified. If he had just told me they were removing me from the anchor job because they didn't like me anymore, it would have been a different feeling. I might have been depressed, but I wouldn't have been this angry. Ridge Shannon had just told me that he was taking away my job because I wouldn't pretend to be stupid in order to make my male peers look smarter. If that wasn't a blatant example of sex discrimination, I didn't know what was. For the moment, I only knew that the situation was clearly unacceptable. Still stunned when Ridge asked if I would stay on as a reporter, I told him I couldn't imagine working in a place where I was apparently so disliked. He told me to go home and think about it over the weekend. . . .

. . . As we walked up the courthouse steps in the 100-degree weather, cameras recorded every step as they did each time we exited or entered the building during the entire eleven days of the trial. We, of course, could not talk to them as they shouted questions. Our answers and our own questions would be fielded in the courtroom. The moment of truth had arrived. I felt wonderful, rumors of canine ancestry notwithstanding. I knew that many newspeople just wanted to play up the "sexy" aspect of the story. Was I really too old and too unattractive to do the news? I also knew that others like Fred Graham, the revered legal correspondent at CBS, would zero in on the Title VII issue of the case, the meat of the matter. I knew the local stations, including KMBC, would be competing to cover the story and that I would be able to watch it all. It had taken two difficult years to get these corporate defendants to this point. All their money hadn't kept them out of round one. With all the world watching, we realized that this was going to be one hell of a collective day in court.

The end of our case drew closer. Providing some less weighty moments after all the statistical testimony was Sherry Chastain, a woman who had been a news producer at Channel 9 before my arrival. Sherry had worked for both Ridge Shannon and Kent Replogle and without hesitation she described how appearance had always been the most important thing at the Metromedia station. She said Ridge had instructed her to monitor the appearance of female anchors and reporters, but never males. He had flown into a fit when one woman had worn her hair pulled back for a newscast, complaining that she looked like a "frumpy housewife." He observed of the same woman that he hoped she wouldn't turn sideways because she had a "big honker." The male counterpart of that particular anchor team was bald, with a bad toupée and thick glasses, yet nothing was ever said about monitoring his appearance.

Before they ever sought to hire me, KMBC's practice of hounding its women on-air employees about appearance had been long established. Sherry Chastain was not allowed by Judge Stevens to testify that, as a Channel 9 news producer, she had been paid considerably less than the male producers for the same job.

It was fine consolation to know that Sherry later went on to use that particular fiscal experience as one inspiration for her bestselling nonfiction book, *Winning the Salary Negotiation Game. . . .*

. . . Letters revealed that what had happened to me was far from unusual. From Iowa, another female anchor wrote she had discovered that her co-anchor was making 45 percent more than she. "To date, that has never been rectified. I could file a complaint with the Iowa Civil Rights Commission. But instead, I have chosen to get completely out of the business because of the trends I see in broadcast journalism . . . appearance over intellect."

I had a number of letters from people in broadcasting who had actually filed EEOC charges only to settle out of court, usually because they were too poor to proceed. All of those people were left with a hope that someday someone would stick it out.

Another woman anchor wrote to thank me for "taking this first momentous step that will encourage all women to fight back when they are degraded and humiliated in this cold and cosmetic business." . . .

On the flipside of all the positive input, I was literally floored by a quote that seemed to doom me to an eternal blacklist. It appeared, ironically enough, in an issue of *Ms.* magazine. In a cover edition devoted to the progress of women in TV news, mention was made of the Craft case. Discussing how to deal with the pervasive breed of sex discrimination and sexual harassment that still permeates the broadcast workplace, Nina Totenberg, a radio correspondent for National Public Radio, advised, "You can either take it like we all do, or sue like Christine Craft and never have a career."

I phoned Ms. Totenberg, determined she should understand that I had *resigned* from my Santa Barbara job. She spoke of her support for my stand but added that she had talked with her friends who were women executives at the networks. They had seen my work during the Democratic Convention and thought I was good on the air. However, they told Nina none of them would ever hire me, of course, "for all the wrong reasons." I asked Ms. Totenberg to ask her friends to please refrain from putting me on any blacklists, at least until I asked to be on a list.

The whole incident was reminiscent of Metromedia's pointed comments to me that it was the women viewers in Kansas City who didn't want to give me a chance. Maybe there was the resentment factor operative in all this. I dared to say "hold it" to sexist practices to which most of these network women had at some point acquiesced. If the handful of network women executives was only able to say "no" and not "yes," then they were still only tokens. Men continued to hold every position of real power in the network superstructures.

Jane Pauley, the "Today Show" anchor, put it extremely well to the *New York Post*: "Christine Craft has made television executives publicly accountable for private attitudes that should have been retired ten years ago." . . .

35

When an Anchor's Face
Is Not Her Fortune

Eleanor Randolph

In television news, as in entertainment, a pretty face can't hurt. Still, a few, mostly belonging to the males in the business, age more lucratively than others. Take Tom Brokaw, Dan Rather and Peter Jennings, for example. The visual effect of gravity on these three famous faces has been to add another layer of gravitas.

As any woman in television is often ready to admit, usually in private, the camera sees the aging female quite differently. For all the talk about more baby boomers trusting their peers as TV anchors, the top women stars have to keep stretching the fantasy that they remain perpetually in early middle age. Lest that sound overblown, think about our most famout TV-divas—Barbara Walters, Diane Sawyer, Connie Chung, Lesley Stahl and Judy Woodruff—and then ask yourself: Is there a gray hair among them?

All of which brings us to the case in Hartford of a blonde television anchor, Janet Peckinpaugh, who is arguing that she was booted from the co-anchor's chair when her managers thought they spotted her first wrinkle. Overnight, Ms. Peckinpaugh, Connecticut's superstar, went from being an asset to an albatross at her CBS affiliate. The station bought out her contract and she moved from a salary of $250,000 a year (plus a makeup consultant, a wardrobe allowance and a hairdresser) to $45,000 for an early morning news show at a slightly downmarket station across town.

In a Federal court case now being heard in Hartford, the 48-year-old Ms. Peckinpaugh is charging that her bosses promised in the 1980's to allow her to age gracefully in her job because she had rebuffed earlier offers elsewhere and remained loyal to WFSB, then owned by Post-Newsweek Stations, a division of The Washington Post Company. Company officials don't remember any such promises, and they are calling this case a mere contract dispute.

Ms. Peckinpaugh is also charging that her co-anchor Al Terzi groped her and that after she complained he tried to have her bumped as co-anchor. Mr. Terzi insists that it was a fraternal hug, not a grope, but his denial on the witness stand last week helped focus on the very issue she has raised in court: he is a 56-year-old man who still has both his gray hair and his job.

Despite gains for some older women at the anchor level, what makes Ms. Peckinpaugh's plight so disturbing is that it is not new. The Christine Craft case in the 1980's let any aspiring young woman know how station managers view aging blondes. After a focus group for her Kansas City television station showed that she wasn't drawing the customers as well as her younger sisters, Ms. Craft was demoted. She filed for damages, which she finally lost on appeal. The tape of one focus group shows a man suggesting that Ms. Craft looked like a dog. "Is she a mutt?" he mocked.

The sampling of public opinion is undoubtedly a little more sophisticated these days. "They probably don't ask which one you'd like to have sex with anymore," says Ms. Craft, who is now a lawyer and radio talk show host in California. Probably not, but in Ms. Peckinpaugh's case, a market reseracher for the station polled shoppers at an area mall. Her job prospects slipped drastically after they found that she ranked last among viewers in something they labeled the "net enjoyment score."

36

Black Man with a Nose Job: How We Defend Ethnic Beauty in America

Lawrence Otis Graham

. . . For my entire life, until yesterday, I had displayed my father's same nostrils, bridge, and profile. Tomorrow I wouldn't. Tomorrow I'd look like someone else. Staring up at the back of my father's head, I realized that the success of my operation would be measured in direct proportion to how much differently my nose looked from his. It was a shameful contrast to make with someone I loved so much, but when looking at my sketches, it was an accurate one nevertheless. . . .

Having torn more than fifty or sixty shots of sharp-nosed, square-jawed, model-handsome, near-black-looking or practically black-looking men from some of the best store catalogs and hippest fashion magazines in New York, I felt I'd done more than my share of the legwork. I was now ready to pay whatever it cost and submit myself to whatever tests, X rays, computer imaging, or painful surgical procedures were necessary. . . .

"Mr. Graham," the sensitive doctor began as he reached for my chin and turned my head to either side. "There is only a certain amount of alteration that is possible, or even desirable, for any one nose." . . .

He looked down at the brownest of all my men. "Mr. Graham, that nose would never be in harmony with your lips and chin. They would never work together."

"My lips and chin?" I asked. I had to pause a few seconds and consider the significance of his remark. "Then change them," I finally howled. "Change them, I'll pay whatever it costs. Change them. Just change them!"

Sometimes it takes very little to send some of us down the slippery slope toward black self-hatred.

Eventually I entered a hospital on Manhattan's Upper West Side to undergo that common surgical procedure we all call rhinoplasty. While this procedure is performed nearly a hundred thousand times each year, I had the feeling that my case was different. It was shortly after being wheeled into the large, brightly lit recovery room that I became certain that I had just launched an assault on my identity and my people. But now it was too late to go back. I was, forever, a black man who had gotten a nose job.

Although I'd grown up in a white neighborhood where male and female adolescents got their noses narrowed, chins and cheeks enhanced, and skin chemically peeled as a coming-of-age ritual during junior high and high school vacations, I had never seriously considered plastic surgery for myself. Yes, I wanted to be thought of as more handsome, but no one in my family had ever undergone cosmetic surgery. For these white friends and classmates who had undergone surgical changes, their explanations focused simply on cosmetics: They wanted to look "better." Not surprisingly, no one ever seemed to impute any other motive or to psychoanalyze the real meaning of "better." For me and my family, physical appearance and its alteration were issues of ethnicity and heritage. Black people had wide nostrils, thick lips, protruding mouths, and dark skin—and any desire to change those features was, by definition, a negative commentary on our people and our own racial identity.

For the most part, I never even compared my looks to those of the white kids or white adults around me. During my adolescence, I did, however, draw contrasts with the young blacks in my own world of black professionals and their families who socialized in our black social clubs and vacation places. There were numerous occasions as a child, and later as an adult, when hosting summer cookouts in Sag Harbor, Long Island, or Oak Bluffs, Martha's Vineyard; attending our Jack & Jill family gatherings; or partying at the Sisters of Ethos all-black dances at Wellesley College, when I'd run into dozens of well-to-do, light-skinned, straight-haired, thin-featured black childhood friends. After returning to the security of my own bedroom mirror, I would critique my features against those other blacks in my life who had "sharper," "nicer," "finer" (all words that meant more attractive and less Negroid) physical characteristics. . . .

My color ambivalence manifested itself in many different ways during my adolescence. I'm reminded of the Hasbro G.I. Joe army and astronaut set I used to play with. One afternoon I put brown shoe polish all over my 1967 G.I. Joe astronaut's entire pink body and later melted his tiny nose away with the heat from my Mattel "Creepy Crawlers" cooking iron. I don't know if I can ascribe my actions to black pride or a desire to punish Joe, but I never took him out in public after that.

Finally, after considering hundreds of magazine and catalog layouts and doctor's sketches, after writing a check for $4,000 to a black surgeon, and after having the operation, I still sometimes feel like I've upset the standard of blackness that I'd been raised to accept and appreciate.

When I told a black former classmate about my operation, she accused me of trying to pass out of the black race. It was hardly the sympathetic response I had expected from an intelligent woman who had been one of the my first friends in law school. In fact, her contempt was so great and questions so numerous, I really began to wonder if she was right about my motives.

Did I have this operation in order to become less black—to have features that were more white? Had I bought into the white definition of beauty—the sharp nose, the thin lips, the straight hair? Did I think that my less Negroid-looking black friends were more attractive than me?

My wife says my decision is personal and that I shouldn't feel compelled to defend it or explain it to anyone else. I'd like to think she is right. Maybe she's right about not needing to justify my acts to white coworkers or white neighbors. But what about my black relatives, my black friends, my black coworkers, my black secretary? Don't I owe them an explanation? Don't I have to let them know I wasn't saying that I wanted to be white when I pared down my wider, rounder Negroid nose?

Of course, I could take the easy way out and tell onlookers that one's racial identity is not embodied in one's nose. It certainly should be obvious in my case. After all, my dark brown skin and curly black hair are still intact. A different nose won't make me look white. But that's really not the point I need to address, is it?

For two years prior to my operation, I agonized over the ethnic ramifications of cosmetic surgery. According to the American Society of Plastic and Reconstructive Surgeons, 640,000 cosmetic procedures were performed in the United States in 1994. Since the preponderance of those patients were white, I am fairly certain that many of them felt no obligation to justify their surgery to members of their ethnic group.

All of this leads me to conclude that my defenses are a wasted effort. While my white friends have guiltlessly selected profiles and implants with their surgeons, I was making a futile attempt to validate my ethnic loyalty by developing arguments to prove that a nose job would not make me less black.

I shouldn't have to defend my surgery any more than those 640,000 patients who pass under the scalpel each year—or for any person who makes any type of cosmetic changes in his or her natural appearance. After all, an Italian person rarely feels guilty for turning his brown hair blond. Few Jewish people apologize for having their noses shaved down. Not many Asian people have to justify putting waves into their straight hair. Many people, in fact, are surprised to learn that in both Japan and Korea, as well as in the United States, it is quite common for male and female Japanese and Korean people of all ages to have their eyes done (for less than $1,500, a surgeon creates a more westernized eye by creating a fold in the eyelid that makes it appear rounder) and their noses enhanced (for about $2,500, a surgeon creates a more Caucasian nose by raising the bridge and tip by inserting a plastic or cartilage implant). With so many other groups undergoing the same procedures, it is ludicrous for black cosmetic surgery to be taken as a form of heresy against the race.

I am discovering that many whites as well as blacks perceive a black person's cosmetic surgery as a sign of self-hatred or the desire to be less black—an accusation often aimed at singer Michael Jackson, who in spite of his claims about rare skin diseases and naturally changing bone structure, pinched his nose, bleached his skin, tattooed his eyes, enhanced his chin, and straightened his hair. Even black talk-show host Montel Williams felt compelled to explain his nose job to his viewers. His claim: He'd done it because he'd had difficulty breathing. Whether we believe his explanation or not, none of us have the right to challenge such a decision.

An equally presumptuous attitude prevailed a while back with regard to colored contact lenses. No one objected when white actors, models, and consumers wore the cosmetic lenses, but when black talk-show host Oprah Winfrey wore them on TV, there was an immediate avalanche of attacks from both whites and blacks who could not understand why a black person would wear green contacts. White people seemed to be threatened by the notion that black people could actually avail themselves of cosmetic advances and appropriate the beauty characteristics that white people had theretofore defined as exclusively their own. Black audiences, too, looked at rich, powerful, and famous Oprah and feared that she was somehow about to "buy" herself out of the black race and leave us bereft of one more black heroine and role model. In the end, when the host held her ground on her black identity, black and white viewers wised up and realized that the ever dedicated and down-to-earth Winfrey wasn't going anywhere she didn't belong. Colored contacts weren't going to change her.

Black plastic-surgery patients or lens-wearers should not have to address the issue of ethnicity any more than white people who go to a tanning salon or get a collagen shot to thicken their lips—as so many white actors, models, and fashion-conscious citizens are doing today. Black people who get their hair straightened each month should be able to do so just because they want to sample a noncurly style.

Because I've narrowed my nose, some of my black friends say I have sought to deny my ethnicity, and oddly enough, some of my white friends—even those who have had nose jobs themselves—say I'm representative of the young black professional who wants to assimilate into the white culture. Perhaps it is true that the media images and the white kids who surrounded me as a child sometimes caused me to judge my own attractiveness on some other group's standard of beauty, but I dismiss the suggestion that any black who seeks to alter his natural physical characteristics has turned on his people and attempted to "pass" as a member of some other race.

Once the bandages were finally taken off (a few years ago), friends discovered that I am no less black than I was before the operation. I still had the same black friendships, still supported the same black causes, and still maintained the same black consciousness. As my father, the stoic black southerner, was able to do, my friends continue to allow me to take pleasure in my new appearance. For them to view this as anything more than a cosmetic procedure would be to suggest that the culture, feelings, and history of black people are awfully superficial.

Part Eleven

Patriarchy and Its Consequences

37

The Subjection of Women

John Stuart Mill

The object of this Essay is to explain as clearly as I am able, the grounds of an opinion which I have held from the very earliest period when I had formed any opinions at all on social or political matters, and which, instead of being weakened or modified, has been constantly growing stronger by the progress of reflection and the experience of life: That the principle which regulates the existing social relations between the two sexes—the legal subordination of one sex to the other—is wrong in itself, and now one of the chief hindrances to human improvement; and that it ought to be replaced by a principle of perfect equality, admitting no power or privilege on the one side, nor disability on the other.

The very words necessary to express the task I have undertaken, show how arduous it is. But it would be a mistake to suppose that the difficulty of the case must lie in the insufficiency or obscurity of the grounds of reason on which my conviction rests. The difficulty is that which exists in all cases in which there is a mass of feeling to be contended against. So long as an opinion is strongly rooted in the feelings, it gains rather than loses in stability by having a preponderating weight of argument against it. For if it were accepted as a result of argument, the refutation of the argument might shake the solidity of the conviction; but when it rests solely on feeling, the worse it flares in argumentative contest, the more persuaded its adherents are that their feeling must have some deeper ground, which the arguments do not reach; and while the feeling remains, it is always throwing up fresh intrenchments of argument to repair any breach made in the old. And there are so many causes tending to make the feelings connected with this subject the most intense, and most deeply-rooted of all those which gather round and protect old institutions and customs, that we need not wonder to find them as yet less undermined and loosened than any of the rest by the progress of the great modern spiritual and social transition;

nor suppose that the barbarisms to which men cling longest must be less barbarisms than those which they earlier shake off. . . .

In the first place, the opinion in favour of the present system, which entirely subordinates the weaker sex to the stronger, rests upon theory only; for there never has been trial made of any other; so that experience, in the sense in which it is vulgarly opposed to theory, cannot be pretended to have pronounced any verdict. And in the second place, the adoption of this system of inequality never was the result of deliberation, or forethought, or any social ideas, or any notion whatever of what conducted to the benefit of humanity or the good order of society. It arose simply from the fact that from the very earliest twilight of human society, every woman (owing to the value attached to her by men, combined with her inferiority in muscular strength) was found in a state of bondage to some man. Laws and systems of polity always begin by recognising the relations they find already existing between individuals. They convert what was a mere physical fact into a legal right, give it the sanction of society, and principally aim at the substitution of public and organized means of asserting and protecting these rights, instead of the irregular and lawless conflict of physical strength. Those who had already been compelled to obedience became in this manner legally bound to it. Slavery, from being a mere affair of force between the master and the slave, became regularized and a matter of compact among the masters, who, binding themselves to one another for common protection, guaranteed by their collective strength the private possessions of each, including his slaves. In early times, the great majority of the male sex were slaves, as well as the whole of the female. And many ages elapsed, some of them ages of high cultivation, before any thinker was bold enough to question the rightfulness and the absolute social necessity, either of the one slavery or of the other. . . .

If people are mostly so little aware how completely, during the greater part of the duration of our species, the law of force was the avowed rule of general conduct, any other being only a special and exceptional consequence of peculiar ties—and from how very recent a date it is that the affairs of society in general have been even pretended to be regulated according to any moral law; as little do people remember or consider, how institutions and customs which never had any ground but the law of force, last on into ages and states of general opinion which never would have permitted their first establishment. Less than forty years ago, Englishmen might still by law hold human beings in bondage as saleable property; within the present century they might kidnap them and carry them off, and work them literally to death. This absolutely extreme case of the law of force, condemned by those who can tolerate almost every other form of arbitrary power, and which, of all others, presents features the most revolting to the feelings of all who look at it from an impartial position, was the law of civilized and Christian England within the memory of persons now living: and in one half of Anglo-Saxon America three or four years ago, not only did slavery exist, but the slave trade, and the breeding of slaves expressly for it, was a general practice between slave states. Yet not only was there a greater strength of sentiment against it, but, in England, at least, a less amount either of feeling or of interest in favour of it than of any other of the customary abuses of force: for its motive was the love of gain, unmixed and undisguised; and those who profited by it were a very small numerical fraction of the country, while the natural feeling of all who were not personally interested in it, was unmitigated abhorrence. So extreme an instance makes it almost superfluous to refer to any other; but consider the long duration of absolute monarchy. In England at present it is the almost universal conviction that military despotism is a case of the law of force, having no other origin or justification. Yet in all the great nations of Europe except England it either still exists, or has only just ceased to exist, and has even now a strong party favourable to it in all ranks of the people, especially among persons of station and consequence. Such is the power of an established system, even when far from universal, when not only in almost every period of history there have been great and well-known examples of the contrary system, but these have almost invariably been afforded by the most illustrious and most prosperous communities. In this case, too, the possessor of the undue power, the person directly interested in it, is only one person, while those who are subject to it and suffer from it are literally all the rest. The yoke is naturally and necessarily humiliating to all persons, except the one who is on the throne, together with, at most, the one who expects to succeed to it. How different are these cases from that of the power of men over women! I am not now prejudging the question of its justificableness. I am showing how vastly more permanent it could not but be, even if not justifiable, than these other dominations which have nevertheless lasted down to our own time. Whatever gratification of pride there is in the possession of power, and whatever personal interest in its exercise, is in this case not confined to a limited class, but common to the whole male sex. Instead of being, to most of its supporters, a thing desirable chiefly in the abstract, or, like the political ends usually contended for by factions, of little private importance to any but the leaders; it comes home to the person and hearth of every male head of a family, and of every one who looks forward to being so. The clodhopper exercises, or is to exercise, his share of the power equally with the highest nobleman. And the case is that in which the desire of power is the strongest: for every one who desires power, desires it most over those who are nearest to him, with whom his life is passed, with whom he has most concerns in common, and in whom any independence of his authority is oftenest likely to interfere with his individual preferences. If, in the other cases specified, powers manifestly grounded only on force, and having so much less to support them, are so slowly and with so much difficulty got rid of, much more must it be so with this, even if it rests on no better foundation than those. We must consider, too, that the possessors of the power have facilities in this case, greater than in any other, to prevent any uprising against it. Every one of the subjects lives under the very eye, and almost, it may be said, in the hands, of one of the masters—in closer intimacy with him than with any of her fellow-subjects; with no means of combining against him, no power of even locally overmastering him, and, on the other hand, with the strongest motives for seeking his favour and avoiding to give him offence. In struggles for political emancipation, everybody knows how often its champions are bought off by bribes, or daunted by terrors. In the case of women, each individual of the subject-class is in a chronic state of bribery and intimidation combined. In setting up the standard of resistance, a large number of the leaders, and still more of the followers, must make an almost complete sacrifice of the pleasures or the alleviations of their own individual lot. If ever any system of privilege and enforced subjection had its yoke tightly riveted on the necks of those who are kept down by it, this has. . . .

All causes, social and natural, combine to make it unlikely that women should be collectively rebellious to the power of men. They are so far in a position different from all other subject classes, that their masters require something more from them than actual service. Men do not want solely the obedience of women, they want their sentiments. All men, except the most brutish, desire to have, in the woman most nearly connected with them, not a forced slave but a willing one; not a slave merely, but a favorite. They have therefore put everything in practice to enslave their minds. The masters of all other slaves rely, for maintaining obedience, on fear; either fear of themselves, or religious fears. The masters of women wanted more than simple obedience, and they turned the whole force of education to effect their purpose. All women are brought up from the very earliest years in the belief that their ideal of character is the very opposite to that of men; not self-will, and government by self-control, but submission, and yielding to the control of others. All the moralities tell them that it is the duty of women, and all the current sentimentalities that it is their nature, to live for others; to make complete abnegation of themselves, and to have no life but in their affections. And by their affections are meant the only ones they are allowed to have—those to the men with whom they are connected, or to the children who constitute an additional and indefeasible tie between them and a man. When we put together three things—first, the natural attraction between opposite sexes; secondly, the wife's entire dependence on the husband, every privilege or pleasure she has being either his gift, or depending entirely on his will; and lastly, that the principal object of human pursuit, consideration, and all objects of social ambition, can in general be sought or obtained by her only through him, it would be a miracle if the object of being attractive to men had not become the polar star of feminine education and formation of character. And, this great means of influence over the minds of women having been acquired, an instinct of selfishness made men avail themselves of it to the utmost as a means of holding women in subjections, by representing to them meekness, submissiveness, and resignation of all individual will into the hands of a man, as an essential part of sexual attractiveness. Can it be doubted that any of the other yokes which mankind have succeeded in breaking, would have subsisted till now if the same means had existed, and had been as sedulously used, to bow down their minds to it? If it had been made the object of the life of every young plebeian to find personal favour in the eyes of some patrician, of every young serf with some seigneur; if domestication with him, and a share of his personal affections, had been held out as the prize which they all should look out for, the most gifted and aspiring being able to reckon on the most desirable prizes; and if, when this prize had been obtained, they had been shut out by a wall of brass from all interests not centering in him, all feelings and desires but those which he shared or inculcated; would not serfs and seigneurs, plebeians and patricians, have been as broadly distinguished at this day as men and women are? and would not all but a thinker here and there, have believed the distinction to be a fundamental and unalterable fact in human nature?

The preceding considerations are amply sufficient to show that custom, however universal it may be, affords in this case no presumption, and ought not to create any prejudice, in favour of the arrangements which place women in social and political subjection to men. But I may go farther, and maintain that the course of history, and the tendencies of progressive human society, afford not only no presumption in favour of this system of inequality of rights, but a strong one against it; and that, so far as the whole course of human improvement up to this time, the whole stream of modern tendencies, warrants any inference on the subject, it is, that this relic of the past is discordant with the future, and must necessarily disappear.

For, what is the peculiar character of the modern world—the difference which chiefly distinguishes modern institutions, modern social ideas, modern life itself, from those of times long past? It is, that human beings are no longer born to their place in life, and chained down by an inexorable bond to the place they are born to, but are free to employ their faculties, and such favourable chances as offer, to achieve the lot which may appear to them most desirable. Human society of old was constituted on a very different principle. All were born to a fixed social position, and were mostly kept in it by law, or interdicted from any means by which they could emerge from it. As some men are born white and others black, so some were born slaves and others freemen and citizens; some were born patricians, others plebeians; some were born feudal nobles, others commoners and *roturiers*. A slave or serf could never make himself free, nor, except by the will of his master, become so. In most European countries it was not till towards the close of the middle ages, and as a consequence of the growth of regal power, that commoners could be ennobled. Even among nobles, the eldest son was born the exclusive heir to the paternal possessions, and a long time elapsed before it was fully established that the father could disinherit him. Among the industrious classes, only those who were born members of a guild, or were admitted into it by its members, could lawfully practise their calling within its local limits; and nobody could practise any calling deemed important, in any but the legal manner—by processes authoritatively prescribed. Manufacturers have stood in the pillory for presuming to carry on their business by new and improved methods. In modern Europe, and most in those parts of it which have participated most largely in all other modern improvements, diametrically opposite doctrines now prevail. Law and government do not undertake to prescribe by whom any social or industrial operation shall or shall not be conducted, or what modes of conducting them shall be lawful. These things are left to the unfettered choice of individuals. Even the laws which required that workmen should serve an apprenticeship, have in this country been repealed: there being ample assurance that in all cases in which an apprenticeship is necessary, its necessity will suffice to enforce it. The old theory was, that the least possible should be left to the choice of the individual agent; that all he had to do should, as far as practicable, be laid down for him by superior wisdom. Left to himself he was sure to go wrong. The modern conviction, the fruit of a thousand years of experience is, that things in which the individual is the person directly interested, never go right but as they are left to his own discretion; and that any regulation of them by authority, except to protect the rights of others, is sure to be mischievous. This conclusion, slowly arrived at, and not adopted until almost every possible application of the contrary theory had been made with disastrous result, now (in the industrial department) prevails universally in the most advanced countries, almost universally in all that have pretensions to any sort of advancement. It is not that all processes are supposed to be equally good, or all persons to be equally qualified for everything; but that freedom of individual choice is now known to be the only thing which procures the adoption of the best processes, and throws each operation into the hands of those who are best qualified for it. Nobody thinks it necessary to make a law that only a strong-armed man shall be a blacksmith. Freedom and competition suffice to make blacksmiths strong-armed men, because the weak-armed can earn more by engaging in occupations for which they are more fit. In consonance with this doctrine, it is felt to be an overstepping of the proper bounds of authority to fix beforehand, on some general presumption, that certain persons are not fit to do certain things. It is now thoroughly known and admitted that if some such presumptions exist, no such presumption is infallible. Even if it be well grounded in a majority of cases, which it is very likely not to be, there will be a minority of exceptional cases in which it does not hold; and in those it is both an injustice to the individuals, and a detriment to society, to place barriers in the way of their using their faculties for their own benefit and for that of others. In the cases, on the other hand, in which the unfitness is real, the ordinary motives of human conduct will be on the whole suffice to prevent the incompetent person from making, or from persisting in, the attempt.

If this general principle of social and economical science is not true; if individuals, with such help as they can derive from the opinion of those who know them, are not better judges than the law and the government, of their own capacities and vocation; the world cannot too soon abandon this principle, and return to the old system of regulations and disabilities. But if the principle is true, we ought to act as if we believed it, and not to ordain that to be born a girl instead of a boy, any more than to be born black instead of white, or a commoner instead of a nobleman, shall decide the person's position through all life—shall interdict people from all the more elevated social positions, and from all, except a few, respectable occupations. Even were we to admit the utmost that is ever pretended as to the superior fitness of men for all the functions now reserved to them, the same argument applies which forbids a legal qualification for members of Parliament. If only once in a dozen years the conditions of eligibility exclude a fit person, there is a real loss, while the exclusion of thousands of unfit persons is no gain for if the constitution of the electoral body disposes them to choose unfit persons, there are always plenty of such persons to choose from. In all things of any difficulty and importance, those who can do them well are fewer than the need even with the most unrestricted latitude of choice; and any limitation of the field of selection deprives society of some chances of being served by the competent, without ever saving it from the incompetent.

At present, in the more improved countries, the disabilities of women are the only case, save one, in which laws and institutions take persons at their birth, and ordain that they shall never in all their lives be allowed to compete for certain things. . . .

The social subordination of women thus stands out an isolated fact in modern social institutions; a solitary breach of what has become their fundamental law; a single relic of an old world of thought and practice exploded in everything else, but retained in the one thing of most universal interest. . . .

The least that can be demanded is, that the question should not be considered as prejudged by existing fact and existing opinion, but open to discussion on its merits, as a question of justice and expediency; the decision on this, as on any of the other social arrangements of mankind, depending on what an enlightened estimate of tendencies and consequences may show to be most advantageous to humanity in general, without distinction of sex. And the discussion must be a real discussion, descending to foundations, and not resting satisfied with vague and general assertions. It will not do, for instance, to assert in general terms, that the experience of mankind has pronounced in favour of the existing system. Experience cannot possibly have decided between two courses, so long as there has only been experience of one. If it be said that the doctrine of the equality of the sexes rests only on theory, it must be remembered that the contrary doctrine also has only theory to rest upon. All that is proved in its favour by direct experience, is that mankind have been able to exist under it, and to attain the degree of improvement and prosperity which we now see; but whether that prosperity has been attained sooner, or is now greater, than it would have been under the other system, experience does not say. On the other hand, experience does say, that every step in improvement has been so invariably accompanied by a step made in raising the social position of women, that historians and philosophers have been led to adopt their elevation or debasement as on the whole the surest test and most correct measure of the civilization of a people or an age. Through all the progressive period of human history, the condition of women has been approaching nearer to equality with men. This does not of itself prove that the assimilation must go on to complete equality; but it assuredly affords some presumption that such is the case.

Neither does it avail anything to say that the *nature* of the two sexes adapts them to their present functions and position, and renders these appropriate to them. Standing on the ground of common sense and the constitution of the human mind, I deny that any one knows, or can know, the nature of the two sexes, as long as they have only been seen in their present relation to one another. If men had ever been found in society without women, or women without men, or if there had been a society of men and women in which the women were not under the control of the men, something might have been positively known about the mental and moral differences which may be inherent in the nature of each. What is now called the nature of women is an eminently artificial thing—the result of forced repression in some directions, unnatural stimulation in others. It may be asserted without scruple, that no other class of dependents have had their character so entirely distorted from its natural proportions by their relation with their masters; for, if conquered and slave faces have been, in some respects, more forcibly repressed, whatever in them has not been crushed down by an iron heel has generally been let alone, and if left with any liberty of development, it has developed itself according to its own laws; but in the case of women, a hot-house and stove cultivation has always been carried on of some of the capabilities of their nature, for the benefit and pleasure of their masters. . . .

Hence, in regard to that most difficult question, what are the natural differences between the two sexes—a subject on which it is impossible in the present state of society to obtain complete and correct knowledge—while almost everybody dogmatizes upon it, almost all neglect and make light of the only means by which any partial insight can be obtained into it. This is, an analytic study of the most important department of psychology, the laws of the influence of circumstances on character. For, however great and apparently ineradicable the moral and intellectual differences between men and women might be, the evidence of their being natural differences could only be negative. Those only could be inferred to be natural which could not possibly be artificial—the residuum, after deducting every characteristic of either sex which can admit of being explained from education or external circumstances. The profoundest knowledge of the laws of the formation of character is indispensable to entitle any one to affirm even that there is any difference, much more what the difference is, between the two sexes considered as moral and rational beings; and since no one, as yet, has that knowledge, (for there is hardly any subject which, in proportion to its importance, has been so little studied), no one is thus far entitled to any positive opinion on the subject. Conjectures are all that can at present be made; conjectures more or less probable, according as more or less authorized by such knowledge as we yet have of the laws of psychology, as applied to the formation of character.

Even the preliminary knowledge, what the differences between the sexes now are, apart from all questions as to how they are made what they are, is still in the crudest and most incomplete state. . . .

One thing we may be certain of—that what is contrary to women's nature to do, they never will be made to do by simply giving their nature free play. The anxiety of mankind to interfere in behalf of nature, for fear lest nature should not succeed in effecting its purpose, is an altogether unnecessary solicitude. What women by nature cannot do, it is quite superfluous to forbid them from doing. What they can do, but not so well as the men who are their competitors, competition suffices to exclude them from; since nobody asks for protective duties and bounties in favour of women; it is only asked that the present bounties and protective duties in favour of men should be recalled. If women have a greater natural inclination for some things than for others, there is no need of laws or social inculcation to make the majority of them do the former in preference to the latter. Whatever women's services are most wanted for, the free play of competition will hold out the strongest inducements to them to undertake. And, as the words imply, they are most wanted for the things for which they are most fit; by the apportionment of which to them, the collective faculties of the two sexes can be applied on the whole with the greatest sum of valuable result.

The general opinion of men is supposed to be, that the natural vocation of a woman is that of a wife and mother. I say, is supposed to be, because, judging from acts—from the whole of the present constitution of society—one might infer that their opinion was the direct contrary. They might be supposed to think that the alleged natural vocation of women was of all things the most repugnant to their nature; insomuch that if they are free to do anything else—if any other means of living, or occupation of their time and faculties, is open, which has any chance of appearing desirable to them—there will not be enough of them who will be willing to accept the condition said to be natural to them. If this is the real opinion of men in general, it would be well that it should be spoken out. I should like to hear somebody openly enunciating the doctrine (it is already implied in much that is written on the subject)—"It is necessary to society that women should marry and produce children. They will not do so unless they are compelled. Therefore it is necessary to compel them." The merits of the case would then be clearly defined. It would be exactly that of the slaveholders of South Carolina and Louisiana. "It is necessary that cotton and sugar should be grown. White men cannot produce them. Negroes will not, for any wages which we choose to give. *Ergo* they must be compelled." An illustration still closer to the point is that of impressment. Sailors must absolutely be had to defend the country. It often happens that they will not voluntarily enlist. Therefore there must be the power of forcing them. How often has this logic been used! and, but for one flaw in it, without doubt it would have been successful up to this day. But it is open to the retort—First pay the saviors the honest value of their labour. When you have made it as well worth their while to serve you, as to work for other employers, you will have no more difficulty than others have in obtaining their services. To this there is no logical answer except "I will not": and as people are now not only ashamed, but are not desirous, to rob the labourer of his hire, impressment is no longer advocated. Those who attempt to force women into marriage by closing all other doors against them, lay themselves open to a similar retort. If they mean what they say, their opinion must evidently be, that men do not render the married condition so desirable to women, as to induce them to accept it for its own recommendations. It is not a sign of one's thinking the boon one offers very attractive, when one allows only Hobson's choice, "that or none." And here,

I believe, is the clue to the feelings of those men, who have a real antipathy to the equal freedom of women. I believe they are afraid, not lest women should be unwilling to marry, for I do not think that any one in reality has that apprehension; but lest they should insist that marriage should be on equal conditions; lest all women of spirit and capacity should prefer doing almost anything else, not in their own eyes degrading, rather than marry, when marrying is giving themselves a master, and a master too of all their earthly possessions. And truly, if this consequence were necessarily incident to marriage, I think that the apprehension would be very well founded. I agree in thinking it probable that few women, capable of anything else, would, unless under an irresistible *entrainement,* rendering them for the time insensible to anything but itself, choose such a lot, when any other means were open to them of filling a conventionally honourable place in life: and if men are determined that the law of marriage shall be a law of despotism, they are quite right, in point of mere policy, in leaving to women only Hobson's choice. But, in that case, all that has been done in the modern world to relax the chain on the minds of women, has been a mistake. They never should have been allowed to receive a literary education. Women who read, much more women who write, are, in the existing constitution of things, a contradiction and a disturbing element: and it was wrong to bring women up with any acquirements but those of an odalisque, or of a domestic servant.

38

Real Rape

Susan Estrich

MY STORY

In May 1974 a man held an ice pick to my throat and said: "Push over, shut up, or I'll kill you." I did what he said but I couldn't stop crying. When he was finished, I jumped out of my car as he drove away.

I ended up in the back seat of a Boston police car. I told the two officers I had been raped by a man who came up to the car door as I was getting out in my own parking lot (and trying to balance two bags of groceries and kick the car door open). He took the car, too.

They asked me if he was a crow. That was their first question. A crow, I learned that day, meant to them someone who is black. That was the year the public schools in Boston were integrated.

They asked me if I knew him. That was their second question. They believed me when I said I didn't. Because, as one of them put it, how would a nice (white) girl like me know a crow?

Now they were really listening. They asked me if he took any money. He did; but though I remember virtually every detail of that day and night, I can't remember how much. It doesn't matter. I remember their answer. He did take money; that made it an armed robbery. Much better than a rape. They got right on the radio with that.

We went to the police station first, not the hospital, so I could repeat my story (and then what did he do?) to four more policemen. When we got there, I borrowed a dime to call my father. They all liked that. . . .

In many respects I am a very lucky rape victim, if there can be such a thing. Not because the police never found him: looking for him myself every time I crossed the street, as I did for a long time, may be even harder than confronting him in a courtroom. No, I am lucky because everyone agrees that I was "really" raped. When I tell my story, no one doubts my status as a victim. No one suggests that I was "asking for it." No one wonders, at least out loud, if it was really my fault. No one seems to identify with the rapist. His being black, I fear, probably makes my account more believable to some people, as it certainly did with the police. But the most important thing is that he was a stranger; that he approached me not only armed but uninvited; that he was after my money and car, which I surely don't give away lightly, as well as my body. As one person put it: "You really didn't do anything wrong." . . .

But most rape cases are not as clear-cut as mine, and many that are, like mine, simply are never solved. It is always easier to find the man when the woman knows who he is. But those are the men who are least likely to be arrested, prosecuted, and convicted. Those are the cases least likely to be considered real rapes.

Many women continue to believe that men can force you to have sex against your will and that it isn't rape so long as they know you and don't beat you nearly to death in the process. Many men continue to act as if they have that right. In a very real sense, they do. That is not what the law says: the law says that it is rape to force a woman "not your wife" to engage in intercourse against her will and without her consent. But while husbands have always enjoyed the greatest protection, the protection of being excluded from rape prohibitions, even friends and neighbors have been assured sexual access.[1] What the law seems to say and what it has been in practice are two different things. In fact, the law's abhorrence of the rapist in stranger cases like mine has been matched only by its distrust of the victim who claims to have been raped by a friend or neighbor or acquaintance.

The latter cases are cases of "simple rape." The distinction between the aggravated and simple case is one commonly drawn in assault. It was applied in rape in the mid-1960s by Professors Harry Kalven and Hans Zeisel of the University of Chicago in their landmark study of American juries.[2] Kalven and Zeisel defined an aggravated rape as one with extrinsic violence (guns, knives, or beatings) or multiple assailants or no prior relationship between the victim and the defendant. A simple rape was a case in which none of these aggravating circumstances was present: a case of a single defendant who knew his victim and neither beat her nor threatened her with a weapon. They found that juries were four times as willing to convict in the aggravated rape as in the simple one. And where there was "contributory behavior" on the part of the woman—where she was hitchhiking, or dating the man, or met him at a party—juries were willing to go to extremes in their leniency toward the defendant, even in cases where judges considered the evidence sufficient to support a conviction for rape.[3]

Juries have never been alone in refusing to blame the man who commits a "simple rape." Three centuries ago the English Lord Chief Justice Matthew Hale warned that rape is a charge "easily to be made and hard to be proved, and harder to be defended by the party accused, tho' never so innocent."[4] If it is so difficult for the man to establish his innocence, far better to demand that a woman victim prove hers; under Hale's approach, the one who so "easily" charges rape must first prove her own lack of guilt. That has been the approach of the law. The usual procedural guarantees and the constitutional mandate that the government prove the man's guilt beyond a reasonable doubt have not been considered enough to protect the man accused of rape. The crime has been defined so as to require proof of actual physical resistance by the victim, as well as substantial force by the man. Evidentiary rules have been defined to require corroboration of the victim's account, to penalize women who do not complain promptly, and to ensure the relevance of a woman's prior history of unchastity. . . .

Although rape has emerged as a topic of increasing research and attention among feminists in recent years,[5] the law of rape, particularly of the "simple rape," has not been widely addressed.[6] When I began law school, a few months after being raped, I expected to learn the law of rape. I was wrong. Rape was, I discovered, just not taught. When I started teaching, seven years later, rape was still not being taught. When I asked why, I was told that it was not interesting enough, or complicated enough, or important enough to merit a chapter in a criminal law casebook or a week in a course. That attitude is, at long last, beginning to change. But it is not enough that lawyers begin to understand the law of rape as a serious subject. Rape law is too important, too much a part of all of our lives, and too much in need of change, to leave to the lawyers. . . .

IS IT RAPE?

. . . The man telling me this particular story is an assistant district attorney in a large Western city. He is in his thirties, an Ivy League law school graduate, a liberal, married to a feminist. He's about as good as you're going to get making decisions like this. This is a case he did not prosecute. He considers it rape—but only "technically." This is why.

The victim came to his office for the meeting dressed in a pair of tight blue jeans. Very tight. With a see-through blouse on top. Very revealing. That's how she was dressed. It was, he tells me, really something. Something else. Did it matter? Are you kidding!

The man involved was her ex-boyfriend. And lover; well, ex-lover. They ran into each other on the street. He asked her to come up and see *Splash* on his new VCR. She did. It was not the Disney version—of *Splash*, that is. It was porno. They sat in the living room watching. Like they used to. He said, let's go in the bedroom where we'll be more comfortable. He moved the VCR. They watched from the bed. Like they used to. He began rubbing her foot. Like he used to. Then he kissed her. She said no, she didn't want this, and got up to leave. He pulled her back on the bed and forced himself on her. He did not beat her. She had no bruises. Afterward, she ran out. The first thing she did was flag a police car. That, the prosecutor tells us, was the first smart thing she did.

The prosecutor pointed out to her that she was not hurt, that she had no bruises, that she did not fight. She pointed out to the prosecutor that her ex-boyfriend was a weightlifter. He told her it would be nearly impossible to get a conviction. She could accept that, she said: even if he didn't get convicted, at least he should be forced to go through the time and the expense of defending himself. That clinched it, said the D.A. She was just trying to use the system to harass her ex-boyfriend. He had no criminal record. He was not a "bad guy." No charges were filed.

Someone walked over and asked what we were talking about. About rape, I replied; no, actually about cases that aren't really rape. The D.A. looked puzzled. That was rape, he said. Technically. She was forced to have sex without consent. It just wasn't a case you prosecute.

This case is unusual in only one respect: that the victim perceived herself to be a victim of rape and was determined to prosecute. That is unusual. The prosecutor's response was not.

. . . A recent study in Seattle found that prior relationship was the single most important factor in the underreporting of rape to the police.[7] The author found a positive correlation between prior relationship and other variables (force, injury, circumstances of initial contact) that were positively related to reporting. But notably, even those women raped by friends or relatives, who did experience serious threats, force, or injury, were less likely to report. Similarly, a study of women who contacted rape crisis centers in Massachusetts found that nearly two-thirds knew their attackers and that the majority did not report the victimization to the police. The closer the relationship between victim and assailant, the less likely the woman was to report.[8]

What is most noteworthy about such studies is not the reporting rates themselves but the extent to which, contrary to the picture of the official victimization surveys, nonstranger rapes outnumber assaults by strangers. In both Massachusetts and Seattle the overwhelming majority of women who contacted rape centers had been attacked by men they knew. And women who contact these centers are women who at least perceive themselves to be "rape" victims, even if they do not report to the police. It appears that most women forced to have sex by men they know see themselves as victims, but not as legitimate crime victims. . . .

The reasons given in these studies for the failure to perceive forced sex as rape, let alone report it as such, reflect an understanding of rape that discounts the "simple" case. Some women do not report because they were "successful" in resisting the actual penetration, suggesting an erroneous belief that sexual aggression is a crime only when it ends in unwanted intercourse.[9] Other women do not report because they ended up "giving in" to the sexual pressure without a "fight," suggesting the equation of nonconsent with utmost or at least reasonable physical resistance.[10] And many young women believe that sexual pressure, including physical pressure, is simply not aberrant or illegal behavior if it takes place in a dating situation. Thus, one study concluded that most adolescent victims do not perceive their experience of victimization "as legitimate," meaning that "they do not involve strangers or substantial violence." Forced sex does not amount to criminal victimization "unless it occurs outside a dating situation or becomes especially violent."[11]

These findings confirm what has been learned through tests posing hypothetical examples. In those tests almost no one has any difficulty recognizing the classic, traditional rape—the stranger with a gun at the throat of his victim forcing intercourse on pain of death—as just that. When the man in the hypothetical (even a stranger) "warns her to do as he said" and "tells her to lie down" instead of "slashing her with a knife" or at least "waving" it in the air and shoving her down, those who are certain that a "rape" has taken place decrease significantly in every category except women who generally held "pro-feminist" views.[12] In situations where a woman is presented as being forced to engage in sex after a "date with a respected bachelor" or with a man she met in a bar who takes her to a deserted road (instead of home) or with her boss after working late, less than half of the female respondents in another survey were certain that a "rape" had occurred. Notably, where the two were strangers and the circumstances of the initial contact were involuntary—accosted in parking lots, house break-ins—nearly everyone was certain that a rape had occurred.[13] Adolescents in one survey were least likely to label clearly forced sex as "rape" when the couple was presented as dating. According to that study, "teenagers of both genders are quite accepting of forced sex between acquaintances and often don't view it as rape."[14] . . .

Why would fully half of the women who not only perceived themselves to be the victims of nonstranger rape but also went so far as to report it to the police remain silent when asked about criminal victimization by a survey interviewer? One possibility is that they were simply tired of talking about it and considered it too private or too painful to discuss with a stranger who wanted the information for a survey. But that possibility would seem to apply equally to all rape victims, not only to those raped by non-strangers; it does not explain why the stranger victims were so willing to disclose and the nonstranger victims so unwilling. A second possibility does: that the victims who did not disclose were those who had in effect been told that they were not legitimate victims by the police and the criminal justice system.

The woman raped by her ex-boyfriend the weightlifter, in the "technical" rape my acquaintance so easily dismissed, clearly thought she had been raped. She flagged down a police car; she went to meet with the prosecutor; she was willing to persist, regardless of the odds. The response from the system was negative. I wonder what she would say if a survey interviewer came to her house one day and asked if she had been victimized in the last year. I would not be surprised if she said nothing at all. . . .

Distrust by Definition

... Nonconsent has traditionally been a required element in the definition of a number of crimes, including theft, assault, battery, and trespass.[15] Rape may be the most serious crime to allow a consent defense, but it is certainly not the only one.[16] Rape *is* unique, however, in the definition that has been given to nonconsent—one that has required victims of rape, unlike victims of any other crime, to demonstrate their "wishes" through physical resistance. And the law of rape is striking in the extent to which nonconsent defined as resistance has become the rubric under which all of the issues in a close case are addressed and resolved.

Brown v. State, a 1906 Wisconsin decision,[17] is a classic statement of the definition of nonconsent in rape as "utmost resistance."[18] It is also a classic simple rape.

The victim in *Brown*, a sixteen-year-old (and a virgin), was a neighbor of the accused. She testified at the trial that on a walk across the fields to her grandmother's house, she greeted the accused. He at once seized her, tripped her to the ground, and forced himself upon her. "I tried as hard as I could to get away. I was trying all the time to get away just as hard as I could. I was trying to get up; I pulled at the grass; I screamed as hard as I could, and he told me to shut up, and I didn't, and then he held his hand on my mouth until I was almost strangled." Whenever he removed his hand from her mouth she repeated her screams. The jury found the defendant guilty of rape.

On appeal, the Supreme Court of Wisconsin did not reverse Brown's conviction on the ground that the force used was insufficient to constitute rape. Nor did they conclude that he lacked the necessary *mens rea* or criminal intent for rape. Rather, they reversed his conviction on the grounds that *the victim* had not adequately demonstrated her nonconsent: "Not only must there be entire absence of mental consent or assent, but there must be the most vehement exercise of every physical means or faculty within the woman's power to resist the penetration of her person, and this must be shown to persist until the offense is consummated."[19]

Here the victim failed to meet that standard: she only once said "let me go"; her screams were considered "inarticulate"; and her failure actually to "resist"—to use her "hands and limbs and pelvic muscles," obstacles which the court noted that "medical writers insist . . . are practically insuperable"—justified reversal of the conviction.[20] In fact, the court noted that "when one pauses to reflect upon the terrific resistance which the determined woman should make," her absence of bruises and torn clothing was "well-nigh incredible."[21] . . .

Still, such courts' equation of nonconsent with resistance was questionable even on their own terms. A system of law that truly celebrated female chastity, which is the system that these judges purported to uphold, should have erred on the side of less sex and presumed nonconsent in the absence of affirmative evidence to the contrary. The resistance test accomplished exactly the opposite. Chastity may have been celebrated, but consent was presumed. A system of law which at that time treated women, in matters ranging from ownership of property to the pursuit of the professions to participation in society, as passive and powerless, nonetheless demanded that in matters of sex they be strong and aggressive and powerful.[22]

That is only the half of it. It was bad enough to say—and the cases do—that seizing and tripping a woman, and telling her to shut up and covering her mouth with your hands (the *Brown* case) is the sort of romantic foreplay that neighborhood teenagers must endure; or that sex with the master comes with the job, at least where there is no gun or beating (the *Dohring* case). . . .

What is worse is that the resistance requirement accomplished this not by judging the man and finding his behavior legitimate, but by judging the woman and finding her conduct substandard. She failed to behave as judges thought a chaste woman would; therefore she consented; she wanted it; she was unchaste. It was her behavior that was scrutinized, and her conduct that was found wanting. By choosing to resolve these cases of simple rape under the resistance standard, rather than standards of force or intent, the common law courts chose the course most punitive toward the woman victim. . . .

The virtue of the woman and the force used by the man obviously are factors to be taken into account, but they are not the only ones; the "appropriateness" of the relationship may be equally important. Strangers need not be resisted, even if unarmed; dates must be.[23] A stepdaughter is not required to resist her stepfather, but she is required to resist the boy or man next-door.[24] Adult women are required to resist when the man is an adult neighbor, but not when he is a drunken youth.[25] White women are not required to resist black men, but black women are.[26]

Thus, the broadened sexual access permitted by the resistance requirement generally applied only in "appropriate" relationships. The genius of these common law judges, if it can be called that, was in framing and applying the requirement so as to ensure just such access, no more and no less, while at the same time protecting men like themselves from the dreaded lies of the appropriate women they spurned. . . .

By the 1950s and 1960s, the "utmost resistance" standard had been generally replaced by a reasonable resistance standard.[27] Chastity was still valuable, but judges no longer suggested that it was more valuable than life itself. . . .

. . . In the literature of the 1950s and 1960s special scrutiny of women complaining of simple rape was required because men understood women to be confused and ambivalent in these potentially appropriate relationships. According to an article published in the *Stanford Law Review* in 1966:

> Although a woman may desire sexual intercourse, it is customary for her to say, "no, no, no" (although meaning "yes, yes, yes") and to expect the male to be the aggressor. . . . It is always difficult in rape cases to determine whether the female really meant "no." . . .[28]

In order to remedy these problems, the *Stanford Law Review* concludes that the resistance standard, at least as applied in simple rape cases involving a single unarmed defendant, must be "high enough to assure that the resistance is unfeigned and to indicate with some degree of certainty that the woman's attitude was not one of ambivalence or unconscious compliance and that her complaints do not result from moralistic afterthoughts." At the same time, the standard must be "low enough to make death or serious bodily injury an *unlikely outcome* of the event."[29] That death or serious bodily injury remains a *possible* outcome of ignoring a woman's words is, apparently, not too great a price to pay.

Perhaps the most influential of all such commentary is the often-cited *Yale Law Journal* article on what women want.[30] Relying on Freud, the author points out that it is not simply that women lie, although there is an "unusual inducement to malicious or psychopathic accusation inherent in the sexual nature of the crime."[31] Even the "normal girl" is a confused and ambivalent character when it comes to sex with men she knows. Her behavior is not always an accurate guide to her true desires, for it may suggest resistance when in fact the woman is enjoying the physical struggle:

> When her behavior looks like resistance although her attitude is one of consent, injustice may be done the man by the woman's subsequent accusation. Many women, for example, require as a part of preliminary "love play" aggressive overtures by the man. Often their erotic pleasure may be enhanced by, or even depend upon, an accompanying physical struggle. . . .[32]

And if a woman is ambivalent about sex, it follows that it would be unfair to punish the man who was not acting *entirely* against her wishes:

> [A] woman's need for sexual satisfaction may lead to the unconscious desire for forceful penetration, the coercion serving neatly to avoid the guilt feeling which might arise after willing participation. . . . Where such an attitude of ambivalence exists, the woman may, nonetheless, exhibit behavior which would lead the fact finder to conclude that she opposed the act. To illustrate . . . the anxiety resulting from this conflict of needs may cause her to flee from the situation of discomfort, either physically by running away, or symbolically by retreating to such infantile behavior as crying. . . .[33]

The problem accordingly is not only Hale's fear that some women simply lie, but that many women do not know what they want, or mean what they say—at least when they say no to a man they know. And the presence of force hardly proves rape since many women enjoy, and even depend for their "pleasure" on "an accompanying physical struggle." . . .

Resistance therefore emerges not only as a test that ensures male access, but as an imperative to ensure adequate notice. A man is free to ignore a woman's words (for his own pleasure, as well as the woman's), but resistance signifies that no, in this case, means no. Resistance thus serves to give notice that sex is unwelcome, that force is just that, and that the man has crossed the line.

The requirement that the victim of a simple rape do more than say no was virtually without precedent in the criminal law. Many other crimes encompass a consent defense; none other has defined it so as to mandate actual physical resistance. In trespass, the posting of a sign or the offering of verbal warnings generally suffices to meet the victim's burden of nonconsent; indeed, under the Model Penal Code, drafted by the elite American Law Institute and followed by many states, the offense of trespass is aggravated where a defendant is verbally warned to desist and fails to do so.[34] A defendant's claim that the signs and the warnings were not meant to exclude *him* generally serves to indicate his intent or *mens rea* in committing the act, not the existence of consent.[35]

In robbery, claims that the victim cooperated with the taking of the money or eased the way, and thus consented, have been generally unsuccessful.[36] Only where the owner of the property actively participates in planning and committing the theft will consent be found; mere "passive submission"[37] or "passive assent"[38] does not amount to consent[39]—except in the law of rape. . . .

. . . In spite of the law's supposed celebration of female chastity, a woman's body was effectively presumed to be offered at least to any appropriate man she knows, lives near, accepts a drink from, or works for. The resistance requirement imposed on her the burden to prove otherwise and afforded courts a convenient vehicle to reverse convictions of simple rape where the woman had, in the words of the *Yale Law Journal*, done no more than "retreat" to "such infantile behavior as crying." But as important as the resistance requirement was to the accomplishment of these goals, it was not the only tool available to the common law courts. If the definition of the crime did not exclude the simple rape, the rules of proof would.

Evidentiary Distrust

. . . The requirement that the victim's testimony be corroborated in order to support a conviction was, in its heyday, formally applied in a significant minority of American jurisdictions. In practice, it continues to be a critical factor in determining the disposition of rape charges even today.[40] The justification for the formal rule was, quite explicitly, that women lie. As the *Columbia Law Review* explained in the late 1960s: "Surely the simplest, and perhaps the most important, reason not to permit conviction for rape on the uncorroborated word of the prosecutrix is that that word is very often false. . . . Since stories of rape are frequently lies or fantasies, it is reasonable to provide that such a story, in itself, should not be enough to convict a man of a crime."[41] The writer felt no need to cite a single authority for the long-held, if never-tested, proposition that women frequently lie, voluntarily exposing themselves to the potential humiliation of a rape prosecution.

Rhetorically a number of courts agreed. Without the corroboration rule, "every man is in danger of being prosecuted and convicted on the testimony of a base woman, in whose testimony there is no truth."[42] The corroboration rule is required because of the "psychic complexes" of "errant young girls and women coming before the court," which take the form "of contriving false charges of sexual offences by men."[43] If proof of opportunity to commit the crime were alone sufficient to sustain a conviction, no man would be safe."[44] Corroboration is required because "sexual cases are particularly subject to the danger of deliberately false charges, resulting from sexual neurosis, phantasy, jealousy, spite, or simply a girl's refusal to admit that she consented to an act of which she is now ashamed."[45] . . .

. . . The key question is not simply whose intent should govern, but what we should expect and demand of men in the "appropriate" and "ambiguous" situations where rape has been most narrowly defined. It is not unfair, *Morgan* notwithstanding, to demand that men behave "reasonably" and to impose criminal penalties when they do not. Even more important, the reasonable man in the 1980s should be one who understands that a woman's word is deserving of respect, whether she is a perfect stranger or his own wife. . . .

In holding a man to a higher standard of reasonableness, the law would signify that it considers a woman's consent to sex significant enough to merit a man's reasoned attention and respect. It would recognize that being sexually penetrated without consent is a grave harm; and that being treated like an object whose words are not even worthy of consideration adds insult to injury. In effect, the law would impose a duty on men to open their eyes and use their heads before engaging in sex—not to read a woman's mind, but to give her credit for knowing it herself when she speaks it, regardless of their relationship. . . .

Many feminists would argue that so long as women are powerless relative to men, viewing a "yes" as a sign of true consent is misguided. For myself, I am quite certain that many women who say yes to men they know, whether on dates or on the job, would say no if they could. I have no doubt that women's silence sometimes is the product not of passion and desire but of pressure and fear. Yet if yes may often mean no, at least from a woman's perspective, it does not seem so much to ask men, and the law, to respect the courage of the woman who does say no and to take her at her word.

In the nineteenth century and on into the twentieth courts celebrating female chastity in the abstract were so suspicious of the women who actually complained of simple rape that they adopted rules that effectively presumed consent. I have heard the same response justified in the 1980s by those who would seize on women's liberation as a basis to celebrate female unchastity. I could not disagree more. If in the 1980s more women do feel free to say yes, that provides more reason—not less—to credit the word of those who say no. The issue is not chastity or unchastity, but freedom and respect. What the law owes us is a celebration of our autonomy, and an end at long last to the distrust and suspicion of women victims of simple rape that has been the most dominant and continuing theme in the cases and commentary. . . .

. . . In sentencing a man who pled guilty to the aggravated rape of his fourteen-year-old stepdaughter in exchange for the dismissal of charges of sexual assault on his twelve-year-old stepson, a Michigan trial judge in 1984 commented:

> On your behalf, there are many things that you are not. You are not a violent rapist who drags women and girls off the street and into the bushes or into your car from a

parking lot, and I have had a lot of these in my courtroom. . . . You are not a child chaser, one whose obsession with sex causes him to seek neighborhood children or children in parks or in playgrounds, and we see these people in court. You are a man who has warm personal feelings for your stepchildren, but you let them get out of hand, and we see a number of people like you in our courts.[46]

The judge is absolutely wrong. What makes both the "violent rapist" and the stepfather whose feelings "get out of hand" different and more serious offenders than those who commit assault or robbery is the injury to personal integrity involved in forced sex. That injury is the reason that forced sex should be considered a serious crime even where there is no weapon or beating. Whether one adheres to the "rape as sex" school or the "rape as violence" school, the fact remains that what makes rape, whether "simple" or "aggravated," different from other crimes is that rape is a sexual violation—a violation of the most personal, most intimate, and most offensive kind.

Conduct is labeled criminal "to announce to society that these actions are not to be done and to secure that fewer of them are done."[47] It is time—long past time—to announce to society our condemnation of simple rape, and to enforce that condemnation "to secure that fewer of them are done." The message of the law to men, and to women, should be made clear. Simple rape is real rape.

NOTES

1. Even today, husbands remain completely immune from rape prosecutions in at least nine states; only ten states allow prosecution under all circumstances. In the rest, husbands can be prosecuted only in limited circumstances, as where they are living separately under court order or where one spouse has filed for divorce. See generally Note, "To Have and To Hold: The Marital Rape Exemption and the Fourteenth Amendment," *Harvard Law Review,* 99 (1986): 1258–1260; *People v. Liberta*, 65 N.Y.2d 152, 474 N.E.2d 567 (1984), *cert. denied,* 105 S.Ct. 2029 (1985).

2. Harry Kalven and Hans Zeisel, *The American Jury* (Boston: Little, Brown, 1966).

3. Ibid., pp. 252–255.

4. Sir Matthew Hale, *The History of the Please of the Crown,* I (London: Professional Books, 1971), LVIII: *635. This statement is the usual basis, if not the exact wording, of the "cautionary" instruction given to juries in rape cases.

5. See, for example, Susan Brownmiller, *Against Our Will: Men, Women and Rape* (New York: Simon & Schuster, 1975); Diana E. H. Russell, *The Politics of Rape* (New York: Stein & Day, 1975); Nancy Gager and Cathleen Schurr, *Sexual Assault: Confronting Rape in America* (New York: Grosser & Dunlap, 1976); Andra Medea and Kathleen Thompson, *Against Rape* (New York: Farrar, Straus and Giroux, 1974); Susan Griffin, "Rape: The All-American Crime," *Ramparts,* September 1971, pp. 26–36; Catharine MacKinnon, "Feminism, Marxism, Method, and the State," *Signs,* 8 (1983): 635.

6. There are "major" articles in the late nineteenth and early twentieth century on the problems of consent in the law of rape. But what fascinated Professors Beale and Puttkammer, the leading authors, was not the consent of competent, adult women, but rather the prob-

lem of "consent" when a snake-oil salesman convinces a woman that he is really her husband and that sex is really a physical examination of her wooden leg. I am exaggerating, but only a very little. See Joseph Beale, "Consent in the Criminal Law," *Harvard Law Review*, 8 (1895): 317, Ernst Wilfred Puttkammer, "Consent in Rape," *Illinois Law Review*, 19 (1925): 410. With few exceptions—as, for example, Vivian Berger, "Man's Trial, Woman's Tribulation: Rape Cases in the Courtroom," *Columbia Law Review*, 77 (1977): 1—the best of the more modern writing in the legal literature is found in "notes" prepared by students. See, for example, Note, "The Rape Corroboration Requirement: Repeal not Reform," *Yale Law Journal* 81 (1972): 1365; Note, "Recent Statutory Developments in the Law of Rape," *Virginia Law Review*, 61 (1975): 1500; Comment, "Towards a Consent Standard in the Law of Rape," *University of Chicago Law Review*, 43 (1976): 613.

7. Linda S. Williams, "The Classic Rape: When Do Victims Report?" *Social Problems*, 31 (April 1984): 464. See also Menachem Amir, *Patterns in Forcible Rape* (Chicago: University of Chicago Press, 1971); Diana E. H. Russell, *Sexual Exploitation* (Beverly Hills, Calif.: Sage, 1984), pp. 96–97; Richard L. Dukes and Christine L. Mattley, "Predicting Rape Victim Reportage," *Sociology and Social Research*, 62 (October 1977): 63; K. Weiss and S. S. Borges, "Victimology and Rape: The Case of the Legitimate Victim," *Issues in Criminology*, 8 (1973): 71.

8. Candace Waldron and Elizabeth Dodson-Cole, "An Analysis of Sexual Assaults Reported to Rape Crisis Centers in Massachusetts" (Boston: Mass. Department of Public Health, 1986). See also Judy Foreman, "Most Rape Victims Know Assailant, Don't Report to Police, Report Says," *Boston Globe,* April 16, 1986, p. 27.

9. See, for example, Ageton, *Sexual Assault among Adolescents*, pp. 129–130.

10. See, for example, David Knox and Kenneth Wilson, "Dating Problems of University Students," *College Student Journal*, 17 (1983): 226.

11. Ageton, *Sexual Assault among Adolescents*, p. 48.

12. Judith E. Krulewitz and Elaine Johnson Payne, "Attributions about Rape: Effects of Rapist Force, Observer Sex and Sex Role Attitudes," *Journal of Applied Social Psychology*, 8 (1978): 291.

13. Susan H. Klemmack and David L. Klemmack, "The Social Definition of Rape," in Marcia J. Walker and Stanley L. Brodsky, eds., *Sexual Assault: The Victim and the Rapist* (Lexington, Mass.: Lexington Books, 1976), pp. 135–146.

14. Gail L. Zellman and Jacqueline D. Goodchilds, "Becoming Sexual in Adolescence," in Elizabeth Rice Allgeier and Naomi B. McCormick, eds., *Changing Boundaries: Gender Roles and Sexual Behavior*, 1st ed. (Palo Alto, Calif.: Mayfield, 1983), pp. 60–61. See also Kathellen L'Armand and Albert Pepitone, "Judgments of Rape: A Study of Victim-Rapist Relationship and Victim Sexual History," *Personality and Social Psychology Bulletin*, 8 (March 1982): 134.

15. See Graham Hughes, "Consent in Sexual Offences," *Modern Law Review*, 25 (November 1962): 673–676; Glanville Williams "Consent and Public Policy," *Criminal Law Review,* 1962 (February–March 1962): 74, 154; Ernst Wilfed Puttkammer, "Consent in Criminal Assault," *Illinois Law Review*, 19 (1925): 617.

By contrast, sexual offenses are deservedly criticized examples of "morals" offenses for which consent is no defense. See Sanford H. Kadish, "The Crisis of Overcriminalization," *The Annals of the American Academy of Political and Social Science*, 374 (November 1967): 157. "Deviant" sex punishable by law has included homosexual sex, sex with children, oral sex, sex for money, let alone, under older laws, sex outside of marriage, or at least adultery.

But in the long list of prohibited sexual relations, a separate category of "consensual" violent heterosexual sex is conspicuously absent; to the extent such sex has been prohibited, it is because it is sex (as fornication or adultery), not because it is violent, and both man and woman are considered equally guilty.

16. Virtually the only exception to the rule requiring nonconsent in cases of rape or sexual assault is one oft-cited (and criticized) English case. In *The King v. Donovan*, [1934] 2 K.B. 498, the accused was charged with caning a girl of seventeen "in circumstances of indecency" for purposes of sexual gratification. His defense was consent, and he appealed his conviction on the ground that the trial judge had failed to instruct the jury that the burden was on the prosecution to establish lack of consent as an element of the offense of indecent assault. The court quashed his conviction on the grounds of misdirection of the jury, but in doing so it held that where the blows were likely or intended to do bodily harm, consent was no defense. It treated as an exception those cases of "cudgels, foils, or wrestling" which are "manly diversions, they intend to give strength, skill and activity, and many fit people for defence," as well as cases of "rough and undisciplined sport or play, where there is no anger and no intention to cause bodily harm." According to the court, "nothing could be more absurd or more repellent to the ordinary intelligence than to regard his conduct as comparable with that of a participant in one of those 'manly diversions'. . . . Nor is his act to be compared with . . . rough but innocent horse-play." For criticism of *Donovan's* "breadth," see, for example, Williams, "Consent and Public Policy," pp. 154, 155.

17. 127 Wis. 193, 106 N.W. 536 (1906).

18. See also *Reynolds v. State*, 27 Neb. 90, 91, 42 N.W. 903, 904 (1889); *Moss v. State*, 208 Miss. 531, 536, 45, So.2d 125, 126 (1950), "resistance [must] be unto the uttermost"; *People v. Dohring*, 59 N.Y.374, 386 (1874), "until exhausted or overpowered"; *King v. State*, 210 Tenn. 150, 158, 357 S.W.2d 42, 45 (1962), "in every way possible and continued such resistance until she was overcome by force, was insensible through fright, or ceased resistance from exhaustion, fear of death, or great bodily harm." In effect, the "utmost resistance" rule required that the woman resist to the "utmost" of her capacity and that such resistance not have abated during the struggle. See Note, "Recent Statutory Developments in the Definition of Forcible Rape," *Virginia Law Review*, 61 (November 1975): 1506.

19. 127 Wis. at 199, 106 N.W. at 538.

20. 127 Wis. at 199–200, 106 N.W. at 538. According to the court, a woman "is equipped to interpose most effective obstacles by means of hands and limbs and pelvic muscles. Indeed, medical writers insist that these obstacles are practically insuperable in absence of more than the usual relative disproportion of age and strength between man and woman, though no such impossibility is recognized as a rule of law." The latter qualification is, by the court's own opinion and holding, open to question. The view that an unwilling woman could not physically be raped was not limited to Wisconsin or to the nineteenth century; and it provided support for insisting that the least women should do was resist to the utmost. See W. Norwood East, "Sexual Offenders—A British View," *Yale Law Journal*, 55 (1946): 543.

21. 127 Wis. at 201, 106 N.W. at 539.

22. See, for example, *Muller v. Oregon*, 208 U.S. 412 (1908), upholding an Oregon law restricting hours of work for women by invoking scientific and sociological materials linking female biology and female dependency; *Goesart v. Cleary*, 335 U.S. 464 (1948), upholding legislative judgment that women who were not the wives or daughters of tavern owners should not be permitted to work as bartenders. It was not until 1971 that the United States Su-

preme Court for the first time struck down a state law as sex discrimination: *Reed v. Reed,* 404 U.S. 71 (1971).

23. See, for example, *People v. Kinne,* 76 P.2d 714 (Cal. App. 1938), conviction in a stranger case upheld, notwithstanding the absence of resistance; *State v. Dizon,* 390 P.2d 759 (Hawaii 1964), the same as the preceding; *People v. Blankenship,* 225 P.2d 835 (Cal. App. 1951), a repeat rapist convicted on four counts, notwithstanding the absence of resistance; *State v. Hunt,* 135 N.W.2d 475 (Neb. 1965), the requirement of "utmost resistance" was not applied where a woman was attacked by three men. For a particularly strict application of the resistance requirement to reverse a conviction in the context of a date, see *State v. Hoffman,* 280 N.W. 357 (Wis. 1938). See also *Territory v. Nishi,* 24 Hawaii 677 (1919), reversing for lack of resistance because the defendant and the victim were "friends and companions" and she voluntarily accompanied him to the park.

24. See *Bailey,* 82 Va. at 111; *Lewis v. State,* 154 Tex. Crim. 329, 226 S.W.2d 861 (1950).

25. Compare *Prokop v. State,* 148 Neb. 582, 28 N.W.2d 200 (1947), a drunken youth who broke in, with *People v. Serrielle,* 354 Ill. 182, 188 N.E. 375 (1933), an adult neighbor allegedly invited in.

26. See, for example, *State v. Hinton,* 333 P.2d 822 (Cal. App. 1959). See also *Perez v. State,* 94 S.W. 1036, 1038 (Tex. Crim. App. 1906), conviction reversed in a case involving Mexicans on the ground that "something more was required of the prosecutrix. . . . A virtuous woman and her companions would naturally be expected to exercise more force in opposition to the alleged outrage than is manifested by the testimony in this record."

27. See, for example, *Satterwhite v. Commonwealth,* 201 Va. 478, 111 S.E.2d 820 (1960), "woman is not required to resist to the utmost of her physical strength, if she reasonably believes resistance would be useless and result in serious bodily injury"; *People v. Tollack,* 233 P.2d 121 (Cal. App. 1951), utmost resistance not required; *State v. Herfel,* 49 Wis.2d 513, 518–19, 182 N.W.2d 232, 235 (1971), good-faith resistance measured by total circumstances; Note, "Towards a Consent Standard in the Law of Rape," *University of Chicago Law Review,* 43 (1976): 613, 620.

28. Note, "The Resistance Standard in Rape Legislation," *Stanford Law Review,* 18 (February 1966): 682; citing Gray and Mohr, "Follow-Up of Male Sexual Offenders," in Ralph Slovenko, ed., *Sexual Behavior and the Law* (Springfield, Ill.: Charles C. Thomas, 1965), pp. 742, 746; Ralph Slovenko, "A Panoramic Overview: Sexual Behavior and the Law," in ibid., pp. 5, 51.

29. Note, "The Resistance Standard in Rape Legislation," p. 685; emphasis added.

30. Note, "Forcible and Statutory Rape: An Exploration of the Operation and Objectives of the Consent Standard," *Yale Law Journal,* 62 (December 1952): 55. This note is cited, and its influence apparent, not only in the Model Penal Code provisions adopted in the 1950s but in the comments to them edited in the 1970s and published in 1980. See American Law Institute, *Model Penal Code and Commentaries,* part II (Philadelphia: American Law Institute, 1980), vol. 1, sec. 213.1, pp. 301–303. The Code cites the Yale article for the proposition that overemphasis on nonconsent would compress into a single statute conduct ranging from "brutal attacks . . . to half won arguments . . . in parked cars." The Code, echoing the earlier commentary, goes on to note that: "often the woman's attitude may be deeply ambivalent. She may not want intercourse, may fear it, or may desire it but feel compelled to say 'no.' Her confusion at the time may later resolve into nonconsent. . . . The deceptively simple notion of consent may obscure a tangled mesh of psychological com-

plexity, ambiguous communication, and unconscious restructuring of the event by the participants."

31. Note. "Forcible and Statutory Rape," p. 61. This and subsequent citations to the article reprinted by permission of The Yale Law Journal Company and Fred B. Rothman & Company from *The Yale Law Journal*, Vol. 62.

32. Ibid., p. 66.

33. Ibid., pp. 67–68.

34. See Model Penal Code, sec. 221.2(2) (1980), defiant trespasser.

35. The Model Penal Code requires that the person enter the place, "knowing that he is not licensed or privileged to do so." It also provides an affirmative defense that the "actor reasonably believed that the owner of the premises, or other person empowered to license access thereto, would have licensed him to enter or remain." Model Penal Code, sec. 221.2(3) (c).

36. In *Smith v. United States*, 291 F.2d 220 (9th Cir. 1961), for example, a bank teller pretended to agree, but told the manager, who instructed him to hand the defendant a bag when he was "held up." On appeal, the defendant argued that the bank had consented to giving him the money, thus there was no robbery. The court of appeals rejected the argument and affirmed the conviction, concluding that the bank had not consented but merely smoothed the way for the crime's commission.

37. *State v. Neely*, 90 Mont. 199, 300 P. 561 (1931).

38. *State v. Natalle*, 172 La. 709, 135 So. 34 (1931).

39. See also *Alford v. Commonwealth*, 240 Ky. 513, 42 S.W.2d 711 (1931); *People v. Teicher*, 52 N.Y.2d 638, 422 N.E.2d 506, 439 N.Y.S.2d 846 (1981); *Carens v. State*, 134 Tex. Crim. 8, 113 S.W.2d 542 (1938). Nor is contributory behavior afforded exculpatory significance in property crimes. Leaving keys in the ignition does not exculpate from motor vehicle larceny, nor does leaving a front door unlocked excuse the trespass. See *State v. Plaspohl*, 239 Ind. 324, 157 N.E.2d 579 (1959); *State v. Moore*, 129 Iowa 514, 106 N.W. 16 (1906); Wayne LaFave and Austin Scott, *Handbook on Criminal Law* (St. Paul, Minn.: West, 1972).

40. See Chapter 2; corroboration is a key factor in virtually every study in determining the disposition of rape complaints.

41. Note, "Corroborating Charges of Rape," *Columbia Law Review*, 67 (1967): 1137–1138.

42. *Davis v. State*, 120 Ga. 433, 48 S.E. 180, 181 (1904).

43. *State v. Wulff*, 194 Minn. 271, 260 N.W. 515, 516 (1935).

44. *Power v. State*, 43 Ariz. 329, 332, 30 P.2d 1059, 1060 (1934).

45. *State v. Anderson*, 272 Minn. 384, 137 N.W.2d 781, 783, n. 2 (1965), quoting Glanville Williams, "Corroboration—Sexual Cases," *Criminal Law Review*, 1962 (October 1962): 662–671.

46. The defendant was sentenced to probation, conditional on his receiving experimental drug treatment with Depo-Provera. Both the defendant and the state appealed, and the sentence was reversed on appeal. *People v. Gauntlett*, 134 Mich. App. 737, 352 N.W.2d 310, 313 (Mich. Ct. App. 1984).

47. Hart, *Punishment and Responsibility*, p. 6.

39

Clarence Thomas, Patriarchal Discourse and Public/Private Spheres

Mary F. Rogers

. . . Generically, patriarchy is a system of domination whereby men dominate women, with high-status men dominating other men as well. In contemporary Western societies, high-status men are white, heterosexual, able-bodied, and upper class or, at least, upper-middle class professionals commanding enviable salaries and benefits. . . .

My interest lies in exploring the empirical shape of "patriarchal discourse," that is, any network of meanings that both justifies male dominance, whether in general or in specific institutions, and is widely used as an interpretive resource among members of a given society or community. In societies where men control all the major institutions—government, religion, economy, education, family, and so forth—patriarchal discourse would seem commonplace. Indeed, it is. As the Hill-Thomas hearings illustrate, however, this widespread discourse is plied with a benign cast that paints patriarchy as a fair and humane way of organizing social life. . . .

To some extent all men share in masculine privilege and the institutionalized subordination of women. Yet masculine privilege varies with class, age, race, able-bodiedness, and sexual orientation. Put differently, gender cannot be experienced apart from these and other circumstances of our lives. Thomas thus came to the extended hearings patriarchally disadvantaged. Minimally, his race and class of origin mark him as less than elite. He could not assume that the fourteen white men on the Senate Judiciary Committee would consider him fully entitled to masculine privilege. Not surprisingly, Thomas invoked imagery whereby he could claim a masculinity, albeit racialized, commensurate with theirs for all practical and political purposes.

With testimony framed in narrowly patriarchal terms, Thomas established grounds whereon his fellow males could seem reasonable in sympathizing with him while also

Reprinted from *The Sociological Quarterly* 39, no. 2: 289–308, by permission. Copyright © 1998 by *The Midwest Sociological Society*.

appearing appropriately concerned about Hill. Significantly, the patriarchal imagery he and most of the other participants put into play left Hill no clear-cut place to stand. Nowhere does her gender resound with its full subordinate force; nowhere does her race scream out for attention the way Thomas's did. Hill was "constructed . . . as a generic or universal woman with no race or class (or with race or class being unimportant to her experience)" (Brown 1995, p. 105).

METHOD

In 1994, the transcripts of the Thomas/Hill hearings became available in softcover (Miller 1994). They include only the testimony, affidavits, and other evidence gathered in response to Hill's allegations that Thomas sexually harassed her, first at the Department of Education and then at the Equal Employment Opportunity Commission (EEOC). That part of the confirmation process—its "extended" or "reopened" hearings—occurred October 11, 12, and 13, 1991.

I treat the transcripts broadly as an expression of what Dorothy E. Smith (1990, p. 6) calls the "relations of ruling," which include "the complex of discourses . . . that intersect, interpenetrate, and coordinate the multiple sites of ruling." I was curious about what types of discourse predominated in the words of Hill, Thomas, committee members, and various witnesses. So I sought narrative patterns in this mass of words about the workplace, professionalism, careers, and government service, about Hill's and Thomas's "backgrounds," careers, and "propensities," about power, privilege, and the politics of upward mobility. I approached the transcripts, then, as a knot of narratives reflective of how the relations of ruling are structured not only around gender but also around race and heterosexuality (among other axes). . . .

. . . I found that the masculinity of Thomas and his interlocutors emerged early and strongly, while the femininity of Hill and other female witnesses was less easily pinpointed. The transcripts show that masculinity means being a "protector" and "provider," especially in connection with literal and figurative families. In large measure, then, this article focuses on narrative data about heterosexual men's claims about their protection, provisioning, and power in connection with their real or rhetorical families. Following Adrienne Rich (1977, p. xvi), I treat "family" in terms "defined and restricted under patriarchy," that is, as an institution built up around heterosexual pairing where the man typically dominates the woman in socially accepted, culturally prescribed ways.

As I have implied, one learns little by looking at only one axis of patriarchal domination. In other terms, the "matrix of domination" demands attention alongside the relations of ruling. As Patricia Hill Collins (1991) defines it, that matrix comprises overlapping but distinct axes, such as gender and race, whereby some members gain advantages and others incur disadvantages. Collins's conceptualization implies that most of us are both privileged *and* disprivileged to some degree. It also implies that

The way in which race, gender, and class categories are constructed in political discourse reinforces inequalities, obscures common interests, and denies the experiences
of many women (and men). When both the dominant and the oppositional discourse
tend to construct *women, Blacks,* and *labor* as separate and distinct categories or constituencies, the underlying interconnections are distorted. (Deitch 1993, p. 201)

Thomas had a vested interest in distorting those interconnections; he could
scarcely come across as privileged and oppressive. Alleged to have harassed his col-
league/supervisee with claims about his sexual prowess and details from pornographic
films, Thomas needed to make a presentation of self (Goffman 1959) as an oppressed
individual less interested in his own advancement than in the welfare of "subordinates" such as Hill. What better way than to present himself as a loving father? And
what better way to seal that image than by extending it into the workplace? As protector, provider, and power wielder, Thomas spoke a language widely accepted in
American life. His was the language of "family values" associated with backlash and
traditionalism as well as patriarchy. . . .

PROTECTOR

From beginning to end, Thomas presents himself as a "family man." First, in his
opening statement, he insists that "this apparently calculated public disclosure has
caused me, my family, and my friends enormous pain and great harm." He goes on,
"My family and I have been done a grave and irreparable injustice" (Miller 1994, p.
16). Soon Thomas mentions his mother, jarred enough by the turn of events to be
"confined to her bed, unable to work and unable to stop crying." He asks, "Let me
and my family regain our lives." Later, Thomas reiterates how his "family has been
harmed, [his] friends have been harmed" (p. 18).

Thomas illustrates how men in patriarchal society can speak as victims while claiming their masculinity. By focusing on how events victimize those for whom he is
responsible, the male victim deflects attention from his vulnerability while bolstering his status as patriarchal protector. Not surprisingly, then, Thomas recurrently
refers to his family's pain and suffering: "This has devastated me and it has devastated my family"; "I can't tell you what my wife has lived through or my family. I
can't tell you what my son has lived through"; "My family has been harmed"; "I don't
think that my family and I should have been put through this kind of ordeal"; "This
has caused me great pain—and my family great pain"; "My family has suffered
enough" (pp. 140, 155, 160, 161, 190, 195). Indeed, Thomas says the instigators
of the extended hearings "should at some point have to confront [his] family" (p.
183).

. . . In the end, Thomas sits before the Judiciary Committee narratively and visually constructed not primarily as a careerist eager to reach the pinnacle of the
American judicial system but as a family man: "I am here for my name, my family,
my life and my integrity" (p. 117).

Second, Thomas presents himself as a "family man" in the workplace. As Homi K. Bhabba (1992, p. 236) puts it, Thomas translates the workplace into "familial space." Repeatedly, he offers variations of the following:

> I tend to be the proud father type who sees his special assistants go on and become successful and feels pretty good about it. (Miller 1994, p. 137)

> I view my special assistants as charges of mine. They are students, they are kids of mine and I have an obligation to them. It is the same way I feel toward interns and individual co-ops or stay-in-school students. (p. 142)

> I have had some [interns] who were nineteen or twenty years old who I would treat more like my son or daughter. (p. 172)

Among his workplace "charges" was Hill, whom Thomas says he treated "the same" as his "other special assistants *who were successful or who performed well*" (p. 217, emphasis added). Note how Thomas implies that patriarchal protection presupposes compliance with the patriarch's expectations. In any case, Thomas reports that because a mutual friend recommended Hill, he felt a "special responsibility" for her. He "felt very strongly that [he] could discharge" it, in part by "be[ing] careful about her career." Thus did Hill join Thomas's special assistants: "They are family. My clerks are my family. They are my friends" (p. 151). Thomas claims he "looked out for" his workplace kin (p. 169). In the process, he "paint[s] a picture of a fatherly relationship" with Hill (Muir and Young 1996, p. 62). . . .

Before long, Thomas reiterates,

> These are people who are like family to me. These are not—these are former special assistants . . . and individuals who were in the inner confines of my office. And again, as I indicated, my staff and I are family. (p. 153)

. . . By themselves, Thomas's invocations of family, country, and protective responsibilities might seem woefully contrived. The senators interrogating him, however, articulated parallel stances that lent credibility to Thomas's claims. They did this, first, by expressing sympathy for him and his family, thereby bolstering his protective stance.

The chair of the judiciary committee, Joseph Biden (D-DE), said no one could fully appreciate how Thomas was feeling (Miller 1994, p. 223). Orrin Hatch (R-UT) noted that the president himself had asked Thomas whether he and his "family could take what would follow in the process" (p. 203). . . .

Fully half (N = 7) of the committee explicitly expressed sympathy for Thomas, and four included his family in their expression. Whatever their motives, these senators gave Thomas what he rhetorically needed, namely, acknowledgment of his family-man characteristics. Thomas the protector thus gained rhetorical life partly from the teamwork (Goffman 1959) of senators broadly playing that same family-man role. . . .

Yet patriarchy generally disallows the public destruction of a woman, even a woman of color in white-supremacist society who commands professional credentials and exhibits a feminine (neither assertive nor self-centered) demeanor. Since Hill never did "lose her poise, become angry, or break into tears" (Phelps and Winternitz 1992, p. 328), she came across as a properly feminine professional woman. Thus, the senators needed to appear to "protect" her in order to maintain their patriarchal standing. They did so by speaking to, about, and for Anita Hill in seemingly protective ways. In the process, they strengthened Thomas's rhetorical hand.

When they speak *to* Hill, the senators inject two topics traditionally linked with women: feelings and family. [Herbert] Kohl [(D-WI)] tells Hill, "I am sure this has been very painful for you" (p. 217). Paul Simon (D-IL) reports, "I sensed you were really agonizing on this whole thing" (p. 108). Howard Metznbaum (D-OH) tells Hill he is "sure" that "areas so sensitive . . . are so difficult for you to talk about" (p. 99). Arlen Specter's [(R-PA)] protective stance is similar: "I can understand that it is uncomfortable and I won't want to add to that. If any of it—if there is something you want to pause about, please do" (p. 39). Other senators ask Hill about her feelings. Biden wants to know how she "felt at the time" of the alleged harassment: "Were you uncomfortable, were you embarrassed, *did it not concern you?*" (p. 34, emphasis added) [Patrick] Leahy [D-VT] is interested in her current feelings: "Now, that was years ago. . . . How do you feel today? (p. 95) [Dennis] DeConcini's [D-AZ] query is diagnostic: "Do you feel put upon? Do you feel exposed?" (p. 101). . . .

Besides concerning themselves with her feelings, committee members sometimes cast Hill in the role of daughter or sister in sharp contrast to Thomas as *head* of a family. After Hill's opening statement, Biden turns attention to her family before questioning her: "Professor Hill, . . . would you be kind enough to introduce your primary family members to us?" (p. 26). After Hill introduces her parents, four sisters, and a brother, she faces Biden's first question: "You are the youngest in the family, is that correct?" Like Biden, Simon acknowledges Hill's family before asking her anything: "First, Professor Hill, let me say to your parents, you have a daughter you ought to be very, very proud of" (p. 107). . . .

Another way the senators constituted a supportive chorus for Thomas's patriarchal rhetoric was by directing protective remarks to other female witnesses. DeConcini says to J. C. Alvarez, a Thomas witness, "Nobody would call you arrogant. You are such a very nice lady" (p. 347). Generally, Biden excels along this dimension. He thanks [Susan] Hoerchner "for coming all the way across the country" from California but gives [John] Doggett no thanks for traveling from Arizona. At another gendered juncture, Biden says, "I am going to ask the women on the panel whether they need a break. They have been sitting there a long time" (p. 345). . . .

PROVIDER AND POWER WIELDER

With the role of protector recurrently invoked on both sides of the table, Thomas was narratively positioned to invoke its correlates: provider and power wielder. His rhetoric illustrates that one can presume to protect only if one appears to have more power than the protected. Moreover, one can protect with the greatest legitimacy if one dispenses desirable resources. All the while, patriarchs' protection goes hand in hand with subordinates' compliance. As his former colleague Alvarez said of Thomas,

> With his immediate staff, he was very warm and friendly, sort of like a friend or a father. You could talk with him about your problems, go to him for advice, but, like a father, he *commanded* and he *demanded* respect. He *demanded* professionalism and performance, and he was *very strict* about that. (p. 296, emphasis added)

. . . With reference to Hill, Thomas claims the role of provider but abjures the role of power wielder. He describes her as someone he "helped at every turn in the road," someone who "sought [his] advice and counsel" (p. 16). . . .

Missing from this picture of collegiality and mentoring is power. That Thomas was the boss and that, by his own report, his "staffs were almost invariably predominantly women" (p. 174) are circumstances that his rhetoric obscures. Thomas the power wielder surfaces in the hearings but *not* in connection with Hill. For example, he claims to have taken "swift and decisive action when sex [*sic*] harassment raised or reared its ugly head" (p. 16). When he "was in a position to do something about it," he "did something about it" (p. 149). Thomas's assertions speak not to procedures but abrupt decisions, not to fair hearing but quick outcomes. His are the words of power, not leadership or fair play as such.

Nowhere do his words have that cast more than when he says, "I terminated [Angela Wright] very aggressively a number of years ago. And very summarily" (p. 196). Wright worked with Thomas as director of public affairs at the EEOC. Having made allegations strikingly similar to Hill's, she was only interviewed over the telephone by staff from six committee members' offices.

Wright describes coming to work one day and finding "a letter in [her] chair" saying "your services here are no longer needed" (p. 388). Consistent with the implications of Thomas's recollection, Wright reports no prior discussion—indeed, no discussion at all except the one she immediately demanded. Asked about dismissing her, Thomas said, "That is the way I am with conduct like that, whether it is sex [*sic*] harassment or slurs [alleged in Wright's case] or anything else, I don't play games" (p. 209). . . .

Not only on but also off the job Thomas openly wielded power. For instance, Wright says he once came to her apartment uninvited and unannounced (pp. 384, 396). [Rose] Jourdain recalls that Wright had seen Thomas's visit as "rather presumptuous" (p. 423). Such presumptuousness also punctuated the hearings, as when Thomas advised the senators: "If you really want an idea of how I treated women, then ask the majority of the women who worked for me" (p. 125). Why only the "majority"? The power wielder is not asked.

That Thomas is not asked such hard questions implies how much narrative momentum he built up during the hearings. Judith K. Bowker (1996, p. 160) notes.

"Using race as the vehicle, he established a relationship of power where he had authorization to indict his prosecutors." Particularly in collaboration with Orrin Hatch, as we will see, Thomas made "race trump sex" (Roper, Chanslor, and Bystrom 1996, p. 52; cf. Jordan 1995, p. 38). To some extent, then, "gender-based (Hill) and race-based (Thomas) frames vied" with each other during the hearings (Robinson and Powell 1996, p. 297). Yet Thomas's was a gendered as well as a racialized rhetoric. As David Frye (1996, p. 11) emphasizes, "maleness is not marked in the national politician"; it is presumed. Thus, a man in Clarence Thomas's position "faces the peculiar problem of keeping his gender invisible by keeping it sufficiently 'male'" (Frye 1996, p. 11).

Overall, Thomas's power was underplayed during the hearings. His was a "masked power agenda" (Robinson and Powell 1996, p. 298). As Wahneema Lubiano (1992, p. 329) puts it, "Thomas's . . . power and the state power that supported him throughout the debate were naturalized as his 'dignity,' 'character,' and 'integrity.'" . . .

PATRIARCHY, RACE, AND CLEAN HETEROSEXUALITY

. . . Thomas describes the alleged harassment as "grotesque conduct" and thrice refers to its "grotesque language" (pp. 149, 155, 156). He describes the allegations about it as "impossible to wash off" (p. 156). Thomas refers to "this whole affair" as "garbage" (p. 161). Besides casting the alleged behavior into the profane realm of dirt, sleaze, garbage, trash, and the grotesque and gross (p. 218), Thomas casts it beyond the pale of normality by later calling it "sick" (p. 161). . . .

A brief exchange ensues, with Hatch querying Thomas about whether various of Hill's allegations invoke stereotypes of black men. As that exchange nears its end, Thomas says,

> I feel as though I have been abused in this process. . . . I feel as though something has been lodged against me and painted on me and it will leave an indelible mark on me. This is something that . . . plays into the worst stereotypes about black men in this society. And I have no way of changing it and no way of refuting the charges. (Miller 1994, p. 158)

Thomas's use of the "discourse of dirt and defilement" (Thomas 1992, p. 383) put the finishing rhetorical touch on his and Hatch's teamwork. Drawing from Joel Kovel (1984), Kendall Thomas (1992, pp. 384–385) emphasizes the cultural association of black bodies with dirt, filth, bodily wastes, and contamination. By using metaphors of dirt, sleaze, and filth during a discussion of racial stereotypes, Thomas alludes to those cultural meanings and thus bolsters his charge that the hearings are fundamentally racist. Rhetorically, he dares his interlocutors to make judgments of him consistent with stereotypes of black men. In effect, Thomas claims his masculinity by judiciously racializing it and then challenging the stereotypes making nonwhite masculinity profoundly problematic. All the while Thomas lays grounds for claiming, in tandem with the senators, a clean heterosexuality.

Most of the senators fall into rhetorical line with Thomas. They sensationalize the allegations enough to support a perception of monstrosity and, therefore, the need for a perceptible monster. In Thomas the family man—protector and provider on and off the job—they find no monster. The senators cannot, then, see a peddler of sleaze, dirt, and trash any more than they can see a sick, perverted, or emotionally disturbed person sitting across from them. . . .

PATRIARCHY DISCOURSE AND THE PUBLIC/PRIVATE DIVIDE

Throughout the hearings, Thomas insists on his right to a private life. He refuses to discuss conversations "about my personal life or my sex life with any person outside the workplace" (pp. 149–150). He says, "I didn't want my personal life and allegations about my sexual habits or anything else broadcast in every living room in the United States" (p. 211). When [Howell] Heflin [D-AL] asks whether Thomas continues to "refuse to answer any questions other than what may have occurred in employment," Thomas responds, "Oh, absolutely, Senator" (p. 212). . . .

Lurking beneath most such comments are assumptions about a reliable, if not clear-cut, boundary between people's private and public lives. Thomas claims, for instance, "I do not and did not co-mingle my personal life with my work life nor did I co-mingle [staff members'] personal life with the work life" (p. 176). Yet Thomas brought his son to the office; he listened to colleagues' "personal" problems; he regarded them as "family" and "friends." Even Thomas's insistence that "my relationship with my staff, although I care about them, is in the workplace" fails to hold up. By his own admission he visited Hill's apartment several times; Wright says he once dropped by her apartment.

Only Metzenbaum latches onto the inconsistencies in Thomas's public/private rhetoric. He comments to [Phyllis] Berry-Myers that Thomas "says that he kept his personal life extremely private. You seem to indicate that it was sort of public" (p. 333). In fact, Berry-Myers reports that she "got to know [Thomas's] private life, his private travails and things." She says that was the case, though, because her job entailed "preparing him for processes like this one" (p. 333). Further, Alvarez admits that she and Thomas "had been friends for many, many years" but says that "at the office [they] were colleagues" (p. 351). Her stance reflects a discourse about friendship that runs through the transcripts. . . .

In these and other ways, "a discussion of sexual harassment . . . takes us back to private/public distinctions" (Brown 1995, p. 119). One reason is that privacy is "connected to a politics of *domination*." As hooks (1994, p. 224) sees it, we cannot undercut the matrix of domination until we "challenge the notions of *public* and *private*." Like many other feminist theorists, hooks points to how much nastiness in our lives is anchored in the so-called private sphere—child abuse, wife battering, elder abuse, temper tantrums, emotional neglect, cheating, betrayal, violation. When such wrongs occur in one's "home" or behind "closed doors" in the workplace, they become much harder to talk about, let alone "prove." To say in public—to mere acquaintances and even strangers—that intimates and close acquaintances have done us wrong is to tell a most painful story under circumstances likely to feel traumatic.

From the standpoint of those who abuse power and violate trust, though, privacy is crucial. As Cynthia Fuchs Epstein (1988, p. 235) explains:

> Behind barriers, closed doors, in secret meetings, behind masks, men have parlayed insider information to create institutions that disproportionately generate for them windfall profits of opportunity and advantage.

As the sine qua non of respectable "public" personae, privacy gives the powerful grounds for acting offended or even victimized when called to give an accounting. That the very notion of a private sphere serves patriarchal interests seems straightforward enough, though in need of continual reworking under shifting material and social conditions. That that idea also falsifies people's experiences is less clear and more in need of theoretical clarification and empirical grounding. . . .

. . . Notions about public life and private life, publicity and privacy, and being "in the world" or staying "at home" make for gendered ambiguity in law, ethics, journalism, architecture, and (auto)biography as well as in social theory. In feminist theory lie strategies for untangling such conceptual knots. . . .

Thus, feminists aim to extend into the "private" sphere those standards of conduct mandated by law and custom in the "public" sphere. Their theorizing suggests the fruitfulness of conceptualizing the private sphere as that arena where the law falters and civility becomes unreliable. . . .

. . . Like center/margin and inside/outside, which have been problematized by a number of theorists (Fuss 1991; hooks 1994; Smith 1992), public/private no more stands up under the weight of people's lived experiences than do body/mind, feminine/masculine, emotion/cognition, or desire/need. Like other oppositional dualisms, this one rides roughshod over lived experiences while serving the interests of the powerful. . . .

. . . "As an aspect of liberal theory" privacy certainly entails "a right to exclude others" (Young 1990, p. 108), but its *focus* cannot be exclusion for the sake of greater control or firmer domination. In principle, the private sphere is socially permeable (and often congenially so). It is not radically discontinuous with the public sphere, as Thomas and some of his interlocutors portrayed it. Indeed, when it is—when a household's members rarely interact with neighbors and rarely invite guests into their home—we suspect abuse of some sort or, more generally, a "dysfunction" household. Thus, feminists commonly contest the dualism that stamps the public sphere as "formalized, calculating, and hierarchical" while romanticizing the private sphere as its polar opposite (Kalberg 1987, p. 160). . . .

Yet the private sphere broadly revolves around needs and desires that by definition (and often by law) cannot be satisfied in public. The private sphere thus concerns those social regions where we slough off our formal roles as best we can and are "ourselves"—"off" in Goffman's (1959) terms—without fearing censure of any palpable sort. Thus conceptualized, privacy is dramatically curtailed when one moves from home to the workplace, school, or mall where opportunities for intimacy plummet along with opportunities to be "known" as a biographically unique person. In this conceptual light, sexual harassment is a violation of privacy, an attempt within a predominantly impersonal sphere to introduce personal matters conventionally associated with intimacy or the prospect thereof. Thus, sexual harassment mangles privacy.

Alternatively, sexual harassment comprises efforts by one person to impose his—occasionally, her—privacy on some part of another person's public life. From this vantage point sexual harassment is deformed privacy, a holdover from a prefeminist age when male privilege equally left its stamp beyond and within the home. It is exclusionary for the sake of augmenting control and ensuring deniability, not for the sake of promoting intimacy. Sexual harassment denies women the privacy routinely granted men in the workplace. It is the workplace equivalent of the whistles, catcalls, and worse that women often face on the street.

Thus, during the reopened hearings on Thomas's nomination "the law's definition of public and private spheres . . . was at stake and under scrutiny." Ironically, "in the course of the hearings, the public import of sexual harassment was consistently privatized, in Hill's case," while "Thomas's attempt to protect his privacy was consistently respected." All the while, much in line with the separate spheres ideology consigning women to the "private" sphere, Hill was portrayed "as an essentially private individual, with private motives" (Ross 1992, pp. 56–57). The extended hearings thus illustrate that "in the public imagination the feminine world has the same flavor as a fictional world. It is present but not entirely real" (Griffin 1993, p. 2).

In this light, Thomas's insistence on his privacy entails a great deal more than restricting access to the details of his "personal" life. Above all, such insistence allows him to present a radically privatized self centered on protecting, providing, and power wielding on behalf of his literal and figurative families. In that same discursive space, Thomas could public-ize a heavily gendered family-man persona alongside a racially problematic clean-heterosexual persona. His construction of those personae heavily involved the rhetorical cooperation (Hatch, Specter, Biden) or relative silence (Kennedy, Grassley, Brown) of the senators across the room. . . .

I conclude that the private/public dichotomy is as central to patriarchal discourse as notions about protection, provision, and power. Indeed, that dichotomy allows men ultimately to privatize their public responsibilities and thus dodge accountability. Until the public/private dichotomy is fully interrogated and reworked in our culture, men such as Clarence Thomas will continue to have the upper hand whenever "private" violations of trust and abuses of power precipitate "public" occasions for separating victims from victimizers. To that extent, the relations of ruling remain undisturbed, and the matrix of domination is reinforced.

REFERENCES

Bhabba, Homi. 1992. "A Good Judge of Character: Men, Metaphors, and the Common Culture." Pp. 232–250 in *Race-ing Justice, En-Gendering Power*, edited by Toni Morrison. New York: Pantheon Books.

Bowker, Judith K. 1996. "Believeability: Narratives and Relational Messages in the Strategies of Anita Hill and Clarence Thomas." Pp. 149–167 in *The Lynching of Language*, edited by Sandra L. Ragan et al. Urbana: University of Illinois Press.

Brown, Elsa Barkley. 1995. "Imaging Lynching: African American Women, Communities of Struggle, and Collective Memory." Pp. 100–124 in *African American Women Speak Out*, edited by Geneva Smitherman. Detroit, MI: Wayne State University Press.

Collins, Patricia Hill. 1991. *Black Feminist Thought: Knowledge, Consciousness, and the Politics of Empowerment*. New York: Routledge.

Deitch, Cynthia. 1993. "Gender, Race, and Class Politics and the Inclusion of Women in Title VII of the Civil Rights Act." *Gender & Society* 7:183–203.

Epstein, Cynthia Fuchs. 1988. *Deceptive Distinctions: Sex, Gender, and the Social Order*. New Haven, CT, and New York: Yale University Press and the Russell Sage Foundation.

Frye, David. 1996. "The Gendered Senate: National Politics and Gendered Imagery after the Thomas Hearings." Pp. 3–15 in *Outsiders Looking In*, edited by Paul Siegel. Cresskill, NJ: Hampton Press.

Fuss, Diana. 1991. "Inside/Out." Pp. 1–10 in *Inside/Out*, edited by Diana Fuss. New York: Routledge.

Goffman, Erving. 1959. *The Presentation of Self in Everyday Life*. New York: Anchor Books.

Griffin, Susan. 1993. "Red Shoes." Pp. 1–11 in *The Politics of the Essay: Feminist Perspectives*, edited by Ruth-Ellen B. Joeres and Elizabeth Mittman. Bloomington: Indiana University Press.

hooks, bell. 1994. *Outlaw Culture: Resisting Representations*, New York: Routledge.

Jordan, Emma Coleman. 1995. "The Power of False Racial Memory and the Metaphor of Lynching." Pp. 37–55 in *Race, Gender, and Power in America*, edited by Anita Faye Hill and Emma Coleman Jordan. New York: Oxford University Press.

Kalberg, Stephen. 1987. "The Origin and Expansion of *Kulturpessimismus*: The Relationships Between Public and Private Spheres in Early Twentieth Century Germany." *Sociological Theory* 5: 150–165.

Kovel, Joel. 1984. *White Racism: A Psychohistory*. New York: Columbia University Press.

Lubiano, Wahneema. 1992. "Black Ladies, Welfare Queens, and State Minstrels: Ideological War by Narrative Means." Pp. 323–363 in *Race-ing Justice, En-gendering Power*, edited by Toni Morrison. New York: Pantheon Books.

Miller, Anita., ed. 1994. *The Complete Transcripts of the Clarence Thomas-Anita Hill Hearings: October, 11, 12, 13, 1991*. Chicago: Academy Chicago Publishers.

Muir, Janette Kenner, and Marilyn J. Young. 1996 "Evidence, Credibility, and Narrative Structures: The Case of Anita Hill." Pp. 57–77 in *Outsiders Looking In*, edited by Paul Siegel. Cresskill, NJ: Hampton Press.

Phelps, Timothy M., and Helen Winternitz. 1992. *Capitol Games: Clarence Thomas, Anita Hill, and the Story of a Supreme Court Nomination*. New York: Hyperion.

Rich, Adrienne. 1977. *Of Woman Born: Motherhood as Experience and Institution*. New York: Bantam.

Robinson, Cherylon, and Lawrence Alfred Powell, 1996. "The Postmodern Politics of Context Definition: Competing Reality Frames in the Hill-Thomas Spectacle." *The Sociological Quarterly* 37:279–305.

Roper, Cynthia S., Mike Chanslor, and Diane G. Bystrom. 1996. "Sex, Race, and Politics: An Intercultural Communication Approach to the Hill/Thomas Hearings." Pp. 44–60 in *The Lynching of Language,* edited by Sandra L. Ragan et al. Urbana: University of Illinois Press.

Ross, Andrew. 1992. "The Private Parts of Justice." Pp. 40–60 in *Race-ing Justice, En-gendering Power,* edited by Toni Morrison. New York: Pantheon Books.

Smith, Dorothy. 1990. *Texts, Facts, and Femininity: Exploring the Relations of Ruling.* New York: Routledge.

———. 1992. "Sociology from Women's Experience: A Reaffirmation." *Sociological Theory* 10: 88–98.

Thomas, Kendall, 1992. "Strange Fruit." Pp. 364–389 in *Race-ing Justice, En-gendering Power,* edited by Toni Morrison. New York: Pantheon Books.

Young, Iris Marion. 1990. *Throwing Like a Girl and Other Essays in Feminist Philosophy and Social Theory.* Bloomington: Indiana University Press.

Part Twelve

Equality and the Millennium:
The Crisis in Education Has
Consequences for the *Isms*

40

Downsizing Higher Education: Confronting the New Realities of the High-Tech Information Age Global Economy

Walda Katz-Fishman

EDUCATION AS GATEKEEPER OR LIBERATOR? KNOWLEDGE AND FACULTY JOBS FOR WHOM?

The mythology of American democracy has rested squarely on the assertion that education—and especially higher education—is the key to achieving the American dream, that education is the great equalizer. The American dream has turned into the American nightmare for the working class and the poor and has begun to turn even for the more privileged middle class. As we take a sober look at what is going on, we find that while higher education was never what it was alleged to be, that it, too, is under siege. Colleges and universities are being restructured and downsized. Staff are fired with no notice. Intense efforts are underway to cut full-time faculty and eliminate faculty tenure and, with this, academic freedom and faculty governance. Faculty are overworked—they teach more and larger classes with less support staff under deteriorating conditions. The flow of government research funds is slowing sometimes to a trickle; and sometimes to an end. Teaching hospitals, mired in the economic crisis of health care, are being downsized, closed, or spun off from universities. Graduate student teaching assistants are being forced to do basically full-time faculty teaching, at one fraction the compensation. Tuition is soaring, student aid is falling behind, and enrollments are beginning to drop off. If and when students graduate, they are drowning in debt. Censorship is on the rise in subtle and not so subtle ways. Why?

From "Downsizing Higher Education: Confronting the New Realities of the High Tech Information Age Global Economy" by Walda Katz-Fishman (Atlanta: Project South, Institute for the Elimination of Poverty & Genocide, 1995). Reprinted with permission.

In reality, education perpetuates rather than transforms the social order and its inequalities of class, race, ethnicity, nationality, and gender. In turn, the economic revolution and crisis of the larger society are expressed within the institutions of higher education and in the day-to-day operations of colleges and universities. Thus, to better understand the attack on higher education—which is really an attack on faculty, students, and staff and the communities from which we come—we must examine the economic and political realities of this historic moment.

The global integration of the market economy (driven by the necessity for maximum profits) and the high technology revolution are at the very heart of the transformation and crises in our society—including that within higher education. America's 128 million workers today compete in a global labor market with more than 3 billion workers worldwide, including over 900 million un/underemployed. The once high paid American workers have seen their real wages steadily decline over the last 20 years as they compete with low-waged labor in the developing world. Computers and automation are eliminating millions of jobs, leading to reengineering (downsizing) in manufacturing, the service sector, government, and even the knowledge sector. This creates a further surplus of workers who further drive down wages as they compete for fewer and fewer good jobs—full-time secure jobs at a living wage with benefits.

The political attack spearheaded by today's politicians—both Democrats and Republicans—is a reflection of this new economic reality. The reform agenda of the New Deal and civil rights eras—including government support for health, education, and welfare—is being shredded. White supremacy is intensifying. The prison industrial complex is mushrooming. Censorship and cultural repression are at a new high. The right wing is in elected office. And the danger of a police state is upon us. . . .

EDUCATION, SOCIETY AND THE ECONOMY— SOME ENDURING RELATIONSHIPS

Education, including higher education, is a key institution in the reproduction of the existing social order and the maintenance of the *status quo*. This occurs in two critical spheres: 1. in the material sphere of work, the labor force, and the struggle for survival (the social relations of production)—with their inequalities of class dynamically and historically related to race, ethnicity, nationality, and gender; and 2. in the ideological sphere of knowledge, ideas, theories, and values that legitimate or challenge the existing social order—and give direction to political motion in society.

Education, at its various levels of varying quality, prepares the current and future generations to do the work that needs to be done in society. Unskilled workers rarely, if ever, go to college and many do not even complete high school. In contrast, the most skilled technical and professional workers in our society often go to graduate and professional school and earn advanced degrees. As industry expanded from the 1940s through the 1970s, and the service and knowledge sectors of the economy grew—the development of this mass work required a corresponding development of mass education and higher education. This period saw the expansion of public education and of higher education—of land grant colleges and universities and historically black colleges and universities, which had historically served "special" groups in the society, as well as of public 2 and 4 year colleges and private colleges and universities. The new expanding work force needed a new kind of education for the post–World War II industrial and service economy that was taking off.

All that has changed in the 1990s. Today's postindustrial high tech global information society has witnessed the end of "mass labor" and, with it, the end of "mass education." Yesterday's public education, organized in the image of the factory and largely preparing youth for factory jobs, is in deep crisis. Higher education and those aspiring to teach and learn there are also in deep crisis. The shrinking labor markets for all kinds of workers—not just manufacturing workers, but also service, and knowledge workers—means a downsizing of higher education that was, in reality, never available to the masses, but was accessible to the growing middle class and some sections of the working class of all racial ethnic groups.

In the 1990s soaring tuition and student aid that does not keep pace call that accessibility—however limited it may have been—into question. More and more students work one or even two jobs while trying to comlpete their degrees in a reasonable amount of time. With fewer jobs available for college graduates, there is less and less reason for those in power to ensure easy and affordable access to higher education for today's youth.

Faculty who entered or have maintained their position in the middle class as knowledge workers to do the research needed by government and the corporate sector and to teach the next generation in our colleges and universities are less and less needed as the number of students going to college begins to decline. Full-time faculty are being increasingly replaced by part-time, contingent academic workers—mirroring the dynamics occurring in the larger labor force. A multi-tiered academic work force for faculty brings home to the academy the harsher realities of work in the larger society. The top tier consists of privileged full-time tenured faculty, the second tier of full-time tenure track faculty in the race for tenure, and the bottom tier of part-time and contract faculty often working multiple jobs at subsistence wages with no benefits. For those doing research, some funds are still available. But they are most available for researchers willing to do the bidding of the corporate class and its drive for maximum profits and maximum social control—however much these purposes may be disguised or denied—often at unimaginable expense to the quality of life on the planet and to the dignity and freedom of the world's peoples. . . .

Whenever there have been changes in the economic foundation of society—how we produce and distribute the goods and services necessary for social life—there have been corresponding changes in the institutions of education and in the production and application of knowledge. If we examine higher education in the United States historically and today, we find a definite relationship between the social and economic order and changes within it and the quantity and quality of higher education. . . .

The types and number of institutions of higher education

In 1970 there were 891 2-year colleges and 1,665 4-year+ colleges and universities, for a total of 2,556. Between 1970 and 1992 the biggest jump in the number of institutions was in 1980. The number of 2-year colleges increased by almost 50% to 1,274 and of 4-year+ institutions to 1,957, for a total of 3,231. By 1992 there was some additional increase to 1,469 2-year colleges and 2,169 4-year+ colleges and universities, for a total of 3,638 institutions (US Bureau of the Census 1994, p. 180, Table No. 274). This greater increase in 2-year colleges suggests that even though the overall number of higher education institutions increased dramatically, the greatest increase was at the low end of 2-year colleges—hardly preparation for the high-tech information-age jobs of the future.

Who's in college? Who graduates when?

In 1972 total student enrollment in all higher education institutions was 9.1 million, including 8.2 million whites, 727,000 blacks, and 242,000 Latina/os (US Bureau of the Census 1994, p. 179, Table No. 272). By 1982 these figures had increased to 12.4 million total students: 10 million whites, 1.1 million blacks, 519,000 Latina/os, 351,000 Asian Americans, and 88,000 American Indians. In 1992 they further increased to 14.5 million total students: 10.9 million whites, 1.39 million blacks, 955,000 Latina/os, 697,000 Asian Americans, and 119,000 American Indians. . . . The patterns for 1994 are similar to those for 1993. Overall enrollment declined .2% to 14.28 million, with white enrollment declining 1.7% to 10.42 million, black enrollment increasing 4.9% to 3.42 million, Latina/o enrollment increasing 6.9% to 1.06 million, Asian American enrollment increasing 6.8% to 774,000 and American Indian enrollment increasing 5% to 52,400 (Carter & Wilson 1996, p. 60, Table 3).

We can also look at college enrollment as a percentage of the 18- to 24-year-old population and as a percentage of high school graduates. Thus, in 1973 24% of all 18–24 year olds were in college—which was 29.7% of high school graduates (80.7% of those in high school). For whites this represented 25% of all 18–24 year olds, or 30% of high school graduates (82.8% of those in high school). For blacks this represented 16% of all 18–24-year-olds, or 24% of high school graduates (66.8% of those in high school). For Latina/os this represented 16% of all 18–24-year-olds, or 29% of high school graduates (55% of those in high school) (Carter & Wilson 1995, pp. 62-3, Table 1).

These figures steadily increased through 1992, when 34.4% of all 18–24-year-olds were in college—which was 41.9% of high school graduates (82.1% of those in high school). For whites this was 35.2% of all 18–24-year-olds, or 42.2% of high school graduates (83.3% of those in high school). For blacks this was 25.3% of all 18–24-year-olds, or 33.8% of high school graduates (74.6% of those in high school). For Latina/os this was 21.3% of all 18–24-year-olds, or 37.1% of high school graduates (57.3% of those in high school) (Carter & Wilson 1995, pp. 62–3, Table 1).

In 1994, 34.6% of all 18–24-year-olds were in college—which was 42.4% of high school graduates (81.5% of those in high school). For whites, 35.3% of all 18–24-year-olds were in college, or 42.7% of high school graduates (82.6% of those in high school). For blacks, 27.3% of all 18–24-year-olds were in college, or 35.5% of high school graduates (77% of those in high school). For Latina/os, 18.8% of all 18–24-year-olds were in college, or 33.2% of high school graduates (56.6% of those in high school) (Carter & Wilson 1996, pp. 54–55, Table 1).

We do not yet know the patterns of college enrollment in the new high tech global economy. College education in this period is much like a high school education was in the earlier expanding industrial era—it is essential for obtaining the skills needed for employment. The problem, however, is that high technology is eliminating more and more jobs so that even if every youth 18–24 years old got a college degree, many would still be unemployed and underemployed. In addition, it seems that the increases in enrollment that characterized the earlier years have slowed significantly and that those students who make it to college accumulate much greater debt that those who graduated prior to the 1990s. And, despite their increasing enrollment, students of color remain a long way from parity with white students. In addition, many of us may have thought that going to college was far more widespread that it actually is and has been. At its best, roughly one-third of all 18–24 year olds are in college, or 42% of high school graduates. This still excludes two-thirds of the youth in this age group and well over half of those who graduate from high school.

Class position and family income are critical in terms of who will graduate from college by age 24. The lowest income youth (whose family income is less than $21,300) have a 6% or 1 in 16 chance of graduating by age 24. This figure has been constant since 1970. Youth whose family income is between $21,300 and $38,700 have between an 8% and 12% chance—fluctuating over the period from 1970 to 1993. Youth whose family income is between $38,700 and $63,800 have seen their chances of earning a college degree by age 24 increase from 14% in 1980 to 23% in 1993. *Those most likely to earn a college degree by age 24 are, of course, the youth whose families have the highest income—above $63,800. Their chances went from 29% in 1980 to 81% in 1993.* (Common Agenda Coalition and National Priorities Project [CAC & NPP] 1995, pp. 20–21).

Given the disproportionate number of blacks at the low end of the class structure, we find that half as many—or fewer—blacks as whites had completed 4 or more years of college among those 25 years and older from the late 1950s through 1990. In 1957 these percentages were 2.9% for blacks and 8% for whites. By 1964 these percentages increased slightly to 3.9% for blacks and 9.6% for whites. They increased more dramatically to 6.4% of blacks and 14.5% of whites by 1975. These figures almost doubled by 1989 to 11.8% of blacks and 21.8% of whites. For blacks this number decreased to 11.3% in 1990 (the latest year for which these data are available), though it continued to increase for whites to 22% (Kominski & Adams 1992, p. 96).

The bleakest picture is for African American working class youth, especially men. It has been much noted in recent years that more young black men are in the criminal injustice system (in prison or jail, on probation or parole) than are in college. More precisely, in 1989 19.6% of black men 18–24 years old were in college while 23% were under criminal "justice" supervision. While the proportion of young black men in college increased to 22.8% by 1993 (the latest year for which data are available), the proportion of young black men 20–29 years old under criminal "justice" supervision soared to 30.2% in 1994 and to 32.2% in 1995 (Carter & Wilson 1995, pp. 66, Table 2; Mauer & Huling 1995, p. 4).

How much does it cost? Who pays?

The Sentencing Project estimates the cost of criminal "justice" control for the 827,440 young black men in the system in 1995 to be $6 billion a year (Mauer & Huling 1995, p. 1). Consider how much cheaper it would be to send a young man to college (average cost of tuition and fees, and room and board at a public 4 year college was about $5,400 in 1993) compared to the cost of prison at about $35,000 (US Bureau of the Census 1994, p. 184, Table No. 280; Joint Center for Political and Economic Studies [JCPES] 1995, p. 2). From 1980 to 1995 the federal government has decreased the education budget by $59 billion and increased the "corrections" budget in the criminal "justice" system by the same $59 billion (CAC & NPP 1995, p. 7). Is this a coincidence? Probably not! In the last decade alone the government spent $34.6 billion of our tax dollars to build 1000 new prisons and jails to hold the soaring inmate population—now over 1.5 million (*Washington Post* 1995, p. A25).

These numbers suggest that it is surely much cheaper and more cost effective to educate a young black man than to put him in jail. Yet those in power who insist on jail rather than college know the danger of educating those for whom there is no good job and no future! A study for the Justice Policy Institute, *From Classrooms to Cell Blocks* (1997), found that states have dramatically cut their funding for higher education. In the 1980s state expenditures for higher education decreased 6% while expenditures for corrections increased 95%. From 1987 to 1995 higher education state spending decreased 18.2%, while corrections gained 30% (Ambrosio and Schiraldi 1997, p. 6). In the 1994–95 period state bond fund expenditures for higher education declined in the amount of $954 million, and expenditures for corrections increased $926 million—almost an identical amount (Ambrosio and Schiraldi 1997, p. 10). The ruling class, despite its rhetoric about education, is pouring millions and billions into the prison-industrial complex at the expense of higher education for the youth of this country.

In addition, the cost of a college education, while affordable relative to the cost of prison, has soared in recent years. Between 1980 and 1993 the average cost of a college education increased roughly 300%. Average tuition and fees for all public institutions (2- and 4-year colleges and other 4 year schools) more than tripled from $583 in 1980 to $1,787 in 1993.[1] If room and board are included, these figures go from $2,165 in 1980 to $5,394 in 1993.[2] Average tuition and fees for all private institutions also tripled from $3,130 in 1980 to $10,031 in 1993. When room and board are included, the average cost goes from $4,912 in 1980 to $14,741 in 1993 (US Bureau of the Census 1994, p. 184, Table No. 280).

While college costs were tripling, the average Pell Grant—the largest federal program for grants to college students, did *not* triple. In 1980 the average Pell Grant was $882, which represented 41% of average college costs (tuition, fees, room and board at a public institution). By 1993 the average Pell Grant had increased to $1,418, but college costs had tripled; thus Pell Grants covered only 26% of average college costs (US Bureau of the Census 1994, p. 183, Table No. 278).

The remainder of student aid in the 1990s comes from student loans, work study, or just plain work. In 1980 the federal government spent $2.4 billion on Pell Grants and a total of $10.3 billion on all student financial assistance programs. In 1993 it spent $6.1 billion on Pell Grants and a total of $24.7 billion on all assistance (US Bureau of the Census 1994, p. 183, Table No. 278). Clearly, with only a quarter of college costs for only 30% of college students covered by Pell Grants, most students are drowning in debt if and when they graduate. This is a strange way to show the next generation how important a college education is to their success and well-being and to that of society as well. Or, are they lying to us?

How many faculty (full-time/part-time)? What's the pay?

Much is made by college administrators and some corporate elites of the drain placed on the resources of our society by the full-time tenured faculty of the country. When we actually look at the numbers, we find that this charge is much exaggerated. Not only are there *not* that many tenured faculty, but faculty salary and benefits are modest compared to that of many corporate CEOs and even that of college administrators and professional workers in the corporate sector.

The total number of college faculty went from 474,000 in 1970 to 686,000 in 1980, to 840,000 in 1990, (the latest year for which these data are available). In *toto* this is less than 1 million faculty. But wait—of these, in 1970 78% were full-time and 22% part-time. In 1980 66% were full-time and 34% part-time, and in

1990 only 61% were full-time and 39% part-time (US Bureau of the Census 1994, p. 180, Table No. 274). Thus in 1990 512,400 faculty (slightly over 1/2 million) were full-time while 327,600 were part-time. If this trend continues—as is happening—by the early years of the 21st century more college faculty will be part-time contingent workers than full-time. This hardly speaks to a societal (or governmental) priority on the importance of a quality college education for all our youth. . . .

DISMANTLING HIGHER EDUCATION AS WE KNOW IT: HIGHER EDUCATION CONFRONTS THE CORPORATE MODEL OF MAXIMUM PROFITS AND "LEAN & MEAN"

The high technology revolution in the productive process that has been eliminating jobs in the manufacturing and service sectors by the millions has finally hit the knowledge industry and higher education itself, including the Ivy League. In the larger economy, twenty-five million jobs were lost from the 1960s to the 1990s, some of these quality jobs in "blue chip" companies (Mills 1996; Rifkin 1995). By early in the next century another 35 million jobs are slated for elimination. In general, the new jobs created—when they are created—tend to be part-time and contingent jobs with low wages, no security and no benefits. This shrinking of economic opportunity means a shrinking need for educational preparation.

The corporate model of lean and mean that has swept the corporate and government sectors—that will do whatever is necessary to maximize profits even if it means destroying the social fabric of our communities and creating chaos—is being implemented in higher education. The corporate class and those who represent its interests in government are setting the agenda locally, regionally, nationally, and internationally. If there are no good jobs for middle class and working class youth, the government and corporate sectors will not support their education. This is the reality rather than other way round—as it is presented by the ruling class with their individualistic and the blame the victim ideology and propaganda.

It is essential that we understand how these processes of change operate in society, that we expose the lies constantly put forth by the power elite and its scholar "experts." They assert that poor and working class youth and young adults cannot get jobs because they lack the necessary education. The truth is that the number of youth in college and with college degrees has nothing to do with the number of jobs in the economy locally, nationally or globally. The massive elimination of jobs in recent years has proceeded despite roughly the same proportion of youth in college and an increase in their actual numbers. And many of those thrown out of good jobs as a result of downsizing have college degrees and often advanced degrees.

The truth is that *because* there are fewer and fewer good jobs for today's college graduates, those in power are making higher education less and less accessible for the majority of our youth—with working class youth and youth of color especially hard hit. Thus, the elimination of good jobs and the shrinking job market for college graduates is what is at the root of the attack on higher education and the thorough restructuring and downsizing being imposed under the guise of fiscal accountability and "rightsizing."

For faculty this means fewer and fewer good jobs—part-time and contract work replacing full-time tenured positions, more and larger classes, deteriorating laboratory and teaching conditions, and graduate teaching assistants replacing faculty. Increasingly, too, research funds come only to those who ask the "right" questions—from the point of view of profits, domination and control. Censorship is intensifying. This includes both self-censorship for fearful faculty looking over their shoulder trying to hold onto their jobs and, more and more, overt censorship through hiring committees, tenure committees (where they exist), publishing venues, and various political groupings set loose on campuses to terrorize faculty—and students—if they persist in teaching and discussing truth from the perspective of those at the bottom of society.

EDUCATION AS LIBERATION: TAKING IT TO THE STREETS

. . . On the one hand fewer workers must be trained—in traditional blue collar as well as white collar, professional and technical jobs. As important, if not more so, the ideological function of higher education—to search for knowledge and understanding—is increasingly dangerous when that search is calling into question the viability of the economic, political, social structures of the last 500+ years of capitalist world hegemony. Now that the world is on a trajectory of revolutionary transformation, this knowledge and understanding contain fighting words and ideas, theories and findings. And the ruling corporate class has no intention of allowing faculty the tenure and academic freedom, the well stocked and staffed institutions of higher education to educate the people. Nor will it fund students to acquire this critical and transformative understanding of the world. Within this context, the attack on higher education makes sense from the point of view of the ruling class. . . .

Today we live in a new world—the reforms we fought for have been eliminated and the root causes of our social problems stand more exposed than ever and in greater need than ever of being addressed. The challenge is ours. If we are truly educators, as I trust we are—then I am sure we will work in our communities to create a new learning environment with the teachers, the youth, and those who have already been discarded by this brutal system. This process must inform our research and communications among ourselves as we organize those scholars and students who will, in unity with our communities, develop the popular education and action necessary to win. Our fight for a liberatory research and education agenda must be against the same forces that have created untold poverty and misery among working class peoples in the United States—Native Americans, African Americans, Latina/os, Asian Americans, and European Americans—and throughout the world. We will get only what we are organized to take. Together we can make it happen!

NOTES

1. These figures are for the entire academic year for in-state students.
2. The board figures beginning in 1990 are for 20 meals a week rather than meals served 7 days a week previously. Also, these figures do *not* include the cost of books, supplies, and travel—estimated at about $1,000.

REFERENCES

Ambrosio, Tara-Jen & Vincent Schiraldi
1997 *From Classrooms to Cell Blocks: A National Perspective,* Washington, DC: The Justice Policy Institute.

Aronowitz, Stanley & W. DiFazio
1994 *The Jobless Future: Sci-Tech and the Dogma of Work.* Minneapolis: U of Minnesota Press.

Beck, Allen J.
1995 "Prisoners in 1994" in *Bureau of Justice Statistics Bulletin* (August) p. 1. Washington, DC: US Department of Justice.

Carter, Deborah & Reginald Wilson
1996 *Minorities in Higher Education: 1995–6 - 14th Annual Report.* Washington, DC: American Council on Education.

1995 *Minorities in Higher Education: 1994 - 13th Annual Report.* Washington, DC: American Council on Education.

Chait, Richard
1995 "The Future of Academic Tenure" in *AGB Priorities* (Spring) p. 1–12.

Common Agenda Coalition & National Priorities Project (CAC & NPP)
1995 *Creating a Common Agenda: Strategies for Our Communities.* Washington, DC: Common Agenda Coalition.

Ewen, Lyna, W. Katz-Fishman & G. Slaughter
1990 *Murder of the Mind,* Atlanta, GA (250 Georgia Ave, Ste 344, 30312): Project South.

Greenberg, Daniel S.
1995 "Surplus in Science" in *The Washington Post* (December 12) p. A25.

Joint Center for Political and Economic Studies (JCPES)
1995 "Political TrendLetter" in *Focus* (October/November). Washington, DC: JCPES.

Katz-Fishman, Walda & Jerome Scott
1994 "Diversity and Equality: Race and Class in America" *Sociological Forum* V. 9, No. 4 (Nov) pp. 569–581.

Kominiski & Adams
1992 [cited in 1996 draft dissertation by Paula Snyder, Dept of Sociology & Anthropology, Howard University]

Kuumba, M. Bahati, Jerome Scott & Walda Katz-Fishman
1995 "Liberation Research and Project South: Weapons in the Hands of the Oppressed" in

Selected Proceedings of the First National Conference on Urban Issues—Crossing Boundaries: Collaborative Solutions to Urban Problems edited by D. Koritz, et al, SUNY College at Buffalo: Center for Multidisciplinary Applied Research in Urban Issues.

Mauer, Marc & Tracy Huling
1995 *Young Black Americans and the Criminal Justice System: Five Years Later.* Washington, DC: The Sentencing Project.

Mills, Mike
1996 "Reorganized AT&T to Cut 40,000 Jobs" *The Washington Post* (Jan 3): A1, A21.

Mishel, Lawrence & J. Bernstein
1995 *The State of Working America. 1994–1995.* New York: ME Sharpe.

Peery, Nelson
1993 *Entering an Epoch of Social Revolution.* Chicago: Workers Press (PO Box 3705, zip 60654).

Rifkin, Jeremy
1995 *The End of Work: The Decline of the Global Labor Force and the Dawn of the Post-Market Era.* New York: Tarcher/Putnam.

Soley, Lawrence C.
1995 *Leasing the Ivory Tower: The Corporate Takeover of Academia.* Boston: South End Press.

US Bureau of the Census
1994 *Statistical Abstract of the United States: 1994 (114th edition).* Washington, DC. Washington Post.
1995 "Nation's Prison Population Soars Above 1 Million" *The Washington Post* (August 10): A25.

Woodson, Carter G.
1990 (1933) *The Mis-education of the Negro.* Trenton, NJ: Africa World Press.

Epilogue

Social scientists, for the most part, go about the business of researching and teaching in an unbiased, objective manner. Further, Sociology 101 teaches us that sociology is *not* about presenting what *should* be, but what *is*. Through the words of the distinguished scholars assembled in this text, you have read what *is*. You have been given information about the differential treatment members of minority groups experience in a variety of situations and under varying conditions. It is for you to decide if this is the way it *should be*. It is for you to decide whether discriminating against members of minority groups or excluding white males is the best way to organize a society. It is for you to decide whether denying people jobs, promotions, or neighborhoods in which to live because of the shape in or the color of their skin is the sign of a just society or an unjust society. If you feel disturbed by some or all of what you have read, then it is for you to change what *is* and decide what *should be*.

When I step into the classroom at the beginning of each semester my goal is to make students think out of the box for the fifteen weeks we spend together. Through this text you have been a student in my classroom. By reading the selections you have been exposed to another view, another angle from which to think about old social problems. If you have begun to think out of the box I hope it will not end with the reading of the final entry. Many, many former students tell me that once they stepped out of the box, it was impossible to get back inside!

A final note: In this space I had planned to discuss the report on the President's Race Initiative and connect it to the readings; however, as of this writing, the report has not been completed. Once it is, I urge the executive branch to continue its quest for racial/ethnic equality. However, I challenge the current administration as well as the ones that follow to broaden the focus to include a national initiative to examine the complex set of issues related to sexism in our everyday lives, many of which have been addressed in this text.

Permissions

Index

357

and the private sector, 331; and the unruly woman, 273; and violation of social and physical boundaries, 223; and vote as autonomy, 216

Ferree, Myra Marx, 237

film and aging, xxi, 254–59

Fine, Michelle, xviii, 83–90

Fischer, D. H., 264

Fonda, Jane, xx–xxi, 243–47, 249; and control of the body, 245–46

force, law of, 300

"Forcible and Statutory Rape" (Hale), 316–17, 320n21

Fortune 500 list, 182–83, 189

Foucault, Michel, 133, 135n5, 279

Freud, Sigmund, 273, 274, 283–84, 318

Friedan, Betty, 227

From Classrooms to Cell Blocks (Justice Policy Institute), 344

Frost, Katherine, 195

Frye, David, 330

Furstenberg, F. F., 94

Gambino, Erica-Lynn. *See* Huberty, Erica-Lynn

Gambino family and ethnic stereotyping, 36–39

Garrels, Anne, 289

Gaylin, Willard, 199–200

Gebbie, Kristine M., 176

gender, xix, 157, 232; athletics and male dominance, 68, 70–71, 72, 138–40; biology and ideology and power, 137–42; and black women's involvement in discussion of, 23; and business executives, xx, 189–97; and child custody, 94; construction of and sexuality, xix, 129–36; conversational styles and workplace, 173–81; and differences between the sexes, 306–7; and the educational system, 159–60, 232; equality and difference, 235; and genitalia, 137, 138; and housework, 234–35; inability to separate from race/ethnicity and class, xvii; and mating, 233; and network of socializing agents, 158–59; and older

men, 259–60; as socially constructed, xix; and sports, 67–73; and structured inequality, xix; and technological competence, 138, 140–42; and the workplace, xx, 235–36

Gender and Later Life (Arber and Ginn), 265

"gender order," 68

George, Phyllis, 289

Gerson, Kathleen, 201–2

Ghiloni, Beth, 183–84, 187

Gilbert, Matthew, 191, 192

Ginn, J., 265

girls and gender performance, xix, 157–60

Gittlin, Todd, 222

Goffman, Erving, 9–10, 275–76, 332

Golub, Sharon, 168

Goodman, John, 280

good old boys' networks, 191, 193–94, 196

Goodstein, Laura, xvi, 33–35

Gore, Jennifer M., 79

graduate degrees and corporate success, 184, 195

Graham, Lawrence Otis, xxi, 293–96

Grey, Mary, 125

Griswold, Robert L., 200–201

gynecological research, xix, 161–68

Hale, Matthew, 310–11, 316

Hall, J. D., 35

"Hallway Hangers," 3, 4, 6, 8

Hannerz, U., 100

Hare, J. and N., 67–68

Harris, Caleigh, xxi, 254–60

Harrison, Nancy, 194

Haskell, Molly, 141

Hatch, Orrin, 327, 330

Hayakawa, Sam, 44

Henley, Nancy, 280

Hill, Anita, xxi, 279, 325–33

Hirsch, E. D., 48

Hispanics: birthrate of, 47; and conceptions of masculinity, 148; and crime control policies, 107; and enrollment in higher education, 342–344; family behavior and living

About the Editor

Barbara A. Arrighi is an associate professor of sociology at Northern Kentucky University. Professor Arrighi's research and teaching have focused on gender, work, and family. She can be contacted at arrighi@nku.edu.